D1522185

Human–Computer Interaction Series

Human–Computer Interaction is a multidisciplinary field focused on human aspects of the development of computer technology. As computer-based technology becomes increasingly pervasive – not just in developed countries, but worldwide – the need to take a human-centered approach in the design and development of this technology becomes ever more important. For roughly 30 years now, researchers and practitioners in computational and behavioral sciences have worked to identify theory and practice that influences the direction of these technologies, and this diverse work makes up the field of human–computer inter-action. Broadly speaking, it includes the study of what technology might be able to do for people and how people might interact with the technology.

In this series, we present work which advances the science and technology of developing systems which are both effective and satisfying for people in a wide variety of contexts. The human–computer interaction series will focus on theoretical perspectives (such as formal approaches drawn from a variety of behavioral sciences), practical approaches (such as the techniques for effectively integrating user needs in system development), and social issues (such as the determinants of utility, usability and acceptability).

Author guidelines: www.springer.com/authors/book+authors > Author Guidelines

For other titles published in this series, go to
http://www.springer.com/series/6033

Jennifer Golbeck

Editor

Computing with Social Trust

 Springer

Editor
Jennifer Golbeck
University of Maryland, MD
USA
jgolbeck@umd.edu

ISSN: 1571-5035
ISBN: 978-1-84800-355-2   e-ISBN: 978-1-84800-356-9
DOI 10.1007/978-1-84800-356-9

British Library Cataloguing in Publication Data
A catalogue record for this book is available from the British Library

Library of Congress Control Number: 2008939871

Springer Science+Business Media
springer.com

Preface

This book has evolved out of roughly five years of working on computing with social trust. In the beginning, getting people to accept that social networks and the relationships in them could be the basis for interesting, relevant, and exciting computer science was a struggle. Today, social networking and social computing have become hot topics, and those of us doing research in this space are finally finding a wealth of opportunities to share our work and to collaborate with others.

This book is a collection of chapters that cover all the major areas of research in this space. I hope it will serve as a guide to students and researchers who want a strong introduction to work in the field, and as encouragement and direction for those who are considering bringing their own techniques to bear on some of these problems.

It has been an honor and privilege to work with these authors for whom I have so much respect and admiration. Thanks to all of them for their outstanding work, which speaks for itself, and for patiently enduring all my emails. Thanks, as always, to Jim Hendler for his constant support. Cai Ziegler has been particularly helpful, both as a collaborator, and in the early stages of development for this book. My appreciation also goes to Beverley Ford, Rebecca Mowat and everyone at Springer who helped with publication of this work. Finally, thanks to the many people who helped me and the book along the way, including Allison Druin, Mariya Filippova, James Finlay, Irene, John, Tom, Michelle, Kaitlyn, Emily, Bo, Ike, Wrigley, and Crystal Golbeck, Paul Jaeger, Ugur Kuter, Dan Norton, Dagobert Soergel, and, as always, π and K .

College Park, Maryland   Jennifer Golbeck

Contents

Contributors

Paolo Avesani Fondazione Bruno Kessler, Via Sommarive 18, Povo (TN), Italy avesani@fbk.eu

Pamela Briggs Northumbria University, School of Psychology and Sport Sciences, Newcastle upon Tyne, UK, p.briggs@unn.ac.uk

Cristiano Castelfranchi Institute of Cognitive Sciences and Technologies-CNR, Rome, Italy c.castelfranchi@istc.cnr.it

Rino Falcone Institute of Cognitive Sciences and Technologies-CNR, Rome, Italy r.falcone@istc.cnr.it

Jennifer Golbeck College of Information Studies, 2118F Hornbake Building, University of Maryland, College Park, MD 20742, USA, jgolbeck@umd.edu

Ugur Kuter UMIACS, University of Maryland, College Park, MD, 20742, USA ukuter@cs.umd.edu

Ming Kwan nGenera (Formerly New Paradigm) 145 King St. East, Toronto, Ontario, Canada M5C 2Y7, mkwan@ngenera.com, Deepak@newparadigm.com

K. Faith Lawrence University of Southampton, Southampton, UK, kf03r@ecs.soton.ac.uk

Raph Levien UC Berkeley, Berkeley, CA, USA, raph.levien@gmail.com

Emiliano Lorini Institute of Cognitive Sciences and Technologies-CNR, Rome, Italy; Institut de Recherche en Informatique de Toulouse (IRIT), France e.lorini@istc.cnr.it

Stephen Marsh National Research Council Canada, Institute for Information Technology, Ottawa, Ontario, Canada, steve.marsh@nrc-cnrc.gc.ca

Paolo Massa Fondazione Bruno Kessler, Via Sommarive 18, Povo (TN), Italy massa@fbk.eu

Nolan Miller Kennedy School of Government, Harvard University, Cambridge, MA, USA, nolan_miller@harvard.edu

John O'Donovan Department of Computer Science, University of California, Santa Barbara, California, USA, jod@cs.ucsb.edu

Deepak Ramachandran New Paradigm 133 King St. East, Toronto, Ontario, Canada M5C 1G6, Deepak@newparadigm.com

Paul Resnick School of Information, University of Michigan, Ann Arbor, MI 48109, USA, presnick@umich.edu

Jean-Marc Seigneur University of Geneva and Venyo, Geneva, Switzerland, Jean-Marc.Seigneur@gmail.com.org

Richard Zeckhauser Kennedy School of Government, Harvard University, Cambridge, MA, USA, richard_zeckhauser@harvard.edu

Cai-Nicolas Ziegler Siemens AG, Corporate Technology, Otto-Hahn-Ring 6, Geb. 31, Raum 260, D-81730 München, Germany, cai.ziegler@siemens.com

Chapter 1
Introduction to Computing with Social Trust

Jennifer Golbeck

The Web is deep into its second decade of life, and since 1991 it has dramatically changed the way the connected world operates. As the Web has shifted to an inter-active environment where much content is created by users, the question of whom to trust and what information to trust has become both more important and more difficult to answer. One promising solution is using *social* trust relationships. In this book, we examine challenging research problems on computing with social trust, including the computation of trust relationships and the use of these relationships in applications.

1.1 The Need for Social Trust

There are two important entities on the web: people and information. The numbers of both are in the billions. There are tens of billions of Web pages and billions of people with Web access.[1] Increasingly, average Web users are responsible for content on the web. Netcraft shows Google's Blogger service adding around a million new blogs every month.[2] Technorati reports tracking over 113 million blogs in September, 2008. They also report tracking 1.5 million new posts per day. LiveJournal, another popular blogging site, has millions of new posts per day. This means that every day, users are creating enough blog posts to equal the size of the entire Web in mid-1995.

Blogs are only the beginning. User-generated content is everywhere: discussion boards in online communities, social network profiles, auction listings and items for sale, video and photo feeds, reviews and ratings of movies, hotels, restaurants, plumbers, and more. While this content can be very helpful to users, the volume can

J. Golbeck (✉)
College of Information Studies, University of Maryland, College Park, College Park, MD 20742, USA
e-mail: jgolbeck@umd.edu

[1] http://www.internetworldstats.com/stats.htm
[2] http://news.netcraft.com/archives/web_server_survey.html

J. Golbeck (ed.), *Computing with Social Trust,* Human-Computer Interaction Series, DOI 10.1007/978-1-84800-356-9_1 © Springer-Verlag London Limited 2009

be overwhelming. For example, many movies on the Internet Movie Database have well over 1,000 user reviews.

With so much user-interaction and user-generated content, trust becomes a critical issue. When interacting with one another, users face privacy risks through personal information being revealed to the wrong people, financial risks by doing business with unreliable parties, and certainly inconvenience when spam or other unwanted content is sent their way. Similarly, information provided by users can be overwhelming because there is so much of it and because it is often contradictory. In some cases, it is simply frustrating for users to try to find useful movie reviews among thousands or to find a news report that matches the user's perspective. In other cases, such as when considering health information, finding insight from trusted sources is especially important. While users could formely judge the trustworthiness of content based on how "professional" a website looked [1, 2], most of this new content is on third party sites, effectively eliminating visual clues as helpful factors.

There are, of course, plenty of cases where popular opinion or a central authority can help establish trust. A website with Verisign credentials, for example, can be given some added degree of trust that it will protect the user's sensitive information. Peer-to-peer networks use measures of reliability for each peer as a measure of trust. However, these instances say more about the broad definition of "trust" than a solution to the problems described earlier. In the cases of user interaction on the Web or user-generated content, trust is often not an issue of security or reliability, but a matter of opinion and perspective. When looking at book reviews, for example, titles will often have a wide range of positive and negative reviews. Even dismissing the most misguided ones will leave a large set of valid opinions. Establishing trust, in this case, means finding people whose opinions are like the user's, that is, *social trust*.

In interactions with users or user-generated content, social trust can aide the user. Approximations of how much to trust unknown people can become a factor in interactions with them. In the case of user-generated content, trust in the users can serve as an estimate of how much to trust that information. Thus, content from more trusted people should be weighed more or considered more strongly than content from less trusted people. Trust can be used to sort, filter, or aggregate information, or to visibly score content for the benefit of the users.

1.2 Challenges to Computing with Social Trust

Each user knows only a tiny fraction of all the people they encounter online, either directly or through the information they produce. If we are to use trust as a way to evaluate people and information, we must be able to compute trust between people who do not know one another and translate the result into a form that is helpful to users. However, social trust is a fuzzy concept. Unlike probabilities or trust derived as a measure of successful interactions between agents, *social* trust comprises all sorts of unmeasurable components. Because of this imprecision, computing with social trust is particularly challenging. This book addresses three broad computational challenges to working with trust: models of trust, propagation of trust, and applications of trust.

Modeling trust for use in computation is difficult, particularly when working in a Web context. Trust is a complex relationship based on a wide range of factors. Between two individuals, trust may be affected by their history of interactions, similarity in preferences, similarity in background and demographics, information from third parties about the reputation of one another, and each individual's separate life experiences that may impact their propensity to trust are only a few factors. Furthermore, trust depends on context; someone may trust a friend to recommend a restaurant, but not to perform heart surgery. And finally, trust changes over time for a variety of reasons. If that weren't enough, these factors are compounded on the web. Relationships online often have different features than relationships in real life; for example, people tend not to drop friendships in web-based social networks when those relationships are often long dead in reality [4]. The anonymous nature of the Web makes identity an important factor.

There are good models that respect these aspects of trust (e.g. [6]), but often, the information necessary to implement these models is missing. At the same time, web-based social networks offer a rich source of data that may be used. The benefits are clear: there are hundreds of social networks with over a billion user accounts among them[3] [4]. Many of these networks have indications of trust between the users, either explicitly or implicitly. However, these networks generally provide only a simple trust rating between users; there is none of the information on history of interactions or other background data that a more complex trust model would require. Still, if trust can be propagated through the network, so two people who are not directly connected can be given estimates of how much to trust one another, then this ample source of social data can be exploited to provide trust information for later use. Computing trust accurately, avoiding attacks by untrustworthy users, and understanding the differences between trust inference algorithms, all are important research problems that must be addressed if these values are to be useful.

Trust derived from simple or complex models becomes important when used in applications. As described earlier, there are many scenarios where an estimate of trust in a user can be important. Specifically, trust can help in judging the quality of user-generated content or determining whether or not to enter into a transaction with a person online. Exactly how to apply trust estimates to these tasks is challenging. Depending on the context, trust should be indicated in different ways (as in feedback systems for online auctions) or hidden from the user all together (as in recommender systems). How to use estimates of social trust to build actual trust in people, content, and systems is also important.

This book is organized into three sections, corresponding to these major challenges:

---

[3] http://trust.mindswap.org/SocialNetworks

- Section 1 presents research on models of trust that address issues of identity, dynamics, and past interactions.
- Section 2 addresses trust propagation methods for use in social networks.
- Section 3 discusses many applications that use trust, covering many of the potential uses discussed here.

1.3 Future Questions

The work presented here provides a broad overview of the cutting edge research on computing with social trust. However, there are many more challenges that must be addressed. In particular, methods of evaluation, additional applications, and integration of techniques are all under researched areas.

Evaluation is very difficult when working with social trust, particularly in modeling, propagation, and other estimation methods. Because trust is sensitive, users do not publicly share these values. Nearly all social networks and other applications with trust ratings from their users keep this data hidden. On one hand, this is good for the users, because they are more likely to provide honest information when they know that it is private. From a research perspective, this is challenging because there are no open sources of data available to work with. For researchers who are fortunate enough to have access to their own social networks (e.g. the FilmTrust system [3] used in the chapter by Golbeck and Kuter, or the Advogato network [5] used in the chapter by Levien), they are still testing on only *one* network. Any analysis using a single network cannot make claims about robustness or scalability. In fact, this lack of data means that frequently research on trust models and inference algorithms is published with very little empirical analysis.

For work in this space to progress and have significant impact in large Web environments, we must develop new and better ways of evaluating our work. A possible solution would be a trust network generator, which could generate simulated networks of varying size, structural dynamics, and with realistic trust properties. While simulated networks will not work as well as natural ones, they offer an opportunity to do basic testing of scalability and performance of the algorithms. Another approach would be to gather as many social networks as possible with trust data, and generate anonymized versions for use in benchmark data sets. There are undoubtedly more solutions, and additional research in this space would be a great benefit to the community.

More applications are also necessary to understand when and how trust is useful. This book contains five chapters on applications that use trust for their functionality, and there are a handful of other applications that have been either prototyped or fully implemented and analyzed. It is still an open question as to which applications see the best improvement for the user from these values and where trust is not as reliable as it needs to be to add significant value. This understanding can only come from further development and evaluation of a wide range of applications.

Finally, how to best match trust algorithms with the requirements of a specific application is a problem that has received very little attention. The organization of this book separates trust models and inference algorithms from applications of trust. This is quite reflective of the way research has progressed. While many researchers develop both algorithms and applications (including many chapter authors in this book), the interface between the two is not well analyzed. There are major differences among types of trust algorithms and their outputs—which one works best for which applications is largely unstudied. When work develops, both an algorithm and an application, there is rarely consideration of other algorithms that could be used in that application. With a wider range of applications available, and more advanced methods of evaluation for trust algorithms, this next question of how to best couple the two can be answered.

1.4 Conclusions

The Web is providing an ever-growing set of applications and environments where users interact with one another directly or through content. In these virtual, often anonymous interactions, trust is a critical component to building effective systems. Unlike traditional computing environments that treat reliability, responsiveness, or accuracy as measures of trust, the fuzzier *social* trust is particularly well suited to these new Web settings. Computing with social trust—whether modeling it, inferring it, or integrating it into applications—is becoming an important area of research that holds great promise for improving the way people access information.

This book is a collection of work from top researchers in this exciting area, assembled with the goal of providing full coverage of these interrelated topics. As with any nascent research area, much work remains to be done. It is clear that the information problems that motivate this work will continue to grow, and social trust is likely to increase in its importance as an approach to addressing them.

References

1. Paul Alexandru Chirita, Stratos Idreos, Manolis Koubarakis, and Wolfgang Nejdl. Publish/subscribe for rdf-based p2p networks. In *In Proceedings of 1st European Semantic Web Symposium*, 2004.
2. Cynthia L. Corritore, Beverly Kracher, and Susan Wiedenbeck. On-line trust: concepts, evolving themes, a model. *Int. J. Hum.-Comput. Stud.*, 58(6):737–758, 2003.
3. Jennifer Golbeck. Generating predictive movie recommendations from trust in social networks. In *Proceedings of the Fourth International Conference on Trust Management*, 2006.
4. Jennifer Golbeck. The dynamics of web-based social networks: Membership, relationships, and change. *First Monday*, 12(11), 2007.
5. Raph Levien and Alex Aiken. Attack-resistant trust metrics for public key certification. In *7th USENIX Security Symposium*, pp. 229–242, 1998.
6. Stephen Marsh. *Formalising Trust as a Computational Concept*. PhD thesis, University of Stirling, Department of Mathematics and Computer Science, November 1994.

Part I
Models of Social Trust

Chapter 2
Examining Trust, Forgiveness and Regret as Computational Concepts

Stephen Marsh and Pamela Briggs

Abstract The study of trust has advanced tremendously in recent years, to the extent that the goal of a more unified formalisation of the concept is becoming feasible. To that end, we have begun to examine the closely related concepts of regret and forgiveness and their relationship to trust and its siblings. The resultant formalisation allows computational tractability in, for instance, artificial agents. Moreover, regret and forgiveness, when allied to trust, are very powerful tools in the Ambient Intelligence (AmI) security area, especially where Human Computer Interaction and concrete human understanding are key. This paper introduces the concepts of regret and forgiveness, exploring them from social psychological as well as a computational viewpoint, and presents an extension to Marsh's original trust formalisation that takes them into account. It discusses and explores work in the AmI environment, and further potential applications.

2.1 Introduction

Agents, whether human or artificial, have to make decisions about a myriad of different things in often difficult circumstances: whether or not to accept help, or from whom; whether or not to give a loan to a friend; which contractor to choose to install a new kitchen; whether to buy from this online vendor, and how much money to risk in doing so and so on. As has been pointed out [15], invariably trust is a component of these decisions. Trust is a central starting point for decisions based on risk [59], and that's pretty much all decisions involving putting ourselves or our resources in the hands (or whatever) of someone, or something, else.

We can see trust as exhibiting something of a duality – in many decisions one trusts or does not, whereas in others one can trust *this much*, and no more, and decide

S. Marsh (✉)
National Research Council Canada, Institute for Information Technology, Ottawa, Ontario, Canada
e-mail: steve.marsh@nrc-cnrc.gc.ca

P. Briggs (✉)
Northumbria University, School of Psychology and Sport Sciences, Newcastle upon Tyne, UK
e-mail: p.briggs@unn.ac.uk

J. Golbeck (ed.), *Computing with Social Trust,* Human-Computer Interaction Series, DOI 10.1007/978-1-84800-356-9_2 © Springer-Verlag London Limited 2009

where to go from there. To make the study of trust somewhat more interesting, as well as this duality, trust exhibits a behaviour that is singular in that it is seen only in its consequences – that is, I may say 'I trust you' but until I do something that *shows* that I trust you, the words mean nothing. Like light, trust is seen in its effect on something, and inbetween truster and trustee, there is simply nothing to see.

Trust provides a particularly useful tool for the decision maker in the 'shadow of doubt' [50], and indeed "distrust" provides useful analysis and decision making tools in its own right (cf. [70, 30, 71, 67]). That said, the dynamics of trust seem far from simple, in that trust is itself influenced by, and influences, many other social phenomena, some of which are the subjects of study in their own right, including, for instance, morality, apologies and ethics [18, 90, 21, 43, 76, 8, 5]. The recent interest in trust (brought on mainly from the eCommerce field, and the rapid convergence of technologies and 'social' connections of people across distance) has resulted in a much greater understanding of trust as a single object of study. We believe that the time is right to expand that study into the counterparts of trust.

We are working toward an over-arching theory and model of artificial trust-based behaviour for a specific culture[1] in a human-populated social setting. In such a setting, it is important to be able to reason with and about the social norms in operation at that time. As such, while there exist many promising angles of study, the logical next step for us is to attempt to incorporate into our understanding of trust a deeper understanding of what it can lead to, and what happens next.

What trusting (or failing to trust) can lead to, amongst other things, is *regret*: regret over what was, or might have been, what was or was not done and so on. What comes next may well be *forgiveness*: for wrongs done to us, or others, by ourselves or others. We conjecture that a deeper understanding of, and at least pseudo-formal model of, trust, regret and forgiveness and how they may be linked is a necessary step toward our goal. The reasons why regret and forgiveness are worth studying will be discussed further below, but that they have both been the objects of study of philosophers and psychologists for many years (or centuries) [2, 16, 7, 55, 26, 49, 27, 87, 37], and moving into the present day they provide ever more compelling topics for discussion and examination, for instance, in areas where humans work and play virtually (cf. [86]).

This chapter shows the enhancement of a model of trust that was first introduced in 1992 [62, 65, 63]. At that time, the model incorporated a great deal of input from the social sciences and philosophies, and although it was aimed at being a computationally tractable model, and indeed was implemented, it had its difficulties, as many observers have since pointed out. This work marks the first major enhancement of the model, and incorporates previously published work on the 'darker' side of trust [67] as well as recent forays into regret management and punishment [26].

---

[1] When one comes from a largely western-oriented judaeo-christian culture, one tends to look in that direction. However, trust and its application across cultures is not an ignored topic at all [45, 54, 74, 14]

Accordingly, the first part of the chapter delves into the whys and wherefores of trust itself, and why it's worth studying, before setting the stage in Section 2.3 with a parable for the modern age that brings regret and forgiveness into the frame of Ambient Intelligence and Information Sharing. Following diversionary comments related to human factors, which explain to an extent why we followed the less formal path in the first place, the original model is briefly presented in Section 2.4.

Section 2.6 presents a discussion of the dark side of trust: distrust and its siblings, untrust and mistrust. They must be incorporated into the model before we can proceed further because ultimately regret and forgiveness and betrayal of trust will lead us into areas where trust is more murky. In Section 2.7, we present a thorough examination of regret, its roots and uses, and incorporate it into the model in Section 2.8, while Sections 2.9 and 2.10 accomplish much the same for forgiveness. A worked example of the phenomena in practice is given in Section 2.11, along with a brief discussion of some of the current work in which we are applying the concepts. Conceding that this is not the final word on trust, we discuss related work and future work in trust as is may be in Sections 2.12 and 2.13 before concluding.

2.1.1 Caveats

This chapter is not going to state how trust works. To an extent, what is being looked at in this work is not actually *trust* at all, as we see it in everyday life, but a derivative of it. In much the same way that Artificial Intelligence is not *real* intelligence, the computational concept of trust isn't *really* trust at all, and if the reader wants other views of real trust, there are many excellent tomes out there (for instance, [73, 72, 85, 24, 15, 33], to name a few). For some time, we felt that the artificial concept needed a name that was different enough from the original to remove the need for preconceptions, and introduce the opportunity for ingenuity (and let's be fair, some cost-cutting in definitions), and a foray into other names resulted in the *Boing* concept [66] as an attempt to do just that. Still, there is something to be gained from using a term close to the original from a human factors point of view, as is discussed later in this chapter. That given, at this time, we remain with the term 'trust'.

Some of this chapter may seem overly philosophical, or even quasi-religious, for a book on Computing with Trust. We make no apology for this—the foundations of trust go a long way back into many spheres, and when one considers the concept of forgiveness in particular, there is much to learn from a great many of the world's religions. If our ultimate aim is the attainment of socially viable 'automation' (call it an agent) of sorts, extant in the worlds, both physical and artificial, where humans also exist, a solid interpretation of human social norms is necessary. Trust, Forgiveness and Regret are merely steps along this way, but a strong model incorporating all three is necessary, and this is what we are attempting here. This is, of course, not to say that Trust, Regret and Forgiveness are the most *important* or even *timely* objects of study. In a world where opportunities for 'betrayal' of trust keep multiplying and the precious shadow of the future keeps shrinking [15, p. 3], we see that thinking about regret and forgiveness is at least moving in a right direction.

2.2 Why Is Trust Important? Why a Formalization?

> ... trust is a social good to be protected just as much as the air we breathe or the water we drink. When it is damaged, the community as a whole suffers; and when it is destroyed, societies falter and collapse.
>
> Bok, 1978, pp 26 and 27.

Trust is so all pervasive in all of our lives, online or not, that it sometimes seems strange to either have to ask or answer the question of why trust is important. Despite the need for more control, especially with regard to technology [15], trust remains a paramount part of our daily lives. This is especially true when other people are involved, thus, when making decisions about using a babysitter to buying a house, trust, and confidence, are elements in the decision, even if sometimes managed more by regulation. An absence of trust in a society seems to result in the death of that society, however small (cf. [9, 52].)

For an artificial entity extant in a social world where humans are present, this is a fact: humans must be considered in terms of trust, and while the considerations are many, they include the following:

- How much they might trust an entity or what the entity gives them (for instance, information);
- How much they might trust each other in a social network;
- How much they can be trusted in a given situation, either by the entity or by someone else working with them;
- What can be done to augment the trust in order to achieve a higher level of confidence;

The key thing to note here is that allowing technology, the artificial entity, to consider trust, amongst the other factors at its disposal in decision making, can be nothing other than positive. As Gambetta states, 'if behaviour spreads through learning and imitation, then sustained distrust can only lead to further distrust. Trust, even if always misplaced, can never do worse than that, and the expectation that it might do at least marginally better is therefore plausible.' [34]. If this is true for us as humans, it may as well be true for the artificial entities that we allow into our societies and that, crucially, we allow to make decisions for us.

It may follow then that introducing a way for these entities to reason with and about trust, and its allied phenomena, such as regret and forgiveness, gives them a more solid footing in the human societies into which they are introduced. Any computational formalism or formalization of trust is a step in that direction. While some are used, for instance, to judge the reliability or manage the reputation of strangers; others, such as that proposed here, are more generalized (and as a result perhaps less tractable).

It is possible to argue that of course, we cannot trust machines, merely rely on them to operate as promised, indeed that 'people trust people, not technology' [32], but that is of course exactly the point—in designing a scheme for computational trust we are allowing the technology to reason about trust between people. That the agents in the deliberation may be human *or* technological, as Cofta states [15], and can reason about trust within *each other* is an added bonus.

What should be clear from the preceding discussion is that this work is not in itself the development of a Trust Management system, where social agents consider each other using potentially shared, inferred and transitive trust or reputation (for instance, [38, 47, 81]). While naturally, considering how much you might trust another necessitates such a system when the other is a stranger, it is not the focus of our work, which is the individual considerations and internal workings of trust. Without both, there is a lack of *completeness* for agents making social trust deliberations.

2.3 A Parable of the Modern Age

Consider Ambient Intelligence (AmI).

AmI is a big thing. Stemming from Weiser's [88] vision of ubiquitous computing, and from there through the European Union's Information Society Technologies Program Advisory Group, it has become a vision of 'intelligent and intuitive interfaces embedded in everyday objects [..] responding to the presence of individuals in an invisible way' [3]. A good vision, no doubt, but one that is nevertheless still some way away. The technical aspects of AmI are within our grasp, but what of the social? In particular, since in such a vision information will be flowing around us—invisible, and highly personal—how are we to ultimately trust what is said about us? More, how are we to ensure that the systems that 'represent' us will reflect our values when deciding whether and how to share information.

These questions are not new, but in general, the assumption is that it'll all be alright on the night and we can convince people to trust the systems because they will be built to be trustworthy. A great many advances have taken place in the field of trust management dedicated to exactly this concept, and they will result in better and more trustable systems. However, we are forgetting that the other side of the trust coin is risk.

The question is, what really is going on? Ultimately, the AmI goal is about sharing, and reasoning with, enough knowledge and information that sensible, socially appropriate things can happen for individuals. As individuals, then, we can help the AmI environment make the correct decisions, and potentially avoid some of the worst pitfalls. Trust, as has been pointed out elsewhere [56], is an excellent tool in this regard.

Consider then, this conceptual story about granting access to information. At most levels, Steve is happy with lots of people to see lots about him. Some information is more private, yet more is more private still. Steve can say all this to his agent in the AmI environment and let it get on with things. In a truly artificial society, the likes of which AmI aims to support, his agent will share data with, and get data from, other agents (Steve need not see this happening, and Steve need not see the data). The sharing of this data can be based on trust.

Imagine that Steve's friend Alice also has a device on which is an agent. Alice is a close friend and so their agents are also in close contact. One day Alice's agent requests some information about Steve that is private, but for a legitimate reason. Maybe it's a credit card number, maybe it's a health information, or maybe it is just a password for Steve's private photo site. The point is not that the information is *necessarily* harmful, it is just private as far as Steve is concerned. Given their (and Alice and Steve's) closeness, Steve's agent reasons (we'll get to that) that it can trust Alice's agent with that information. Now, Alice's agent knows this fact.

One fine weekend, Alice, Bob and Steve are out canoeing and kayaking in Algonquin Park. Alice's agent, still humming away back in town, inadvertently lets that snippet of private information out into the wider community. There's obviously no bringing it back, the damage is done.

Steve does not know about all of this, but his agent, being a member of that community itself, does. Feeling that trust has been betrayed. It contacts Alice's agent to request an exlanation. Alice's agent expresses regret, stating that the leak was unintentional and a result of a faulty decision in response to a request made by an external agency.

Based on, and mitigated by, Alice's agent's expressions of regret, Steve's agent reduces the amount of trust it has in that agent, effectively removing it from his closest circle of friends. This trust information is propagated to other close friends' agents (say, those in a direct contact with Steve). Because this information is shared, the other agents in Steve's circle of friends respect this decision and act accordingly, ensuring that no further information about him is shared with Alice's agent, and revising their own trust levels (although it is reasonable to assume that some might not alter their levels at all whilst still respecting the information block.)

Time passes, and depending on the severity of the leak, and the regret Steve's agent feels, coupled with that of Alice's agent, a forgiveness process kicks into play. Slowly, Alice's agent is trusted with more information (but monitored more closely, because of this), and eventually, at least potentially, allowed back into the circle of close friends. All is well.

Until Steve comes home and find out what happened.

Steve may wish to censure the agent myself, or even Alice for buying such a terrible implementation of an agent (she always was a cheapskate) but he has two choices here. His agent can explain its reasoning, he can accept its judgment and carry on. Otherwise, he can instruct it to censure Alice's agent once more, and be subject to his own decision about forgiveness. Steve will have to sort it out with Alice herself, but that's what people do. Alice can express her own regret, and ultimately the relationships, both human and artificial, can be repaired.

As an aside, Steve can also censure his own agent, revisiting the amount of 'trust' he had in it and revising it as he sees fit. Perhaps next time Steve won't be daft enough to let a connected machine hold sensitive personal information.

2.3.1 A Brief Sojourn to 'Human Factors': Why Not Call It Trust After All

Of course, one may argue that the agent isn't *really* trusting others, or even regretting what it did in sharing that information, but it certainly acts *as if* it is. So what's the difference? While that is largely a discussion for philosophy, there is one thing we can learn here: the agent can justify its decision in terms that Steve can understand. He knows what trust is, or at least, like most people, has an idea of how it works *for him*. So when he requests an explanation of why his agent shared this data with Alice's agent in the first place, as well as how it handled the situation, it uses words and concepts Steve readily understands—regret, forgiveness and trust. The agent may or may not be trusting, or feeling forgiveness, that's ultimately for Steve to decide, but the explanations are understandable. There are some parallels here with expert systems and the way in which they justify their own decisions via backtracking, but ultimately the use of the loaded terms of trust and other human understandable phenomena is, we conjecture, a more comfortable 'relationship' between user and technology.

There is much at stake here. As noted earlier, the acceptance of using trust as a means of helping make decisions means that sometimes trust gets misplaced. Mistakes are made. Risk is inherent in the consideration. As well, trust is vague: it's not the same thing to all people, and even if it was, my high trust may be equivalent to your low trust, depending on our personalities, because trust is seen in action, not thought. It may be possible to set up a 'soft secure' system using nothing more than trust values, but the risk is that they may be misinterpreted, or interpreted differently than the way Steve would have liked. This will happen. Trust and its siblings are not a panacea for technological ills.

2.4 Trust as Was

Trust has been extensively studied as a computational phenomenon in the past decade or so, and various models exist (e.g., [1, 75, 83, 38, 51]). All of them have different yet related ways of looking at trust, even different values for expressing the phenomenon. For coherence with our thoughts, we will extend our own in this chapter, although the concepts of regret and forgiveness are as applicable to the other models. Marsh's model appeared first in 1992 [62] and in revised form in 1994 [63]. While it has its problems, it remains as a standalone model capable of being adapted, revised and revisited. This chapter in fact revisits and alters the formalisation for ease of incorporation of regret and forgiveness, and in line with what we have learned in the past few years. However, it seems prudent to explore what is being revised before actually doing so. This section, then, presents the model before we move on to the matter of making it in some way different.

As we have mentioned in Section 2.1.1, the key here is to note that the purpose of this formalisation is not to accurately model social trust, but rather to give a piece for discussion and better understanding of the behaviour of the phenomenon, either artificial or real.

Bearing in mind that distinct trust levels are ambiguous at best (at least in terms of semantics and subjectivity [1, p. 124]), we will use them anyway. We believe their benefits far outweigh their disadvantages, and include the ability to narrow down and discuss subconcepts (as is shown below), (computational) tractability and the ability to discuss and compare to some extent, and given a limited amount of space here, we will argue the point at length elsewhere.

From [63] we use the notation shown in Table 2.1. For more information and discussions on the use of values and their ultimate frailties, see [63, 75, 84], amongst others.

Some explanation is in order before continuing. We see time in this system as a set of discrete states, at each of which an agent may find itself in a given *situation*—a need to carry out some task, get some information, send some and so on. In this situation, an agent has decisions to make about who it might trust, and how much, in order to carry out its task. The passage of time, the introduction of new agents, the changing of priorities and more can all have an effect, and create what is ultimately a new situation for that agent.

We do not think that this is ultimately very different from 'real' life. Others may disagree.

The formalisations are [63] attempted to answer questions about trust in cooperative situations. That is, given the choice between cooperation and non-cooperation, whether to cooperate with a specific trustee or not. We make a simplifying assumption, for the purpose of the consideration, that there are two protagonists. The systems work for more, however: just figure out which you trust the most in this situation.

Table 2.1 Summary of notation ('Actors' are truster, trustee and others)

Description	Representation	Value Range
Situations	$\alpha, \beta, \ldots$	
Actors	$a, b, c, \ldots$	
Set of Actors	$\mathscr{A}$	
Societies of Actors	$\mathscr{S}_1, \mathscr{S}_2 \ldots$	
	$\mathscr{S}_n \in \mathscr{A}$	
Knowledge (e.g., x knows y)	$K_x(y)$	True/False
Importance (e.g., of α to x)	$I_x(\alpha)$	$[0, +1]$
Utility (e.g., of α to x)	$U_x(\alpha)$	$[-1, +1]$
Basic Trust (e.g., of x)	T_x	$[-1, +1)$
General Trust (e.g., of x in y)	$T_x(y)$	$[-1, +1)$
Situational Trust (e.g., of x in y for α)	$T_x(y, \alpha)$	$[-1, +1)$

Two formulae are used, the first being to estimate Situational Trust, the second to estimate a Cooperation Threshold. To estimate situational trust, an entity x uses:

$$T_x(y, \alpha) = U_x(\alpha) \times I_x(\alpha) \times \widehat{Tx(y)} \tag{2.1}$$

The $\widehat{T_x(y)}$ here emphasises that x can use previous trust-based knowledge in y in this calculation, whether related to this situation or not [63]. Thus, *at this time, in this situation*, x has *this much* trust in y. It's important to make this clear because in a different situation, this may be very different—if the situation is more important to x, for instance.

This is, though, only half the story. Regardless of how much x might trust y, any given situation might put x in an interesting decisional position. The consideration is how much do I *need* to trust you to cooperate with you in this situation? The answer lies within the *Cooperation Threshold*:

$$\text{Cooperation\_Threshold}_x(\alpha) = \frac{\text{Perceived\_Risk}_x(\alpha)}{\text{Perceived\_Competence}_x(y, \alpha) + \widehat{T_x(y)}} \times I_x(\alpha)$$
$$\tag{2.2}$$

This gives us a means of seeing what is necessary for x to accept any cooperation with (help from) y in this situation. We can state that,

$$T_x(y, \alpha) \geq \text{Cooperation\_Threshold}_x(\alpha) \Rightarrow \text{Will\_Cooperate}(x, y, \alpha)$$

It is a truism to say that, when trust is upheld, it is strengthened. When betrayed, it is weakened. Most practitioners accept this statement, with caveats here and there. In our earlier work [63], we proposed that: If:

$$\text{Helped}(x, y, \alpha)^{t-\delta} \wedge \text{Defected}(y, \beta)^t \tag{2.3}$$

Then:

$$T_x(y)^{t+1} \ll T_x(y)^t$$

Informally, if x helped y in the past, and y responded at this time by defecting, the trust x has in y will reduce by a large amount. The converse is if:

$$\text{Helped}(x, y, \alpha)^{t-\delta} \wedge \text{Cooperated}(y, \beta)^t \tag{2.4}$$

Then:

$$T_x(y)^{t+1} \geq T_x(y)^t$$

Informally, if x helped y in the past, and y reciprocated at this time with cooperation, then the amount of trust x has in y will remain the same or increase only by a small amount.

In other words, the amount of trust x has in y substantially decreases following y not reciprocating [10]. However, y's reciprocation merely confirms to x that she (x) was correct in helping y in the first place [52]. This being the case, x had every right to *expect* y to help. So, although y's reciprocation may lead x to trust her *judgement* of people more, she may revise her trust in y only slightly, if at all [52].

However, beyond these musings, little was said about how much was a lot, or a little, with respect to how to alter trust values. We revisit this below.

2.5 What Can't Trust Give Us?

It would be wise to consider trust as a part of a solution for any artificial (or natural) socially or culturally embedded entity. Just as humans are more than trusting or untrusting creatures, and use trust as a part of their decision-making process, the same applies to artificial agents.

Most importantly, trust cannot give us *certainty*—it is a judgment based on evidence, potentially 'irrational' feelings (in humans), and is often skewed in one way or another. In fact, to trust inherently holds with it the risk of betrayal [59]—if certainty was what was sought (and achieved), trust would not be necessary.

Trust cannot give us *control*. Control is the antithesis of a trusting relationship because it implies that one is not putting oneself into another's hands (which is what trust is), but that one has the right and the power to enforce behaviour in others. That is not to say that trusting others does not bring some form of control, at least in a moral sense (as in fact does forgiveness, if taken to extremes). Thus, if I say 'I trust you' and you are trustworthy and a moral person, you will feel obligated to work in my best interests. Needless to say this control is flimsy and easily ignored if you're not a morally righteous person!

Trust can't give us *confidence*. It can give us a sense of risk-laden comfort about the path we have chosen, but it isn't the same as knowing (being confident) that someone you are buying online from will deliver the goods and not overcharge (cf. [15]). Confidence is often achieved through rules and regulations that are backed up by a trustworthy legal or social system (the irony in that sentence is not lost to us).

In short, trust gives us little more than a soft relationship with another entity. If that entity values the relationship, understands the meaning and culture of trust *and is trustworthy*, we're likely okay to trust. If any of these pre-requisites fails, we might well be in trouble. Ultimately the same applies to other soft notions as regret, forgiveness and morality. That doesn't make them useless – they have a power that is not physical or, usually, legally binding, and convey upon the trustee weighty responsibilities which, all things being equal, are not easily ignored. Certainly, we feel that they can be the *basis* for social behaviour and decision making in a moral social world, and potentially have strength even in a darker society, as long as there are some trustworthy agents out there. Various experiments with trust uphold this view well enough (see [89, 4, 79], amongst others).

2.6 Trust as Is, Part Zero: The Dark Side

In [67] we presented to the trusting agent the concepts of distrust, untrust and mistrust. Distrust has in fact become a much more popular object of study, although given the number of definitions of trust [15, 69, 70], distrust is at least as difficult to pin down. Distrust is often considered as the 'negative mirror-image of trust' [85, page 26], a 'confident negative expectation regarding anothers conduct' [54 page 439] in a situation entailing risk to the trusting party. In situations where trust 'betrayals' happen, trust can easily move toward distrust or untrust. Thus, since they bear relevance to our discussions of forgiveness and regret, the concepts are summarised here.

Trust is a continuously assessed, continuously variable measure, or relationship, between actors. It has positive and negative aspects, and indeed positive and negative values, at least in our model. Indeed, we can see trust as a continuum (see also Cofta's trust cube [15, p. 109] for a more dimensional model). Figure 2.1 illustrates the continuum, with negative trust values being seen as 'distrust' while positive trust values are seen as 'trust'. But there are gaps, in both the figure and our understanding, that are addressed in this work.

In [63] we stated that distrust was negative of trust. Here, we're evolving that definition because of the work that has been done in the area, and a greater understanding of the concept because of this work. That given, it's still surprisingly difficult to find definitions of distrust that don't use mistrust as synonymous. In fact, we believe this is a mistake because it removes a tool for trust researchers to be able to focus on what they are researching. For clarity, in [67] we used a comparison with the concepts of *misinformation* and *disinformation*. From the Oxford English Dictionary, we find that the term 'misinformation' can be taken to mean information that is incorrect. This can be a mistake on the part of the informer, and generally speaking, it can be spotted after the fact. The term 'disinformation' removes all doubt—it is information that is deliberately false and *intended* to deceive. That is, disinformation is misinformation that is deliberately and knowingly planted. From this, we moved to a better understanding of distrust and mistrust, and what untrust is.

A simple comparison between the concepts is probably necessary. For the sake of argument, following [10, 57, 78, 22, 59, 63], let us say that trust, in general, is taken as the belief (or a measure of it) that the trustee will act in the best interests

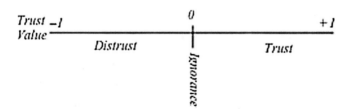

Fig. 2.1 Trust continuum: from distrust to trust

of the truster in a given situation, even when controls are unavailable and it may not be in the trustee's best interests to do so. Given this, we can now present untrust, distrust and mistrust.

2.6.1 Distrust

If we are to take disinformation as deliberately planted, that is, intentional and active misinformation, our extension with distrust is that it is also an active phenomenon, that is to say, when x distrusts y, it is because x has considered the situation, and actively *believes* that y has negative intentions toward her. We can put this semi-formally as:

$$T_x(y, \alpha) \; < 0 \Rightarrow \text{Distrust}(x, y, \alpha) \tag{2.5}$$

So, for this situation, x believes that y does not have her best interests at heart. Not only that, but y will actively seek to work against those best interests (this is not a failure of omission, in other words). As with a measure of trust, the greater the magnitude, the more the certainty and the greater the strength of belief that y will be actively against x's best interests.

2.6.2 Mistrust

Accepting that Misinformation is passive in some form (that is, it may or may not be intentional, and is a judgment usually attained after the fact), we similarly conjecture that *Mistrust* is misplaced trust. That is, following a decision in which there was a positive estimation of trust, and where one is betrayed, we can say that trust has been misplaced (not always 'betrayed,' since the trustee may not have had bad intentions). Thus, the truster *mistrusted* the trustee. As we see in [1] mistrust is defined so 'When a trustee betrays the trust of the truster, or, in other words, defaults on trust, we will say that a situation of mistrust has occured, or that the truster has mistrusted the trustee in that situation.' (p. 47).

Note that this works both ways, and one can mistrust by assuming the other is 'distrustworthy' when in fact they are 'on our side' [15, especially chapter], although it's harder to recover from that, or at least spot it, since in such a situation we're unlikely to give the other the chance to prove it.

This is perhaps something of a departure from traditional english usage, which tends to confuse distrust and mistrust, but we feel that for a computational model, some degree of accuracy and definition is required!

2.6.3 Untrust

As complicated as life is, it's unlikely that there are black and white aspects of trust without a little grey. The reader will have noticed that, given a specific situation, the cooperation threshold puts an artificial barrier somewhere along the trust continuum. It's likely that this barrier exists within the positive side of the spectrum, and so we have a situation where a trustee is viewed positively but not positively enough to cooperate with. Given Barber's [6] view of trust based on continuity, competence and motivation, evidence against any of those may well result in this situation, as we noted in earlier work [63]—I may trust my brother to drive me to the airport, but flying the plane is a different matter. This isn't because I distrust him, it's because I know he can't fly planes. In previous work [67] we stated that 'if we say a trustee is untrusted, then the truster has little confidence (belief, faith) in the trustee acting in their best interests in that particular situation', but that's not strictly true, as my brother's example shows (I presume he has my best interests at heart!). Of course, if he really did have my best interests at heart and knew he couldn't fly a plane, he wouldn't ordinarily offer...

This grey area is what Cofta calls *Mix-Trust* [15], and what we have chosen to call *untrust*.

We can present untrust formally as:

$$T_x(y, \alpha) > 0 \ \& \ T_x(y, \alpha) < \text{Cooperation\_Threshold}_x(\alpha) \Rightarrow \text{Untrust}(x, y, \alpha) \quad (2.6)$$

That is, if $T_x(y, \alpha)$ is less than the Cooperation Threshold but larger than 0, x is in a state of *untrust* in y. That is, x 'doesn't trust' y, but bear in mind that in fact the amount of trust is positive, which perhaps gives x some incentive to try to find a way to cooperate with y. Section 2.6.5 revisits the trust continuum to put untrust in its proper place on the map. The story isn't over for untrust yet either, as we'll see.

2.6.4 Ignorance Is...

Ignorance, the state where x knows nothing of y at all, or the situation she finds herself in, is classed as a zero state, thus $T_x(y, \alpha) = 0$. This is both very unusual and difficult to handle, but nevertheless needs to be acknowledged. It's unusual because, in general, we can conjecture from previous experience either about potential trust in others—so called *Basic Trust* (cf. [63])—and in situations (although this may be more difficult for an artificial entity.)

2.6.5 The Continuum, Revisited

We are now beginning to see how distrust and its siblings in fact are present on the continuum of trust. As we see in Fig. 2.2, we still have negative trust being distrust, and now we can have a new section on the continuum, where untrust lives – below the level, for any given situation, of the cooperation threshold, yet still in the realms of positive trust.

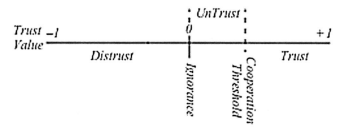

Fig. 2.2 Trust continuum: untrust

The figure does not include *mistrust*, for the simple reason that mistrust is everywhere – in other words, it's possible to make errors in trusting (or distrusting) estimations throughout the continuum. Thus, one can think of mistrust as an overarching *possibility* across the continuum of trust.

We will revisit this continuum later in the chapter.

2.6.6 Continuing a Difficult Relationship

As we have noted previously, distrust and untrust are important not because they may stop some relationships, or cooperation, but because they may in fact allow something to continue [67, p. 21]. Consider a situation where x has little choice but to cooperate in some way with y, even while she distrusts y – the measure of distrust allows x to make hedges in order to achieve a greater comfort (and control [15]) over the errant y. More importantly, if x *un*trusts y there is evidence somewhere (for instance, using Barber's assessment classes [6]) that there is a positive relationship to work on in order to achieve greater comfort or control for x.

Trust and its siblings are not, then, the only decision, or control tool available to an agent, they are just some of many. In the final analysis, they may indeed be little more than pointers to the need for remedial work on a relationship, or a legal contract, or letters of reference, and so on. If this is so, their value is no less than if they were the ultimate arbiters of relationships.

That said, we do believe that trust is simply a part of the decision making puzzle, and that other psycho-social phenomena and/or emotions play a large part in the decisions people make. We have chosen to focus in this work on two of these, regret and forgiveness, and how they interact with trust and each other.

2.7 Regret

Trust is only required if a bad outcome would make you regret your decision.

Luhmann, 1978, p. 98.

Regret has been studied in psychology and economics for some time. In 1982, both Bell [7] and Loomes and Sugden [55] independently introduced the concept of regret theory in economics, itself based on the social psychological theory of counterfactual thinking [82]. In game theory, the Savage/Regret Minimax theory has existed for some time [58], itself based again on interpretation of psychological theories. Further, regret continues to be an active field of study in psychology and economics, as well as philosophy and health care [2, 16, 7, 55, 26]. In many of these works, the concept is analyzed mathematically, as per Bell's work and beyond. Despite its strengths, it is not our intention to extend this economic or game theoretical work [61] into our own. Instead we have chosen to model regret in a much simpler manner, with two main aims:

- The simplicity of the model may become more accessible to non-mathemeticians (perhaps most members of an AmI society in the future!)
- The broad extensibility and interpretation that a very simple model might give may enable further work in very different micro and macro analysis in future.

In one form, regret is a form of cognitive dissonance that an actor feels when what is done is in dissonance with what the actor feels should have been done [31, 42]. After a decision is made, if it is not supported by what we think is 'right,' we will feel 'bad' about it. This is of course not the only aspect of regret that is of importance here, although it does give additional decision-making aspects for trusting agents. Another aspect of regret is experienced following a trusting decision that is betrayed by the trustee. We will attempt to formalise both aspects of regret here.

When a decision is made to trust, effectively in error (a mistrusting decision, here), what happens next is a betrayal of that trust. It is important to consider two types of betrayal – first, where the trustee *knew* they were trusted, and second, where they *did not know*. In the first instance, we propose that the regret felt by the truster is greater than in the second, because the truster has reason to believe the trustee made a conscious decision to betray the trust. Of course, there are both mitigators and exacerbators for both kinds of betrayal and these include the following:

- The regret felt by the trustee post decision;
- (Not the same), acknowledgment of the betrayal by the trustee;
- The magnitude of the 'betrayal' – whether the trustee knows of it or not;
- Reparations;

2.7.1 What Regret Is

Regret allows an action or happening to be looked upon as negative, and further allows the actors, or observers, to reinforce behaviours or associated feelings or emotions (such as trust) to ensure that the likelihood of such a thing happening again is reduced. It is, therefore, a powerful motivational force in interactions with others. Further, because it can have an effect on trust, it is necessary to study, formalise and concretise regret to the extent that it becomes a computational tool similar to the current status of trust.

However, regret, while a tool for hindsight, is also a predictive tool. For instance, it is possible to say I am going to regret this (and then do it anyway!). In this way, regret, as with trust, allows a consideration of possible alternatives in a situation in order to choose the best, or most likely not to cause regret, for instance. Thus regret, like trust, is a powerful tool in the consideration of actions and alternatives. When allied to trust, it becomes much more powerful and predictive.

2.7.2 The Many Faces of Regret

Like most terms that encompass human feelings (including trust), regret is somewhat overloaded. It is possible to regret something that one is personally involved with (or did), and it is possible to regret something that was done, or happened. There are, then, several valid uses of the term. Additionally, it may be possible to feel that something should not have been done without necessarily regretting that it was. Moreover, it is possible to regret something but have seen no choice. For instance, 'I wish I hadn't done that' is not the same as 'I feel bad for having done that,' which might be the same as 'I regret having done that.' But regret can encompass other things too: 'It is with regret that I must announce the death of' is for example not an admission of fault, but is an admission that what has happened is regretted, that the feelings involved are negative. Similarly for statements such as 'That was a regrettable incident.'

2.7.3 Modeling Regret

Largely, in this work, we are concerned with answering the questions:

- What was lost (κ)
- What it meant (λ)
- How it feels (μ)

While the latter question is harder to estimate for an artificial entity, the first two are relatively straightforward if we can also consider what has come before, thus if there is a potential measure of utility, we can use this in determining what was lost, and if there is a measure of importance (and perhaps trust) we can use this in determining what it meant to the agent concerned. The rest, we may have to leave to the owner of an artificial entity, rather than the entity itself.

2.7.3.1 I Regret That You Did That

A truster, when betrayed, can feel regret that they were betrayed. In simple utilitarian terms we can say that the regret felt is based on opportunity cost, or the amount of utility lost from the betrayal as compared to what could have been gained (this is in fact similar to the Savage/regret Minimax criterion [58]). We suggest that there's something more to it than that, simply because there was in fact a trusting decision made. Bear in mind that in much extant work this decision would imply that in fact there is much more to lose than would have been gained in the decision to trust [59, 23] (but this view is somewhat mitigated in [39, 63]). In any case, the decision to trust has put the truster in the trustee's hands at least to some extent [10] and thus the betrayal (whether the trustee knows of it or not) is felt more personally (as a caveat, though, consider that 'trust can only concern that which one person can rightfully demand of another' [44, page 319] when thinking about regret).

Thus, we add considerations not only of utility, but also of the trust that was originally placed in the situation to our regret function:

$$\text{Regret}_x(\alpha) = (U_x(\alpha) - U_x(\alpha^-)) \bullet f(\kappa, \lambda, \mu) \tag{2.7}$$

Where:

- The $\bullet$ denotes some operation (presently, we use multiplication);
- $U_x(\alpha^-)$ is the utility gained from what happened (the 'betrayal' situation) as opposed to what was originally estimated *could have been* gained ($U_x(\alpha)$);

Note that we see regret as a primarily situational phenomenon. It not only simplifies the agent's considerations of what is regretted, but allows a significant amount of control over what is assessed in the regret function.

The function addressing our primary questions (what was lost, what it meant and how it feels) is addressed partly here. We are working continuously on refinements.

There are considerations. First, that the amount of trust that existed, as well as the Cooperation Threshold, are important aspects in the regret measurement, and second, that the relationship itself is of potential importance in the final analysis. This is consistent with [53]'s analysis of Calculus-Based, Knowledge-Based, and Identification-Based Trust, and goes a little way toward not only answering *what it meant*, but also *how it feels*, for our agent.

Thus we propose:

$$f(\kappa, \lambda, \mu) = \text{C\_T}_x(y, \alpha)^t + \text{I}_x(xy) \tag{2.8}$$

- $\text{I}_x(xy)$ is the importance, to x, of the relationship xy – see below for more discussion of this;
- $\text{C\_T}_x(y, \alpha)^t$ is the Cooperation Threshold for x at that situation.

Here, *what it meant* (Cooperation Threshold, which took into account trust in the first place) and *how it feels* ($\text{I}_x(xy)$) are addressed, with what was lost being taken into account via the incorporation of utility.

The importance of the relationship features prominently here.

Clearly, there are times when nothing is known of the other, and so we use, very simply:

$$f(\kappa, \lambda, \mu) = \text{Importance}_x(\alpha) \tag{2.9}$$

Hence, the more important the situation was, the more regret is felt that a betrayal occurred. Don't forget utility is also taken into account. Again, we strive to answer *what was lost* (Utility) and *what it meant* (in this case, Importance).

There is much work to be done here, and we are addressing it. For instance, even when nothing is known of the other, sometimes the relationship is still important (for instance, when dealing with authority).

2.7.3.2 You Regret That You Did That

As noted earlier, the other side of regret is where the transgressor (the trustee) expresses (or feels) a sense of regret for what they have done (this is related to the idea of post-decisional dissonance [80]). We have suggested above that this feeling of regret need not in fact be accompanied by some form of acknowledgment of wrong done. This is more applicable when the regret expressed is over something that was outside the control of the transgressor, for example. More plausible, perhaps, is acknowledgment without regret, which we do not cover here. For the sake of simplicity, we will not be considering these different angles here, focusing only on the expression of, and feeling of, regret, and how it potentially affects trust.

The formula is similar to equation (2.7):

$$\text{Regret}_y(\alpha) = (U_y(\alpha) - U_y(\alpha^-)) \bullet I_y(yx) \tag{2.10}$$

Note that first, the consideration of regret here must be taken from the point of view of the transgressor, but in some what calculated (or transmitted to) the truster (who was betrayed). This is something of a problem area (y could lie, to try preserve the relationship and benefit, perhaps, from more transgressions) and needs to be further addressed.

Here, y may regret having done something, but again expressing this in a purely economic sense is not acknowledging the role of the relationship (and trust in some way). The inclusion of the importance of the relationship to y mitigates any benefit y may have gained from y's betrayal.

Given these measures of regret, it is up to x to decide how to use them in mitigating the initial, and continuing, effect on trust of the transgression. In this work, the regret calculations are simply a part of how forgiveness, the repairing of the trust relationship, works in a computational sense.

2.7.3.3 I Regret That I *Didn't* Do That, and Derivatives

Consistent with findings from counterfactual thinking and regret [36], there is evidence to suggest that we often regret that we *didn't* take more risks, do more things, at least in specific, and so on, as we grow older – a lost opportunity is something none of us appreciate. While this seems somewhat odd to think about in terms of AmI and trust, in fact, the *Anticipated (Anticipatory) Regret* (AR) of not doing (or of refraining from doing) something is potentially a powerful motivational force in actually getting us to take risks and trust more. That being the case, we can incorporate AR into the trust considerations of an agent. Indeed, we feel that AR has a role in determining the Cooperation Threshold for an agent in a given situation.

A development from [63] taking this into account gives a simple proposal for a derivative of AR:

$$\text{Cooperation\_Threshold}_x(\alpha) =$$
$$\frac{\text{Perceived\_Risk}_x(\alpha)}{\text{Perceived\_Competence}_x(y, \alpha) + \widehat{T_x(y)}} \times (I_x(\alpha) - \text{AR}(\alpha^-)) \quad (2.11)$$

Thus, here, the utility of α^- can be taken as a positive motivational force, because α^- may be regretted if *not* done. Note that, the determination of AR in this circumstance is not necessarily different from in, for example, equation (2.7), but a negative regret from that equation would be a positive AR in equation (2.11). Equation (2.11) is in fact more properly *I Will Regret it if I* Don't *Do That*, a much more useful tool for the computational trusting agent.

There is also much work on using this as a tool for trying to avoid doing something that we will regret later (see for example [7, 55, 2]). I may decide against smoking another cigarette, or going out drinking the night before an exam because I know that I'll regret it later (bad health, bad grades and so on). Once again this can be a powerful tool in decision making, although it's more properly characterized as *I Will Regret it if I* Do *Do That*. The calculation is similar to that in equation (2.11).

2.8 Trust as Is, Part One: Building Regret into Trust

Now, it is possible to think about how regret can be used to both mitigate the behaviour of others and to respond to it. We have in the past [63, 64] considered the adjustment of trust values following transgressions or cooperation, particularly as regards optimism and pessimism. It is the adjustment of trust, in fact, that both forgiveness and regret will have an impact on.

As a start, consider the following:

$$T_x(y^{t+n}) = T_x(y^t) \pm f(\text{Cooperation\_Threshold}_x(\alpha)^t, T_x(y\alpha)^t) \quad (2.12)$$

Thus, the amount of trust x will have in y at a subsequent timestep $(n > 0)$ will be dependent on the situation x was in, via some analysis of the relationship between the cooperation threshold and situational trust – intuitively, and for the sake of argument, the greater the difference in one direction or another between these thresholds, the more the effect on the adjustment. In fact, for an upward movement, this may be a reliable method, but there is general agreement, at least for what [53] call *Calculus Based Trust* and *Knowledge Based Trust*, that trust is in fact relatively fragile – that is, hard to build up and easy to lose. A sensible function in equation (2.12) will naturally have to take this into account. In the past we have also used a simple percentage calculation, thus the more y was trusted, the more the movement in trust (downward, at least).

Taking into account a transgression, it's now possible to enhance this equation to take into account regret:

$$T_x(y)^{t+n} = T_x(y^t) - f(\text{Cooperation\_Threshold}_x(\alpha)^t,$$
$$T_x(y\alpha)^t, \text{Regret}_x(\alpha), \text{Regret}_y(\alpha)) \qquad (2.13)$$

In our current work, for this important function, we use:

$$f = \frac{\text{C\_T}_x(\alpha) + T_x(y\alpha)^t}{\Xi_x} \times (\text{Regret}_x(\alpha) - \text{Regret}_y(\alpha)) \qquad (2.14)$$

The value of Ξ_x is anything x chooses. The higher it is, the more 'volatile' the agent is, and the less 'understanding.' For this reason, we call Ξ the *understanding constant* for an agent. The lower the understanding constant, the more understanding the agent. In our work we use a value between 1 and 10, but really, most values go, as long as the result isn't too (rationally) challenging.

The outcome of such a calculation is that the agent may pass from 'trust' through untrust and on to distrust. The magnitude of the change is dependent on the magnitude of (or importance of) the situation, betrayal, regret and so forth. Here. the more y is trusted, the greater the loss of trust. However, it's not a complete loss as postulated by many. That could easily be handled by, for example, stating that if $T_x(y, \alpha)^t$ was above a certain threshold, dependent on the agent, then $T_x(y)^{t+1}$ could simply be reduced by, for instance, the value of $\text{Regret}_x(\alpha)$. There is no easy answer here, as in [53] we find that Identification-Based Trust is potentially strong enough to absorb transgressions without necessarily major alterations. It all depends, in other words, on how you want your agent to behave (and some variability makes for a much more interesting world).

For honest trustees who do not transgress, we continue to use a percentage increase, with the percentage value itself decreasing as we approach a trust limit of 0.99^2.

2.9 Forgiveness and the Blind and Toothless

If we practice and eye for an eye and a tooth for a tooth, soon the whole world will be blind and toothless

Gandhi.

---

[2] We have discussed elsewhere [63] why trust values of 1, indicating blind trust, are not trust at all (since, being blind, they do not by definition take any consideration by the agent about the situation or others in it into account).

If one is to assume that regret can be expressed, shown or made to be felt, it would appear that we have arrived at a situation where there is a great deal of the stuff, but very few things to do with it—we can make decisions, review them and even come to a different understanding of trust. But it's not enough if a 'next step' is not considered. In our work, we see this next step as that of forgiveness.

2.9.1 What Forgiveness Is

> To err is human; to forgive, divine.
>
> Alexander Pope

Forgiveness is something of an enigma. While social psychologists appear more comfortable defining what it is *not* [27] (it isn't forgetting, for example, and it doesn't imply reconciliation, but it is a conscious decision), there is some evidence that they may be out of step with what people actually think it *is* [46]. A good start is given by, Vasalou and Pitt who see forgiveness as a 'prosocial decision to adapt a positive attitude toward another' [86, p. 146], which neatly removes the need to say what it actually results in.

It is through forgiveness that trust can be restored in relationships, and that, consequently, things that were impossible before can become possible. The act, and expression, of regretting, which explicitly acknowledges that some bad thing has happened (but not necessarily culpability), is a major step on the road to forgiveness, and thus to restored trust. Forgiveness is not always required or justified where regret is voiced.

In Vasalou and Pitt's recent work, [86], the concept of forgiveness has been examined in the context of a reputation system. In their DigitalBlush system, expressions of shame, embarrassment and so on are used to elicit potential forgiveness by others in the society. While acknowledging the fact that, applied too swiftly, or incorrectly, it may in fact be more problematic than if it were not applied (especially online), the system reinforces the idea that regret (however expressed) is a precursor to a potential forgiving act. In fact, there is a lively debate on the ethics of forgiveness in psychology [27, 77], but evidence to suggest that forgiveness is good for the forgiver and the forgivee [12, 87, 11].

There is little doubt that forgiveness is a particularly important area where trust is concerned. It is through forgiveness that trust can be repaired, and it is through forgiveness that cooperation can as a result be re-opened. We acknowledge, along with [86], the potential problems forgiveness may create, but we feel that it is too important, and too beneficial, to ignore as a computational concept. In our own work, we are concerned less with helping people forgive that allowing artificial or analytical systems to consider forgiveness as a tool, for example, when making trusting decisions.

2.9.2 A Model of Forgiveness

> The weak can never forgive. Forgiveness is the attribute of the strong.
>
> Gandhi.

For our own model, we are less concerned with the precursors to forgiveness than the mechanisms of the act of forgiving in and of itself. Naturally, we assume the precursors must exist (regret, as we have already discussed, is one of them, and used heavily here), but we see forgiveness as a step along the road to the re-establishment of trust. As a step, it can be seen in its own light. This view of forgiveness may be something of a departure from some views of the topic (it's not always seen as a restorative process, for instance), but it serves well here.

While making no judgment on whether or not forgiveness can happen in any given circumstance, we see two major aspects of forgiveness in an autonomous agent:

- The Forgiveness Trait
- The Forgiveness Function

First, note that these are individual to each agent, and therefore can differ radically between agents.

Consider the Forgiveness Trait for an agent. Put in its simplest form, this trait is an expression of the length of time after a transgression that must pass before the agent will even begin to consider forgiving. When this length of time has passed, the Forgiveness Function can come into play. This is in fact quite a simple parameter to set up in an artificial system, but also slightly proscribed. In fact, it makes much more sense to relate this length of time to the severity of the transgression, coupled with the Forgiveness Trait as an expression of the 'strictness' of the agent's 'moral code', represented as a percentage (this is important in the following equations), and once more this is simple enough to accomplish. Thus, the length of time before forgiveness is:

$$t_{\mathrm{Ft}_x} = \mathrm{Ft}_x \times \mathrm{Regret}_x(\alpha) \tag{2.15}$$

With Ft_x expressed as a number between 1 and 100 – more forgiving agents have lower Ft values.

From this, then, we can calculate a number of timesteps between transgression and forgiveness that is related to the Forgiveness Trait of the agent, coupled with how much the agent regrets what happened (the more regret, the longer it takes to think about forgiving). As will be discussed further below, agent time and human time are subjectively very different things. Your own mileage may vary.

The Forgiveness Function is likewise straightforward. Ultimately, it is an expression of the transgression's severity, regret felt and expressed (the concept of shame and embarrassment is similar in [86]), and the relationship that the agents have had before the transgression occurred. Formally (and normalised in some sensible way, which we discuss further below), the Forgiveness Function for a (very) simple agent is:

$$\text{Fk}_x = \frac{(\text{Regret}_y(\alpha) - \text{Regret}_x(\alpha) + \text{I}_x(xy))}{\text{Ft}_x} \times T_x y \qquad (2.16)$$

Thus, the more regret x has, and the less (or even negative) regret y has, the less forgiveness is forthcoming. Note also that the forgiveness is mitigated by the amount of trust that exists in the relationship (the higher it is, the more forgiveness). This trust could in fact be that which now exists as a result of the transgression, or what existed before – different results will be obtained from each. Consider for example a high trust relationship which after a transgression becomes a very low trust relationship – using the original trust value may be more forgiving, and a reflection of the value of trust, than using the post transgression value. These are considerations, however, for individuals (both agent and human).

2.10 Trust as Is, Part Two: The Incorporation of Forgiveness

Now that the Forgiveness Trait and Function are clarified, we can look at how forgiveness, when adopted, can enter the alteration of trust following a transgression.

Formally, over time, an agent who transgressed *may be* forgiven:

$$T_x(y)^{t+t_{\text{Ft}x}} = T_x(y)^{t+t_{\text{Ft}x}-1} + \text{Fk}_x(\text{Regret}_x(\alpha), \text{Regret}_y(\alpha), \text{I}_x(xy), \alpha^-) \qquad (2.17)$$

Where:

- Ft_x is x's *Forgiveness Trait*;
- Fk_x is x's *Forgiveness Function*;
- t is some time step in the future from the trangression;
- α^- represents the situation in which the trangression took place, and can be used to calculate other aspects, such as thresholds, etc.

We have introduced the Forgiveness Trait and Function above. Note here that any forgiveness consideration must take into account the situation in which the transgression took place, as well as the players (there may be more than two) in the situation.

2.10.1 The Trust Continuum, Revised: The Limits of Forgiveness

Our considerations of forgiveness allow us to revisit what we may have known about the trust continuum – previously we considered untrust to be a positive trust, yet not enough trust for cooperation (see Fig. 2.2). However, it is possible to imagine a situation where a negative trust is not in fact distrust, but the result of a transgression that propels a specific agent's trust values into negativity. It's possible the

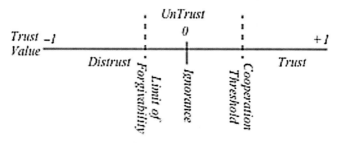

Fig. 2.3 Trust continuum: The limit of forgivability

transgression was minor, or even an honest mistake (consider Alice's agent sharing Steve's information), and it's possible to consider the agent standing in potential of forgiveness and remediation, regardless of the fact that the current trust we have in them is negative.

There are, however, limits. Some things cannot be accepted, and some agents are malicious or non-redeemable. To take this into account we introduce a new concept, the *Limit of Forgivability*, beyond which we might say the agent is truly distrusted, and cannot be considered as other than acting against our best interests. In considerations of forgiveness, this Limit will be used by agents to determine the worth of entering into redemption strategies with others. Note that a single transgression may well put another beyond this pale. Note also that the Limit of Forgiveness is individual and personal (private). Keeping the limit private is in fact important in any situation where knowledge of how trust and forgiveness work can be used against an agent.

The Limit of Forgivability introduces the concept of untrust as a potentially negative phenomenon. This is shown in Fig. 2.3.

2.11 Applications: Revisiting the Parable and Imagining the Future

While interesting in its own right, often, the theory and associated descriptions are not enough to shed light on what is imagined. Our current work is concentrated on the use of trust, regret and forgiveness in information sharing architectures, both as expressed in the parable in Section 2.3 but also in more complex environments where trust amalgamation is key. Much of this work is theoretical, but it is possible to show worked examples, and this section is devoted to such an endeavour. In the first place, we revisit our parable, and work through the example showing how the individual agents work. Following this, we briefly present the wider information sharing concept, and how trust, regret and forgiveness, amongst other social norms, can work to enhance human experiences in this domain. Finally, we present our ideas for Soft Security and Regret Management.

In the course of this work, much of what is conjectured works well enough at first blush, but on application, even in such a limited sense as a worked example, errors and omissions are found. It's worth mentioning here that this is indeed the case in this work, and that the formalisations above have benefitted from such worked examples. In addition, the examples below illustrate some of the 'behind the scenes' considerations that agents and others must make in their deliberations, some of which are trust related, others of which are not.

2.11.1 The Parable at Work

Let us revisit the agents of Alice and Steve. Ordinarily, they consider us to be friends and trusted. Let's say then that the amount of general trust Alice has in Steve (strictly speaking, Alice's agent has in Steve's own) is 0.85 – quite high[3] in other words, and Steve's in Alice is 0.80. We can express this as:

$$T_{\text{Steve}}(\text{Alice}) = 0.80$$
$$T_{\text{Alice}}(\text{Steve}) = 0.85$$

When Alice's agent requests that piece of information, Steve's agent has certain things to consider – the importance of the information to Steve, the utility of revealing it to Alice's agent (which could be based on furthering trusting relations, getting something back later or just being nice because Steve likes Alice), Steve's trust in Alice (as seen by his agent), Alice's (agent's) 'information handling' competence (as seen from experience, and if not, then estimated by other means) and the risks associated with distribution. In this instance, there's little to be concerned about as far as Alice is concerned (little do we know…) Thus

$$T_{\text{Steve}}(Alice, \text{info\_share}) = U_{\text{Steve}}(\text{info\_share}) \times I_{\text{Steve}}(\text{info\_share}) \times \widehat{T_{\text{Steve}}(Alice)}$$

Putting in some sensible numbers (this is relatively important, and Steve stands to gain because he knows Alice needs the info for a book she's working on), we already know how much Steve trusts Alice…

$$T_{\text{Steve}}(Alice, \text{info\_share}) = 0.80 \times 0.85 \times 0.80 = 0.544$$

This may not seem like much, but bear in mind there's another set of considerations:

$$\text{Cooperation\_Threshold}_{\text{Steve}}(\text{info\_share}) =$$

$$\frac{\text{Perceived\_Risk}_{\text{Steve}}(\text{info\_share})}{\text{Perceived\_Competence}_{\text{Steve}}(Alice, \text{info\_share}) + \widehat{T_{\text{Steve}}Alice}} \times I_{\text{Steve}}(\text{info\_share})$$

---

[3] Regardless of how well we may be able to justify a value system, or the choice of a particular value, others will rightly state that 0.85 is way too high for a friend, while still others might say it's not high enough, again rightly. And here we arrive once more at the problem with trust – sharing values is just not going to work. Thus, keep your own, measure it your way, and measure by action, not statement, of values or otherwise.

Again, with sensible numbers (it's risky, because the information is personal, but we see, so far, Alice's agent as competent in all dealings thus far – little do we know that this is because Alice has (human)-fielded all her agent's dealing with others):

$$\text{Cooperation\_Threshold}_{\text{Steve}}(\text{info\_share}) = \frac{0.75}{0.7 + 0.8} \times 0.85 = 0.397$$

And so, since clearly Alice (her agent, at least) is trusted enough in this situation, Steve's agent shares this information.

Time passes and it becomes clear that Alice's agent has transgressed on the understanding, and the information is out there. Trust must be re-evaluated, based on what has happened. Recall from section 2.4 that we have in the past considered a very simple means of reducing trust following a transgression [63], in most cases, this being a percentage of the original trust, with a greater or lesser percentage dependent on the 'personality' of the agent concerned. With the tool of regret, we have an additional means of re-evaluating trust. In this case, we might say that I (Steve's agent) regret that you (Alice's agent) did that, and so we can take a look at equation (2.7) and (2.8):

$$\text{Regret}_{\text{Steve}}(\text{info\_share}) = (U_x(\text{info\_share}) - U_x(\text{info\_share}^-)) \times f(\kappa, \lambda, \mu)$$

Where:

$$f(\kappa, \lambda, \mu) = \text{C\_T}_{Steve}(Alice, \text{info\_share})^t + \text{I}_{Steve}(Steve, Alice)$$

We already know some of the values here, and can fill in the others now. Certainly, Steve stands to lose now that the information is out. In fact, it can potentially cost him, so there is a negative utility to the current situation (say, -0.1, because it's not a huge cost, but will take time and effort to fix). Steve and Alice are good friends, and he values the relationship. Thus:

$$[\text{Regret}_{\text{Steve}}(\text{info\_share}) = (0.8 - (-0.1)) \times (0.397 + 0.75) = 1.03$$

This is greater than 1, and that's fine, but we could normalize it if needed. In this case, we can use the regret to calculate how much trust is lost. From equation (2.13) and (2.14), we have:

$$T_{\text{Steve}} Alice^{t+n} =$$
$$T_{\text{Steve}} Alice^t -$$
$$\left(\frac{\text{C\_T}_{Steve}(\text{info\_share}) + T_{\text{Steve Alice}}\text{info\_share}^t}{\Xi_{Steve}} \times \right.$$
$$(\text{Regret}_{\text{Steve}}(\text{info\_share}) - \text{Regret}_{\text{Alice}}(\text{info\_share}))$$

Now, Steve is a nice guy and understands that mistakes happen, and he doesn't like to punish people unnecessarily for that, so the *understanding constant* for his agent is set to 5. As noted earlier, it's an arbitrary choice, and to be determined by the agent's owner (we use anything between 1 and 10). So:

$$T_{Steve}Alice^{t+n} = 0.8 - \left(\frac{(0.397 + 0.544)}{5} \times (1.03 - Regret_{Alice}(info\_share)) \right)$$

We're almost there. We just need to figure out how much Alice's agent regrets what happened. Of course, we needn't, and can set this to 0, giving an adjustment of 0.19. That's okay, but we give the agent a chance to express regret and see.

As discussed above in Section 2.7.3, it's not so easy to figure out if what we're *being told* is actually what *is*. We do have a potential formula from equation 2.10:

$$Regret_{Alice}(info\_share) = (U_{Alice}(info\_share) - U_{Alice}(info\_share^-))$$
$$\bullet I_{Alice}(Alice, Steve)$$

It's possible for Steve's agent to estimate much of these values in a pinch, and these may tally with Alice's agent's estimates or they may not. This is in fact not as important as it might sound, since the trust we are re-evaluating is Steve's agent's in Alice's agent, and this is inherently personal. If Steve or his agent was to get feedback from Alice's agent *that he or his agent considered valid* this *may* make a difference, but he could just as easily choose to discard it. In this instance, because his agent knows the relationship is important, and the previous trust was high (for Steve), it makes the decision to believe what it is given. In addition, for consistency, it calculates its own $Regret_{Alice}(info\_share)$ value, which we call $Steve(Regret_{Alice}(info\_share))$:

$$Steve(Regret_{Alice}(info\_share)) = (0.5 - 0)times0.8 = 0.4$$

Alice's own calculations are similar, and show a regret of 0.45. Being a nice agent, Steve's agent takes this to be true. Then, we can finally work out how to adjust the trust value:

$$T_{Steve}(Alice)^{t+n} = 0.8 - (\frac{(0.397 + 0.544)}{5} \times (1.03 - 0.45) = 0.8 - 0.109 = 0.691$$

This final value has an effect on how Steve's agent sees Alice's agent. For example, next time she asks to get some information, the original trust and cooperation threshold calculations above result in 0.47 for trust and 0.535 for the cooperation threshold (all other things, except for Alice's agent's competence being revised drastically down to 0.5 here). Clearly, it's not going to happen again. Distributing this data amongst Steve's agent's circle of friends is not complicated either.

So what happens next?

Alice's agent regrets what happened, that much is clear. In the final analysis, this regret may be higher than the formulae predict here (there is a loss over and above that situation). Eventually, it's time, then, for forgiveness to be considered.

A brief aside is necessary here. At what time does one consider forgiveness? In equation (2.17), recall, it's our *Forgiveness Trait*. For some, it's a more or less instantaneous action,[4] for others less so. Some never consider it. For our part, with no moral judgment on the matter, we have given our agents the *Forgiveness Trait* in order to allow agent owners, if this system is incorporated within them, to decide for themselves. However, there is a difference in subjective times for agents and humans – agents in this example if not others work on 'internet time,' and things happen fast there. 'Human time,' however perceived, is always slower than this. Thus, if we visit the parable once more, we see that forgiveness is entered into before Steve emerges from the bush, kayak in hand (so to speak). This could be a week later or a month later. Perhaps, even less time has passed. For Steve's agent, it seems a lot longer...

Steve's agent has a *Forgiveness Trait* of 75. Recall from equation (2.15) that regret mitigates the length of time to wait – the more regret, the longer the time. Here the agent's regret is 1.03, giving a timescale of 77.25 for the agent. That's 77.25 timesteps. For the sake of nothing other than arbitrariness, let us say that each step on that scale equates to one hour[5] of real time. Thus, in 77 hours and 15 minutes, Steve's agent is *ready to consider* forgiving Alice's agent. When that time arrives, his agent considers the *Forgiveness Function*, from equation (2.16):

$$Fk_{Steve} = \frac{(Regret_{Alice}(info\_share) - Regret_{Steve}(info\_share) + I_{Steve}(Steve, Alice))}{Ft_{Steve}} \times T_{Steve}(Alice)$$

Then, with our new level of trust, but still considering the relationship important:

$$Fk_{Steve} = \frac{(0.4 - 1.03) + 0.75}{75} \times 0.691 = 0.0011$$

So, from equation (2.17) Steve's agent can now trust Alice to a value of 0.6921. This can take some time.... Of course, we can now look at this in a couple of different ways – every timestep, since this is a positive value, we can reconsider forgiveness and increase trust, and should circumstances, such as cooperation in other endeavours, permit, increase the $T_{Steve}(Alice)$ value in that way also. Or, as with the grey areas of untrust, state that since the forgiveness function came up with a positive figure, forgiveness is assured and wipe the slate clean (returning the trust value to its previous figure of 0.80). We prefer the more gradual approach and use it in our work. Consider that if we re-evaluate every hour (time step), then after 53 hours, all other things being equal, cooperation can resume on the information sharing situation. Even with a more punishing revising of the competence of Alice's agent to 0.3, cooperation can resume within 217 hours (time steps). 5–12 days in real time.

---

[4] Gordon Wilson, in life, and Michael Berg respectively were and are prominent among them.,

[5] Yes, it could be a minute or a second. This is one parameter an owner of such an agent should consider, amongst many others.

Forgiveness then, in this circumstance, appears to do what it's supposed to – give time for reflection and the rebuilding of trust.

2.11.2 Regret Management

In [26] we introduced the concept of *Regret Management*, and here will take it a little further with the discussion of a simple Regret Management system.

The purpose of a Regret Management system is to ensure that transgressors in a previously trusted situation are held to account for their transgressions. There are many examples of where and how this could be achieved, from a posteriori access control [13] to blacklisting in online auction sites, or from our own example of the parable above taken through Alice's agent's eyes, through advanced Trust Management system techniques that ensure accountability.

In [26], we postulated that a Regret Management system would have the following properties (now numbered, in no particular order):

1. It is capable of assessing to some value the amount of regret a truster has after a trustee transgresses.
2. It is capable of ensuring that the transgressor is 'assigned' that regret – that is, punished in some material (meaningful to the transgressor) way in a form proportional to the truster's regret.
3. It is open and clear enough, and 'trusted' by both parties to be able to make these things happen. An 'untrusted' regret management system is as good as no system at all.

For item 1, the formalisations for regret above correctly fulfill this role – there is an assessment of regret. Item 2 depends more on the system, but consider that given the assessment, any system where communication of some form is possible would be able to assign that regret. Note, for instance, that in the example, the regret is assigned by my agent, and further by my agent's broadcasting this to its own close acquaintances. Given the gamut of possibilities for systems, item 3 is more difficult, but what is necessary is for the transgressor to know that the truster is not above making their own 'failings' in trusting 'badly' known to the world in some way. *All* trust-based systems, human or otherwise, will fail in the face of reluctance in this instance – embarrassment is the con-man's greatest weapon.

If we can revisit the worked example above for a moment, we note that Alice's agent is capable of expressing regret, and that my own agent is capable of making it regret its actions (by shutting it out of my community for a time, and by broadcasting that to the community). A reasonable start for a Regret Management system. However, a more formal approach is required in order to achieve our second and third requirements.

We propose that the system should:

- Calculate regret for each agent in the relationship, independently of the agents' calculations;

- (If possible) ascertain the regret calculations from each agent for corroboration – this in fact can be used also to determine the truthfulness of each agent's deliberations;
- Ensure all agents are aware of the calculations and results;
- Apportion reparations based on the results of the calculations
- Enforce reparations;

We are currently implementing such a system based on the ACORN architecture [68] with trust additions.

2.12 Related Work

There is a great deal of work, this volume amongst it, that deals with the phenomenon of trust in a computational setting. Approaches range from Trust Management [38, 48, 25, 41], where there is a need to determine trust or its propagation via trusted others, to trust models [63, 1, 83], which enable individual agents to model other with trust as at least a component, if not the major one, of the model. Additionally, regret is, as has been noted above, not a new phenomenon of study, particularly in the economic sciences [7, 55, 16, 35, 91]. It is nothing new to suggest that an agent can and does use regret, anticipatory or otherwise, in decision making. Forgiveness, while extensively studied in religious and philosophical fields [27, 46, 77, 12, 12, 87, 11, 17], is much less popular a field of study in computational settings. Indeed, [86] is premiere in this field, discussing the application of forgiveness in a computer-mediated communication setting.

While to our knowledge there is no work combining the three phenomena to further the development of truly social agents, the effect obtained, at least when we consider autonomous agents working in specific environments for humans, is similar to the concept of *Adjustable Autonomy*, in which humans retain a meta-level control over their more-or-less autonomous agents [28, 40, 29]. In this work, however, the control is given back to the agents in order to allow them to adjust the amount of leeway (or autonomy) other agents have with their resources, as well as the human. Moreover, there is a built-in, via forgiveness, mechanism for re-attaining autonomy when adequate guarantees are given or behaviour observed.

The quest for more socially oriented agents and the phenomena studied here are related to Danielson's concept of Artificial Morality [19], where a game theoretical approach is used to balance rationality and morality in a social setting. As well, Dautenhahn's Social Intelligence concept [20] maintains a viewpoint similar to our final goal.

2.13 Trust as Will Be: Future Work and Conclusions

The model of trust presented in this chapter is not in itself new, but the way in which it interacts with regret and forgiveness is. In this work, Trust, Regret and Forgiveness form an *internal triangle*. Trust allows agents tools in making decisions, regret allows them yet more, but also gives them a means to, and a measure for, adapting to current circumstances. Forgiveness allows the society (of agents, as well as humans) to continue operating in a reasonable, cooperative fashion.

While the study of the phenomena in their own right is interesting, they point the way to powerful tools in a practical sense. To that end, we have presented the design of the trust, forgiveness, regret triangle in the context of Ambient Intelligence. Our current work is focused on further refining the models, including the incorporation of a consideration of Decision Justification (cf. [16]), implementing the triangle in an information sharing architecture (ACORN [68]), an AmI interface and Regret Management systems.

We have stated that trust is not the panacea for all technological ills. It is, however, necessary for the development of a *complete* social agent. The same goes for regret and forgiveness as computational concepts.

Regret and forgiveness are not the only phenomena with which a social agent can be equipped – other rational decision aids exist. For our part, without presuming to theorise about what *correct*, or *moral* behaviour is, we are beginning to examine the concept of *Integrity* – doing the 'right' thing for the 'right' reason. This is something of a departure from a trusting, or even a moral, agent, but integrity is in itself a decision-making strategy. Moreover, we conjecture that trusting an integrity-based agent would be rather simpler than one who is not, since we would expect the integrity-based agent to behave in accordance with its principles (which could be public) at all times.

Current work involving trust is both promising and worthwhile, but represents only a small portion of the picture that needs to be uncovered. If the systems we build are to be capable of sustained interactions in the (our) social world, there is a need for them to be able to understand, or at least represent, much more than just trust. This work is a step along that road.

References

1. Alfarez Abdul-Rahman. *A Framework for Decentralised Trust Reasoning*. PhD thesis, Department of Computer Sceince, University College London, 2004.
2. Charles Abraham and Paschal Sheeran. Deciding to exercise: The role of anticipated regret. *British Journal of Health Psychology*, 9:269–278, 2004.
3. Jari Ahola. Ambient intelligence. *ERCIM News*, 47, October 2001.
4. Robert Axelrod. *The Evolution of Cooperation*. Basic Books, New York, 1984.
5. Annette Baier. Trust and antitrust. *Ethics*, 96(2):231–260, January 1986.
6. Bernard Barber. *Logic and Limits of Trust*. Rutgers university Press, New Jersey, 1983.
7. David E. Bell. Regret in decicion making under uncertainty. *Operations Research*, 30: 961–981, 1982.
8. George David Birkhoff. A Mathematical approach to ethics. In James R. Newman, editor, *The World of Mathematics, Volume 4*, pages 2198–2208. Simon and Schuster, New York, 1956.
9. Sissela Bok. *Lying: Moral Choice in Public and Private Life*. pantheon Books, New York, 1978.
10. Susan D. Boon and John G. Holmes. The dynamics of interpersonal trust: resolving uncertainty in the face of risk. In Robert A. Hindle and Jo Groebel, editors, *Cooperation and Prosocial Behaviour*, pp. 190–211. Cambridge University Press, 1991.

11. Lesley A. Brose, Mark S. Rye, Catherine Lutz-Zois, and Scott R. Ross. For-giveness and personality traits. *Personality and Individual Differences*, 39:627–638, 2005.

12. Ryan P. Brown and April Phillips. Letting bygones by bygones: further evidence for the valid-ity of the tendency to forgive scale. *Personality and Individual Differences*, 38:627–638, 2005.

13. Jan G. Cederquist, Ricardo J. Corin, Marnix A. C. Dekker, Sandro Etalle, Jerry. I. den Hartog, and Gabriele Lenzini. Audit-based compliance control. *International Journal of Information Security*, 6(2–3):133–151,2007.

14. John Child and Guido Möllering. Contextual confidence and active trust development in the chinese business environment. *Organization Science*, 14(1):69–80, January–February 2003.

15. Piotr Cofta. *Trust, Complexity and Control: Confidence in a Convergent World*. Wiley, 2007.

16. Terry Connolly and Marcel Zeelenberg. Regret in decision making. *Current Directions in Psychological Science*, 11(6):212–216, December 2002.

17. Jim Consedine. Forgiveness as public policy. *Australian EJournal of Theology*, 9, March 2007.

18. Peter Danielson. *Artifical morality: Virtuous Robots for Virtual Worlds*. Routledge, London, 1992.

19. Peter A. Danielson. Is Game Theory Good for Ethics?: Artificial High Fedility. Corrected version of a paper presented at an invited symposium on Game Theory at the APA Pacific Division meeting, San Francisco, 29 March, 1991.

20. Kerstin Dautenhahn, Bond Alan H, lola Canamero, and Bruce Edmonds, editors. *Socially Intelligent Agents: Creating Relationships with Computers and Robots*. Kluwer Academic Publishers, Amsterdem 2002.

21. Paul Davis. On apologies. *Journal of Applied Philosophy*, 19(2):169–173, 2002.

22. Morton Deutsch. Cooperation and trust: Some theoretical notes. In M. R. Jones, editors, *Nebraska Symposium on Motivation*. Nebraska University, 1962.

23. Morton Deutsch. *The Resoltion of Conflict*. Yale University Press, New Haven and London, 1973.

24. Mark R. Dibben. *Exploring Interpersonal Trust in the Enterpreneurial Venture*. MacMillan, London, 2000.

25. Changyu Dong, Giovanni Russello, and Narakner Dulay. Trust transfer in distributed systems. in Sandro Etalle and Stephen Marsh, editors, *Trust Management: Proceedings of IFIPTM 2007*, pp. 17–30, 2007.

26. Sandro Etalle, Jerry den Hartog, and Stephen Marsh. Trust and punishment. In *International Conference on Autonomic Computing and Communication Systems (Autonomics), 28–30 octo-ber 2007*. ACM Press, October 28–30 2007.

27. Julie Juola Exline,Everett L. Worthington JR., Peter Hill, and Michel E. McCullogh. Forgive-ness and justice: A research agenda for social and personality psychology. *Personality and social psychology Review*, 7(4):337–348,2003.

28. Rino Falcone and Cristiano Castelfranchi. Levels of delegation and levels of adoption as the basis for adjustable autonomy. In Evelina Lamma and Mello, editors, *AI*IA99:Advances in Artificial Intlligence: 6th Congress of the Italian Association for Aritfical Intelligence, Bologna Italy, September 1999. Selected papers, volume LNAI 1792*, pp. 273–284. Springer, 2000.

29. Rino Falcone and Cristino Castefranchi. The human in the loop of a delegated agent: athe theory of adujstable social autonomy. *IEEE Transactions on Systems, Man and Cybernetics*, 31(5):406–418,2001.

30. Rino Falcone and Cristino Castefranchi. The socio-cognitive dynamics of trust: Does trust creat trust? In R. Falcone, M. Singh, and Y.-H. Tan, editors, *Trust in Cyber-socities, volume 2246 of lecture Notes in Aritficial Intelligence*. Springer Verlag,2001.

31. Leon Festinger. *A Theory of Cognitive Dissonance*. Stanford University Press, CA, 1957.

32. Batya Friedman, Peter H. Kahn, and Daniel C. Howe. Trust online. *Communications of the ACM*, 43(12):34–40, 2000.

33. Francis Fukuyama. Trust: *The Social Virtues and the Creation of Prosperity*. Simon and Suhuster, 1996.
34. Diego Gambetta.Can we trust trust? In Diego Gambetta, editor, *Trust*, chapter 13, pp. 213–237. Blackwell, Oxford, 1990.
35. Daniel T. Gilbert, Carey K. Morewedge, Jane L. Risen, and Timothy D. Wilson. Looking forward to looking backward: The misprediction of regret. Psychlogical Scince, 15(5): 346–350, 2004.
36. Thomas Gilovich and Victoria Husteed Medvec. The temporal pattern to the experince of regret. *Journal of personality and Social Psychology*, 6(3):357–365, 1994.
37. H.C.J. Godfray. The evolution of Forgiveness. *Nature*, 355:206–207, 16th January 1992.
38. Jennifer Golbeck. *Computing and Applying Trust in web-based Social*, 15(5):346–350, 2004.
39. Robert T. Golembiewski and Mark McConkie. The centrality of interpersonal trust in group process. In Cary L. Cooper, editor, *Theories of group Processes*, chapter 7, pp. 131–185. Wiley, New York, 1975.
40. Michael A. Goodrich, Dan Olsen Jr., Jacob W.Crandall, and Thomas J.Palmer.Experiments in adustable autonomy. In *IJCAI-01 Workshop on Autonomy Delegation,and Control:Interaction with Autonomous Agents*, 2001.
41. Andess Guster.A trust model for an open, decentralized reputation system. In Sandro Etalle and Stephen Marsh, editors, *Trust Management: Proceedings of IFIPTM 2007*, pp. 285–300, 2007.
42. Diane F. Halpern. *Thought and Knowledge: An Introduction to Critical Thinking*. Lawerence Erlbaum Associates, Hillsdale, NJ, 1984.
43. Nicoli Hartman. *Ethics II – Moral Values*. Geroge Allen and Unwin, London,1932.
44. Lars Hertzberg. On the attitude of trust. *Inquiry*, 3(3):307–322, September 1988.
45. Natsuko Hikage,Yuko Murayama, and Carl Hauster. Exploatory survey on an evaluation model for a sense of security. In H. Venter, M. Eloff, L. Labuschangne, J. Eloff, and R. von Solms, editors, *IFIP International for Information Processing, Volume 232, New Approaches for Security, Privacy and Trust in Complex Environments* Volume 232, pp. 121–132. Springer, 2007.
46. Robert Jeffress. When Forgiveness *Doesn't Make Sense*. Waterbrook Press, Colorado, 2001.
47. Audun Josang, Roslan Islami, and Coin Boyd. A survey of trust and reputation system for online sevice provision. *Decision Support System*, 473(2):618-644,2007.
48. Audun Jusang, Stephen Marsh, and Simon Pope. Exploring different types of trust propagation. In Ketil Stolen, Wlliam Winsborough, Fabio Massacci, editors, *Trust Management: Proceedings of the 4th International Conference on Trust Management (iTrust'06), volume 3986 of Springer Lecture Noted in Computer Science*, pp. 197–192, 2006.
49. Daniel Krahmer and Rebecca Stone. Regret in dynamic decision problems.Technical report 71, GESY – Governce and the Efficiency of Economic System Dicussion Paper 71,www.gesy.uni-mannhein.de,July 2005.
50. Roderick M Kramer. Trust for dilemmas: How decision makers and act in the shadow of doubt. In R. Falcone, M. Singh, and Y.-H, editors, *Trust in Cyber Socities*, Lecture Notes in Artifical intellingece, Springer Verlag, LNAI 2246, pp. 9–26 2001.
51. Karl Kruknow. *Towards of trust for the global Ubiquitous Computer*. PhD thisis, University of Aartus,2006.
52. Olli Lagensptez. Legitimacy and trust. *Philosophical Investigations*, 15(1):1–21, January 1992.
53. Roy J. Lewicki and Barbara B. Bunker. Trust in releationship; A model of trust, development and decline. In B B. Bunker and J.Z. Rubin, editors, *Conflict, Cooperation and Justice*, pp. 133–173. Josey Bass, San Franciso 1985.
54. Roy J. Lewiciki, D. J. Bies McAllister, and R. J. Bies. Trust and distrust: New releationship and realities. *Acadamy of Management Review*, 23:438–458, 1998.

55. LG. Loomes and R. Sugden. Regret theory: An alternative theory of rational choice under uncertainty. *Economic Journal*, 92:805–824, 1982.

56. Steve Love, Pamela Briggs, Linda Little, Stephen Marsh, and Lynne Coventry. Ambient intelligence: Does public mean private? In *Proceedings of HCI 2005: The Bigger Picture. Edinburgh, 5–9 September*, 2005.

57. M. Low and V. Srivatsan. What it mean to trust an entreprenur? In S. Birley and I.C. MacMillion. editors, *International Entrepreneurship*, Routeledge, London, New York, pp. 59–78, 1995.

58. R.Duncan Luce and Howard Raiffa. *Games and Decisions*. Dover Publications, New York, 1957.

59. Niklas Luhmann. *Trust and Power*. Wiley, Chichester,1979.

60. Niklas Luhmann. Familiarity, confidence, trust: Problems and alternatives. In Diego Gambetta, editor, *Trust* chapter 6, Blackwell, pp. 94–107 1990.

61. Jason R. Marden, Gurdal Arslan, and Jeff S.Shamma Regret-based dynamics: Convergence in weakly acyclic games. In *Proceedings of AAMAS 2007*, pages 194–201, 2007.

62. Stephen Marsh. Trust and reliance in multi-agent systems: A preliminary report. In *MAA-MAW'92, 4th European Workshop on modeling Autonomous Agents in a Multi-Agent World, Rome*, 1992.

63. Stephen Marsh. *Formalising Trust as a Computational Concept*. PhD thesis, Departement of Computing Scince, Univercity of Stirling,1994.Available online Via http://ww.stephenmarsh.ca/Files/pubs/Trust-thises.pdf.

64. Sterhen Marsh. Optimism and pessimism in trust. In J. Ramirez, editor, *Proceedings Iberoamerican Conference on Artifical Intelligence/National Conference on Artifical Intelligence (IBERMIASE94/CNAISE94)*. McGraw-Hill, October 1994.

65. Stephen Marsh. Trust in Distributed Artificial Intelligence. In Cristiano Castelfranchi and Eric Werner, editors, *Artifical Social System*, Lecture Notes in AI, Springer Verlag, Vol. 830, pp. 94–112, September 1994.

66. Stephen Marsh. Trust, regret, forgiveness, and boing. Seminar, University of St Andrews, Scotland, UK, October 2005.

67. Stephen Marsh and Mark R. Dibben. Trust, untrust, distrust and mistrust—an exploration of the dark(er)side. In Peter Hermann, Valerie Issarny, and Simon Shiu, editors, *Trust Management:Proceedings of iTrust 2005*. Lecture Notes in Computer Science, Springer Verlag, LNCS 3477, 2005.

68. Stephen Marsh, Ali A. Ghorboni, and Virendra C. Bhavsar. The ACORN Multi-Agent System. *Web Intelligence and Agent Systems*, 1(1):65–86, Marsh 2003.

69. D. Harrison McKnight and Norman L. Chervany. The meaning of trust. Working paper, MISRC, 1996.

70. D. Harrison McKnight and Norman L. Chervany. Trust and distrust definitions: One bite at a time. In R. Falcone, M. Singh, and Y.-H. Tan, editors, *Trust in Cyber-Socities*, volume 2246 of *Lecture Notes in Arifical Intelligence*. Springer-Verlag, Berlin, Heidelberg, 2001.

71. D. Harrison McKnight, Chuck Kacmar, and Vivek Choudhury. Whoops...Did I use the Wrong conceptto Predict E-Commerce Trust? Modeling the Risk-Releated Effects of Trust versus Distrust Concepts. In *36th Hawaii International Conference on Systems Scinces*, 2003.

72. Barba A. Mistal. *Trust in Modern Societies,*. Blackwell, Oxford 1996.

73. Guidö Mollering. *Trust: Reason,Routing, Reflexivity*. Elsevier Scince, 2006.

74. Guidö Mollering. The nature of trust:From gerog simmel to a theroy of expectation and suspension. *Sociology*, 35(2):403–420, 2001.

75. Lik Mui. *Computional Models of Trust and Reputation: Agents, Evolutionary Games,and Social Networks*. PhD thesis, Massachusetts Institute of Technology, Departement of Electrical Engineering and computer Science, 2002.

76. J. G. Murphy. Forgiveness, mercy and the retribtive emotions. *Critical Justice Ethics*, 7:3–15.

77. J. G. Murphy. Forgiveness in counseling: A philosophical perspective. In S. Lamb and J. G. Murphy, editors, *Before forgiving: cautionary views of forgiveness in psychotherapy*. Oxford University Press, Oxford, 2002.

78. B. Noteboom, H. Berger, and N. Noordehaven. Effects of trust and governance on relational risk. *Academy of Management Journal*, 40(2):308–338, 1997.
79. Peter A. Pang. Experiments in the evolution of cooperation, Master's thesis, University of String, Departements of Computing Science, 1990.
80. Scott Plous. *The psychology of judgement and decision making*. McGraw-Hill, New York, 1993.
81. Paul Resnick, Richard Zeckhauser, Eric Friedman, and Ko Kuwabara.Reputation systems. *Communications of the ACM*, 43(12):45–48,2000.
82. Neal J. Roese and James M. Olson, editors. *What Might Have Been:The Social Psychology of Counterfactual Thinking*. Lawrence Erlbaum Associates, Mahwah, NJ, 1995.
83. Jean-Marc Seigneur and Privacy in Global Computing. PhD thesis, Trinity College,Dublin,2005.
84. Jean-Marc Seigneur and Christian Damsgaard Jensen. The role of identify in pervasive computational trust. In Philip Robinson, Harald Vogt, and Wagealla, editors, *Privacy, Security and Trust within the Context of Pervasive Computing*, volume 780 of *Kluwer International Series in Engineering and Computer Science*. Kluwer, Dorderch 2005.
85. Pitor Sztompka. *Trust: A Sociology Theory*. Cambridge University Press, 2000.
86. Asmina Vasalou and Jeremy Pitt. Reinventing forgiveness: A formal investigation of moral facilitation. In Peter Hermann, Valerie Issarny, and Simon Shiu, editors, *Trust Management: Third Internation Conference iTrust 2005, Proceedings*, volume 3477 of *Lecture Notes in Computer Science*. Springer, Berlin Heidelberg, 2005.
87. D. F. Walker and R. L. Gorsuch. Forgiveness awithin the big five personslity model. *Personality and Inividual Differences*, 32:1127–1137, 2002.
88. M. Weiser. The computer for the 21st century. *Scientific American*, 265(3):66–75, September 1991.
89. D. J. Wu, Steven O. Kimbrough, and Fang Zhong, Artifcial agents play the "mad mex trust game": A computatinal approach. In *Proceedings of the 35th Hawaii International Conference on System Sciences*, 2002.
90. Yutaka Yamamoto.A Morality Based on Trust: Some Reflections on Japanese Morality. *Philosophy East and West*, XL(4):451–469, October 1990.
91. Marcel Zeelenberg and Rik Pieters. A theory of regret regulation 1.0. *Journal of Consumer Psychology*, 17(1):3–18,2007.

Chapter 3
A Non-reductionist Approach to Trust

Cristiano Castelfranchi, Rino Falcone, and Emiliano Lorini

Abstract We develop in this chapter a conceptual and logical model of social trust. We first present a modal logic of mental attitudes and action in which the concepts of plausible belief, certain belief, and a possibility order over formulas can be characterized. Then, we apply the logic to the formalization of the truster's expectation about some fundamental properties of the trustee (trustee's opportunity to accomplish a given task, his skills, abilities, and willingness to perform a given action for the accomplishment of the task). A, part of this chapter is devoted to discuss and formalize some concepts related to trust such as distrust, mistrust, lack of trust, and delegation. Finally, a concept of comparative trust is presented.

3.1 Introduction

Is trust just reducible to subjective probability, to a simple numeric measure based on frequency and experience? Is this reduction of trust efficient and sufficient for Computing with trust? Can trust be just derived from personal experience and direct interaction, or from reputation and recommendations, or it has other fundamental sources? Is trustworthiness just a single dimension or is a multi-dimensional notion? These fundamental issues must be clarified in order to have a grounded approach to trust phenomena also in/for ICT, in HCI, agent–agent interaction, for the web, for virtual organizations, and so on. The core dimension of trust on which the decision to delegate a task depends is of course its epistemic component: the quantified belief (more precisely the expectation) that the trustee will act in an appropriate and successful manner. There are computational models of trust in which trust is conceived as an expectation sustained by the repeated direct interactions with other agents under the assumption that iterated experiences of success strengthen the truster's confidence [24, 38]. Generally, in this kind of experiences to each success of the trustee corresponds an increment in the amount of the truster's trust in the trustee, and vice versa, to every trustee's failure corresponds a

C. Castelfranchi (✉)
Institute of Cognitive Sciences and Technologies-CNR, Rome, Italy
e-mail: c.castelfranchi@istc.cnr.it

J. Golbeck (ed.), *Computing with Social Trust,* Human-Computer Interaction Series,
DOI 10.1007/978-1-84800-356-9_3 © Springer-Verlag London Limited 2009

reduction of the truster's trust in the trustee. More sophisticated models of social trust have been developed in which reputational information is added to information obtained via direct interaction. In these models, an agent can exploit the information obtained from the reports of other agents who had previous experiences with a given target in order to assess the trustworthiness of the target (e.g. [21, 36]).

However, all these trust models are in our view over-simplified, since they do not consider the indirect supports for this expectation. In our opinion, trust cannot be reduced to mere subjective probability which is updated in the light of direct interaction with the trustee and reputational information. A model of social trust must account for the truster's attribution process, that is, it must account for the truster's ascription of internal properties to the trustee (abilities, willingness, dispositions, etc.) and the truster's ascription of properties to the environment in which the trustee is going to act (will the environmental conditions prevent the trustee from accomplishing the task that the truster has delegated to him?). From this perspective there is a pressing need for elaborating richer models of social trust in which the truster's expectation and its components are explicitly modeled. To this end, we continue our previous work [7, 8] by presenting in this chapter a conceptual and logical model of social trust which shows that trust is not a unitary and simplistic notion. In fact, two fundamental distinctions should be introduced: (1) between an internal attribution (i's trust *in* j) and an external attribution (the environmental trust); (2) between many dimensions of the truster's evaluation and expectation about the trustee's properties, in particular, the expectation about the certainty of the expected/desired behaviour of the trustee (i.e., the truster's expectation that the trustee will be willing to act in a certain way), his quality due to his skills and abilities. We will show that the trust phenomenon involves several fundamental categories which must be carefully distinguished and their properties investigated. In fact, there is not only trust as an evaluation and as an expectation (*core trust*), but also trust as a preference and decision to rely and betting on a given agent (*decision to trust*). The latter is tightly linked with the concept of *delegation*.

The chapter is organized as follows. In Section 3.2, we discuss some fundamental desiderata for a logical model of social trust by specifying the concepts that must be defined in order to have a logical characterization of social trust and social trust reasoning. Section 3.3 is devoted to present a logic of social trust (called $\mathcal{STL}$) in which the goals of an agent and a qualitative notion of plausible belief can be specified. In Section 3.4, the logic $\mathcal{STL}$ will be exploited for a logical analysis of social trust. In Section 3.5, we will present a notion of comparative trust.

3.2 Desiderata for a Logical Model of Social Trust

There is a pressing need for elaborating more precise models of reasoning about trust. Formal logic is an useful tool for developing such a kind of models. But the specification of trust reasoning is typically in the province of this discipline. Indeed, logical models of trust have been focused almost exclusively on informational trust, that is, trust in information sources. In these logics, a certain agent is said to trust another agent if the former agent believes what the other agent says or that the information communicated to him by the other agent is reliable [26, 23, 12]. Some authors have introduced trust as a primitive concept [26], whereas other authors have reduced trust to a particular kind of belief of the truster that the trustee has a given property like sincerity, cooperativity, reliability, and so on [12]. In our view (see also [7, 8]), trust in information sources is only a particular subcase of the more general notion of social trust. From this perspective there is still no logical system in which the conceptual core of social trust can be formalized and its logical properties could be studied.

We think that the following are necessary desiderata for a logical model of social trust.

- A logic of trust must enable reasoning about goals of agents. In fact, agent i's trust in agent j necessarily involves a main and primary motivational component which is a goal of the truster. If i trusts agent j, then necessarily i trusts j because i has some goal and thinks that j has the right properties to ensure that such a goal will be achieved.
- A logic of trust must enable to specify several properties of the trustee on which the truster can rely before deciding to delegate a given task to the trustee. As emphasized earlier, trust is nothing more than an expectation of the truster about internal properties of the trustee (skills, abilities, willingness, etc.) and about the external (environmental) conditions in which the trustee is going to operate. This expectation is based on the truster's evaluation of good/bad properties of the trustee. In this sense, a logic of trust must enable to characterize formally such fundamental components of the truster's expectation.
- A logical model of trust must account for a concept of comparative trust. Indeed, it is fundamental for a model of trust to compare how the truster evaluates and compares the trustworthiness of different agents. For example, given two potential partners j and z to which agent i can decide to delegate a given task, we would like to say whether i trust more j than z or vice versa.

In the following Section 3.3 we will present a modal logic that in our perspective meets the previous desiderata for a formal model of social trust. In Section 3.4 we apply this logic to the formalization of the concept of trust (core trust and decision to trust) and the related concepts of distrust, mistrust, and delegation.

3.3 A Logic for Trust Reasoning

3.3.1 Syntax and Semantics

The basic logic of social trust ($\mathcal{STL}$) combines the expressiveness of dynamic logic in which actions are first-class citizens in the formal language [17] with the expressiveness of a logic of mental attitudes [10, 35, 30, 27, 18]. The syntactic primitives of the logic are the following:

- a nonempty finite set of agents $AGT = \{i, j, \ldots\}$;
- a nonempty finite set of *atomic actions* $ACT = \{\alpha, \beta, \ldots\}$;
- a nonempty finite set of n integers $I = \{k \mid 1 \leq k \leq n\}$ with $n > 1$;
- a set of atomic formulas $ATM = \{p, q, \ldots\}$.

We denote with $PROP$ the set of propositional formulas.

The language of the logic $\mathcal{STL}$ is given by the following BNF:

$$\varphi ::= p \mid \neg\varphi \mid \varphi \vee \varphi \mid After_{i:\alpha}\varphi \mid [i:k]\varphi \mid Goal_i\varphi$$

where $p \in ATM, \alpha \in ACT, i \in AGT$, and $k \in I$. Given an arbitrary integer $k \in I$ and agent $i \in AGT$, $[i{:}k]\varphi$ stands for " φ is true in all worlds that according to i are possible at least degree k". The standard reading of $After_{i:\alpha}\varphi$ is "after agent i does action α, it is the case that φ" (or "φ holds after agent i does action α"). Hence, $After_{i:\alpha}\bot$ expresses "agent i does not do α". A formula $Goal_i\varphi$ has to be read "agent i has the chosen goal that φ". In fact, in the present chapter we focus only on goals that an agent has decided to pursue. Chosen goals (differently from mere desires and wishes) have to satisfy two fundamental properties: they must be consistent (i.e., an agent cannot have the chosen goal that φ and the chosen goal that $\neg\varphi$ in the same time), and they must be compatible with beliefs (i.e., an agent cannot have the chosen goal that φ when, according to i, $\neg\varphi$ is likely true). This point will be better illustrated in Section 3.3.2. For the sake of simplicity we will often shorten the reading of $Goal_i\varphi$ to "agent i has the goal that φ" or "agent i wants φ to be true". The classical Boolean connectives $\wedge, \rightarrow, \leftrightarrow, \top$ (tautology), and $\bot$ (contradiction) are defined from $\vee$ and $\neg$ in the usual manner. The following three abbreviations are given.

$$\langle i{:}k\rangle\, \varphi \stackrel{\text{def}}{=} \neg\,[i{:}k]\,\neg\varphi$$

$$Does_{i:\alpha}\varphi \stackrel{\text{def}}{=} \neg After_{i:\alpha}\neg\varphi$$

$$Int_i(\alpha) \stackrel{\text{def}}{=} Goal_i Does_{i:\alpha}\top$$

$\langle i{:}k\rangle\, \varphi$ has to be read "φ is true in at least one world that according to i is possible at least degree k". Since in our logic $\mathcal{STL}$ it is supposed that all actions of the same agent and all actions of different agents occur in parallel (see below), a formula $Does_{i:\alpha}\varphi$ can be read "agent i does α and φ holds afterward". Thus, a formula $Does_{i:\alpha}\top$ can be read "agent i does α". These are different from the standard readings of propositional dynamic logic where $Does_{i:\alpha}\varphi$ has to be read "it is possible that agent i does action α and φ is true after action α's occurrence" and $possatti{:}\alpha\top$ would be read "it is possible that agent i does action α". Finally, $Int_i(\alpha)$ is read "agent i intends to do α".

$\mathcal{STL}$ models are tuples $M = \langle W, R, P, G, V \rangle$ where:

- W is a set of possible worlds or states.
- R is a collection of binary relations $R_{i:\alpha}$ on W, one for every couple $i{:}\alpha$ where $i \in AGT$ and $\alpha \in ACT$. Given an arbitrary world $w \in W$, if $w' \in R_{i:\alpha}(w)$ then w' is a world which is reachable from world w through the occurrence of agent i's action α.
- P is a collection of binary relations $P_{i:k}$ on W, one for every couple $i{:}k$ where $i \in AGT$ and $k \in I$. Given an arbitrary world $w \in W$, if $w' \in P_{i:k}(w)$ then w' is a world that at world w agent i considers possible at least degree k.
- G is a collection of binary relations G_i on W, one for every agent $i \in AGT$. Given an arbitrary world $w \in W$, if $w' \in G_i(w)$ then w' is a world which is compatible with agent i's goals at world w.
- $V : ATM \longrightarrow 2^W$ is a valuation function.

We suppose that all $\mathcal{STL}$ models satisfy the following semantic conditions. For any $w \in W, i \in AGT$ and $k, l \in I$ such that $l < k$:

$$P_{i:k}(w) \subseteq P_{i:l}(w). \quad (S.1)$$

According to property $(S.1)$, for any $k, l \in I$ such that $l < k$ the set of worlds that agent i considers possible at least degree k is a subset of the set of worlds that agent i considers possible at least degree l. In this sense worlds in a model are ordered according to their possibility degrees in a way similar to Lewis's sphere systems [25]. By way of example, suppose that there are four different possibility degrees as in Fig. 3.1, that is, $I = \{1, 2, 3, 4\}$. The eight worlds $v_1 - v_8$ are ordered as follows:

- $P_{i:1}(w) = \{v_1, v_2, v_3, v_4, v_5, v_6, v_7, v_8\}$;
- $P_{i:2}(w) = \{v_3, v_4, v_5, v_6, v_7, v_8\}$;
- $P_{i:3}(w) = \{v_5, v_6, v_7, v_8\}$;
- $P_{i:4}(w) = \{v_7, v_8\}$.

This means that worlds $v_1 - v_8$ are worlds that at w agent i considers possible at least degree 1, worlds $v_3 - v_8$ are worlds that at w agent i considers possible at least degree 2, worlds $v_5 - v_8$ are worlds that at w agent i considers possible at least degree 3, worlds v_7 and v_8 are the two worlds that at w agent i considers possible at least degree 4. The previous four items contain even more information: v_1 and v_2 do not belong to $P_{i:2}(w)$, hence they are worlds that at w agent i considers less than degree 2; $v_1 - v_4$ do not belong to $P_{i:3}(w)$, hence they are worlds that at w agent i considers less possible than degree 3; $v_1 - v_6$ do not belong to $P_{i:4}(w)$, hence they are worlds that at w agent i considers less possible than degree 4. For any $w \in W, i \in AGT$:

$$P_{i:n}(w) \neq \emptyset. \quad (S.2)$$

According to the semantic property $(S.2)$, for any world w and agent i, the set of worlds that at w agent i considers possible at least maximal degree n is never

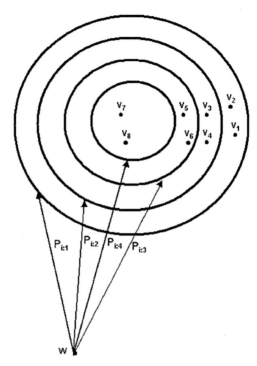

Fig. 3.1 Possibility order over worlds

empty. This means that there is always at least one world to which an agent i assigns a maximal degree of possibility.

The following are two semantic conditions over $\mathcal{STL}$ models about action occurrences. For any $w \in W$, $i \in AGT$ and $\alpha \in ACT$:

$$if \; w' \in R_{i:\alpha}(w) \text{ and } w'' \in R_{j:\beta}(w) \text{ then } w' = w''. \quad (S.3)$$

$$\bigcup_{i \in AGT, a \in ACT} R_{i:\alpha}(w) \neq \emptyset. \quad (S.4)$$

Semantic constraint $(S.3)$ says that all actions of the same agent and all actions of different agents occur in parallel, that is, all actions of the same agent and all actions of different agents correspond to transitions to the same world. This explains why we are allowed to read $Does_{i:\alpha}\varphi$ as "i does α and φ is true after α's occurrence" and to read $Does_{i:\alpha}\top$ as "agent i does α". Semantic constraint $(S.4)$ says that for any world w there is at least one action α and an agent i such that i performs α at w. Constraints $(S.3)$ and $(S.4)$ together ensure that for every world w there is exactly one next (future) world. Thus, it is reasonable to define a new relation $Next$ in order to identify the next world of every world w. $Next(w)$ is defined as the unique world which is reachable from w by the occurrence of some agent's action. Formally, we suppose that for every $w \in W$:

$$Next(w) = \bigcup_{i \in AGT, a \in ACT} R_{i:a}(w)$$

Therefore, $Next$ is nothing but the relation used to interpret the $next$-operator in standard temporal logic.

We conclude with a semantic condition about possibility and goals. For any $w \in W, i \in AGT$:

$$P_{i:n}(w) \cap G_i(w) \neq \emptyset. \quad (S.5)$$

According to the semantic property $(S.5)$, the intersection between the set of worlds that are compatible with i's goals at w and the set of worlds that at w agent i considers possible at least maximal degree n is never empty.

Given a $\mathcal{STL}$ model M, a world w and a formula φ, we write $M, w \models \varphi$ to mean that φ is true at world w in M, under the basic semantics. Truth conditions for atomic formulas, negation, and disjunction are entirely standard. The following are truth conditions for $After_{i:\alpha}\varphi$, $[i:k]\varphi$ and $Goal_i\varphi$.

- $M, w \models After_{i:\alpha}\varphi$ iff $M, w' \models \varphi$ for all w' such that $w' \in R_{i:\alpha}(w)$.
- $M, w \models [i:k]\varphi$ iff $M, w' \models \varphi$ for all w' such that $w' \in P_{i:k}(w)$.
- $M, w \models Goal_i\varphi$ iff $M, w' \models \varphi$ for all w' such that $w' \in G_i(w)$.

We write $\models_{STL} \varphi$ if φ is $valid$ in all $\mathcal{STL}$ models, i.e. $M, w \models \varphi$ for every $\mathcal{STL}$ model M and world w in M. Finally, we say that φ is $satisfiable$ if there exists a $\mathcal{STL}$ model M and world w in M such that $M, w \models \varphi$.

3.3.2 Axiomatization

The following are the axioms and inference rule schemas of our logic $\mathcal{STL}$.

- 0. All tautologies of propositional calculus.
- **Axioms of Possibility**.
  1a. $[i:k](\varphi \rightarrow \psi) \rightarrow ([i:k]\varphi \rightarrow [i:k]\psi)$
  2a. $[i:k]\varphi \rightarrow [i:l]\varphi$ for $l > k$
  3a. $\neg[i:n]\bot$
- **Axioms of Action**.
  1b. $After_{i:\alpha}(\varphi \rightarrow \psi) \rightarrow (After_{i:\alpha}\varphi \rightarrow After_{i:\alpha}\psi)$
  2b. $Does_{i:\alpha}\varphi \rightarrow After_{j:\beta}\varphi$
  3b. $\bigvee_{i \in AGT, a \in ACT} Does_{i:a}\top$
- **Axioms of Goal**.
  1c. $Goal_i(\varphi \rightarrow \psi) \rightarrow (Goal_i\varphi \rightarrow Goal_i\psi)$
- **Interaction Axioms between Goal and Possibility**.
  1d. $[i:n]\varphi \rightarrow \neg Goal_i\neg\varphi$
- **Inference rules**
  R1. $\dfrac{\vdash\varphi \quad \vdash\varphi \rightarrow \psi}{\vdash\psi}$ (Modus Ponens)

R2. $\dfrac{\vdash \varphi}{\vdash [i:k]\varphi}$ ($[i:k]$-Necessitation)

R3. $\dfrac{\vdash \varphi}{\vdash After_{i:\alpha}\varphi}$ ($After_{i:\alpha}$-Necessitation)

R4. $\dfrac{\vdash \varphi}{\vdash Goal_i\varphi}$ ($Goal_i$-Necessitation)

The rest of the section contains explanations of the axioms. Axioms 1a, 1b, 1c, and 1d and rules of inference R2-R4 corresponds to the fact that every operator $[i:k]$, $After_{i:\alpha}$, and $Goal_i$ is a normal modal operator. The following correspondence relations exist between the previous axioms and the semantic constraints given in Section 3.3: Axiom 2a corresponds to constraint (S.1), Axiom 3a to constraint S.2, Axiom 2b to constraint (S.3), Axiom 3b to constraint (S.4). Finally, Axiom 1d corresponds to condition (S.5). According to Axiom 2a, for any $k, l \in I$ such that $l > k$ if φ is true in all worlds, which are for agent i possible at least degree k then φ is in all worlds which are for agent i possible at least degree l. According to Axiom 3a, it is never the case that φ and $\neg\varphi$ are both true in all worlds which are for agent i possible at least maximal degree n. According to Axiom 2b, if an agent i will possibly ensure φ by doing action α then after agent j does action β, it is the case that φ. This means that all actions of the same agent and all actions of different agents starting in a world w occur in parallel. Axiom 3b says that always there exists some agent i and action α such that i performs α (i.e., the world is never static). According to Axiom 1d, if φ is true in all worlds which are for agent i possible at least maximal degree n, then i cannot have the (chosen) goal that $\neg\varphi$. This is similar to the *weak realism* principle discussed in [34, 39, 5]. According to this principle, if an agent is rational, he cannot decide to pursue things that are impossible according to his beliefs.

We call $\mathcal{STL}$ the logic axiomatized by Axioms 1a–3a, 1b–3b, 1c, 1d and rules of inference R1-R4. We write $\vdash_{\mathcal{STL}} \varphi$ if formula φ is a theorem of $\mathcal{STL}$. Since the set of agents AGT and the set of atomic actions ACT is supposed to be finite, we can prove that $\mathcal{STL}$ is *sound* and *complete* with regard to the class of $\mathcal{STL}$ models.

Theorem 1. $\mathcal{STL}$ *is determined by the class of models of* $\mathcal{STL}$.

Proof. It is a routine to prove soundness, whereas completeness is obtained by Sahlqvist's completeness theorem [3].

The rest of this section is devoted to define a "next time" operator X which is used to specify facts that are true in the next state. Furthermore, we will present some theorems of our logic $\mathcal{STL}$ concerning goals and possibility. By the semantic constraints (S.3) and (S.4) given in Section 3.3.1 it is reasonable to conceive world w' as the unique temporal successor of w. The *next* operator is defined according to the following abbreviation.

$$X\varphi \overset{\text{def}}{=} \bigwedge_{i \in AGT, a \in ACT} After_{i:\alpha}\varphi$$

where $X\varphi$ is read "φ will be true in the next state". Clearly, the operator X can be interpreted according to the relation $Next$ defined in Section 3.3.1, that is, for any $w \in W$ we have:
$M, w \models X\varphi$ iff $M, w' \models \varphi$ for every $w' \in Next(w)$. Therefore, X is a normal modality. It can be proved that the formula $X\varphi \leftrightarrow \neg X \neg \varphi$ is a theorem of our logic.

The following Theorem 2 highlight some additional properties of goals and possibility.

Theorem 2. *Let $i \in AGT$ and $k \in I$. Then:*

1. $\vdash_{STL} \neg(Goal_i\varphi \wedge Goal_i\neg\varphi)$
2. $\vdash_{STL} \neg([i{:}k]\varphi \wedge [i{:}k]\neg\varphi)$

Theorem 2.1 says that an agent cannot have conflicting chosen goals. According to Theorem 2.2, for every integer $k \in I$ it never the case that φ and φ are both true in all worlds, which are for agent i possible at least degree k.

3.3.3 Possibility Orders over Formulas

On the basis of the formal constructions of the logic STL, we can define a preferential relation over formulas of type "φ is for agent i at least as possible as ψ", denoted by $\psi \leq_i \varphi$. Formally, for any agent $i \in AGT$ we have:

$$\psi \leq_i \varphi \stackrel{\text{def}}{=} \bigwedge_{k \in I}(\langle i{:}k \rangle \psi \rightarrow \langle i{:}k \rangle \varphi)$$

According to this definition "φ is for agent i at least as possible as ψ" if and only if for every integer $k \in I$ if ψ is true in at least one world which is for agent i possible at least degree k then φ is also true in at least one world which is for agent i possible at least degree k. We can easily prove that $\psi \leq_i \varphi$ satisfies reflexivity, transitivity and completeness (i.e. for any two formulas φ_1 and φ_2 either φ_1 is for agent i at least as possible as φ_2, or φ_2 is for agent i at least as possible as φ_1). Indeed, the following theorems and rule of inference can be derived.

Theorem 3. *Let $i \in AGT$. Then:*

1. $\vdash_{STL} \psi \leq_i \psi$
2. $\vdash_{STL} (\varphi_1 \leq_i \varphi_2) \wedge (\varphi_2 \leq_i \varphi_3) \rightarrow (\varphi_1 \leq_i \varphi_3)$
3. $\vdash_{STL} (\varphi_1 \leq_i \varphi_2) \vee (\varphi_2 \leq_i \varphi_1)$
4. $\vdash_{STL} \bot \leq_i \top$
5. *From* $\vdash_{STL} \varphi \rightarrow (\psi_1 \vee \ldots \vee \psi_s)$ *infer* $\vdash_{STL} (\varphi \leq_i \psi_1) \vee \ldots \vee (\varphi \leq_i \psi_s)$

Theorems 3.2, 3.3, 3.4 are exactly the three fundamental Axioms of Lewis's conditional logic (called VN) [25]. The language of Lewis's logic VN is that of classical logic augmented with a dyadic connective $\leq$. In this sense our logic STL

can be seen as a generalization of $\mathcal{VN}$. A similar result has been proved by Del Cerro & Herzig [11]. The two authors have developed a modal logic of possibility called $\mathcal{PL}$ in which a normal operator of the form $[x]$ for every parameter x in a set of parameters P is introduced (the dual of $[x]$ is noted $\langle x \rangle$). In a way similar to a $\mathcal{STL}$ formula $[i{:}k]\varphi$, a $\mathcal{PL}$ formula $[x]\varphi$ is read "the necessity of formula φ is at least degree x". $\mathcal{PL}$ have the standard axioms and rules of inference of system K for every operator $[x]$ plus the following two Axioms:

PL1 $\neg[1]\bot$
PL2 $([x]\varphi \to [y]\varphi) \vee ([x]\varphi \to [y]\varphi)$ for every $x, y \in P$

where 1 is a particular element in the set of parameters P. The two authors reconstruct Lewis's preferential operators by means of the following translation from $\mathcal{PL}$ to Lewis's conditional logic:

$$\psi \leq \varphi \stackrel{\mathrm{def}}{=} \bigwedge_{x \in P}(\langle x \rangle \psi \to \langle x \rangle \varphi).^1$$

We can easily prove that our logic $\mathcal{STL}$ satisfies the previous two properties of $\mathcal{PL}$. Indeed, PL1 is our Axiom 3a (i.e., $\neg[i{:}n]\bot$). Moreover, by our Axiom 2a we can infer the following Theorem.

Theorem 4. *Let* $k, l \in I$. *Then:*

$$\vdash_{\mathcal{STL}} ([i{:}k]\varphi \to [i{:}l]\varphi) \vee ([i{:}l]\varphi \to [i{:}k]\varphi)$$

Theorem 4 corresponds to Axiom PL2 of $\mathcal{PL}$. On the contrary in $\mathcal{PL}$ we cannot infer a theorem that corresponds to our Axiom 2a, that is, in $\mathcal{PL}$ we cannot infer as a theorem something like $[x]\varphi \to [y]\varphi$ if $x < y$. In this sense, the fragment of our logic $\mathcal{STL}$ with preferential operators of type $[i{:}k]$ can be seen as a generalization of $\mathcal{PL}$.

Now, let us define from $\psi \leq_i \varphi$ a notion of strict preference of the form $\psi <_i \varphi$, where $\psi <_i \varphi$ means "φ is for agent i strictly more possible than ψ". Formally:

$$\psi <_i \varphi \stackrel{\mathrm{def}}{=} (\psi \leq_i \varphi) \wedge \neg(\varphi \leq_i \psi)$$

We can prove that according to this definition of strict preference, if φ is for agent i strictly more possible than ψ then it is not the case that ψ is for agent i strictly more possible than φ.

Theorem 5. *Let* $i \in AGT$. *Then:*

$$\vdash_{\mathcal{STL}} (\psi <_i \varphi) \to \neg(\varphi <_i \psi)$$

The following Theorem shows that in our logic φ is for agent i strictly more possible than $\neg\varphi$ if and only if φ is true in all worlds which are for agent i possible at least maximal degree n.

---

[1] An additional result proved by the two authors is that Lewis's conditional logic is nothing more that the logic of qualitative possibility developed in [13]. On this see also [4].

Theorem 6. *Let $i \in AGT$. Then:*

$$\vdash_{STL} (\neg\varphi <_i \varphi) \leftrightarrow [i{:}n]\,\varphi$$

In the rest of the analysis we will use the following abbreviations to simplify the reading of our possibilistic operators.

$$Plaus_i\varphi \stackrel{\text{def}}{=} [i{:}n]\,\varphi$$
$$Certain_i\varphi \stackrel{\text{def}}{=} [i{:}1]\,\varphi$$

$Certain_i\varphi$ has to be read "agent i is certain that φ is true", and $Plaus_i\varphi$ has to be read "agent i thinks that φ is plausible". Our assumption is that, on the one hand, an agent i can be said to have a plausible belief that φ (or even better to think that φ is plausible) if and only if φ is true in all worlds that according to i are possible at least maximal degree n. Therefore, according to the previous Theorem 6, an agent i thinks that φ is plausible (noted $Plaus_i\varphi$) if and only if he thinks that φ is *strictly more possible than* $\neg\varphi$. On the other hand, an agent i can be said to be *certain* that φ is true if and only if φ is true in all worlds that according to i have possibility at least minimal degree 1. Obviously, if an agent is *certain* that φ is true then he must think that φ is also *plausible*. This property is verified in our logic. Indeed, from $Certain_i\varphi$ we can infer $Plaus_i\varphi$.[2]

The concept of plausible belief expressed by the operator $Plaus_i$ is fundamental for the sake of the present analysis. Indeed, in Section 3.4 we will exploit the operator $Plaus_i$ to formalize the notion of trust. The basic idea is that trust is nothing more than i's *plausible* expectation that j (the trustee) has a set of properties $\Gamma_j(\varphi)$, which guarantee that he will accomplish a given task φ that i (the truster) wants to achieve in the next state (i.e., $Goal_i X\varphi$). The operator $Plaus_i$ will be used to model such a mental attitude of the truster. We will call *core trust*, the truster's cognitive configuration whose components are the truster's goal that φ will be true in the next state, noted $Goal_i X\varphi$, and the truster's plausible expectation that the trustee satisfies all properties in $\Gamma_j(\varphi)$, noted $Plaus_i\Gamma_j(\varphi)$. According to the previous Theorem 6, to say that truster has a plausible expectation that the trustee satisfies all properties in $\Gamma_j(\varphi)$ is equivalent to say that, according to the truster, the fact "the trustee satisfies the properties $\Gamma_j(\varphi)$" is strictly more possible than the fact "the trustee does not satisfy the properties $\Gamma_j(\varphi)$" (noted $\neg\Gamma_j(\varphi) <_i \Gamma_j(\varphi)$). In Section 3.4 we will provide an explicit characterization of the trustee's properties $\Gamma_j(\varphi)$.

---

[2] Note that in principle we could define a notion of graded plausible belief in our logic, where $Plaus_i$ is used to define a concept of plausible belief with minimal degree, $Certain_i$ is used to define a concept of plausible belief with maximal degree and for every k such that $1 < k < n$, the operator $[i{:}k]$ is used to define a concept of plausible belief with degree $(n+1) - k$. In this case, $Plaus_i\varphi$ (which is an abbreviation for $[i{:}n]$) could also be read "agent i thinks that φ is plausible with minimal degree 1" and $Certain_i\varphi$ (which is an abbreviation for $[i{:}1]$) could also be read "agent i thinks that φ is plausible with maximal degree n". For every k such that $1 < k < n$, $[i{:}k]$ could be read "agent i thinks that φ is plausible with intermediate degree k".

3.3.4 Execution Preconditions for Action Execution

We suppose that to every agent i and action α there are associated a formula $IPre(i,\alpha)$ and $EPre(i,\alpha)$ describing respectively the *internal preconditions* for the execution of action α by agent i and the *external preconditions* for the execution of action α by agent i. Let us call *closed action formulas* constructions of the form $Does_{i:\alpha}\top$ and denote with Δ the set of such a kind of formulas, that is, $\Delta = \{Does_{i:\alpha}\top | i \in AGT, \alpha \in ACT\}$. From Δ and the set of atomic formulas ATM, the set of *objective formulas* OBJ is defined as follows.

Definition 1. OBJ is the smallest superset of ATM and Δ such that: if $\varphi, \psi \in OBJ$ then $\neg\varphi, \varphi \vee \psi \in OBJ$

$IPre$ is supposed to be a function, which assigns a propositional formula to every agent i and action α, whilst $EPre$ is supposed to be a function, which assigns an objective formula to every agent i and action α. Formally:

$$IPre : AGT \times ACT \longrightarrow PROP$$
$$EPre : AGT \times ACT \longrightarrow OBJ$$

The idea is that whenever $IPre(i,\alpha)$ and $EPre(i,\alpha)$ hold and agent i intends to perform α, then i will successfully perform action α, and whenever i successfully performs action α, both $IPre(i,\alpha)$ and $EPre(i,\alpha)$ hold. For the sake of simplicity, suppose that there are only two agents in AGT called Bill and Bob and there are only two types of atomic actions $graspObj$ (the action of grasping an object) and $block$ (the action of blocking) in ACT. In this scenario one might suppose that the internal preconditions for Bob to grasp object Obj is that Bob's hand is not paralyzed, that is, $IPre(Bob,graspObj) = \neg BobHandParalyzed$, and the external preconditions for Bob to grasp object Obj is that Bob's hand is not tied up, the object is in front of Bob and Bill does not block Bob's movement, that is, $EPre(Bob,graspObj) = \neg BobHandTied \wedge ObjInFrontBob \wedge \neg Does_{Bill:block}\top$. This means that if *Bob* has the intention to perform the action $graspObj$ and the internal and external preconditions for Bob to perform action $graspObj$ hold, then *Bob* will successfully perform action $graspObj$, that is, $(IPre(Bob,graspObj) \wedge EPre(Bob,graspObj) \wedge Int_{Bob}(graspObj)) \rightarrow Does_{Bob:graspObj}\top$. Moreover, if *Bob* successfully performs action $graspObj$, then both the internal and external preconditions for Bob to perform action $graspObj$ hold, that is, $Does_{Bob:graspObj}\top \rightarrow (IPre(Bob,graspObj) \wedge EPre(Bob, graspObj))$.
More generally, for every agent $i \in AGT$ and action $\alpha \in ACT$ the following two global axioms in Fitting's sense [15] are given:

$$(IPre(i,\alpha) \wedge EPre(i,\alpha) \wedge Int_i(\alpha)) \rightarrow Does_{i:\alpha} top \quad (GAxiom1)$$
$$Does_{i:\alpha} top \rightarrow (IPre(i,\alpha) \wedge EPre(i,\alpha)) \quad (GAxiom2)$$

Therefore, formulas $IPre(i,\alpha)$ and $EPre(i,\alpha)$ together include all facts: (a) which are necessary conditions for agent i's successful performance of action α; (b) which are, together with the fact that agent i intends to perform α, sufficient conditions for agent i's successful performance of action α. The term *internal preconditions* for action execution refers to internal states to an agent's body, whereas the term *external preconditions* for action execution refers to external states to an agent's body. In particular, formula $IPre(i,\alpha)$ expresses the following general fact: there are no impairments that prevent agent i from moving his body in a certain way α, agent i has the ability and skills to move his body in the way α. For example, the internal preconditions of the action of moving a leg for Jack include the fact "Jack's leg is not paralyzed", that is, $IPre(Jack,moveLeg) \rightarrow \neg JackParalyzedLeg$; the internal preconditions of the action of jumping 2 meters in the air for Bob include the facts "Bob has the skill to jump 2 meters in the air", that is, $IPre(Bob,Jump2M) \rightarrow BobSkilledJump2M$. Formula $EPre(i,\alpha)$ expresses the following three general facts: there are no physical obstacles that make it physically impossible for agent i to perform action α; there are no external events and actions of other agents that parallely interfere with the execution of action α by i and prevent agent i from performing α in a successful way; agent i has everything he needs to perform α and is in the right position in a physical space to perform α. For example, the external preconditions of the action of raising an arm for Mary include the two facts "Mary's arm is not tied up" and "Bill does not block Mary's arm", that is, $EPre(Mary,raiseArm) \rightarrow (\neg MaryTiedArm \wedge \neg Does_{Bill:block}\top)$. Finally, the external preconditions of the action of grasping an object for Mary include the fact "there is an object in front of Mary", that is, $EPre(Mary,graspObj) \rightarrow ObjInFrontMary$.

3.4 A formal Ontology of Trust

The following sections are devoted to develop a formal ontology of trust. We will try not only to individuate the basic mental ingredients of trust (responding to the question: which are them?) but also to give an interpretation of the kind of interaction among these elements (responding to the question: how do they interact?) and how the final decision to trust or not is taken. As we emphasized in our previous works [7, 8], we conceive trust as an expectation of the truster about the trustee's behavior, about the status (and dynamics) of the environment in which the trustee is going to operate. We will exploit the logic $\mathcal{STL}$ presented in Section 3.3 to formalize some fundamental concepts for a model of social trust. In particular, we will define and study the properties of the concepts of *core trust*, *delegation*, and *decision to trust*. Furthermore, we will distinguish trust from the related notions of *distrust*, *lack of trust*, and *mistrust*.

3.4.1 Core Trust

In our perspective trust is a complex expectation, in which there is a main and primary motivational component (the principal reason activating the truster's delegating behavior): the goal to achieve some state of affairs φ (the trust in the trustee is always relative to some interest, need, concern, desire of the truster); and a complex configuration of truster's expectations about the qualities of the trustee and the environment in which the trustee is going to operate. More precisely, we suppose the following definition of trust in which the trustee's action is specified.

Definition 2. CORE TRUST. An agent i trusts agent j to ensure φ by performing α if and only if:

1. i wants to achieve φ;
2. i expects that

   - agent j has the opportunity to ensure φ by doing action α AND
   - j is willing (i.e. intends) to do action α AND
   - the internal preconditions for the execution of action α by agent j hold AND
   - the external preconditions for the execution of action α by agent j hold.

The previous items constitute the *core* of social trust. The second and third items concern what the truster thinks about the trustee's qualities and dispositions, whereas the first and fourth items concern what the truster thinks about the environmental conditions in which the trustee is going to operate for achieving the task φ. The first item may also be written as "after agent j does action α, it is the case that φ". More generally, the second and third items are based on the truster's attribution of *internal properties* to the trustee. In this sense they are the essential elements of i's trust *in* j. The first and fourth items are based on the truster's attribution of *external properties* to the trustee, that is, on the truster's attribution of properties to the environment in which the trustee is going to act. Definition 2 can be generalized by placing an existential quantification over the trustee's actions.

Definition 3. (GENERALIZED) CORE TRUST. An agent i trusts agent j to ensure φ if and only if:

- there exists some action α such that agent i trusts agent j to ensure φ by doing α (see Definition 3).

Let us exploit the formal framework presented in Section 3.3 in order to capture the logical form of the notion of *core trust* defined above. We first present a formal translation of Definition 2 with four arguments (truster, trustee, truster's goal, and trustee's action). For any $i, j \in AGT, \alpha \in ACT$ we have:

$$CoreTrust(i, j, \alpha, \varphi) \stackrel{\text{def}}{=}$$
$$Goal_i X\varphi \wedge Plaus_i(After_{j:\alpha}\varphi \wedge Int_j(\alpha) \wedge IPre(j,\alpha) \wedge EPre(j,\alpha))$$

Thus, "i trusts j to ensure φ by doing α" (noted $CoreTrust(i, j, \alpha, \varphi)$) if and only if i wants φ to be true in the next state (noted $Goal_i X\varphi$) and, according to i, it is plausible that after j does action α, it is the case that φ, j intends to perform action α and both the internal and external preconditions for the execution of α by j hold (noted $Plaus_i X(After_{j:\alpha}\varphi \wedge Int_j(\alpha) \wedge IPre(j,\alpha) \wedge EPre(j,\alpha)))$.

Example 1. Suppose that Bill trusts Mary to kill Bob in the next state by performing the action of shooting him:

$$CoreTrust(Bill, Mary, shoot, \neg BobAlive).$$

This implies that Bill wants Bob to die in the next state:

$$Goal_{Bill} X \neg BobAlive.$$

Moreover, according to Bill, it is plausible that Mary has the opportunity to kill Bob in the next state by shooting him now, Mary intends to shoot Bob and both the internal and external preconditions for the execution of the action of shooting by Mary hold (e.g., $IPre(Mary, shoot) = \neg MaryArmParalyzed$, $EPre(Mary, shoot) = \neg MaryBlockedArm$):

$$Plaus_{Bill}(After_{Mary:shoot} \neg BobAlive \wedge$$
$$Int_{Mary}(shoot) \wedge IPre(Mary, shoot) \wedge EPre(Mary, shoot)).$$

A logical translation of Definition 3 is obtained straightforwardly.

$$CoreTrust(i, j, \varphi) \stackrel{\text{def}}{=} \bigvee_{\alpha \in ACT} CoreTrust(i, j, \alpha, \varphi)$$

$CoreTrust(i, j, \varphi)$ is meant to stand for "i trusts j to ensure φ". The following theorem shows that trusting an agent with respect to a goal that φ implies having a positive expectation that φ will be true in the next state.[3]

Theorem 7. *Let $i, j \in AGT$, $\alpha \in ACT$. Then:*

1. $\vdash_{STL} CoreTrust(i, j, \alpha, \varphi) \rightarrow Goal_i X\varphi \wedge Plaus_i X\varphi$
2. $\vdash_{STL} CoreTrust(i, j, \varphi) \rightarrow Goal_i X\varphi \wedge Plaus_i X\varphi$

3.4.2 Distrust, Lack of Trust, and Mistrust

The opposite of *trust* is *distrust*. In our view, an agent i distrusts another agent j to ensure φ by performing action α when i has reasons to believe that j cannot ensure φ by performing α either because j is lacking the opportunities to ensure φ by performing α or because j is not willing to perform such an action or because

---

[3] We suppose that agent i has a positive expectation that φ if and only if i wants φ to be true in the future and according to i it is plausible that φ will be true in the future (see [6, 9, 31] for a theory of positive and negative expectations).

the internal preconditions or the external preconditions for the execution of α by agent j do not hold. In this sense, agent i distrusts in agent j can be based either on i's belief that j is lacking some internal properties, which are needed to accomplish the task or in i's belief that j is not under the right environmental conditions for accomplishing the task by doing α. The concept of distrust can be defined more formally.

Definition 4. DISTRUST. Agent i distrusts j to ensure φ by performing α if and only if:

1. i wants to achieve φ;
2. i expects that

   - j has not the opportunity to ensure φ by performing action α OR
   - j is not willing (i.e., does not intend) to perform action α OR
   - the internal preconditions for the execution of action α by agent j do not hold OR
   - the external preconditions for the execution of action α by agent j do not hold.

As for core trust, a notion of generalized distrust can be given.

Definition 5. (GENERALIZED) DISTRUST. Agent i distrusts j to ensure φ if and only if for all actions α:

- agent i distrusts j to ensure φ by performing α (see Definition 4).

The previous two versions of the concept of distrust are formally defined as follows. Let $i, j \in AGT, \alpha \in ACT$. Then:

$$Distrust(i, j, \alpha, \varphi) \overset{\text{def}}{=}$$
$$Goal_i X\varphi \wedge Plaus_i(\neg After_{j:\alpha}\varphi \vee \neg Int_j(\alpha) \vee \neg IPre(j,\alpha) \vee \neg EPre(j,\alpha))$$
$$Distrust(i, j, \varphi) \overset{\text{def}}{=} \bigwedge_{\alpha \in ACT} Distrust(i, j, \alpha, \varphi)$$

$Distrust(i, j, \alpha, \varphi)$ is meant to stand for "i distrusts j to ensure φ by performing α", while $Distrust(i, j, \varphi)$ is meant to stand for "i distrusts j to ensure φ". The following Theorem highlights the relationship between distrust and (core) trust by stating that if i distrusts j to ensure φ by performing α (resp. i distrusts j to ensure φ) then it is not the case that i trusts j to ensure φ by performing α (resp. i trusts j to ensure φ).

Theorem 8. *Let $i, j \in AGT, \alpha \in ACT$. Then:*

1. $\vdash_{STL} Distrust(i, j, \alpha, \varphi) \rightarrow \neg CoreTrust(i, j, \alpha, \varphi)$
2. $\vdash_{STL} Distrust(i, j, \varphi) \rightarrow \neg CoreTrust(i, j, \varphi)$

It has to be noted that the concept of *distrust* is different from the concepts of *lack of trust*. [4] Indeed, it is reasonable to say that i lacks trust in j with respect to his goal that φ when i wants φ to be true and he does not think to be plausible that j satisfies the internal and external conditions to ensure φ by doing α (i.e., i does not think to be plausible that j has the opportunity to ensure φ by doing α, i intends to do α and the internal and external preconditions for the execution of α by j hold). According to this perspective, lack of trust can be formalized as follows. Let $i, j \in AGT, \alpha \in ACT$. Then:

$$LackTrust(i, j, \alpha, \varphi) \stackrel{\text{def}}{=}$$

$$Goal_i X\varphi \wedge \neg Plaus_i(After_{j:\alpha}\varphi \wedge Int_j(\alpha) \wedge IPre(j,\alpha) \wedge EPre(j,\alpha))$$

$$LackTrust(i, j, \varphi) \stackrel{\text{def}}{=} \bigwedge_{\alpha \in ACT} LackTrust(i, j, \alpha, \varphi)$$

$LackTrust(i, j, \alpha, \varphi)$ is meant to stand for "i lacks trust in j to ensure φ by performing α", while $LackTrust(i, j, \varphi)$ is meant to stand for "i lacks trust in j to ensure φ". It is straightforward to prove that distrust implies lack of trust but not vice versa, that is,

$Distrust(i, j, \alpha, \varphi) \rightarrow LackTrust(i, j, \alpha, \varphi)$ and
$Distrust(i, j, \varphi) \rightarrow LackTrust(i, j, \varphi)$
are theorems of $\mathcal{STL}$, but
$\neg Distrust(i, j, \alpha, \varphi) \wedge LackTrust(i, j, \alpha, \varphi)$ and
$\neg Distrust(i, j, \varphi) \wedge LackTrust(i, j, \varphi)$
are satisfiable in $\mathcal{STL}$.

The concepts of *distrust* and *lack of trust* must be distinguished from the concept of *mistrust*. Indeed, if i mistrusts j then i thinks that j is in condition to harm i and is willing to perform the action which will harm i.

Definition 6. MISTRUST. Agent i mistrusts j to ensure $\neg\varphi$ by performing α if and only if:

1. i wants to achieve φ;
2. i expects that

   - j has the opportunity to ensure $\neg\varphi$ by performing action α AND
   - j intends to perform action α AND
   - the internal preconditions for the execution of action α by agent j hold AND
   - the external preconditions for the execution of action α by agent j hold.

According to this definition, the doxastic component involved in mistrust and core trust is the same: in both cases i expects that j has the right properties to ensure φ by doing α. The only difference between core trust and mistrust is in the

---

[4] The need to distinguish the three concepts of *trust*, *distrust*, and *lack of trust* is also stressed in [37].

motivational component. Indeed, in mistrust the content of agent i's goal is $\neg\varphi$, while in core trust i has the goal that φ. [5] The following definition capture a notion of generalized mistrust.

Definition 7. (GENERALIZED) MISTRUST. Agent i mistrusts j to ensure $\neg\varphi$ if and only if there exists an action α such that:

- agent i mistrusts j to ensure $\neg\varphi$ by performing α (see Definition 6).

Stated formally, for any $i, j \in AGT, \alpha \in ACT$ we have:

$$Mistrust(i, j, \alpha, \varphi) \stackrel{\text{def}}{=}$$

$$Goal_i X\varphi \wedge Plaus_i(After_{j:\alpha}\neg\varphi \wedge Int_j(\alpha) \wedge IPre(j,\alpha) \wedge EPre(j,\alpha))$$

$$Mistrust(i, j, \varphi) \stackrel{\text{def}}{=} \bigvee_{\alpha \in ACT} Mistrust(i, j, \alpha, \varphi)$$

$Mistrust(i, j, \alpha, \varphi)$ is meant to stand for "i mistrusts j to ensure $\neg\varphi$ by performing α", while $Mistrust(i, j, \varphi)$ is meant to stand for "i mistrusts j to ensure $\neg\varphi$". It is straightforward to prove that mistrust implies distrust but not vice versa, that is,
$Mistrust(i, j, \alpha, \varphi) \rightarrow Distrust(i, j, \alpha, \varphi)$ and
$Mistrust(i, j, \varphi) \rightarrow Distrust(i, j, \varphi)$
are theorems of $\mathcal{STL}$, but
$\neg Mistrust(i, j, \alpha, \varphi) \wedge Distrust(i, j, \alpha, \varphi)$ and
$\neg Mistrust(i, j, \varphi) \wedge Distrust(i, j, \varphi)$
are satisfiable in $\mathcal{STL}$. Moreover, as the following theorem shows, i's mistrust in j involves a negative expectation of i.

Theorem 9. Let $i, j \in AGT, \alpha \in ACT$. Then:

1. $\vdash_{\mathcal{STL}} Mistrust(i, j, \alpha, \varphi) \rightarrow Goal_i X\varphi \wedge Plaus_i X\neg\varphi$
2. $\vdash_{\mathcal{STL}} Mistrust(i, j, \varphi) \rightarrow Goal_i X\varphi \wedge Plaus_i X\neg\varphi$

Example 2. Suppose that Bill mistrusts Mary to kill Bob in the next state by performing the action of shooting him:

$$Mistrust(Bill, Mary, shoot, BobAlive).$$

This implies that Bill wants Bob to be alive in the next state:

$$Goal_{Bill} X BobAlive.$$

Moreover, according to Bill, it is plausible that Mary has the opportunities to kill Bob in the next state by shooting him now, Mary intends to shoot Bob and both the internal and external preconditions for the execution of the action

---

[5] Therefore, if i's goal that $\neg\varphi$ transforms into the goal that φ (under the assumption that i's beliefs do not change after this transformation), i's mistrust in j transforms into i's trust in j.

of shooting by Mary holds (e.g. $IPre(Mary,shoot) = \neg MaryArmParalyzed$, $EPre(Mary,shoot) = \neg MaryBlockedArm$):

$$Plaus_{Bill}(After_{Mary:shoot}\neg BobAlive \wedge$$
$$Int_{Mary}(shoot) \wedge IPre(Mary,shoot) \wedge EPre(Mary,shoot)).$$

According to the previous Theorem 9, Bill thinks to be plausible that *Bob* will die in the next state:

$$Plaus_{Bill}X\neg BobAlive.$$

3.4.3 Delegation and Decision to Trust

The concept of *core trust* concerns only the truster's beliefs and expectations about the properties of the trustee and of the environment in which the trustee will operate. It says nothing about the truster's decision to delegate the task to the trustee. In our perspective the notion of *delegation* (or *reliance*) should be conceived as the active counterpart of the notion of *core trust*. When agent i delegates to agent j the performance of action α, i has the goal that j will perform α, i relies on j's action α in his plan. Therefore, the term "deciding to trust" does not only concern the truster's beliefs and expectations about the properties of the trustee and of the environment in which the trustee will operate (the *core trust*), but also his decision to exploit the action of the trustee (the act of *delegation*).

It is reasonable to suppose that an agent i delegates to agent j the achievement of some result φ when i wants φ to be true and wants to achieve φ by exploiting j [28, 14]. Delegation consists in deciding and wanting to exploit the actions of other agents in order to achieve our goals. This can be expressed more formally.

Definition 8. DELEGATION (or **RELIANCE**). Agent i delegates to agent j the performance of action α for the achievement of φ (or i relies on j's action α for the achievement of φ) if and only if:

1. i wants φ to be true AND
2. i wants that j will do α and that j, by doing α, contributes to the fact that φ holds.

In a way similar to core trust, Definition 8 can be generalized by placing an existential quantification over the trustee's actions.

Definition 9. (GENERALIZED) DELEGATION. Agent i delegates to agent j the achievement of φ (or i relies on j for the achievement of φ) if and only if there exists some action α such that:

- agent i delegates to agent j the performance of action α for the achievement of φ (see Definition 8).

Again we exploit the logic presented in Section 3.3 in order to give a formal translation of Definitions 8 and 9. For any $i, j \in AGT, \alpha \in ACT$ we have:

$$Delegate(i, j, \alpha, \varphi) \overset{\text{def}}{=} Goal_i Does_{j:\alpha}\varphi$$

Thus, "i delegates to j the performance of action α for the achievement of φ" (noted $Delegate(i, j, \alpha, \varphi)$) if and only if i wants that j performs action α and that j, by performing α, contributes to the fact that φ will hold in the next state (noted $Goal_i Does_{j:\alpha}\varphi$).[6] A logical translation of Definition 9 is obtained straightforwardly. For any $i, j \in AGT$ we have:

$$Delegate(i, j, \varphi) \overset{\text{def}}{=} \bigvee_{\alpha \in ACT} Delegate(i, j, \alpha, \varphi)$$

$Delegate(i, j, \varphi)$ is meant to stand for "i delegates to j the achievement of φ".

Example 3. Suppose that Bill delegates to Mary the performance of the action of shooting Bob for the achievement of the result $BobDead$ in the next state:

$$Delegate(Bill, Mary, shoot, BobDead).$$

This means that Bill wants Bob to die in the next state, and Bill wants that Mary performs the action of shooting Bob and that Mary, by shooting Bob, contributes to the fact that Bob will die in the next state:

$$Goal_{Bill} Does_{Mary:shoot} BobDead.$$

As noted earlier, the concept of core trust and the concept of delegation together constitute the general concept of decision to trust. Indeed, in our perspective, a decision to trust has two constituents: a passive constituent and an active constituent. The former is the truster's cognitive configuration of beliefs and expectations about the internal and external properties of the trustee (core trust); the latter is the truster's decision to rely on the trustee's action (delegation). Thus, the concept of decision to trust can be defined as follows.

Definition 10. DECISION TO TRUST. Agent i decides to trust j to ensure φ by performing α if and only if:

1. i trusts agent j to ensure φ by performing α (see Definition 2) AND
2. agent i delegates to agent j the performance of action α for the achievement of φ (see Definition 8).

Definition 11. (GENERALIZED) DECISION TO TRUST. Agent i decides to trust j to ensure φ if and only if there exists some action α such that:

- i decides to trust j to ensure φ by performing α (see Definition 10).

---

[6] Note that $Delegate(i, j, \alpha, \varphi)$ implies $Goal_i X\varphi$.

Formally, for any $i, j \in AGT, \alpha \in ACT$ we have:

$$DecideTrust(i, j, \alpha, \varphi) \stackrel{\text{def}}{=} CoreTrust(i, j, \alpha, \varphi) \wedge Delegate(i, j, \alpha, \varphi)$$

$$DecideTrust(i, j, \varphi) \stackrel{\text{def}}{=} \bigvee_{\alpha \in ACT} DecideTrust(i, j, \alpha, \varphi)$$

$DecideTrust(i, j, \alpha, \varphi)$ is meant to stand for "agent i decides to trust j to ensure φ by performing α", whereas $DecideTrust(i, j, \alpha, \varphi)$ is meant to stand for "agent i decides to trust j to ensure φ".[7] The aim of the following two subsections is to investigate the internal reasons that support an agent i's decision to delegate a task to a certain agent j, and to clarify the relationship between delegation as a decision to exploit the actions of other agents (Definitions 8 and 9) and core trust as a configuration of expectations and beliefs of the truster about the trustee's internal and external properties (Definitions 2 and 3).

3.4.3.1 Dependence-Based Delegation and Preference-Based Delegation

There are two distinct cases in which an agent i can delegate to j the performance of action α for the achievement of φ. These cases correspond to two different reasons for delegating a task to someone. In one case, i delegates to j the performance of action α for the achievement of φ because, according to i, φ will be achieved only if j does action α. This corresponds to a form of *dependence-based delegation*. In *dependence-based delegation*, an agent i delegates the performance of an action α for the achievement of φ to another agent j since i thinks that the occurrence of action α performed by j is a necessary condition for achieving his goal that φ will be true. In the other case i delegates to j the performance of action α for the achievement of φ because i prefers relying on j's action α for the achievement φ than not relying on j's action α. This corresponds to a form *preference-based delegation*. In *preference-based delegation*, i's preference to achieve φ by relying on j's action α is determined by several factors such as: – i's belief that it is more likely to achieve φ if j does action α rather than if he does not and/or, - i's belief that it is more likely to achieve φ *plus* all other i's goals if j does action α rather than if he does not.[8] In order to understand the difference between *preference-based delegation* and *dependence-based delegation* consider the following two examples.

---

[7] It has to be noted that the definition of *decision to trust* given here concerns the *result* of the decision rather than the *mental process* of deciding to trust. In a similar way, the previous definition of *delegation* given above concerns only the *result* of the decision to delegate. In order to have a logical model of the decision process involved in trust and delegation, we should relax some assumptions of our logic $\mathcal{STL}$ such as Axiom 2b. Indeed, every decision process involves a strong form of indeterminism at the level of beliefs that our Axiom 2b prevents from expressing.

[8] If we had utility assigned to goals, i's preference would be based on a calculation of expected utility by i. That is, the expression "i's prefers relying on j's action α for the achievement of φ than not relying" would mean that "i wants φ to be true and expects a greater utility from j doing α than j not doing α".

Example 4. Imagine i has some heart illness and wants to recover from it. To achieve his goal, he must undergo a surgical operation. There are two surgeons j and z to whom i can delegate the action of operating on his heart for the achievement of the result "recovered from heart illness". One might say that i believes to depend on the two surgeons for the achievement of the result "recovered from heart illness". But he does not believe to depend on both surgeons since, according to i, each surgeon can heal him independently from what the other surgeon does.[9] So, if i decides to rely on surgeon j rather than on surgeon z, such a delegation does not correspond to a form of *dependence-based delegation*. On the contrary, we would say that it corresponds to a *preference-based delegation*, where i's preference to recover from the heart illness by relying on j's intervention rather than on z's intervention is determined by the fact that, according to i, it is more likely to recover from the heart illness if j operates on his heart rather than if j does not (but z does).

Example 5. Now, imagine agent i being in a small village and his car crashes. There is only one mechanic in the village called z. So, i thinks that his car will not be repaired unless z tries to repair it. Since i wants his car to be repaired and z is the only person who can help him, he must necessarily delegate to z the action of trying to repair his car. This is a typical case of *dependence-based delegation*.

3.4.3.2 Relationship Between Core Trust and Delegation

As far as the relationship between core trust and delegation is concerned, it has to be noted that, an agent i can delegate to j the performance of action α for the achievement of φ even if agent i does not trust agent j to ensure φ by doing α. More generally, an agent i can delegate to j the achievement of φ even if agent i does not trust agent j to ensure φ. These observations are validated by our logic. In fact, the following formulas are satisfiable in $\mathcal{STL}$:

$Delegate(i, j, \alpha, \varphi) \wedge \neg CoreTrust(i, j, \alpha, \varphi)$;
$Delegate(i, j, \varphi) \wedge \neg CoreTrust(i, j, \varphi)$.

Notably in *dependence-based delegation*, when i thinks that j's intervention is a necessary condition for the achievement of φ and delegates to j the achievement of the task, it might happen that i does not believe that j's intervention will be sufficient for achieving φ. This might also happen in *preference-based delegation* when each alternative to whom the task can be delegated is not completely trustworthy.[10] This means that there can be more or less risky forms of delegation.

Example 6. Let us focus on the previous example of the mechanic in more detail. Agent i wants his car repaired for tomorrow morning:

---

[9] This corresponds to i's weak dependence [22] on each of the two surgeons.

[10] However, in *preference-based delegation*, the task is delegated to the most trustworthy alternative among all alternatives [29].

$$Goal_i XrepairedCar.$$

Moreover, according to agent i, it is plausible that his car will not be repaired tomorrow morning unless the only mechanic in the village (called z) tries to repair it.

$$Plaus_i(XrepairedCar \rightarrow Does_{z:repair} \top).$$

This is the reason why i delegates to z the action of trying to repair his car:

$$Delegate(i, z, repair, repairedCar).$$

As noted earlier, this is an instance of dependence-based delegation. Nevertheless, according to i, it is not plausible that the mechanic can ensure that tomorrow the car will be repaired by trying to repair it. Indeed, according to i, there is a serious possibility that z will turn out to be incompetent in repairing cars:

$$\neg Plaus_i After_{z:repair} repairedCar.$$

So, according to our formal definition of core trust, we can infer that i does not trust j to ensure that tomorrow the car will be repaired:

$$\neg CoreTrust(i, z, repair, repairedCar).$$

Although delegation does not necessarily involve trust, it is never the case that an agent i delegates to an agent j the performance of action α for the achievement of φ and i distrusts j to ensure φ (resp. mistrusts j to ensure $\neg\varphi$) by performing α. Indeed, i's delegation of action α to j for the achievement of φ involves at least i's hope that j will ensure φ by doing α (note that by Axiom 1d of $\mathcal{STL}$ $Delegate(i, j, \alpha, \varphi)$ implies $\neg Plaus_i After_{j:\alpha}\neg\varphi$). This point is illustrated by the following Theorem of our logic.

Theorem 10. *Let $i, j \in AGT$, $\alpha \in ACT$. Then:*

1. $\vdash_{\mathcal{STL}} Delegate(i, j, \alpha, \varphi) \rightarrow \neg Distrust(i, j, \alpha, \varphi)$
2. $\vdash_{\mathcal{STL}} Delegate(i, j, \alpha, \varphi) \rightarrow \neg Mistrust(i, j, \alpha, \varphi)$
3. $\vdash_{\mathcal{STL}} Delegate(i, j, \varphi) \rightarrow \neg Distrust(i, j, \varphi)$
4. $\vdash_{\mathcal{STL}} Delegate(i, j, \varphi) \rightarrow \neg Mistrust(i, j, \varphi)$

It has to be noted that, the other direction of the implication is not valid either, that is, an agent i might trust agent j to ensure φ by performing α, even if i does not delegate to j the performance of action α for the achievement of φ (i.e., i does not rely on j's action α). This is typical of situations where i thinks that the occurrence of j's action α will ensure φ while thinking that the occurrence of j's action α will make him incur additional costs. Again, these observations are validated by our logic. In fact, the following formula are satisfiable in $\mathcal{STL}$:

$\neg Delegate(i, j, \alpha, \varphi) \wedge CoreTrust(i, j, \alpha, \varphi);$
$\neg Delegate(i, j, \varphi) \wedge CoreTrust(i, j, \varphi).$

The following example illustrates this point.

Example 7. Now suppose that Bill trusts Mary to kill Bob in the next state by shooting him now:

$$CoreTrust(Bill, Mary, shoot, BobDead).$$

But, according to Bill, it is plausible that if Mary shoots Bob then (as a side effect), the police will discover that he is the instigator of Bob's murder:

$$Plaus_{Bill} After_{Mary:shoot} policeDiscover.$$

Since Bill does not want to go to jail, he does not want Mary to shoot Bob:

$$\neg Goal_{Bill} Does_{Mary:shoot} \top.$$

Thus, according to our formal definition of delegation, Bill should not delegate to Mary the action of shooting Bob as a means for killing Bob in the next state:

$$\neg Delegate(Bill, Mary, shoot, BobDead).$$

To summarize, we have shown that not necessarily core trust implies delegation and not necessarily delegation implies core trust. Moreover, we have shown that delegation and distrust (resp. mistrust) are incompatible.

3.4.3.3 More Specific Forms of Delegation and Decision to Trust

Often an agent i's decision to trust an agent j to ensure φ by doing an action α is supported by i's belief that j is aware that i has delegated to him action α for the achievement of φ. Under this additional condition, if the trustee does not perform the action α that the truster wants and expects him to do, then the truster will feel betrayed by the trustee [20].

Example 8. Suppose that agent i is in a serious financial crisis and decides to trust agent j to help him to solve his financial problems. Moreover, i is certain that j is aware to be delegated by i to help him to solve his financial problems:

$$DecideTrust(i, j, help, \neg financialCrisis) \wedge$$
$$Certain_i Certain_j Delegate(i, j, help, \neg financialCrisis).$$

If j does not help i (i.e., $After_{j:help} \bot$), then i will feel betrayed by j.

Moreover, there are particular situations in which i's decision to trust j is based on i's reliance on j's goodwill towards him. In these situations i (the truster) believes that j (the trustee) believes that i has delegated to him action α for the achievement of φ, and i believes that j wants that i will achieve φ and is willing to act in such a way that i will achieve φ. In this sense, i's decision to trust j is based on i's belief that j is willing to act for i's interests, that is, i's decision to trust j is based on i's belief that j has adopted and will act in order to promote his goal.

According to some philosophers [1, 19], these forms of decision to trust—involving the truster's belief that the trustee has adopted his goal—should be conceived as the genuine forms of trust. [11] The following example illustrates this point.

Example 9. Let us extend the previous example. As before, suppose that agent i is in a serious financial crisis and decides to trust agent j to help him to solve his financial problems. According to agent i, agent j is certain that i wants to be helped by j:

$$DecideTrust(i, j, help, \neg financialCrisis) \wedge$$

$$Certain_i Certain_j Delegate(i, j, help, \neg financialCrisis).$$

Moreover, i is certain that j wants to help him so that i will solve his financial crisis:

$$Certain_i Goal_j Does_{j:help} \neg financialCrisis.$$

In this sense i's decision to trust j is based on i's certain belief that j has adopted i's goal that φ and j is willing to act so that i will achieve this goal.

3.5 Comparative Trust

In this last section of the chapter we will try to define a concept of *comparative trust* by exploiting the formal constructs defined in Section 3.3.3. Our aim here is to characterize formally statements like "agent i trusts agent j to ensure φ by doing α more than agent z to ensure φ by doing β" and "agent i trusts agent j more than agent z to ensure φ". The notion of comparative trust is indeed fundamental in social interaction when the truster has to delegate a given task and has to decide who is going to be the delegated agent among several agents in a set of agents $C \subseteq AGT$. In our perspective agent i trusts agent j to ensure φ by doing α more than agent z to ensure φ by doing β if and only if i wants to achieve φ and, according to agent i, the fact that j has the internal and external properties to ensure φ by performing action α is strictly more possible than the fact that z has the internal and external properties to ensure φ by performing action β. This can be stated more formally as follows.

Definition 12. COMPARATIVE TRUST. Agent i trusts agent j to ensure φ by doing α more than agent z to ensure φ by doing β if and only if:

---

[11] Such forms of trust have also been studied in game theory (see e.g. [2, 32, 33]). For instance, in Gambetta's classical book [16], trust is defined as follows: "...When I say that I trust i, I mean that I believe that, put on test, i would act in a way favourable to me, even though this choice would not be the most convenient for him at that moment...". This shows that in Gambetta's view trust concerns the truster's belief that the trustee has adopted his goal that φ and has decided to perform some action α whose occurrence will promote the achievement of φ, even though doing α is not the best thing the trustee can do for his own interests.

1. i wants to achieve φ;
2. i thinks that the following four conditions:

- j has the opportunity to ensure φ by performing action α AND
- j is willing (i.e., intends) to perform action α AND
- the internal preconditions for the execution of action α by agent j hold AND
- the external preconditions for the execution of action α by agent j hold AND

are together strictly more possible than the following four conditions:

- z has the opportunity to ensure φ by performing action β AND
- z is willing (i.e., intends) to perform action β AND
- the internal preconditions for the execution of action β by agent z hold AND
- the external preconditions for the execution of action β by agent z hold.

Our logic $\mathcal{STL}$ is enough expressive to formalize such a notion of comparative trust. This can be represented as follows. For any $i, j, z \in AGT, \alpha, \beta \in ACT$ we have:

$$(z, \beta, \varphi) <_i^{Trust} (j, \alpha, \varphi) \overset{\text{def}}{=}$$
$$Goal_i X \varphi \wedge$$
$$((After_{z:\beta}\varphi \wedge Int_z(\beta) \wedge IPre(z,\beta) \wedge EPre(z,\beta)) <_i$$
$$(After_{j:\alpha}\varphi \wedge Int_j(\alpha) \wedge IPre(j,\alpha) \wedge EPre(j,\alpha)))$$

where $(z, \beta, \varphi) <_i^{Trust} (j, \alpha, \varphi)$ stands for "agent i trusts agent j to ensure φ by doing α more than agent z to ensure φ by doing β".

A notion of generalized comparative trust can also be defined in which the action of j and z are not specified.

Definition 13. (GENERALIZED) COMPARATIVE TRUST. Agent i trusts agent j more than agent z to ensure φ if and only if for all actions α and β:

- agent i trusts agent j to ensure φ by doing α more than agent z to ensure φ by doing β (see Definition 12).

Formally, for any $i, j, z \in AGT$ we have:

$$(z, \varphi) <_i^{Trust} (j, \varphi) \overset{\text{def}}{=} \bigwedge_{\alpha, \beta \in ACT} ((z, \beta, \varphi) <_i^{Trust} (j, \alpha, \varphi))$$

where $(z, \varphi) <_i^{Trust} (j, \varphi)$ stands for "agent i trusts agent j more than agent z to ensure φ".

3.6 Conclusion

A comprehensive logical model of social trust has been developed in this chapter. We have formalized i's trust in j with respect to a given task φ as i's expectation that j has the right properties (willingness, abilities, skills, power, etc.) to ensure φ

by doing a certain action α. We have discussed several concepts involved in social trust theory such as distrust, mistrust, and lack of trust. Moreover, we have defined delegation as the active counterpart of core trust and we have studied the logical relationships between the two concepts. At the end of the chapter we have presented a general notion of comparative trust. We hope that the logical analysis developed in this paper will be useful for improving understanding of social trust as an expectation and evaluation of the truster about some fundamental properties of the trustee.

References

1. A. Baier. Trust and antitrust. *Ethics*, 96:231–260, 1986.
2. P. Battigalli and M. Dufwenberg. Dynamic psychological games. *Working paper, Mimeo, IGIER-Bocconi*, 2005.
3. P. Blackburn, M. de Rijke, and Y. Venema. *Modal Logic*. Cambridge University Press, Cambridge, 2001.
4. C. Boutilier. Modal logics for qualitative possibility and beliefs. In *Proceedings of the Eight Annual Conference on Uncertainty in Artificial Intelligence (UAI'92)*, pp. 17–24. Morgan Kaufmann, 1992.
5. M. Bratman. *Intentions, plans, and practical reason*. Harvard University Press, Cambridge, 1987.
6. C. Castelfranchi. Mind as an anticipatory device: For a theory of expectations. In M. De Gregorio, V. Di Maio, M. Frucci, and C. Musio, editors, *Brain, Vision and Artificial Intelligence, 1st International Symposium on Brain, Vision and Artificial Intelligence (BV & AI 2005)*, pp. 258–276. Springer-Verlag, Berlin, 2005.
7. C. Castelfranchi and R. Falcone. Principles of trust for MAS: Cognitive anatomy, social importance, and quantification. In *Proceedings of the Third International Conference on Multi-Agent Systems (ICMAS'98)*, pp. 72–79. IEEE Press, New York 1998.
8. C. Castelfranchi and R. Falcone. Social trust: A cognitive approach. In C. Castelfranchi and Y. H. Tan, editors, *Trust and Deception in Virtual Societies*, pp. 55–90. Kluwer Academic Publishers, Dordrecht, 2001.
9. C. Castelfranchi and E. Lorini. Cognitive anatomy and functions of expectations. In R. Sun, editor, *Proceedings of the IJCAI'03 Workshop on cognitive modeling of agents and multi-agent interaction*, 2003.
10. P. R. Cohen and H. J. Levesque. Intention is choice with commitment. *Artificial Intelligence*, 42:213–261, 1990.
11. F. Del Cerro and A. Herzig. A modal analysis of possibility theory. In *Proceedings of Fundamentals of Artificial Intelligence Research (FAIR'91)*, pp. 11–18, Springer Verlag, Berlin 1991.
12. R. Demolombe. To trust information sources: A proposal for a modal logic framework. In C. Castelfranchi and Y. H. Tan, editors, *Trust and Deception in Virtual Societies*. Kluwer Academic Publishers, Dordrecht, 2001.
13. D. Dubois and H. Prade. *Possibility theory: an approach to computerized processing of uncertainty*. Plenum Press, New York, 1988.
14. R. Falcone and C. Castelfranchi. Towards a theory of delegation for agent-based systems. *Robotics and Autonomous Systems*, 24:141–157, 1998.
15. M. Fitting. *Proof Methods for Modal and Intuitionistic Logics*. D. Reidel, Dordrecht, 1983.
16. D. Gambetta (Eds.). *Trust: making and breaking cooperative relations*. Basic Blackwell, Oxford, 1988.
17. D. Harel, D. Kozen, and J. Tiuryn. *Dynamic Logic*. MIT Press, Cambridge, 2000.
18. A. Herzig and D. Longin. C&L intention revisited. In D. Dubois, C. Welty, and M.-A. Williams, editors, *Proceedings 9th Int. Conf. on Principles on Principles of Knowledge Representation and Reasoning(KR2004)*, pp. 527–535. AAAI Press, Austin, Tx, 2004.

19. M. Hollis. *Trust whithin Reason*. Cambridge University Press, Cambridge, 1998.
20. R. Holton. Deciding to trust, coming to believe. *Australasian Journal of Philosophy*, 72:63–76, 1994.
21. T. G. Huynh, N. R. Jennings, and N. R. Shadbolt. An integrated trust and reputation model for open multi-agent systems. *Journal of Autonomous Agent and Multi-Agent Systems*, 13:119–154, 2006.
22. N. Jennings. Commitments and conventions: The foundation of coordination in multi-agent systems. *The Knowledge Engineering Review*, 8(3):223–250, 1993.
23. A. Jones and B. Firozabadi. On the characterization of a trusting agent: Aspects of a formal approach. In C. Castelfranchi and Y. H. Tan, editors, *Trust and Deception in Virtual Societies*, pp. 55–90. Kluwer Academic Publishers, Dordrecht, 2001.
24. C. M. Jonker and J. Treur. Formal analysis of models for the dynamics of trust based on experiences. In F. J. Garijo and M. Boman, editors, *Multi-Agent System Engineering: Proceedings of the 9th European Workshop on Modelling Autonomous Agents in a Multi-Agent World*. Springer Verlag, Berlin, 1999.
25. D. Lewis. *Counterfactuals*. Harvard University Press, Harvard, 1973.
26. C. J. Liau. Belief, information acquisition, and trust in multi-agent systems: a modal logic formulation. *Artificial Intelligence*, 149:31–60, 2003.
27. E. Lorini, A. Herzig, and C. Castelfranchi. Introducing "attempt" in a modal logic of intentional action. In M. Fisher and W. Van der Hoek, editors, *Proceedings of the 10th European Conference on Logics in Artificial Intelligence (JELIA'06)*, volume 4160 of *LNAI*, pp. 280–292. Springer, 2006.
28. E. Lorini, N. Troquard, A. Herzig, and C. Castelfranchi. Delegation and mental states. In *Proceedings of 6th International Joint Conference on Autonomous Agents in Multi-Agent Systems (AAMAS'07)*, pp. 622–624. ACM Press, New York, 2007.
29. S. Marsh. *Formalising Trust as a Computational Concept*. PhD thesis, University of Stirling (Scotland), 1994.
30. J. J. C. Meyer, W. van der Hoek, and B. van Linder. A logical approach to the dynamics of commitments. *Artificial Intelligence*, 113(1-2):1–40, 1999.
31. M. Miceli and C. Castelfranchi. The mind and the future: The (negative) power of expectations. *Theory and Psychology*, 12(3):335–366, 2002.
32. V. Pelligra. Under trusting eyes: the responsive nature of trust. In R. Sugden and B. Gui, editors, *Economics and Social Interaction: accounting for the interpersonal relations*. Cambridge University Press, Cambridge, 2005.
33. M. Rabin. Incorporating fairness into game theory and economics. *American Economic Review*, 83:1281–1302, 1993.
34. A. S. Rao and M. P. Georgeff. Asymmetry thesis and side-effect problems in linear time and branching time intention logics. In *Proceedings of the Twelfth International Joint Conference on Artificial Intelligence (IJCAI'91)*, pp. 498–504. Morgan Kaufmann, San Mateo, CA, 1991.
35. A. S. Rao and M. P. Georgeff. Modelling rational agents within a BDI-architecture. In *Proceedings of the Second International Conference on Principles of Knowledge Representation and Reasoning (KR'91)*, pp. 473–484, Morgan Kaufmann Publishers, San Mateo, CA, 1991.
36. J. Sabater and C. Sierra. Regret: a reputation model for gregarious societies. In *Proceedings of the First International Joint Conference on Autonomous Agents and Multi-Agent Systems*, pp. 475–482. ACM Press, New York, 2001.
37. E. Ullmann-Margalit. Trust, distrust, and in between. In R. Hardin, editor, *Distrust*. Russell Sage Foundation, New York, 2004.
38. M. Witkowski, A. Artikis, and J. Pitt. Experiments in building experiental trust in a society of objective-trust based agents. In C. Castelfranchi and Y. H. Tan, editors, *Trust and Deception in Virtual Societies*, pp. 111–132. Kluwer Academic Publishers, Dordrecht, 2001.
39. M. Wooldridge. *Reasoning about rational agents*. MIT Press, Cambridge, 2000.

Chapter 4
Social Trust of Virtual Identities

Jean-Marc Seigneur

Abstract Most other chapters of this book discuss computational models of trust in broader terms, giving definitions of trust, explaining how trust should evolve over time, surveying the different facets of trust .On the other hand, this chapter has a clear focus on the important element of identity in computational trust mechanisms. Trust and reputation are easier to form in face-to-face situations than in situations involving the use of computers and networks because the identity of the trustee is more difficult to verify. In this chapter, the different means to recognise virtual identities are surveyed. Next, their integration into computational trust engines is discussed, especially according to four main requirements: Adaptability, Security, Usability and Privacy (ASUP).

4.1 Introduction

A number of computational trust models assume that the actions reported to have been carried out by a specific trustee are irrevocably true. However, it might not be the case; for example, a malicious entity may have masqueraded the identity of the trustee after having stolen the trustee password. It is one of the main differences of online interactions compared to face-to-face situations where it is obviously less easy to masquerade one's identity. Depending on the authentication technology, it may be more or less difficult to masquerade a trustee identity. This chapter investigates the impact that using one or another of these identity management technologies has on computational models of trust and how those technologies can be integrated in computational trust engines. The remaining of this section clarifies the terminology used in this chapter and ends by detailing the organisation of this chapter.

J.-M. Seigneur (✉)
University of Geneva and Venyo, Geneva, Switzerland
e-mail: Jean-Marc.Seigneur@unige.ch

J. Golbeck (ed.), *Computing with Social Trust,* Human-Computer Interaction Series,   73
DOI 10.1007/978-1-84800-356-9_4 © Springer-Verlag London Limited 2009

4.1.1 Identity Terminology

One of the foundations of security is authentication. Stajano [1] emphasises that without being sure with whom an entity interacts, the three main security properties, Confidentiality, Integrity and Availability (CIA) can be trivially violated. Generally, authentication schemes start with enrolment of entities. Once enrolment is complete, authentication often consists of two steps: The requester claims an identity (a.k.a., identification) and the claimed identity is verified (a.k.a, verification). As Smith chose for the title of his book on authentication, authentication techniques have evolved from "passwords to public keys" [2]. There are three main authentication factors: something that you know, e.g., a password; something that you have, e.g., a smart card token; and something that represents what you are, e.g., biometrics. It may also be based on other factors, for example, where you are. There are roughly two authentication scenarios of use: either it deals with real humans or it is a remote access. There are three main categories of terms related to identity in the authentication process: the entity, the virtual identity and the real-world identity as depicted in the following Fig. 4.1.

The real-world identity spans a broad panel of resources: software objects, software credentials, agents, files, file systems, processes, printers, machines, nodes, network resources, people, organisations [3, 4]. However, when a computing resource is requested by a real-world identity, the link to the real-world identity is initially unknown and the authentication process is started. Based on distinguishing characteristics, the requesting entity is associated with the virtual identity. The link with the real-world entity is usually either known or unknown (it is represented in Fig. 4.1 by the "Yes/No" text in the right arrow).

Legacy security models and mechanisms rely on the assumption of closed computing environments, where it is possible to bind the virtual identities with their real-world identities and fortify a security perimeter, which protects against potentially malicious entities. However, in these models, there is no room for *anytime-anywhere* mobility outside the security perimeter as it is going to increasingly be the case for the users who move from place to place with their wearable computing devices as envisioned in Weiser's ubquitous computing world [5]. Legacy security models suppose that there is a common security infrastructure and jurisdiction where the notion

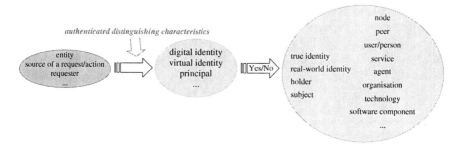

Fig. 4.1 Identity terms

of identity is globally meaningful. The feasibility of this approach is questionable because the Internet and the ubiquitous computing world are open environments with different (possibly conflicting) authorities. Taking the example of binding a real-world identity with a virtual identity via Public Key Infrastructure (PKI) certificates, there is the question of which authority is in charge of certifying the binding with the real-world identity, since there are no unique global authorities. "Who, after all, can authenticate US citizens abroad? The UN? Or thousands of pair wise national cross-certifications?" [6]. Moreover, traditionally, it is assumed that if the actions made by a computing entity are bound to a real-world identity, the owner of the faulty computing entity can be brought to court and reparations are possible. However, due to possibly conflicting jurisdictions in the world, real-world recourse mechanisms, such as insurance or legal actions may be vain. An example where prosecution is ineffective occurs when email spammers do not mind to move operations abroad (Brazil and China according to [7]) to escape any risk of prosecution. There are other issues with security models relying on traditional identity management approaches and solutions. These issues concern the four following overlapping requirements, Adaptability, Security, Usability, and Privacy (ASUP):

- Adaptability: As introduced above, the users are nowadays mobile: they may go outside of their organisation security perimeter or they may become offline without access to their distant home servers. Security solutions need to be adaptable, for example, with identity management that can adapt to the context or the situation, e.g., without requiring the availability of globally known online parties when they are not available.
- Security: When known third-parties are unreachable, which is even more often the case in mobile ad-hoc networks than in traditional fixed networks, security mechanisms requiring access to these third-parties cannot be applied. In this case, security must be created from scratch with reachable/nearby unknown entities. A fundamental requirement is to allow for potential interaction and collaboration with previously unknown entities because they are interdependent, i.e, if they do not collaborate, they achieve less than if they collaborate.
- Usability: Due to the potentially large number of previously unknown entities and simple economic reasons, it makes no sense to assume the presence of a human administrator who configures and maintains the security framework. This means that individual entities must decide about each of these potential interactions themselves. It applies to security decisions too, for example, concerning the enrolment of a large number of unknown entities. However, busy individuals may not have the time to configure security settings or may not be technology-aware enough.
- Privacy: Some entities, such as ubiquitous tiny computing and communicating sensors, will be ambient/invisible but listening – so, it becomes even harder to guarantee private spaces. However, there are privacy protection laws and use of computing technologies must comply with these laws. Even if we assume that computing entities are willing to respect privacy, the burden of countless privacy decisions to be made as the context changes goes against usability.

4.1.2 Computational Trust Terminology

Fortunately, computational trust metrics are able to build trust from scratch without the need of system trust and a priori knowledge – strangers beyond the security perimeter can slowly be granted more resources: interaction after interaction their trustworthiness is formed. In this chapter, the definition of the human notion of trust is Romano's one [8]: "Trust is a subjective assessment of another's influence in terms of the extent of one's perceptions about the quality and significance of another's impact over one's outcomes in a given situation, such that one's expectation of, openness to, and inclination toward such influence provide a sense of control over the potential outcomes of the situation." System trust refers to one of the main types of trust discussed in social research [9]: (1) System trust concerns the external means such as insurance or laws [9, 10]; (2) interpersonal trust, based on past interactions with the trustee; and (3) dispositional trust, provided by the trustor's general disposition towards trust, independent of the trustee. Depending on the situation, a high level of trust in one of these types can become sufficient for the trustor to make the decision to trust. When there is insurance against a negative outcome, or when the legal system acts as a credible deterrent against undesirable behaviour, it means that the level of system trust is high and the level of risk is negligible – therefore the levels of interpersonal and dispositional trust are less important. It is usually assumed that by knowing the link to the real-world identity, there is insurance against harm that may be done by this entity: in essence, this is security based on authenticated identity and legal recourse. In this case, the level of system trust seems to be high but one may argue that in practice the legal system does not provide a credible deterrent against undesirable behaviour, e.g., it makes no sense to sue someone for a single spam email, as the effort expended to gain redress outweighs the benefit. We have already strengthened that due to multiple jurisdictions in global computing, legal recourse is questionable. Of course, scenarios where the level of system trust is low make interpersonal trust more important. The level of dispositional trust may be set due to two main facts. First, the user manually sets a general level of trust, which is used in the application to get the level of trust in entities, independently of the entities. Secondly, the current balance of gains and losses is very positive and the risk policy allows any new interactions as long as the balance is kept positive. Marsh uses the term "basic trust" [11] for dispositional trust; it may also be called self-trust.

A *trust metric* consists of the different computations and communications which are carried out by the trustor (and his/her network) to compute a trust value in the trustee. Ziegler and Lausen [12] discuss global group trust metrics, which compute a global trust value without taking into account personal bias but require the complete trust network information. For example, Google's PageRank [13] can be considered as one of them, where virtual identities and their contacts are replaced by pages and their hyperlinks. Another type of trust metric takes into account personal bias and is called local trust metric [12]. Local trust metrics have two sub-types [12]: local group metrics and local scalar metrics. The local group metrics, such as Appleseed [12] or Levien's trust metric [14] return a subset of the most trustworthy peers from the point of view of the local trustor over a partial view of the trust network, given the amount of trustworthiness desired. Local scalar metrics compute the trust value of a specific virtual identity from the point of view of the local trustor "tracking recommender chains from source to target" [12]. Finally, the computation may be centralised or distributed, meaning that the recommendation received is evaluated before being passed to the successor in the recommender chain.

In this chapter, a computed *trust value* is the digital representation of the trustworthiness or level of trust in the entity under consideration, and defined as a non-enforceable estimate of the entity's future behaviour in a given context based on a combination of evidence. Trust in a given situation is called the *trust context.* When a user is involved in the application scenario and manually sets trust values in specific virtual identities (for example, an email address of a known important contact is whitelisted even if the email address is spoofed from time to time), it must be considered as manual trust values. Another type of evidence are direct observations, the entity has directly interacted with the requesting entity and personally experienced and reported the outcome of an observation. Another type of observation is when a third-party observes an interaction between two parties and infers the type of outcome. A final example of evidence is recommendations [15], when the recommender passes its trust value in the trustee to the trustor. Based on the trust value, security decisions can be made according to the trust policy. For example, the resource is granted to any entities who are associated with a trust value greater than a threshold. The bootstrapping with unknown entities, strangers beyond the security perimeter, can now be carried out without a priori knowledge. The trust value can be formed after an interaction and can be further refined during subsequent interactions. Previous direct interactions may not be obligatory if trustworthy recommenders recommend the newcomer. Since some recommenders are more or less likely to produce good recommendations, even malicious ones, the notion of *recommending trustworthiness* has been added to advanced trust engines [16]. Intuitively, recommendations must only be accepted from senders that the local entity trusts to make judgements close to those that it would have made about others. Assuming the user has a metric for measuring the accuracy of another sender's recommendations, Abdul-Rahman and Hailes [16] and Jøsang [17] have suggested models for incorporating that information into the local trust computation. In many cases, the final trust value, which is used locally, may be different from the recommended one. For example, a recommender with a trust value of *0.6* on a *[0, 1]* scale giving a recommendation of *0.8* provides the adjusted trust value: $0.6 \times 0.8 = 0.48$. However, different trust value formats are possible and some formats are more suitable for evidence-based trust than others. For example, the previous format, a value on a *[0, 1]* scale, may be intuitive for humans in order for them to manually set a value but does not give enough detail on the evidence used to choose this value. The SECURE trust value format [18] is a tree of *(s, i, c)*-triples, corresponding to a mathematical event structure [19, 20]: an event outcome count is represented as a *(s, i, c)*-triple, where *s* is the number of events that supports the outcome, *i* is the number of events that have no information or are inconclusive about the outcome and *c* is the number of events that contradict the expected outcome. This format takes into account the element of uncertainty via *i*.

Thus, security models based on computational trust already address some of the ASUP requirements, such as the adaptation to environments without a priori information about the trustworthiness of the surrounding entities and without possibility of legal prosecutions. However, there is still the assumption of being able to unambiguously authenticate the trustees independently of the underlying authentication schemes. Such an assumption is a too simplistic conception of the identity management layer and the root of a remaining number of ASUP issues as presented in the following section. Section 4.3 describes the entification framework whose goal is to fill the gap between identity management and computational trust. In Section 4.4, an evaluation of the entification framework is carried out with regard to the ASUP requirements and compared to other well-known frameworks. Finally, Section 4.5 concludes this chapter.

4.2 Flawed Trust Computation Due to Simplistic Identity Approach

This section emphasises that the current approach to identity in computational trust is too simplistic and therefore is the root of different issues. The first described issues concern the attacks that are possible on computational trust due to the weak identity approach. Then, the remaining issues with regard to the ASUP requirements are discussed.

4.2.1 Computational Trust Under Identity Usurpation and Multiplicity Attacks

There are two main types of attacks relevant to this related to identity on computational trust: identity usurpation attacks and identity multiplicity attacks.

4.2.1.1 Definitions of Identity Usurpation and Multiplicity Attacks

Identity usurpation attacks mean that legitimate trustworthy virtual identities are compromised and get under the control of the attacker, especially with regard to their statements. Identity usurpation attacks include the *Security Breach Attacks* (SBAs), which mean that the attacker has been able to compromise a specific security perimeter and gain control over all the resources inside this security perimeter. SBAs are a general challenge to computer security, especially because compromising the personal computer of a user is, at the time of writing, feasible due to security vulnerabilities present in common operating systems. According to Twigg and Dimmock [21], a trust metric is γ-resistant if more than γ nodes must be compromised for the attacker to successfully drive the trust value. For example, the trust metric used in Rahman's explicit computational trust framework is not γ-resistant for $\gamma > 1$ (i.e., a successful attack needs only one victim). Indeed, there are a number of specific attacks due to collaboration in order to compromise a majority vote. We do not consider real-world identities, which form an alliance, and use their vote to undermine other entities. On one hand, this may be seen as collusion. On the other hand, one may argue that real-world identities are free to vote as they wish. Instead, we focus on attacks based on vulnerabilities in the identity approach and subsequent use of these vulnerabilities. The vulnerabilities may have different origins, for example, technical weaknesses or topological ones when the attacks use the knowledge that they have on the topology of the social or trust network between the virtual identities. However, these attacks commonly rely on the possibility of identity multiplicity: meaning that a real-world identity uses many virtual identities.

4.2.1.2 The Sybil Attack

A very well-known identity multiplicity attack in the field of computational trust due to collaboration is Douceur's Sybil attack [22]. Douceur argues that in large scale networks where a centralised identity authority cannot be used to control the creation of virtual identities, a powerful real-world entity may create as many virtual identities as it wishes and in doing so challenge the use of a majority vote and flaw trust metrics. This is especially important in scenarios where the possibility to use many pseudonyms is facilitated and provided by the trust engine. In fact, a sole real-world entity can create many pseudonyms who blindly recommend one of these pseudonyms in order to fool the trust engine. The level of trust in the latter virtual identity increases and eventually exceeds a threshold which makes the decision to trust (the semantics of this event depend on the application). In his PhD thesis [14], Levien says that a trust metric is attack resistant if the number of *faked virtual identities*, owned by the same real-world identity, that can be introduced is bounded. Levien argues that to mitigate the problem of Sybil-like attacks it is required to compute "a trust value for all the nodes in the graph at once, rather than calculating the trust value independently for each node". Another approach proposed to protect against the Sybil attack is the use of mandatory "entry fees" associated with the creation of each pseudonym [23, 24]. This approach raises some issues about its feasibility in a fully decentralised way and the choice of the minimal fee that guarantees protection. Also, "more generally, the optimal fee will often exclude some players yet still be insufficient to deter the wealthiest players from defecting" [23]. An alternative to entry fees may be the use of once in a lifetime (1L [23]) pseudonyms, a.k.a. pseudonym commitment, where an elected party per "arena" of application is responsible to certify only 1L to any real-world entity, which possesses a key pair bound to this entity's real-world identity. The technique of blind signature [25] is used to keep the link between the real-world identity and its chosen pseudonym in the arena unknown to the elected party. However, there are still three unresolved questions about this approach: how the elected party is chosen; what happens if the elected party becomes unreachable; and how much the users would agree to pay for this approach. More importantly, a Sybil attack is possible during the voting phase, so the concept of electing a trusted entity to stop Sybil attacks does not seem practical. Bouchegger and Le Boudec envisage the use of expensive pseudonyms [23], cryptographically generated unique identifiers (e.g., CBIDs [26, 27]) and secure hardware modules (e.g., Trusted Platform Modules TPM) to counter the Sybil attack. This may overcome the Sybil attack, but at the same time it may exclude entities that are not TPM-enabled or are too limited to run expensive cryptographic computations fast enough, e.g., on mobile phones. Similarly, Kinateder et al.'s workarounds [28] are two-fold. Firstly, some of the risks of pseudonymity are alleviated via TPM including a trusted Certificate Authority (CA) that would certify the pseudonym without disclosing the real-world identity until legal bodies want to retrieve the link. Secondly, the trust engine should be combined with electronic payment systems, which allow the creation of an originality statement during the payment process which can be included in a recommendation. However, relying on real money turns the trust mechanism into a type of system trust, which is high enough to make the use of interpersonal trust almost superfluous. In the real world, tax authorities are likely to require traceability of money transfers, which would completely break privacy in a money-based system.

A real-world application where the Sybil attack occurs is the email system. The success of spammers has proven it is still cheap enough to create (or spoof) text email addresses, which act as pseudonyms in order to carry out profitable, large-scale spam attacks. It is for this reason that the evaluation of this chapter involves the email and anti-spam domain.

4.2.2 Remaining ASUP Issues Due to Identity Shortcomings

The above section describes the security issues at the identity level. In this section, we survey the remaining ASUP issues, namely, adaptibility, usability and privacy, due to the flaws in current identity management and authentication technologies.

4.2.2.1 Identity Naming Issues in Distributed and Collaborative Settings

When only one computer is used, it is straightforward to use unique identifiers to refer to software entities (such as objects). In distributed computing settings, the issue of naming of entities is more complicated, especially when there is no central naming authority. The deployment and management costs of global name/identifier hierarchies, such as X509 [29] distinguished names, are not always viable. Consequently, the first issue related to identity naming is that it is often required for two different parts of the distributed system to understand that they speak about the same entity: if the two parts have generated local identifiers for the entity under scrutiny, it is very likely that the two local identifiers are different and they fail to realise that they talk about the same entity. Simple Distributed Security Infrastructure (SDSI) [30, 31, 32] and Simple Public Key Infrastructure (SPKI) [30, 33] solve the latter issue through the use of linked local name spaces. "Each principal has its own name space" [30], and can introduce names of its own and issue certificates to define local names. "Name resolution is the process of mapping a principal expression to a global identifier" [32]. Roughly, in SDSI, p_i may be a global identifier, a local name or a compound name. For example, a compound name represented in Abadi's logic [32] is $(Self:p_1 \ldots .p_n)$, which intuitively means p_1's$\ldots p_{n-1}$'s p_n.

A second issue related to identity naming is when the same identifier is picked in two different parts of the system for two different entities. A random generation of identifiers may decrease this kind of naming collision. For example, public keys may be considered as global identifiers [32] because they are assumed to be chosen with a very high degree of randomness and collisions are highly improbable.

Another issue concerning naming is usability. Lampson et al. [34] underline that "when users refer to principals they must do so by names that make sense to people, since users can't understand alternatives like unique identifiers or keys". For example, email addresses can be exchanged orally, digital keys cannot. It is even more problematic when a real-world identity has many virtual identities. Depending on context, the appropriate pseudonym must be selected. Previous work on identity management in ubiquitous computing environments [35, 36] demonstrated that the model of switching identities according to context is appealing and meaningful for users. However, this gain in privacy protection thanks to multiple pseudonyms [28, 7, 38] is undermined by a cost in terms of usability due to the increase of complexity in managing many identities in many contexts.

4.2.2.2 Usability of Identity Management

This task is often time consuming and requires explicit human intervention, such as setting up an account by a system administrator. Enrolling new users may involve considerable work and resources: a random initial secret may be sealed in an envelope and sent to the new user; it can be even more expensive with smart tokens, which can involve two separate activities – token programming and user management [2]. There are already six steps needed for token programming. In the biometrics layer model [39], the enrolment, that is, the first measurement of the biometric characteristics, is crucial and "should be guided by a professional who explains the use of the biometric reader" in order to decrease the number of "fail to enrol" users. The biometric samples are often processed and feature templates are extracted. Then, further authentication is usually fully automated. However, in real biometrics applications, the False Rejection Rate (FRR) is often greater than *10%*, which is a usability issue for legitimate users [39]. "Sometimes biometric authentication systems replace traditional authentication systems not because of higher security but because of higher comfort and ease of use" [39].

The usability issue of authentication mechanisms is still challenging; for example, on average people can remember five to seven items but they are told to use passwords of more than nine meaningless characters. Most of the time, the enrolment (or bootstrapping step at first meeting) is costly in terms of administrative tasks; for example, a public key cannot be exchanged orally or kept in mind. There are protection cost issues in the deployment of cryptographic keys or authentication tokens (what you have): expensive tokens of cryptographic keys may be lost or there are difficulties to span different sites with different authorities. The usability issue of managing and using public keys on a large scale has already shown the limits of approaches based on the exchange of keys that must be bound to real-world identities [40]. For example, in the email domain, previous attempts based on asymmetric encryption and binding of public keys to the identity of the owner of the private key have failed to gain large acceptance and to solve the spam problem. Authentication systems that are designed to run on top of the legacy email system suffer from many usability issues in deployment, use and management. In web of trust style systems [41, 42], the users should carefully check (ideally using an out-of-band channel such as a phone call or attending a key-signing party) that the public key received is really the one sent by the sender due to potential Man-In-the-Middle (MIM[1]) attacks. CA schemes, such as in Privacy Enhanced Mail (PEM) [43] or based on S/MIME [44], replace the onerous need for individual users to check identities, but the charges imposed by the CA act as a barrier to adoption. In all cases, the public key of senders and receivers must be acquired and validated [40]. There is the problem of bootstrapping/first meeting without a computer at hand, which is a significant feature for the wide-spread adoption.

The cost/benefit of security protection at the authentication level is very important. Smith [2] notes that "people are more worried about having their computers available and usable than they are about password cracking". A real challenge concerning the ease of authentication is to facilitate authentication across multiple and different authority domains: this may be achieved by single sign-on or federated identity management [45, 46, 47], where a trusted third party is in charge of managing identity information and ensuring authentication. In user-centric identity management, the users are free to choose their identity management providers. OpenID [48] is a user-centric solution addressing the usability issue of passwords by replacing the use of a password per site by the use of a URL pointing to the user's identity system on all the OpenID-enabled sites. The OpenID technology is still in its infancy, though: For example, the HTTP redirections between the sites and the identity providers open the door for identity usurpation attacks, such as phishing.

Finally, bootstrapping with the real-world identity might not be needed. For example, in SDSI or SPKI, the entity identity can simply be the public key. The public key itself makes declarations by issuing verifiable signed statements that can be certificates or requests for service. Stajano coins the term "anonymous authentication" [1] where "globally unique X.509 "distinguished names" are unnecessary luggage". Thus, personal certification may be envisaged combined with reputation or web of trust [41], which is related to the idea of majority vote and computational trust. However, personal certification facilitates the introduction of multiple virtual identities per real user, which is a problem for computing a majority vote where one real user may vote several times. The possibility to easily introduce new

---

[1] In this chapter, any attack where an attacker can act between the two legitimate entities is called a MIM attack.

virtual identities facilitates that kind of attacks coined as bootstrapping/newcomer attacks.

4.2.2.3 Adaptability of Authentication

In addition to MIM and bootstrapping/newcomer attacks, there are many other attacks that can flaw authentication because it is a reality that authentication products are not perfect. Ideally, an accurate authentication mechanism consistently rejects authentication attempts by people who are not who they claimed to be during identification, while not rejecting authentication attempts by the true people specified during identification. However, the real-world technical constraints may lead to a trade-off between False Acceptance Rate (FAR) and False Rejection Rate (FRR). For example, in biometrics systems, the yes/no decision is based on a threshold, which must be chosen by the administrator. The protection is manually adapted to the application domain.

A biometric system may operate in verification/authentication mode (when a claimed identity must be verified) or identification mode (when there is no claim of identity and search through all the previously known identities). Jain et al. [49] use the word recognition to encompass the verification mode and the identification mode. In verification mode, positive recognition has the aim to prevent multiple people from using the same identity. In identification mode, negative recognition has the aim to prevent a single person from using multiple identities.

The pattern of combination of authentication mechanisms in order to increase security has been proposed in order to adapt the protection to the growing number of attacks at the identity level and the inherent shortcomings of specific authentication mechanisms. For example, a knowledgeable attacker can generally carry out successful probing attacks on authentication tokens and extract critical data from them [2]. In order to solve the problem of lost tokens, a PIN may be added. It follows multimodal authentication, a.k.a. n-factor authentication (e.g., something you know and something you have). Another example is multimodal biometrics [49, 50], which address the issue of non-universality of the biometric characteristic and decrease the risk of successful usurpation attacks thanks to the combination of many biometrics techniques [2, 39, 49].

Usurpation attacks are most likely to succeed when a lot of information about the users is known. A habitual target for attackers is then the user's personal computer because it contains the knowledge required to carry out successful usurpation attacks. If SBA is possible, the ideal counter-measure may be that "no secret information is stored anywhere, including on the host being protected" [51]. For example, S/Key authentication [51], based on Lamport's key-chains, uses secure hash functions (meaning that it is easy to compute $f(x) = y$ but hard to retrieve x by only knowing y and f) and a sequence of hashes starting with a user-chosen password (plus a seed). The last hash of the sequence becomes the first one-time password stored on the server. Each time authentication is required the server checks that the stored hash is equal to the secure hash of the hash provided by the client. Then, the new hash provided by the client becomes the hash stored by the server. A new sequence is generated when the sequence of hashes has been processed. In doing so, only secure hashes are stored.

In this context, certificate revocations are necessary because private keys can be stolen or broken. However, due to the offline nature of asymmetric cryptography, certificate revocation becomes difficult [1]. This aspect of adaptability may be addressed by: revocation lists, online revocation (although this contradicts the offline philosophy), and certificates Time-To-Live (TTL).

The environmental context may change due to an attack. For example, an attacker starts a trial-and-error attack on the authentication scheme used by the application. There is an implicit trust in the level of protection given by this attacked authentication scheme but the point is that it may fall under attack. In the intrusion tolerance approach [52], some intrusions may be allowed, but tolerated: "the system triggers mechanisms that prevent the intrusion from generating a system security failure". There is a need to a dynamic adaptation to the environmental context.

An example where explicit (but static) risk analysis is used to tolerate a number of attacks occurs in the domain of authentication and is called 'weak authentication" [53, 54]. OpenID [48] goes in this direction of improved usability whilst arguably achieving a lower level of authentication. Weak authentication is not really suitable for applications requiring a link/binding to real-world identities or traditional authentication frameworks such as PKI [53]. However, it may still provide means for some form of authentication, without pre-shared secrets, previous enrolment to an infrastructure or manual configuration (especially by a technology-aware administrator). There are four main mechanisms [53]: "spatial separation" (e.g., checking whether or not communication can be made on specific paths or channels); "temporal separation" (for example, it is assumed that no MIM is present at first encounter and common information of previous encounters is verified); "asymmetric costs" (that is, the attack is made more costly to the attacker, e.g., the rich targets can only be found at random); and "application semantics" (for example, the identifier is derived from the public key). Finally, these mechanisms can be combined or orchestrated to increase the level of implicit trust in authentication/recognition, which is in line with multimodal authentication. The distinction between authentication and recognition is made by Weimerskirch and Westhoff [55]. They emphasise that in pervasive scenarios, it is likely that there are no pre-shared secrets or common trusted third parties between two complete strangers. They introduce new schemes, called Zero Common-Knowledge (ZCK) schemes, to "recognise" previously encountered virtual identities based on spatial separation and temporal separation. They claim that in such ad-hoc scenarios "recognition is the best we can achieve" [55]. Arkko and Nikander [53] argue that it may be sufficient if the link/binding with the real-world identity is not needed and some attacks are assumed to remain very unlikely (such as the MIM attack). They mention it "cannot achieve as much as other authentication schemes" [55] and it is one of the reasons it consists of an implicit and static level of trust. Generally, a ZCK uses a C/R based on a public part of a secret, which is stipulated at first interaction. It is based on a standard asymmetric encryption public key followed by crypto-based nonce challenges or a new type of public key based on Lamport's key-chains, which is more efficient for resource-constrained devices.

Weak authentication may not always achieve perfect security but may still significantly increase practical security, or is otherwise good enough for the requirements under consideration. Overall, weak authentication may allow for economic trade-offs between security and usability. So, the economic analysis and threat scenarios of the application domains under consideration give a static implicit initial level of trust, which may be regarded as a level of system trust. For example, the targets are attacked at random among a large community (such as, random large-scale spam attacks without marketed database of email addresses). However, if a dedicated attacker targets a specific entity, the level of trust in these assumptions vanishes. If the attack is detected, mechanisms are needed to adapt the state of the entity. As in intrusion tolerance, the system adapts itself and reacts to the detection of an attack. It is said that with zero risk, no trust is needed. Because in weak authentication, the risk of a successful attack "is also quite small, but not zero" [53] (and it may increase when some events are detected) a dynamic explicit level of trust is needed, even if it is a trust level in a technical component of the underlying technical infrastructure.

4.2.2.4 Privacy and Identity

In computing security terms, privacy is close to confidentiality or secrecy [56], where only authorised persons have access to certain information or how information flows [37, 57]. Privacy is linked to intellectual and philosophical ideas [58]. It is difficult (Langheinrich even claims it is impossible [59]) to provide an all encompassing definition of privacy. Privacy can be seen as a fundamental human right "to enjoy life and be let alone" [60] or a basic need (according to Maslow's hierarchy of needs [61]) for a private sphere protected against others. The most sensitive personal information, called Personally Identifiable Information (PII), is directly associated with the real-world end-user identity. According to Tobias and Olsen [62], "personal data is defined in the EC Directive on Data Protection as any information relating to an identified or identifiable natural person. An "identifiable person" is one who can be identified, "directly or indirectly" within a reasonable time, considering the necessary effort taking account of all the means likely reasonably to be used".

Some invasions of privacy cause annoyance and waste time [63]. For example, personal data can be used to build accurate user profiles for marketing and selling purposes. New privacy vulnerabilities have come along with the creation of the Internet, the World Wide Web and the electronic mail system. To some extent, personal information has become a commodity that can be traded in online commerce. Information can be used to contact the person with the email address even though the person does not want this specific contact. We see email addresses as PII having the property of easily (i.e., for a very low cost) and effectively (i.e., an email delivered in the Inbox will surely obtain human attention, even if it is only for a fraction of time) making contact with the related human. The privacy violation that occurs when a third-party obtains the email addresses of some people without their consent is usually followed by unsolicited messages – known as spam – sent on the open communication channel associated with the email address, that is, the standard electronic mail system. The cost of email privacy violation varies a great deal between users, but the overall cost is known to be very high [64]. With the advance of online worldwide social networking services, such as Facebook, MySpace, LinkedIn or Friend-Of-A-Friend (FOAF) [65], it is even possible to build the social network topology between persons. Therefore, both the individual's private information and the private information of the members of his/her network of collaborators are threatened.

Langheinrich has proposed six useful principles for guiding the design of privacy-friendly systems [59]: notice; choice and consent; anonymity and pseudonymity (that should be provided by default and support the fact that means should be left to the users to be in control of their private data); proximity and locality (it may be sufficient in some applications to rely on the locality of the real-world parties to grant or deny access); access and recourse; adequate security (which emphasises that the security solution should be adapted to the risk involved and resource constraints). Legislative means for privacy protection go from country-specific legislations to higher level legislations (for example, European Union 95/46/CE [66], which deals with the worldwide principle of collection limited to mandatory required data for the purpose of identification [62]). However, legislation has shown its limitations: There may be multiple contradicting jurisdictions and, even in the same jurisdiction, privacy protective laws [62] can be reversed to excessive data retention [67, 68]. Non-physically enforced approaches, based on privacy policies and the good will of the contractor [69], have also shown their limitations: for example, there are known cases where millions of airline passengers information was disclosed in violation of the airline stated privacy policy in order to support research in data mining and screening systems [70]. An important aspect of privacy is that people have dynamic privacy expectations: "our privacy needs change almost constantly in response to our desire to interact with one another and social moral and institutions affect privacy expectations" [58]. The change of the EU position regarding privacy protection after the September 11th terrorist attacks [62, 67, 68] is one example of this dynamic aspect. Privacy is a trade-off "with efficiency, convenience, safety, accountability, business, marketing, and usability" [71]. This great number of changes would require changes to privacy policies. However, to set up and tune policies takes time and effort. Agrawal [72] has questioned if users will be able to tune adequately their policies or simply if, busy as they are, they will make the effort to set up their policies. Frequent and time consuming configurations for privacy protection run counter to the requirement of Weiser's "calm technology" [73] that should not monopolise the attention of the user: security mechanisms should distract the user as little as possible; this again concerns usability. Currently, there is active research on privacy enhancing technologies (PET) [25, 74–77] and one of these PETs concerns the use of pseudonyms. The ordinary definition of a pseudonym is "a fictitious name used when the person performs a particular social role"[2]. Others [37, 78, 79], in domains other than computational trust, have presented how pseudonyms can be used for privacy protection and shown that different levels of pseudonymity and configurations exist. Their work is valuable in the decision to choose the appropriate type of configuration and pseudonymity for the purpose of privacy-friendly computational trust.

4.3 Entification: Bridging Trust and Virtual Identities

In this section, the above attacks and ASUP issues are mitigated by a new framework, called entification, which combines identity and computational trust approaches. Firstly, the authentication process is revised, based on the notion of recognition, to increase dynamic enrolment and auto-configuration. This is followed by the description of the integration of recognition into a trust engine and the means to increase adaptability. Then, we detail how the framework explicitly supports the possibility to use multiple virtual identities per user to protect privacy and to trade privacy for trust. Finally, means to mitigate flaws and attacks at the level of identity are presented.

4.3.1 Recognition Rather than Authentication

The previous sections underline that more usable authentication is required and enrolment is especially important to achieve this goal. To allow for dynamic enrolment of strangers and unknown entities, we propose an entity recognition process. Table 4.1 compares the current Authentication Process (AP) with our Entity Recognition (ER) [80] process.

There is no initial enrolment step at the beginning of the entity recognition process but this does not mean that enrolment cannot be done. Actually, in step E.3, if the entity to be recognised has never been met before, what will be retained is going to be reused the next time this entity is going to be recognised. Depending on the recognition scheme, it should be more or less transparent, that is, more or less like the enrolment step in A.1. Thus, by moving down the enrolment step in the process, we emphasise that the door is still open for interacting with strangers and unknown entities. An authentication process may be seen as an ER scheme by doing enrolment at step E.3. For example, a message-based ER scheme, called "A Peer Entity Recognition" (APER), is described in [80] and one based on vision techniques, called Vision Entity Recognition (VER), is described in [81].

A number of different sensing, recognition and retention strategies can be envisaged for entity recognition schemes. In VER, the context at the time of retrieval is

---

[2] Definition from WordNet Dictionary: http://www.hyperdictionary.com/search.aspx?define= pseudonym

Table 4.1 Authentication and Entity Recognition Side-by-side

Authentication Process (AP)	Entity Recognition (ER)
A.1. Enrolment: generally involves an administrator or human intervention	
A.2. Triggering: e.g., someone clicks on a Web link to a resource that requires authentication to be downloaded	E.1. Triggering (passive and active sense): mainly triggering (as in A.2), with the idea that the recognising entity can trigger itself
A.3. Detective Work: the main task is to verify that the entity's claimed identity is the peer's	E.2. Detective Work: to recognise the entity to be recognised using the negotiated and available recognition scheme(s)
	E.3. Discriminative Retention (optional): "preservation of the after effects of experience and learning that makes recall or recognition possible"[3]
A.4. Action: the identification is subsequently used in some ways. Actually, the claim of the identity may be done in steps 2 or 3 depending on the authentication solution (loop to A.2)	E.4. Upper-level Action (optional): the outcome of the recognition is subsequently used in some ways (loop to E.1)

used to optimise the responsiveness. The detective work depends on which recognition scheme is used. For example, in the APER recognition scheme, it may consist of sending a challenge/response or signature verification. Although Jain et al. [49] use the word recognition, which encompasses verification/authentication and identification, they do not present a full process where enrolment is postponed and not mandatory done as a separate initial step. When they mention that negative recognition cannot be done in non-biometric systems, they fail to present the generic potential of the recognition process. The ER process is designed to also be applicable to authentication schemes which are not based on human biometrics. The reason is that the evaluation is more focused on email message-based recognition.

By self-triggering (step E.1), we mean that the entity takes the initiative to start the recognition process in order to recognise potential surrounding entities, for example it starts the recognition scheme that involves the recogniser monitoring the network and selectively carrying out detective work on (some of) the entities that are observed. Step E.4 is optional since it is not required if the only objective is to gather recognition clues. Step E.3 is also optional but the reason is different: recognition clues need not be retained – say if the entity has been seen before. In our approach, when an entity wants to refer to another virtual identity, it provides recognition clues for other virtual identities to recognise the virtual identity under scrutiny. Each local computing entity interprets these clues in its own way. For example, in the VER scheme, the main clues consist of sequences of images of people passing in front of cameras. In this case, the smart concierge software carries out its own local detective work based on the provided images. To cope with scalability, we propose to *forget* about entities based on context, for example, that we have not collaborated with, after a certain time. We do not specify how the forgetting mechanism is implemented

---

[3] http://www.m-w.com/cgi-bin/dictionary?book=Dictionary&va=retention

at this stage and do not mean that all recognition information is deleted: it may be stored in a storage with less efficiency for retrieval.

4.3.2 End-to-End Trust

Since an authentication scheme can follow the entity recognition process explained above, we already support a considerable set of legacy entity recognition schemes: symmetric and asymmetric keys, biometrics, etc. Moreover, the openness required for enrolment suggests many more schemes to come, for example, the APER scheme. However, it is known that different authentication schemes are more or less difficult to compromise. As in the Gaia framework [82], a level of confidence may be associated to the authentication scheme used. Differences in the strength of recognition schemes obviously raise the question of trust in the underlying technical infrastructure. Dynamic enrolment allows previously unknown virtual identities to become acquaintances. However, trust in a virtual identity cannot be accurate if the information used at the recognition level is imprecise or simply invalid (for example, due to a successful usurpation attack). Therefore, technical trust in the infrastructure must be explicitly taken into account. Furthermore, it is impossible to expect more than what the technical infrastructure provides: applications requiring strong security should not be run with weak ER schemes.

So, there are layers of trust and the two main categories are trust in the underlying technical infrastructure and trust in the requesting or interacting entity. The point is that these layers form an end-to-end trust relationship, a chain of layers of trust. It has been reported that "information security measures reside in the physical layer of the trust model and have interaction with the personal layer" [83]. Similarly, Golbeck et al. [84] notice that "a security measure builds trust about the authenticity of data contained in the network, but does not describe trust between people in the network". The overall level of trust is the result of how much trust is found at each level. Whether the overall level of trust is acceptable or not is a separate issue. Some benefits of autonomous applications make it worth relying on not-so-trustworthy underlying technologies. There is a trade-off between what can be obtained and what can be lost. This trade-off has to be acknowledged and specified. To get the full potential of autonomous computing, the risks of using not-really-trustworthy environments have to be considered explicitly, as it is indeed done in the risk analysis component of trust engines. Thus, we have the following generic function for the calculation of the overall trust value, the *end-to-end trust value* [80]:

$$EndtoEndTrustValue = f(TechnicalTrustValue,$$
$$VirtualIdentityTrustValue)$$

There are different functions that can be used to compute the final end-to-end trust value. For example, in Jøsang's framework [17], the conjunction operator could be used. Another example may be that the two trust values are on a scale between *0* and *1*, where trust may be interpreted as the probability that an entity behaves in the expected manner for the intended purpose. Assuming these trust values are independent, their multiplication would limit the overall trust value. Beyond a simple level of confidence in recognition, manually set by an expert, the recognition scheme can be associated with a technical trust value, which can be based on direct observations and recommendations. The recognition scheme is seen as an entity whose trust value varies dynamically interaction after interaction, which is an improvement compared to static confidence values. In the remainder of this chapter, the underlying technical infrastructure is abstracted to the technical trust of the recognition scheme. However, recognition is only one piece of the underlying technical infrastructure. Other technical elements could be considered, for example, secure communication over networks after authentication.

In fact, Jøsang, with his metric for public keys web of trust [17], did not consider technical trust at the level of the recognition scheme, such as differences between the size of keys. Instead, he focused on the link between the real-world identity and the public key, which corresponds to the virtual identity. In this case, the trust value is set manually by the user. It reminds us that there is also a level of confidence in the association between the real-world identity and the virtual identity. Figure 4.2 presents a revised version of the identity terms and their relations. The authenticated distinguishing characteristics are replaced by recognition clues. A notion of uncertainty has been added to the arrows by the means of the $+/-$ characters. A partial identity is more or less bound to the user's real-world identity, going from an explicit authenticated binding to an implicit guess, for example, based on data mining.

To summarise, the ER process in the light of end-to-end trust consists of four steps:

1. *Triggering* of the recognition mechanism;
2. *Detective Work* to recognise the entity using the available recognition scheme(s); this provides the level of confidence (or technical trust) in recognition;
3. *Discriminative Retention* of information relevant for possible recall or improved future recognition; this is the equivalent of enrolment and constitutes the first main difference with authentication;
4. *Upper-level Action* based on the outcome of recognition, which includes technical trust; this constitutes the second main difference with authentication.

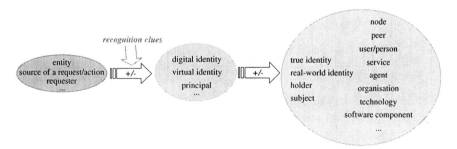

Fig. 4.2 Revised identity terms categorisation

As said above, in some cases, the possibility of prosecution of the real-world identity behind the virtual identity may be low. When the level of system trust is high, the need of a trust value in the entity is less motivated. The link between the real-world identity and the virtual identity seems not mandatory so as to be able to compute the trust value in the entity. The link has its impact on the trusting decisions since more interactions may be allowed if recourse in the real-world is provided, which is equivalent to a high level of system trust. If the decisions change according to the level of system trust, the outcomes of the different interactions also change and therefore the interpersonal trust value in the entity is changed. Still, a strong level of system trust is not mandatory. It means that recognition schemes, which do not link the real-world identity and the virtual identity, are sufficient for the computation of trust in the entity. This is good news from a privacy point of view, especially when means to mitigate attacks at the level of identity are provided.

A parallel can be drawn between intrusion tolerance [52] and the need of dynamic enrolment provided by the ER module, which is followed by the formation and evolution of the level of trust in the entity. The door must be open to strangers but if they behave badly, their level of trust decreases and forbids them to generate major security failures. In intrusion tolerance, another mechanism is used to react to the attack but both approaches provide adaptability.

4.3.3 Means for Recognition Adaptation

According to the above identified ASUP dimensions, the framework must be adaptable. Firstly, the recognition module of the entification framework is pluggable with the broad panel of recognition schemes. The outcomes of the different ER schemes can be combined to define the set of recognised virtual identities, including their level of confidence in recognition. Secondly, the environmental context can be used to tune the Pluggable Recognition Module (PRM) [85], which in turn generates information about the recognition state.

4.3.3.1 Pluggable Recognition Module: Recognised Virtual Identities Set

Choosing a weak recognition scheme, perhaps one allowing for highly dynamic enrolment, is possible but has an impact upon end-to-end trust. The highest level of trust possible is as high as the level of trust in the underlying technology. The recognition module should be pluggable as PAM [86] allows for the use of different legacy authentication schemes. So, we should aim to develop a Pluggable Recognition Module (PRM) where auto-configuration is present and a large spectrum of recognition schemes can be used. Adaptability to an entity's capabilities and to legacy authentication solutions is required. The design of that PRM is leveraged from PAM. The main difference is the use of the level of confidence in recognition in the outcome of the recognition process. Beyond the static technical confidence level used in Gaia's pluggable authentication module, the level of confidence may consist of a dynamic trust value in the technical trustworthiness of the ER scheme, based on the flow of evidence.

In the PRM, many recognition schemes can be used. A set of different virtual identities can be recognised with an associated level of confidence in recognition with each of them. Furthermore, due to the use of different ER schemes with varying strengths, the outcome of recognition carries uncertainty. The uncertainty in the outcome of recognition may be so high that a number of virtual identities may be confused. For example, the VER scheme is proactive: It triggers itself when a new person passes in front of the room Webcam and uses a range of vision techniques which give evidence to compute a probability distribution of recognised entities.

Therefore, the outcome of the ER process can be a set of n virtual identities (vi) associated with a level of confidence in recognition lcr. A range of methods can be used to compute the distribution of the recognised virtual identities, e.g., fuzzy logic or Bayes. In addition, the combination between the level of confidence in recognition in the entity and the technical trust of the ER scheme used can be done in different ways; for example, Jøsang's conjunction operator could be used. The general approach should be to follow the pattern of combination of authentication mechanisms in order to increase security, a.k.a., n-factor (or multimodal) authentication. Jain et al. [49] underline that there are different approaches for the calculation of the output of recognition of biometric techniques.For example, in serial mode, the outcome of each ER scheme is used to narrow down the set of identities. In parallel mode, the information from multiple traits is used simultaneously. In contrast, the ER process provides a set of recognised entities with a level confidence in recognition. It is important to know whether or not the ER schemes use independent recognition mechanisms. For example, one person among n previously recognised enters a room which is equipped with a biometric ER scheme (such as VER). The outcome of recognition hesitates between two people: vi_2 and vi_3, which it believes it recognises with respective levels of confidence 8% and 92%. Other persons are recognised with an lcr of 0%. The outcome of recognition corresponds to:

$$\sum_{i=1}^{n} lcr_i \times vi_i = 0 \times vi_1 + 0.08 \times vi_2 + 0.92 \times vi_3 + 0 \times vi_4 + \ldots + 0 \times vi_n$$

Technical trust (tt) is associated with each ER scheme, such as face template matching in VER. Each technique provides a level of recognition (lr) for each entity. If the sum of (lr) is too low, this suggests that we need to create a new virtual identity, as long as there are enough recognition clues to distinguish the potential new virtual identity. Assuming that we have m ER schemes and that each technique is weighted (with w) compared to the other ER schemes used, we have:

$$lcr = \sum_{j=1}^{m} lr_j \times tt_j \times w_j$$

We have also developed recognition in message-based applications provided by the *Claim Tool Kit (CTK)* [85]: the APER scheme uses cryptographic keys, hashes of previous messages and challenge/responses. Since public keys are used for recognition, at first glance, it appears more secure than with vision techniques. However, depending on the key size, the symmetric cryptographic algorithm used and the time since creation, technical trust may also vary. The more time has elapsed since the key has been generated, the more time attackers have to break the key.

4.3.3.2 A Tuneable/Talkative ER Module

In intrusion-tolerant architectures [52], it is assumed that security faults remain, that is, that security is not perfect. However, faults are mitigated by the presence of error detection mechanisms, which are triggered when a fault is detected, and error handling mechanisms, whose goal is to avoid failures (e.g., network connection is closed if a remote fault source is detected). False alarms are a burden for the administrator, especially if the administrator has no time or skills to be an administrator (e.g., the busy tenant of a smart home, who cannot pay a real administrator). Adaptability makes the life of the users easier.

One objective of "autonomic" [87] models is to increase adaptability. The basic pattern of an "autonomic element" [87] consists of a management unit and a functional unit. When we apply this pattern to our ER process, its four steps (namely Triggering, Detective Work, Discriminative Retention and Upper-level Action) become parts of the functional unit as depicted in Fig. 4.3. The management unit is in charge of monitoring and tuning the ER module.

The type of management unit can vary a great deal: "unlike conventional computing systems, which behave as they do simply because they are explicitly programmed that way, the management unit of an autonomic element will often have a wide range of possible strategies" [87]. The management unit is open to a broad panel of policies and decision-making mechanisms. Of course, in the entification framework, the decision-making is based on computational trust.

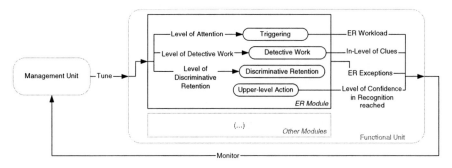

Fig. 4.3 The ER Autonomic functional unit[4]

---

[4] Both management and functional units are represented as rounded rectangles. The black directed arrows represent information from one element to another. The functional unit rounded rectangle contains two module rectangles: the ER module and another one for potential other modules. The ER steps are drawn as rounded rectangles in the ER module rectangle.

The access control of the autonomic element pattern can be enforced by tuning the level of attention: the lower the level of attention, the fewer recognition rounds are processed. When the level of attention changes, the triggering of the ER module becomes more or less sensitive. In return, more or less computation is spent for entity recognition. This is useful when management of computation resources is required. A greater or lower level of detective work means that the ER module spends more or less time and applies more or fewer mechanisms to recognise current entities. A greater or lower level of discriminative retention means that the ER module retains more or less recognition clues for later recognition.

Exceptions occurring during the entity recognition process should be used to update the environmental context in order to react to potential attacks at the recognition level (for example, denial-of-service due to too many triggerings, or trial-and-error attack over a set of possible observable attributes). Each time there is a triggering and not enough recognition clues provided, the ER module can log an optional piece of evidence summarising this exception. Other kinds of ER exceptions may be envisaged. This logging is represented by the loop called Monitor back to the management unit at the bottom of Fig. 4.3. Other optional useful pieces of evidence to be given back to the management unit consist of the level of confidence in recognition reached after each recognition, the in-level of clues (that is, an estimation of the level of clues used by other virtual identities) present and used for reaching these levels of confidence in recognition and the ER current workload. All these pieces of evidence can be used by the management unit, in addition to external information, to choose the most appropriate level inputs for the ER Module. For example, by knowing that the system is under DoS attack, the triggering of the ER process can be made less sensitive in order to decrease resources used for recognition. If more security is required, the level of detective work may be increased in spite of spending more resources. The final element that the management unit can tune is the level of clues to be exhibited to other entities, which may include the selection of the local pseudonym to use as encouraged in the next section.

4.3.4 Encouraging Privacy and Still Supporting Trust

In our view, privacy is a human right or a need that must remain in the hands of each individual. Therefore, we encourage the use of multiple pseudonyms to protect privacy. Still, the entification framework allows the users to trade privacy for increased trust if they wish.

The ER process is presented above as a more general replacement for authentication that does not necessarily bind an identity to the recognised virtual identity. We consider authentication as a special case of recognition that binds a real-world identity to the recognised virtual identity. We argue that the ability to recognise another entity, possibly using any of its observable attributes, is sufficient to establish trust in that entity based on past experience. Our end-to-end trust model starts with recognition where the link with the real-world identity in absolute terms is not needed. Therefore recognition intrinsically favours privacy by divorcing recognition and representational aspects of an identity. Our expectation is that entities are in general virtually anonymous to the extent that the link to the real-world identity alone conveys little information about likely behaviour. What is important as a prerequisite is not really "Who exactly does this entity represent?" but "Do I recognise this entity as a trustworthy collaborator, whomever it represents?" The real-world identity may bring system trust but it is not mandatory for the computation of interpersonal trust values. We assume virtual anonymity and therefore we do not require (but do allow) the ability to establish the real-world identity of a given entity in absolute terms, for example, through globally unique and meaningful certified X.509 "distinguished names" assigned to real-world identities. As already said, in global computing settings, it may not be feasible to enforce penalty mechanisms on the real-world entities due to the lack of a unique legitimate authority.

Information becomes personal when it can be linked back to an individual or when it allows two individuals to be linked together in some way. This means that control of the dissemination of personal information can be exercised through preventing, or at least limiting, linkability of information to individuals. This is illustrated in Fig. 4.4, where a user Alice performs some transactions with another user Bob (neither Alice nor Bob needs to be actual users, but could be clients, servers or part of the computing infrastructure).

In Fig. 4.4, Alice performs two transactions tr_1 and tr_2 with Bob. In order to protect the privacy of Alice[5], it is important that Bob, or anyone who eavesdrops on their communication, is unable to link either transaction tr_1 or tr_2 directly to Alice's real-world identity. However, it is equally important to prevent Bob from linking the two transactions to each other, since this would allow him to compile a comprehensive profile of the other party, which could eventually identify Alice. Moreover, the violation of Alice's privacy would be increased dramatically if any future transaction tr_x can be linked to Alice, since this would allow Bob to link the full profile to Alice and not just tr_x. However, trust is based on knowledge about the other party [88], which directly contradicts the prevention of linkability of information to users, so perfect privacy protection, i.e., preventing actions to be linked to users, prevents the formation, evolution and exploitation of trust in the online world.

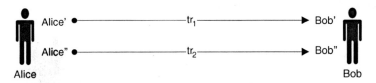

Fig. 4.4 Linkability of transactions

---

[5] The rights/needs to privacy of Alice and Bob are symmetrical, so it may be equally important to prevent Alice from knowing that the two transactions were performed with the same entity.

Recalling the process of trust formation makes apparent the fact that privacy is at stake in trust-based systems. Computational trust is built by linking interactions over time and recommendations between entities. In order to be able to make the decision to trust another entity, the first step is to establish the level of trust in that entity, which is the result of an analysis of the existing knowledge and evidence. If full knowledge is available, it is true that the need for trust vanishes because there is no uncertainty and no risk. To establish the level of trust in the entity requires ways to relate the entity with its trust value. The common way is to use real-world identities to be able to achieve this relation. First of all, privacy is really in danger when identities point to real world users. In this case, they become Personally Identifiable Information (PII). For example, two entities interact and information about the outcome of their interactions is recorded. Depending on the outcome, the trust between each entity is increased or decreased. Further, this trust information may be forwarded to other entities as recommendations. The drawback of this approach is that an entity may disclose arguably private information and compromise the privacy of the targeted entity [89]. Even if trust has only been built with direct observations, PII information stored in another entity may still have to conform to directives, for example, the Fair Information Practices (FIP) [90]. Secondly, when trust built on direct observations is used for further recommendations or reputation, the new trust values created in other entities are by no means part of a common interaction, removing any privacy legitimacy of their source. Trust relies on profiling, where more information is better, because it allows the likely behaviour of the other entity to be more accurately estimated. The trust engines are fuelled with information which aims at building more and more accurate profiles over time. Any link with the real end-user would change this information into sensitive PII. There is an inherent conflict between trust and privacy because both depend on knowledge about an entity, but in opposite ways. There must be a mechanism that can dissociate users from their actions [91]. However, when privacy protection is high, the need of trust is far greater that when full knowledge is available.

From a privacy protection point of view, we argue for the use of multiple virtual identities, acting as pseudonyms as a first technological line of defence. In Kobsa and Schreck's classification [37], transaction pseudonyms (such as a pseudonym used for only one transaction), and anonymity cannot be effectively used because they do not allow linkability between transactions as required when building trust. Pseudonyms appear to be the appropriate solution for protecting privacy in trust-based systems and for achieving some level of privacy and trust. The minimum requirement is a local reference for the formation of trust, which is in turn managed by other components in the trust engine. According to the privacy protection principle of "collection limitation" [59], data collection should be strictly restricted to mandatory required data for the purpose of the collection. Since trustworthiness estimation accuracy increases as information increases, it is not built-in for trust engines to minimise the collection of personal information. Our requirement is to establish the trustworthiness of entities and not their real-world identity. This is why pseudonymity, the level of indirection between trust and the real-world entity, is sufficient. Giving users the option to conceal their identities seems a viable way

to alleviate users' privacy concerns, whilst preserving the benefits of trusted interactions. It is known that "pseudonymization is effective only if identity cannot be
easily inferred from user behaviour" [71]. Ian Goldberg [78] underlined that any
transaction engaged by a person reveals meta-content, especially information about
the identity of the person. Traffic analysis, data triangulation and data-mining, with
some effort, may also associate a pseudonym with the real user. That is why it
is important that we provide multiple pseudonyms that are levels of indirection
between trust and real-world identity. Although trust allows us to accept risk and
engage in actions with potentially harmful outcome, a computational trust engine
must take into account that humans need (or have the right to) privacy. However,
depending on what benefits can be reaped through trustworthiness, people may be
willing to trade part of their privacy for increased trustworthiness: hence, contextual
privacy/trust trade is needed. Due to the division of trust evidence between many
pseudonyms, it takes more time for the entities behind these pseudonyms to reach
the same trustworthiness than for a unique virtual identity. Depending on what they
can get, they may be willing to divulge some of their private data. One may argue
that this is not right [72]. However, business must also be considered [92] along
with technology, legislation and social norms. Therefore, the entification framework
allows for privacy/trust trade based on linkability of pieces of evidence [93] where
the users may choose to disclose the link between several of their pseudonyms in
order to increase the total number of pieces of evidence by aggregating the pieces
of evidence of each pseudonym.

4.3.5 Accuracy and Attack-Resistance of the Trust Values

Usurpation attacks can be mitigated with the level of confidence in recognition or
the technical trust in the recognition scheme used. Still, there are remaining issues,
especially due to the fact that the entification framework encourages the use of many
pseudonyms.

4.3.5.1 Trust Computation Accuracy with Many Pseudonyms

First, we emphasise that care should be taken when linked evidence on multiple
virtual identities is assessed. The most important requirement is to avoid counting
the same evidence twice when it is presented as part of two different pseudonyms or
overcounting overlapping evidence. In some cases, passing recommendations in the
form of a simple trust value, instead of all supporting information,[6] does not fulfill
the latter requirement. Assessing evidence may require analysis and comparison of
each piece of evidence to other pieces of evidence. For example, let us assume that

---

[6] We agree that only passing the trust value may improve performance and may be better from a
privacy point of view than all evidence information. However, it may also decrease interoperability
as highlighted here, and may show how another entity computes trust from evidence. This may
help to mount attacks and may reveal feelings towards other entities, which may not be welcome.

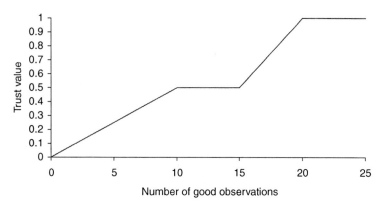

Fig. 4.5 Example relation between observations and trust values

we have the relation depicted in Fig. 4.5 and we know the trust values of two virtual identities vi_1 and vi_2, tvi_1 and tvi_2 respectively. The X axis of Fig. 4.5 represents the number of good observations and the Y axis the resulting trust value.

If $tvi_1 = 0.5$, whatever value tvi_2 is, we cannot compute the combined trust value without knowing the number of good observations, which is at a level of evidence deeper[7] than the level of trust values. In fact, assessing linked evidence requires great care and implementations may vary depending on the complexity of the trust lifecycle [15] and trust dynamics [94]. When recommendations are used, previous self-recommendations are also not easy to take into account. If this is part of a low cost mechanism for introducing new pseudonyms, it may be tolerated to simply discard the recommendations in the calculation. However, this must be part of a risk analysis decision. If this is the case, then it is difficult to determine how to fairly incorporate this into a trust engine based on count of event outcomes, as the self-recommendation is not based on a real history of interactions. In addition, recommendations must be stored separately from direct observations and identified with the recommender name. Another choice might be to consider such recommendations as evidence of untrustworthiness. Permission to make self-recommendations at will, at no cost, paves the way for a Sybil attack.

When using pseudonyms, a means must be present to prevent users from taking advantage of the fact that they can create as many virtual identities as they wish [79]. In a system where there are pseudonyms that can potentially belong to the same real-world entity, a transitive trust process is open to abuse. Even if there is a high discounting factor due to recommending trustworthiness, the real-world entity can diminish the impact of this discounting factor by sending a huge number of recommendations from his/her army of pseudonyms in a Sybil attack.

---

[7] With this case of relation, it is also insufficient to only transfer the trust value in recommendations.

4.3.5.2 Trust Transfer

According to the above Romano's definition of trust, the trustor should be able to increase/decrease the influence of the recommenders according to his/her goals. The goal in our case is to build a trust engine, which allows recommendations without being vulnerable to the Sybil attack, so the mechanism used to control the recommender's influence must achieve this goal. We call this mechanism *trust transfer* [95].

Trust transfer implies that recommendations cause trust on the trustor (T) side to be transferred from the recommender (R) to the subject (S) of the recommendation. A second effect is that the trust on the recommender side for the subject is reduced by the amount of transferred trustworthiness. If it is a self-recommendation, then the second effect is moot, as it does not make sense for a real-world entity to reduce trust in his/her own pseudonyms. Even if there are different trust contexts (such as trustworthiness in delivering on time or recommending trustworthiness), each trust context has its impact on the single construct trust value: they cannot be taken separately for the calculation of the single construct trust value. A transfer of trust is carried out if the exchange of communications depicted in Fig. 4.6 is successful. A local entity's *Recommender Search Policy (RSP)* dictates which contacts can be used as potential recommenders. Its *Recommendation Policy (RP)* decides which of its contacts it is willing to recommend to other entities, and how much trust it is willing to transfer to an entity.

Trust Transfer (in its simplest form) can be decomposed into 5 steps:

1. The subject requests an action, requiring a total amount of trustworthiness TA in the subject, in order for the request to be accepted by the trustor; the actual value of TA is contingent upon the risk acceptable to the user, as well as dispositional trust and the context of the request; so the risk module of the trust engine plays a role in the calculation of TA;
2. The trustor queries its contacts, which pass the RSP in order to find recommenders willing to transfer some of their positive event outcomes count to the

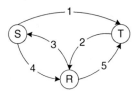

Fig. 4.6 Trust transfer process[8]

---

[8] In this type of figure, the circles represent the different involved entities: S corresponds to the sender, which is the subject of the recommendation and the requester; T is the trustor, which is also the target; and R is the recommender. The directed black arrows indicate a message sent from one entity to another. The arrows are chronologically ordered by their number.

subject. Recall that trustworthiness is based on event outcome counts in trust transfer;

3. If the contact has directly interacted with the subject and the contact's *RP* allows it to permit the trustor to transfer an amount *(A ≤ TA)* of the recommender's trustworthiness to the subject, the contact agrees to recommend the subject. It queries the subject whether it agrees to decrease *A* of trustworthiness on the recommender side;
4. The subject returns a signed statement, indicating whether it agrees or not;
5. The recommender sends back a signed recommendation to the trustor, indicating the trust value it is prepared to transfer to the subject. This message includes the signed agreement of the subject.

Both the *RSP* and *RP* can be as simple or complex as the application environment demands. For now, we limit the policies to simple ones based on trust values. For example, a more complicated *RSP* could be based upon privacy considerations (as is highlighted in the email anti-spam application example below). An advanced *RP* could be based upon the level of participation in the collaborative process and risk analysis.

The trust transfer process is illustrated in Fig. 4.7 where the subject requests an action, which requires *10* positive outcomes (recall that the system uses interpersonal trust based on the outcome of past events). The *RSP* of the trustor is to query a contact to propose to transfer trust if the *balance (s-i-c)* is strictly greater than *2TA*. This is because it is sensible to require that the recommender remains more trustworthy than the subject after the recommendation. The contact, having a balance passing the *RSP (s-i-c=32-0-2=30)*, is asked by the trustor whether he/she wants to recommend *10* good outcomes. The contact's *RP* is to agree to the transfer if the subject has a trust value greater than *TA*. The balance of the subject on the recommender's side is greater than *10 (s-i-c=22-2-2=18)*. The subject is asked by the recommender whether he/she agrees *10* good outcomes to be transferred. Trustor *T* reduces its trust in recommender *R* by *10* and increases its trust in subject *S* by *10*. Finally, the recommender reduces her/his trust in the subject by *10*.

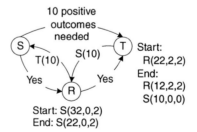

Fig. 4.7 Trust transfer process example[9]

---

[9] In this figure, an entity *E* associated with a SECURE triple, as explained above, *(s,i,c)* is indicated by *E(s,i,c)*.

The recommender could make requests to a number of recommenders until the total amount of trust value is reached (the search requests to find the recommenders are not represented in the figures). For instance, in the previous example, two different recommenders could be contacted, with one recommending 3 good outcomes and the other one 7.

A recommender chain in trust transfer is not explicitly known to the trustor. The trustor only needs to know his/her contacts who agree to transfer some of their trustworthiness. This is useful from a privacy point of view since the full chain of recommenders is not disclosed. This is in contrast to other recommender chains such as public keys web of trust [17]. Because we assume that the entities cannot be compromised, we leave the issue surrounding the independence of recommender chains in order to increase the attack resistance of the trust metric for future work. The reason for searching more than one path is that it decreases the chance of a faulty path (either due to malicious intermediaries or unreliable ones). If the full list of recommenders must be detailed in order to be able to check the independence of recommender chains, the privacy protection is lost. This can be an application-specific design decision.

Thanks to trust transfer, although a real-world identity has many pseudonyms, the Sybil attack cannot happen because the number of direct observations (and hence, total amount of trust) remains the same on the trustor side. Still, local newcomers can be introduced thanks to collaboration. In the previous example, if the subject and the recommender are pseudonyms of the same real-world entity, they remain unlinked. If the proof is given that they can be linked, the compound trust value can be calculated with a guarantee of no overcounting of overlapping evidence or self-recommendations. One may argue that it is unfair for the recommender to decrease the same amount of trustworthiness as specified in his/her recommendation, moreover if the outcome is ultimately good. It is envisaged that a more complex sequence of messages can be put in place in order to revise the decrease of trustworthiness after a successful outcome. This is left for future work, because it can lead to vulnerabilities (for example, based on Sybil attacks with careful cost/benefit analysis). The current approach is still limited to scenarios where there are many interactions between the recommenders and where the overall trustworthiness in the network (that is, the global number of good outcomes) is large enough that there is no major impact on entities when they agree to transfer some of their trust (such as in the email example below). Ultimately, without sacrificing the flexibility and privacy enhancing potential of limitless pseudonym creation, Sybil attacks are guaranteed to be avoided, which is a clear contribution to the field of decentralised, computational trust.

4.4 Entification Framework Evaluation

In order to evaluate trust transfer and its usefulness against identity multiplicity attacks, issues surrounding identity multiplicity in the email domain are explained and empirically estimated in a real-world network of email users. Then, trust transfer is tailored to the email domain in order to mitigate these attacks.

4.4.1 Trust Transfer Applied to the Email Domain

If we apply trust transfer to the email application domain, it is not acceptable to leave the honest email user computers to carry out the recommender search on behalf of the requesting sending spammer. Therefore, we revise the trust transfer process in order to put more work on the spammer side. We slightly modify the search for recommenders needed for trust transfer in order to put more work on the spammer side and take into account privacy considerations. We do not mean it as a strong proof-of-work or bankable postage scheme [24] but it makes more sense to leave the work on the spammer side (when possible), in order to ramp up the per-email cost of spamming. The main idea is to return the list of potential recommenders, that is, the contacts of the receiver, to the sender. Instead of the receiver or recommender contacting further recommenders, the sender will use the list to contact each potential recommender (according to the search algorithm chosen).

There is a potential privacy issue in giving the lists of contacts to be processed by the sender. However, since the sender has no other choice to start with his/her own best friends, the lists of potential recommenders can be adjusted according to the trust value of the sender. If the sender is not trustworthy, no list is returned and it cannot find a path to the receiver. In order to ensure non-repudiation, we assume that all requests and responses are signed. Finally, the receiver has to locally verify the signatures (without having to re-contact the recommenders). We need another protection mechanism related to privacy disclosure. Each time an email is sent to a new receiver, the email sender sets two local values on a *[0, 1]* scale. The first value corresponds to the level of privacy information that the receiver is allowed to see from *0* (none) to *1* (full information). The second value, which is specified in the sender's email when the receiver must change it, corresponds to the level of privacy required by the contacts of the receiver to be allowed to use the sender as a recommender. $Contact_{Privacy}(0.8, 0.7)$ means that the contact has a privacy level of *0.8* and allows the recommender to disclose their relationship to subjects with privacy level greater than (or equal to) *0.7*.

Thus, the default trust transfer is changed to the one in Fig. 4.8 that we call *Proof-of-Friends (PoF) trust transfer* [95] (the search requests for the different recommenders are not represented).

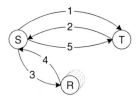

Fig. 4.8 Proof of friends trust transfer

The trust transfer consists of the following steps:

1. The subject requests an action of the trustor;
2. The trustor replies that an amount of trustworthiness, *TA*, is required before it will grant the request; until a complete recommender chain is found (or the search's time-to-live expires):
3. The subject starts to query his/her contact email addresses, who pass the *RSP*, to find a recommender chain to the trustor;
4. If the privacy test is passed and the recommender does not know the receiver, it sends back the list of privacy checked contacts to the sender. This list includes a statement signed by the recommender that he/she is willing to recommend the sender as part of a recommender chain, if one can be found;
   Once the recommender chain is found, every recommender involved confirms that they have transferred trustworthiness accordingly by a signed statement;
5. The subject sends the recommendation to the trustor.

In the example of Fig. 4.9, the sender has only one contact, who does not know the receiver target. However, this contact has one contact who knows the receiver. In this scenario, the *RSP* requires that a potential recommender must have a balance of at least *2TA* on the trustor side. The *RP* is that the subject must have a balance greater than *TA* on the recommender side.

In our default collaboration scheme, the following emails are exchanged:

1. The sender sends an email to a new receiver;
2. The receiver replies that the proof of having sent one legitimate email is needed to get the email out of the spam folder. In other words, *TA* is *(1, 0, 0)*;
3. The sender starts contacting his/her list of contacts; in this case, there is only one contact;
4. The sender's only contact is queried; it does not know the receiver, so it starts checking its list of contacts to see if the privacy test is passed; in this case, the sender has a privacy disclosure trust value of *0.8*, which is higher than the threshold specified by the potential recommender *R2*; therefore, the contact is passed

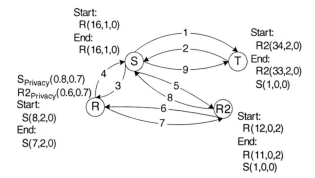

Fig. 4.9 Proof of friends trust transfer example[8,9]

back to the sender: more precisely, the contact signs an email stating that it is inclined to recommend *(1, 0, 0)* for the sender based on a recommender chain including *R2*;

5. The recommender's contact is queried by the sender and is found to be a contact of the receiver; it agrees to recommend *(1, 0, 0)* for the sender to the receiver as long as it receives a confirmation from *R*. This is because *R* has a balance of *10* on *R2*'s side, which is greater than *TA*. *S* has a balance of *6* on *R*'s side, so the *RP* is passed on all nodes in the recommender chain;

6. An email is sent to *R* in order to confirm that the trustworthiness in the sender has been decreased by *(1, 0, 0)* on *R*'s side;

7. The trustworthiness in the sender is decreased by one and a confirmation email is sent back to *R2*;

8. *R2* transfers some trustworthiness (one supporting outcome) from *R* to the sender; then, an email confirming that *R2* recommends *(1, 0, 0)* is sent back to the sender;

9. The recommendation is passed to the receiver, who transfers *(1, 0, 0)* trustworthiness from *R2*'s trust value to the sender's trust value.

In doing so, the spammer has now to endure most of the recommendation work and his/her attacks are more expensive since many more real emails from the spammer are needed.

At first glance, the email infrastructure may be challenged by trust transfer because of the overhead of emails to find potential recommenders. However, in the modified search we present, the spammer must start the search with his/her own friends. As a rule of thumb [24], increasing the cost to the spammer for an attack is desirable and our new trust transfer further increases this cost when engineered attacks are used. This means that the network load is localised to the spammer's network of honest friends (of whom there are unlikely to be many). In addition to this, recommendations are usually only required for newcomers. Finally, the overhead of collaboration is limited by the *RSP* and more intelligent directed search schemes, for example [96] based on local knowledge about similarity between the sender and the local contacts, do not flood the network.

4.4.2 ASUP Evaluation

In this section, related work on identity and trust frameworks is discussed, compared and contrasted according to the ASUP dimensions. In order to get a finer-grained comparison of the related frameworks, each ASUP dimension is given different points of comparison, listed below, including the types of questions that are related to the points. The purpose is to show that the entification framework covers points that other frameworks only cover in part, as evident in Table 4.2. These points are not exhaustive and may overlap because the ASUP requirements intermingle. It is why each point and associated questions must be considered according to its heading ASUP requirement.

Table 4.2 ASUP comparison of previous frameworks

Point of Comparison: strongly addressed (●) approached (○)		JAAS	EAP	PGP	Lampson et al.	ATN	Jini/SESAME	Gaia	Shakhnarovich et al.	YKBB	Marsh	SULTAN	Rahman	J'sang	Kinateder	Golbeck	Appleseed	Eigentrust	Damiani	OpenPrivacy
Adaptability	1	○	●				○	○	○		○				○		○			○
	2		○		○					○	●	●					○			
	3	○	○		○		○	○	○	○	○	○	○	○		○			○	○
	4	●			○		○	○							○		○			
	5	○	○	○	○	○	○							○		○	○			
Security	1						○	○			○	○	○		○	○				○
	2			○				○	○	○	○	○	○		○		○	○		
	3			●	○				●	○	●	●	●	●	○	●	●	●	●	●
	4												○	○		○	○	○		
	5	○		○	○	○						○	○	○					●	○
	6	○	○	○				○					○		●					
	7		○	●		○		○	●	●	●	●	●	●	●	●	●	●	●	●
	8	●	●	○			○	○							○					
	9		○	○							○		○	○			○	○	○	○
	10	●			●		●	●	○					○	●					
	11									○	○	○	○			○	○	○	○	○
Usability	1	○	○		○		○	○		●	○			○					
	2	○			○										○					○
	3					○				○	○	○	○							
	4			●	○	○				○	○	●	○	○		○	○			○
Privacy	1	○			○	○		○			○				●				○	●
	2	○	○		○	○				○	○	○	○		●				○	●
	3		○			●		○												
	4			○		○		○							○	○			●	●

4.4.2.1 Definitions of the ASUP Points of Comparison

Concerning the *adaptability* points of comparison:

1. *to the available technical infrastructure and scalability:* can more or less resource consuming authentication and authorisation schemes be used?; can it handle a large number of virtual identities?;
2. *to the trade-off between security protection and its tolerable cost*: are there means to limit privileges when a weaker technical infrastructure is available?; is there dynamic risk (cost/benefit) analysis?;
3. *to the context*: beyond adapting the decision based on virtual identity, can it be adapted to slightly different application contexts, for example, from trustworthiness for the driving of a car to the driving of a motorcycle?; is the system able to adapt its response to the environmental context, for example, under attack or when normal conditions are perceived?;
4. *to the use of many virtual identities*: is there a problem or a difference when multiple identities per real-world identity are used?; can it handle it without failing?

5. *to new security domains*: are human administrators needed when new security domains are encountered?; can new application domains be used?

Concerning the *security* points of comparison:

1. *cost of the management overhead to be done by the user:* is the user supposed to administer the system?; how often is manual reconfiguration needed?; how often is explicit user intervention needed?;
2. *openness to newcomer*: do newcomers need to be enrolled by a human administrator?; do they have to pay first?; are they considered untrustworthy by default?; what do they have to do to increase their privileges?; is there a mechanism to build trust from scratch?;
3. *through collaboration*: is collaboration and computational trust used to decide about security decisions?; is it only for mere selection of the most trustworthy virtual identities (that is, collaborative filtering)?;
4. *against identity multiplicity attacks*: how does the framework behave against this type of attack?; is the Sybil attack possible?; how is the Sybil attack mitigated?;
5. *against identity usurpation attacks*: how does it behave against these attacks?; what is done against spoofing?; are SBA and MIM attacks discussed?;
6. *uncertainty consideration*: is it assumed that everything is perfect and binary?; what may be uncertain?;
7. *explicit evidence-based trust levels*: are there trust levels?; are they explicitly computed based on evidence?;
8. *based on standards*: has the solution been peer-reviewed?; is it part of a large consortium process?; are old standards reused or new ones accepted?;
9. *possibility of full decentralisation or presence of trusted third parties:* are trusted third parties mandatory?; what changes when they are available?; is it supposed to work in a fully decentralised manner (although it might fail under special circumstances, such as attacks)?;
10. *clear separation between authentication and authorisation:* is there a clear separation between authentication and authorisation?; does identity matter?;
11. *mandatory assumption of effective system trust:* does it rely on the accountability of the real-world identity and successful prosecution?; is there the assumption that the link to the real-world identity guarantees a successful prosecution?; does it rely on real-world recourse such as insurance?

Concerning the *usability* points of comparison:

1. *of bootstrapping/enrolment:* how dynamic are the possible enrolment schemes, especially from an authentication point of view?;
2. *of management of multiple identities*: are there features to ease the management of multiple identities?;
3. *of the specification of privacy policies*: how easy is it for a user to specify privacy policies?;
4. *of the specification of trust policies*: how easy is it for a user to specify trust policies?

Concerning the *privacy* points of comparison:

1. *pseudonymity*: is it possible to use pseudonymity or many virtual identities?;
2. *link to the real-world identity*: is it mandatory?; how hard is it to infer the link?;
3. *negotiation*: is it possible to negotiate the amount of private information to be disclosed?;
4. *user-centric and in control*: is the user in control of his/her privacy?

In addition, for all the compared frameworks, there are a number of shared facts. None of the surveyed frameworks really solves the issue of SBAs. SBAs are indeed very harmful in security through collaboration since compromising one entity may impact its collaborating entities. Further trust dynamics research is needed to overcome this type of attacks. Concerning usurpation attacks, if addressed, the general workaround is to use asymmetric cryptography and to sign transactions and messages. Finally, at the time of writing, there is no computational trust standard. The points of comparison and their number are summarised in Fig. 4.10. The following Table 4.2 presents the comparison of the different frameworks, introduced below, according to the points of comparison determined in this section.

4.4.2.2 List of the Compared Frameworks

1. The first two frameworks can be categorised as adaptable authentication and authorisation frameworks, especially because they are based on standards

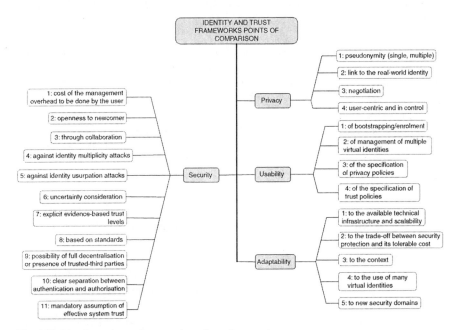

Fig. 4.10 Identity and trust frameworks points of comparison

describing how to plug different authentication schemes. JAAS is a framework and programming interface that enforces in the Java^{TM} platform access control based on the identity of the user who runs the Java application code. The Extensible Authentication Protocol (EAP) [97] is a P2P authentication framework (described in an RFC [97]), which supports multiple authentication methods and takes into account their security strength according to a list of attacks at the authentication level and a static risk analysis.

2. Then, we review three credentials-based authentication and authorisation frameworks. It starts with the influential identity-based framework, PGP [41]. The next framework is Lampson et al.'s framework [34, 98], which relies on "speaks for" relations between a large panel of types of virtual identities (for example, communication channels or roles). The third advanced credentials-based framework is Automated Trust Negotiation (ATN) [99] that takes into account the privacy aspect of credentials released thanks to negotiation. However, ATN "does not address the client's need for trust before it requests service" [100]. Furthermore, because it is required to show credentials in order to start the collaboration, this type of system may have a bootstrapping problem when no credential is already obtained, or cannot be discovered. It also does not help if no third-party is accepted as a common credential provider by both parties. There is a need for additional trust formation mechanisms from scratch, such as computational trust. Credentials may be exchanged or accepted after this trust formation phase, but not before.

3. Al-Muhtadi et al.'s framework [101], called *Jini/SESAME*, tackles the security issues in a smart home with the plug and play technology based on Java called Java Intelligent Network Infrastructure (JINI). The second ubiquitous computing framework is Gaia. The environment of Gaia goes beyond the previous environment of a single smart home. For example, it may be a smart campus. However, there is still the assumption that an infrastructure is present and that technology-aware and dedicated administrators manage this infrastructure. The administrator must set the "confidence" in the security protection given by the different possible authentication schemes. For example, active badge authentication is given *0.6* on a *[0,1]* scale. Depending on how many authentication schemes the user uses to authenticate his/her pseudonym, the final confidence p_n increases or decreases according to the following formula, where n authentication schemes are used and p_i is the confidence of a successfully passed authentication scheme: $p_{final} = 1 - (1 - p_1)...(1 - p_n)$ Another innovative element is to use this final confidence and other context information in the rules used for authorisation decisions. A related framework using biometrics is Shakhnarovich et al.'s framework [102], where face and gait recognition are integrated. Based on experiments on twelve users they found out that multi-modal recognition increases the level of confidence in recognition. Since some recognition schemes may be more or less accurate, they first empirically evaluated the success rates of face and gait classifiers. They found they were similar but face recognition may simply be impossible due to not enough captured images containing the face. Therefore, they computed multi-modal confidence

vectors according to the following formula given the observed sequence of multi-views x:

$$p_{combined}(x) = \left\{ \begin{array}{l} p_{gait}(x), no\_face \\ \left(\frac{p_{gaot}(X)+p_{face}(x)}{2} \right), otherwise \end{array} \right\}$$

4. Concerning explicit evidence-based computational trust frameworks, the six most relevant ones have been selected to be compared according to the same specific points. They are called with the following short names: *YKBB* for [103]; *Rahman* for [10]; *Marsh* for [11]; *SULTAN* for [104]; *Jøsang* for [17] and *Kinateder* for [105]. In YKBB, entities communicate via channels and have a unique identifier and a secret, which can be used for authentication. Some of these entities are supposed to have the role of authentication servers. Each virtual identity is assigned several trust values based on probabilities, which are computed from a number of counters in different trust contexts. These counters are incremented or decremented each time there is an action and its associated outcome (positive or negative) related to the trust context. Marsh's framework [11] is one of the first computational models of trust based on social research. Each trust context is assigned an importance value in the range *[0, 1]* and utility value in the range *[-1, 1]*. Any trust value is in the range *[-1, 1]*. In addition, each virtual identity is assigned a general trust value, which is based on all the trust values with this virtual identity in all the trust contexts. Dispositional trust appears in the model as the basic trust value: it is the total trust values in all contexts in all virtual identities with whom the trustor has interacted so far. Risk is used in a threshold for trusting decision making. The Simple Universal Logic-oriented Trust Analysis Notation (SULTAN) framework provides a simple notation for the writing of policies dealing with trust, risk and recommendation concepts in Internet applications. Rahman's framework consists of a decentralised trust model focusing on the formation and evolution of trust values based on recommendations and direct observations rather than on the use of trust values for decision making. Thus, there is no risk component. There are different levels of trust from very untrustworthy to very trustworthy. Recommending trustworthiness is based on consistency on the "semantic distance" between the real outcomes and the recommendations that have been made. The "recommendation protocol" [16] is used by a trustor to find recommender chains about the trustee. The default recommendation search scheme is related to a depth-first search directed by the recommending trustworthiness of the recommenders if they do not know the subject. Jøsang's framework is called "subjective logic" and integrates the element of ignorance and uncertainty, which cannot be reflected by mere probabilities but is part of the human aspect of trust. In Kinateder's framework, the trust value can be contextualised to the "trust category" (trust context) of concern of the current request (for example, with regard to the context of computer security expertise). This framework takes care of privacy: users are allowed to use virtual identities

to minimise the risk of profiling them based on the history of their transactions. However, as explained above, its mitigation of Sybil attacks introduces new constraints such as the use of trusted hardware.

5. The next frameworks are based on real-world social networks, where users set manual trust values to other users. None of the frameworks explain how the manual trust value could be converted into a trust value based on event outcomes. For example, the Friend-Of-A-Friend (FOAF) [65] initiative can be described as a text format for the online description of the profile of a user (name, contact information, interests, ...) and links to the profiles of users that he/she knows. In Golbeck et al.'s framework [84, 96], that we call Golbeck, the FOAF schema has been extended to include "trust assertions", that is, manual trust values in the individuals targeted by these assertions. They use their network for a kind of anti-spam tool. TrustMail is not supposed to be a spam filter but a layer used to "provide higher ratings to emails that come from non-spam senders" [106]. Emails from known, trustworthy senders are given higher priority in the user's inbox whereas emails from unknown or disreputable senders are given lower priorities. Email senders are given a manual trust value in the range *[1, 10]*; with *1* meaning that the recipient has little or no trust in the sender and *10* meaning that the recipient trusts the sender maximally. In case an email is received from an unknown sender, the recipient attempts to infer the equivalent of a manual trust value for the sender based on recommender chains starting with the recipient's known contacts. Using a Breadth First Search (BFS) in the whole network stored on the TrustMail centralised server, a path from the recipient to the sender is searched for and manual trust values on the path are combined. Ziegler and Lausen's trust metric, called Appleseed [12], is possible because it is assumed that all users make their manual trust values publicly available. This constitutes a threat to privacy since a clear view of the network of acquaintances can be obtained. The manual trust value ranges from *0* (lack of trust) to *1* (blind trust). Recommending trustworthiness does not explicitly appear but it is reflected in the choice of the "spreading factor" [12], which is recommended to be set to *0.85* and "may also be seen as the ratio between direct trust [...] and trust in the ability [...] to recommend others as trustworthy peers". Appleseed's spreading factor highlights that trustworthiness gained by a virtual identity may be passed to another virtual identity. However, this factor is not set by the recommender but by the computing trustor and similar for all virtual identities in the network. In fact, Appleseed is a local centralised group metric.

6. The last type of frameworks covered is the one based on decentralised peer-to-peer (P2P) techniques [107, 108]. They can be built based on two approaches. First, there are unstructured networks, where no index information is maintained, messages with search information (such as, TTL, message identifier or list of already contacted peers) flood the network. Secondly, there are structured networks, where index information is distributed and maintained among the peers according to different solutions (for example, based on a distributed hash table or a binary search tree). From a privacy point of view, the second approach is likely to imply that trust evidence of a user would be maintained by other users, who

cannot be chosen by the user. When the network consists of a social network, a variant of the first approach can be used: the search may be optimised by directing the search according to properties of the target of the search and properties of the direct peers [109]. For example, if an email about movies has been sent by a previously unknown sender, the search for information about the sender would start with the contacts that are known to have an interest in movies. According to Ziegler and Lausen's trust metric classification [12] (explained above), the trust metric used in the Eigentrust [110] framework is a global distributed group metric. The trust values are based on the number of positive and negative outcomes and depend on one (or several) structured P2P networks for the trust value computation. They use the global trust value to increase the quality of P2P file sharing systems (based on an unstructured P2P network). Damiani et al.'s framework [111] add a computational trust metric on top of a P2P unstructured network. The searching follows Gnutella's flooding technique [112], which consists of sending an identified search request message to a number of direct contacts with a TTL. Their first application domain is file sharing. The trust metric is used to choose the most trustworthy peer among the peers who claim to have the sought-after file. In order to minimise the risk of Sybil attacks, recommendations coming from a clique of IP addresses are discarded. Similarly, a number of recommenders are re-contacted to check that they are really the authors of the recommendation.. This double-check is supposed to increase the cost of running faked virtual identities by the same real-world identity. It is also an example of weak authentication. The second application [111] reuses their Gnutella-based computational trust to fight spam in email settings. In order to protect the privacy of the users of a mail server, only the mail servers are considered to be peers in the unstructured network. The mail server aggregates direct observations of its email users about spam emails. Since it is common that spam emails are slightly modified, a fuzzy hash mechanism is used to give the same hash for slightly different spam emails. The peers send updated collection of hashes of spam emails, without reference to the involved email users, to another type of peers, called super-peers. The super-peers maintain a distributed collection of spam hashes and peers can query information about unknown emails. The result of the query is a number of recommendations that are used to compute the final trust value based on the recommenders' trustworthiness and a trust metric, whose choice is left to the future users. Sierra is the implementation of the OpenPrivacy computational trust management framework [113, 114]. Sierra is composed of: the "Nym Manager", which creates, manages and authenticates the pseudonymous certificates; the "Reputation", which is signed by the current local virtual identity and used as recommendation or observation; the "Reputation Calculation Engine (RCE)", which implements the trust metric, computes and maintains reputations; the "Query" package, to query and index data; the "Communication" interface for transparent communication with peers (the type of P2P network can be plugged with this interface); and the "Storage Manager". Any trust metric could be used as long as there is an RCE implementation of the trust metric. Noticeably, there is no risk component in their framework. The

"Nym Manager" has many interesting features although it is limited to public keys for authentication.

4.4.2.3 ASUP Qualitative Frameworks Comparison

Below, the different frameworks are assessed according to the above ASUP points of comparison. First, there is a table summarising the ASUP qualitative assessement of the other frameworks according to the defined points of comparison. Then, the evaluation of the entification framework is detailed.

Concerning the *adaptability* points of comparison of the entification framework, adaptability:

1. *to the available technical infrastructure and scalability:* the set of pluggable recognition schemes is large; in order to scale, specific ER schemes can be used and context is useful to forget/garbage-collect virtual identities unlikely to be met in the current context of interest; collaboration with trustworthy entities can be used to share the load of data;
2. *to the trade-off between security protection and its tolerable cost*: the risk analysis of the trust engine may maintain the right trade-off; ER schemes are associated with the level of confidence in recognition, which can be considered as dynamic technical trust values;
3. *to the context*: the trust value varies across contexts: there are different trust contexts; the ER module generates environmental context evidence and the trust engine can tune the ER module; context can be used to select the appropriate virtual identity;
4. *to the use of many virtual identities*: trust transfer is a means to maintain a safe trust value even in case of multiple virtual identities per user;
5. *to new security domains*: thanks to collaboration and dynamic enrolment, the adaptation to new security domains is smoother; trust may be built from scratch, interaction after interaction.

Concerning the *security* points of comparison of the entification framework:

1. *cost of the management overhead to be done by the user:* once the trust policy is written, the trust value may automatically evolve interaction after interaction; some ER schemes may be more dynamic (but less secure);
2. *openness to newcomer*: newcomer virtual identities can dynamically join the community and their trust value is built interaction after interaction; trust transfer facilitates the consideration of trustworthy newcomers; however, newcomers must have trustworthily interacted with other entities at some stage;
3. *through collaboration*: direct observation, recommendations and collaboration are used; security decisions are possible and should be based on the explicit ER technical trust;
4. *against identity multiplicity attacks*: the Sybil attack is mitigated through trust transfer in case the trust values correspond to the count of event outcomes;

5. *against identity usurpation attacks*: the level of confidence in recognition and technical trust can be used to mitigate spoofing;
6. *uncertainty consideration*: trust values (including technical trust) may have an element of uncertainty, for example, if the SECURE trust value format is used;
7. *explicit evidence-based trust levels*: the trust values based on event outcomes are explicitly computed based on pieces of evidence;
8. *based on standards*: the different parts of the entification framework have been reviewed in a number of publications;
9. *possible full decentralisation or presence of trusted third parties:* a trusted third party is not mandatory: it depends on the ER scheme, new message-based ER schemes, which do not require trusted third parties, have been created; full decentralisation may be achieved thanks to trust transfer in some scenarios as presented above;
10. *clear separation between authentication and authorisation:* there is a clear separation in end-to-end trust and the notion of virtual identity is at the core of the framework;
11. *mandatory assumption of effective system trust:* the assumption is that it is possible to rely on event outcomes and collaboration to build interpersonal trust from scratch; system trust may be used but it is not mandatory.

Concerning the *usability* points of comparison of the entification framework:

1. *of bootstrapping/enrolment:* dynamic enrolment may be provided by some entity recognition schemes since enrolment is postponed in the ER process; in case of a complete newcomer, the potential element of uncertainty in the trust value may be used;
2. *of management of multiple identities*: the disclosure of the appropriate virtual identity can be done based on the trust values and context, for example, automatically switching identities based on location may facilitate the management [38];
3. *of the specification of privacy policies*: context and trust values can be used;
4. *of the specification of trust policies*: the count of event outcomes appears to be intuitive, especially to include the notion of uncertainty when the outcome of the event is yet unknown.

Concerning the *privacy* points of comparison of the entification framework:

1. *pseudonymity*: many virtual identities per user are supported and encouraged;
2. *link to the real-world identity*: the link is not mandatory; recognition is sufficient; many virtual identities make it harder to infer the link to the real-world identity;
3. *negotiation*: the link mechanism is used to trade privacy for trust [93];
4. *user-centric and in control*: the user is in control of his/her trust engine including its pluggable recognition module and related security policy preferences.

4.5 Conclusion

A too simplistic approach to identity management in computational trust leads to different security holes and attacks at the identity level. The entification framework mitigates a number of these security holes and attacks as well as better fulfills the ASUP requirements by carefully bridging identity management and computational trust. Depending on which ASUP requirements are more important, the entification framework can be tuned to better fulfill these most important requirements, possibly at the expense of the other requirements. For example, pure ER schemes may be better for privacy and usability. Adaptability is greater when the range of allowed ER schemes is broader. However, pure ER schemes provide less security since system trust based on the real-world identity cannot be enforced. The combination of convenient user-centric identity management schemes such as OpenID and decentralised computational trust services, such as Venyo [115], seems a promising trade-off.

References

1. F. Stajano, "Security for Ubiquitous Computing," John Wiley & Sons, 2002.
2. R. E. Smith, "Authentication: from passwords to public keys," Addison Wesley, 2001.
3. L. Kagal, J. L. Undercoffer, F. Perich, A. Joshi, T. Finin, and Y. Yesha, "Vigil: Providing Trust for Enhanced Security in Pervasive Systems," University of Maryland Techical Report, 2002.
4. A. Birrell, B. Lampson, R. M. Needham, and M. D. Schroeder, "A Global Authentication Service without Global Trust," Symposium on Security and Privacy: IEEE, pp. 223–230, 1986.
5. M. Weiser, "The Computer for the 21st Century," Scientific American, 1991.
6. R. Khare, "What's in a Name? Trust," 4K Associates, 1999.
7. Postini, "Worldwide Map of Origin of Spam," 2004.
8. D. M. Romano, "The Nature of Trust: Conceptual and Operational Clarification," Louisiana State University, PhD Thesis etd-0130103-070613, 2003.
9. D. H. McKnight and N. L. Chervany, "What is trust? A Conceptual Analysis and an Interdisciplinary Model," presented at the Americas Conference on Information Systems (AMCIS), 2000.
10. F. Rahman,"A Frame work for Decentralised Trust Reasoning", Ph. D. Thesis University College London, 2005.
11. S. Marsh, "Formalising Trust as a Computational Concept," Department of Mathematics and Computer Science, University of Stirling, PhD Thesis 1994.
12. C.-N. Ziegler and G. Lausen, "Spreading Activation Models for Trust Propagation," presented at the International Conference on e-Technology, e-Commerce, and e-Service, 2004.
13. S. Brin and L. Page, "The Anatomy of a Large-Scale Hypertextual Web Search Engine," vol. 30(1–7): Computer Networks, 1998.
14. R. Levien, "Attack Resistant Trust Metrics," UC Berkeley, PhD Thesis 2004.
15. W. Wagealla, M. Carbone, C. English, S. Terzis, and P. Nixon, "A Formal Model of Trust Lifecycle Management," vol. Proceedings of the Workshop on Formal Aspects of Security and Trust (FAST2003), 2003.
16. A. Abdul-Rahman and S. Hailes, "Using Recommendations for Managing Trust in Distributed Systems," Proceedings of the Malaysia International Conference on Communication'97: IEEE, 1997.
17. A. Jøsang, "A Subjective Metric of Authentication," vol. J.- J. Quisquater, Y. Deswarte, C. Meadows, and D. Gollmann, editors, ESORICS'98. Louvain-la-Neuve, Belgium. Bel-

gium: Springer-Verlag, 1998.

18. N. Mogens, M. Carbone, and K. Krukow, "An Operational Model of Trust," SECURE Deliverable 1.2, 2004.

19. M. Nielsen, G. Plotkin, and G. Winskel, "Petri nets, event structures and domains.," *Theoritical Computer Science*, pp. 85–108, 1981.

20. N. Mogens, M. Carbone, and K. Krukow, "Revised Computational Trust Model," SECURE Deliverable 1.3, 2004.

21. A. Twigg and N. Dimmock, "Attack-Resistance of Computational Trust Models," vol. Proceedings of the Twelfth International Workshop on Enabling Technologies: Infrastructure for Collaborative Enterprises: IEEE, 2003.

22. J. R. Douceur, "The Sybil Attack," Proceedings of the 1st International Workshop on Peer-to-Peer Systems, 2002.

23. E. Friedman and P. Resnick, "The Social Cost of Cheap Pseudonyms," Journal of Economics and Management Strategy, pp. 173–199, 2001.

24. M. Abadi, A. Birrell, M. Burrows, F. Dabek, and T. Wobber, "Bankable Postage for Network Services," Proceedings of ASIAN 2003: LNCS, Springer, pp. 72–90, 2003.

25. D. Chaum, "Achieving Electronic Privacy," Scientific American, pp. 96–100, 1992.

26. G. Montenegro and C. Castelluccia, "Statistically unique and cryptographically verifiable(sucv) identifiers and addresses.," Proceedings of the Network and Distributed System Security Symposium, 2002.

27. J. Kleinberg, "Small-World Phenomena and the Dynamics of Information," vol. Advances in Neural Information Processing Systems (NIPS) 14, 2001.

28. M. Kinateder and K. Rothermel, "Architecture and Algorithms for a Distributed Reputation System," Proceedings of the First Conference on Trust Management: LNCS, Springer, 2003.

29. "Public-Key Infrastructure (X.509)." http: //www.ietf.org/html.charters/pkix-charter.html.

30. N. Li, "Local Names In SPKI/SDSI 2.0," Proceedings of The 13th Computer Security Foundations Workshop, 2000.

31. R. L. Rivest and B. Lampson, "SDSI – A Simple Distributed Security Infrastructure," 1996.

32. M. Abadi, "On SDSI's Linked Local Name Spaces," Journal of Computer Security, pp. 3–21, 1998.

33. C. M. Ellison, "SPKI requirements," vol. RFC 2692: IETF, 1999.

34. B. Lampson, M. Abadi, M. Burrows, and E. Wobber, "Authentication in distributed systems: theory and practice," Transactions on Computer Systems: ACM, 1992.

35. U. Jendricke, M. Kreutzer, and A. Zugenmaier, "Pervasive Privacy with Identity Management," Proceedings of the Workshop on Security in Ubiquitous Computing, Ubicomp 2002, 2002.

36. S. Lederer, C. Beckmann, A. K. Dey, and J. Mankoff, "Managing Personal Information Disclosure in Ubiquitous Computing Environments," Intel Research, IRB-TR-03-015, 2003.

37. A. Kobsa and J. Schreck, "Privacy through Pseudonymity in User-Adaptive Systems," vol. ACM Transactions on Internet Technology, pp. 149–183, 2003.

38. J.-M. Seigneur and C. D. Jensen, "Trust Enhanced Ubiquitous Payment without Too Much Privacy Loss," vol. Proceedings of SAC 2004: ACM, 2004.

39. V. Matyas and Z. Riha, "Biometric Authentication – Security and Usability," Masaryk University Brno, Czech Republic.

40. J. Galvin, "(In)Security from End to End," Information Security Magazine, vol. 3, p. 56, 2000.

41. P. R. Zimmerman, "The Official PGP User's Guide," MIT Press, 1995.

42. GnuPG, "The GNU Privacy Handbook," The Free Software Foundation, 1999.

43. S. Kent, "Privacy Enhanced Mail," IETF Working Group, 1996.

44. S/MIME, "S/MIME Mail Security (smime)," IETF Working Group. http://www.ietf.org/html.charters/smime-charter.html

45. IBM/Microsoft, "Federation of Identities in a Web services world," 2003.

46. Liberty Alliance Project, http://www.projectliberty.org/, access date: 29/11/2005.

47. SunMicrosystems, "Identity Grid," SunMicrosystems, 2004.
48. OpenID, http://openid.net/, access date: 09/11/07.
49. A. K. Jain, A. Ross, and S. Prabhakar, "An Introduction to Biometric Recognition," IEEE Transactions on Circuits and Systems for Video Technology, Special Issue on Image- and Video-Based Biometrics, August, 2003.
50. J. Bigun, J. Fierrez-Aguilar, J. Ortega-Garcia, and G.-R. J., "Multimodal Biometric Authentication using Quality Signals in Mobile Communications," Proceedings of the 12th International Conference on Image Analysis and Processing: IEEE, 2003.
51. N. Haller, "The S/KEY One-Time Password System," Proceedings of the Symposium on Network and Distributed System Security, 1994.
52. P. E. Verissimo, N. F. Neves, and M. P. Correia, "Intrusion-Tolerant Architectures: Concepts and Design," vol. Architecting Dependable Systems, R. Lemos, C. Gacek, A. Romanovsky (eds.), LNCS, vol. 2677, Springer Verlag, 2003., 2003.
53. J. Arkko and P. Nikander, "Weak Authentication: How to Authenticate Unknown Principals without Trusted Parties.," vol. Proceedings of the Security Protocols Workshop: LNCS, Springer, 2002, pp. 5–19.
54. R. Volker, "Weak Authentication," Web site, 2004, http://www.igd.fhg.de/
55. A. Weimerskirch and D. Westhoff, "Zero Common-Knowledge Authentication for Pervasive Networks," Proceedings of the Annual International Workshop on Selected Areas in Cryptography, 2004.
56. D. Gollmann, "Computer Security," John Wiley&Sons, 1999.
57. J. Abendroth, "A Unified Access Control Mechanism," Trinity College Dublin, 2004.
58. B. D. Brunk, "Understanding the Privacy Space," First Monday. Chicago: Library of the University of Illinois, 2002.
59. M. Langheinrich, "Privacy by Design - Principles of Privacy-Aware Ubiquitous Systems," Proceedings of Ubicomp 2001: Ubiquitous Computing: Third International Conference, LNCS 2201. Heidelberg: Springer Verlag, pp. 273–291, 2001.
60. T. M. Cooley, "A Treatise on the Law of Torts," Second edition, Chicago: Callaghan, 1888.
61. A. H. Maslow, Motivation and Personality, Harper, 1954.
62. T. Mahler and T. Olsen, "Reputation Systems and Data Protection Law," eChallenges, 2004.
63. D. Work, "Call for A Social Networking Bill of Rights," PlanetWork Journal, vol. 6, 2004.
64. CypherTrust.
65. The Friend-of-a-Friend Project, http://www.foaf-project.org/, access date: 08/04/2006.
66. EU, "Directive 95/46/EC of the European Parliament and of the Council of 24 October 1995 on the protection of individuals with regard to the processing of personal data and on the free movement of such data," 1995.
67. C. o. t. E. Communities, "eEurope Benchmarking Report," 2002.
68. DataProtectionWorkingParty, "Opinion 10/2001 on the need for a balanced approach in the fight against terrorism," The European Commission, 2001.
69. L. Cranor, M. Langheinrich, M. Marchiori, and J. Reagle, "The platform for privacy preferences 1.0 (P3P1.0) specification," W3C Recommendation, 2002.
70. EPIC, "Airline privacy violation cases," 2004.
71. X. Jiang, J. I. Hong, and J. A. Landay, "Approximate Information Flows: Socially Based Modeling of Privacy in Ubiquitous Computing," Proceedings of the 4th International Conference on Ubiquitous Computing (Ubicomp 2002), LNCS 2498. Berlin Heidelberg: Springer-Verlag, pp. 176–193, 2002.
72. R. Agrawal, "Why is P3P Not a PET?," vol. W3C Workshop on the Future of P3P, 2002.
73. M. Weiser and J. S. Brown, "Designing Calm Technology," PowerGrid Journal, vol. 1.01, 1996.
74. O. Berthold and H. Langos, "Dummy Traffic Against Long Term Intersection attacks."
75. T. Aura and C. Ellison, "Privacy and Accountability in Certificate Systems," Helsinki University of Technology, 2000.

76. M. K. Reiter and A. D. Rubin, "Anonymity Loves Company: Anonymous Web Transactions with Crowds," 1999.
77. D. Chaum, "Untraceable Electronic Mail, Return Addresses, and Digital Pseudonyms," Communications of the ACM, 1981.
78. I. Goldberg, "A Pseudonymous Communications Infrastructure for the Internet," University of California at Berkeley, PhD Thesis 2000.
79. R. Hes and J. Borking, "Privacy Enhancing Technologies: The Path to Anonymity," ISBN 90 74087 12 4, 2000.
80. J.-M. Seigneur, S. Farrell, C. D. Jensen, E. Gray, and Y. Chen, "End-to-end Trust Starts with Recognition," Proceedings of the First International Conference on Security in Pervasive Computing: LNCS 2802, Springer-Verlag, pp. 130–142, 2003.
81. J.-M. Seigneur, D. Solis, and F. Shevlin, "Ambient Intelligence through Image Retrieval," Proceedings of the 3rd International Conference on Image and Video Retrieval: LNCS 3115, Springer-Verlag, pp. 526–534, 2004.
82. R. Campbell, J. Al-Muhtadi, P. Naldurg, G. Sampermane, and M. D. Mickunas, "Towards Security and Privacy for Pervasive Computing," Proceedings of the International Symposium on Software Security, Keio University, Tokyo, Japan, November 8, 2002.
83. S. Lo Presti, M. Cusack, and C. Booth, "Trust Issues in Pervasive Environments," Trusted Software Agents and Services for Pervasive Information Environments project, 2003.
84. J. Golbeck and B. Parsia, "Trusting Claims from Trusted Sources: Trust Network Based Filtering of Aggregated Claims," Proceedings of the 3rd International Semantic Web Conference (ISWC2004), 2004.
85. J.-M. Seigneur and C. D. Jensen, "The Claim Tool Kit for Ad-hoc Recognition of Peer Entities," Journal of Science of Computer Programming: Elsevier, vol. 54, 2004.
86. V. Samar and C. Lai, "Making Login Services Independent of Authentication Technologies," Sun Microsystems, 1995.
87. D. M. Chess, C. C. Palmer, and W. S. R., "Security in an autonomic computing environment," IBM Systems Journal,vol 40 2003.
88. A. Jøsang, "The right type of trust for distributed systems," Proceedings of the 1996 New Security Paradigms Workshop: ACM, 1996.
89. O. Olsson, "Privacy protection and trust models," ERCIM News, 2002.
90. CSA, "Model Code for the Protection of Personal Information," Canadian Standards Association, 1995.
91. F. Labalme and K. Burton, "Enhancing the Internet with Reputations," Open Privacy White Paper, 2001.
92. L. Lessig, "The Architecture of Privacy," Taiwan Net'98 Conference, 1998.
93. J.-M. Seigneur and C. D. Jensen, "Trading Privacy for Trust," Proceedings of iTrust'04 the Second International Conference on Trust Management: LNCS 2995, Springer-Verlag, 2004.
94. C. M. Jonker and J. Treur, "Formal Analysis of Models for the Dynamics of Trust based on Experiences," Proceedings of the 9th European Workshop on Modelling Autonomous Agents in a Multi-Agent World : Multi-Agent System Engineering, 1999.
95. J.-M. Seigneur, A. Gray, and C. D. Jensen, "Trust Transfer: Encouraging Self-Recommendations without Sybil Attack," LNCS: Springer, 2005.
96. J. Golbeck and J. Hendler, "Accuracy of Metrics for Inferring Trust and Reputation in Semantic Web-based Social Networks," 2004.
97. B. Aboba, L. Blunk, J. Vollbrecht, J. Carlson, and H. Levkowetz, "Extensible Authentication Protocol (EAP)," vol. RFC3748: Network Working Group, 2004.
98. E. Wobber, M. Abadi, M. Burrows, and B. Lampson, "Authentication in the Taos Operating System," ACM, 1994.
99. M. Winslett, T. Yu, K. E. Seamons, A. Hess, J. Jacobson, R. Jarvis, B. Smith, and L. Yu, "Negotiating Trust on the Web," IEEE, vol. 6, pp. 30–37, 2002.

100. W. H. Winsborough, K. E. Seamons, and V. E. Jones, "Automated Trust Negotiation," vol. DARPA Information Survivability Conference and Exposition, 2000.
101. J. Al-Muhtadi, M. Anand, M. D. Mickunas, and R.H., Campbell, "Secure Smart Homes Using Jini and UIUC SESAME," Technical Report. UMI order Number: UIUCDCS-R-99-2142., University of Illinois at Urbana-Champaign, 2001.
102. G. Shakhnarovich, L. Lee, and T. Darrell, "Integrated Face and Gait Recognition From Multiple Views," Proceedings of IEEE Conference on Computer Vision and Pattern Recognition, 2001.
103. T. Beth, M. Borcherding, and B. Klein, "Valuation of Trust in Open Networks," Proceedings of the 3rd European Symposium on Research in Computer Security, 1994.
104. T. Grandison and M. Sloman, "Trust Management Tools for Internet Applications," Proceedings of iTrust'03: LNCS Springer, 2003.
105. M. P. Kinateder, Siani, "A Privacy-Enhanced Peer-to-Peer Reputation System," Proceedings of the 4th International Conference on Electronic Commerce and Web Technologies, 2003.
106. J. Golbeck and J. Hendler, "Reputation Network Analysis for Email Filtering," Proceedings of the First Conference on Email and Anti-Spam (CEAS), 2004.
107. Z. Despotovic and K. Aberer, "Trust and Reputation Management in P2P Networks," CEC, 2004.
108. D. S. Milojicic, V. Kalogeraki, R. Lukose, K. Nagaraja, J. Pruyne, B. Richard, S. Rollins, and Z. Xu, "Peer-to-Peer Computing," 2002.
109. E. Gray, J.-M. Seigneur, Y. Chen, and C. D. Jensen, "Trust Propagation in Small Worlds," Proceedings of the First International Conference on Trust Management: LNCS 2693, Springer-Verlag, 2003.
110. S. D. Kamvar, M. T. Schlosser, and H. Garcia-Molina, "The EigenTrust Algorithm for Reputation Management in P2P Networks," Proceedings of the Twelfth International World Wide Web Conference, 2003.
111. E. Damiani, S. D. C. d. Vimercati, S. Paraboschi, and P. Samarati, "P2P-Based Collaborative Spam Detection and Filtering," vol. Proceedings of the Fourth International Conference on Peer-to-Peer Computing (P2P'04), 2004.
112. J. Frankel and T. Pepper, "Gnutella," Nullsoft, 2000.
113. K. A. Burton, "Design of the OpenPrivacy Distributed Reputation System," OpenPrivacy.org, 2002.
114. Sierra, http://sierra.openprivacy.org/, access date: 15/11/07.
115. Venyo, http://www.venyo.org, access date: 15/11/07.

Part II
Propagation of Trust

Chapter 5
Attack-Resistant Trust Metrics

Raph Levien

Abstract The Internet is an amazingly powerful tool for connecting people together, unmatched in human history. Yet, with that power comes great potential for spam and abuse. Trust metrics are an attempt to compute the set of which people are trustworthy and which are likely attackers. This chapter presents two specific trust metrics developed and deployed on the Advogato Website, which is a community blog for free software developers. This real-world experience demonstrates that the trust metrics fulfilled their goals, but that for good results, it is important to match the assumptions of the abstract trust metric computation to the real-world implementation.

5.1 Introduction

The Internet is an amazingly powerful tool for connecting people together, unmatched in human history. Yet, with that power comes great potential for spam and abuse. In its early days, when it connected a community of academics and researchers, open email and message board systems were workable, because for the most part everybody who could connect to them was trustworthy.

Today, with nearly the entire world becoming connected, defenses are needed to prevent such systems from being entirely overrun with spam. Also, more and more of the world's business takes place on the Internet, so it is even more vulnerable to disruption by abuse.

The field of computer security is vast, and many technologies are proposed and deployed to make systems less vulnerable. If there is a well-defined list of trusted users, then authentication and encryption technology such as public key cryptography can effectively limit access to only those trusted users. However, many services on the Internet are appealing because they are open to a very large pool of users. It is a shame when that openness is sacrificed because the system would be too vulnerable to attack.

R. Levien (✉)
UC Berkeley, Berkeley, CA, USA
e-mail: raph.levien@gmail.com

J. Golbeck (ed.), *Computing with Social Trust,* Human-Computer Interaction Series, DOI 10.1007/978-1-84800-356-9_5 © Springer-Verlag London Limited 2009

Trust metrics are an attempt to *compute* with some accuracy the set of which people are trustworthy and which are likely attackers. The primary input to this computation is a representation of the *social graph*, the nodes of which are users, and the edges of which are relationships between these users. The basic assumption behind trust metrics is that trustworthy users will generally tend to have relationships (represented by these graph edges) with other trustworthy users. It is well known from sociology that these networks are central in establishing human trust. Further, explicit representation of these networks using the mathematical language of graph theory dates to Jacob Moreno's pioneering work on sociograms from the 1930s [1].

This chapter presents two specific trust metrics developed and deployed on the Advogato Website, which is a community blog for free software developers. This real-world experience demonstrates that the trust metrics fulfilled their goals, but that for good results, it is important to match the assumptions of the abstract trust metric computation to the real-world implementation.

5.2 Attack Resistance

The entire point of computing a trust metric is to reliably make some judgment about whether, say, an action is to be allowed or not. If it is easy for an attacker to force a "yes" answer, then it would have been just as easy to use a much simpler trust metric, or forego it.

The early proposals for trust metrics were not attack resistant. Two such early metrics, Beth, Borcherding and Klein [2] and Maurer [3], fell readily to attacks presented by Reiter and Stubblebine in 1998 [4].

In this context, attack resistance means not succumbing to catastrophic failure once a certain threshold is met for the strength of the attack. Rather, it means that the amount of damage done scales smoothly with the cost of the attack. To be meaningful, this concept requires quantification of both the cost of an attack and the amount of damage done.

It is also important to distinguish between the attack resistance in theory based on an abstract model of attack cost and damage, versus attack resistance in practice. For example, abstract models of attack cost usually assume a unit cost of creating an edge from a "good" node to one controlled by the attacker. Yet, an attack creating a large number of such edges may be viable, for example, by exploiting a security vulnerability in the software, or weak authentication mechanisms. Real-world experience with Advogato underscores the importance of calibrating these models to the real world.

5.2.1 Redundant Certification Paths

A great deal of the early literature on trust metrics was concerned with evaluating a graph of public key certificates attesting to identity relationships. In the standard rooted hierarchy model, all users agree on a root, which issues certificates to delegates (usually termed *Certification Authorities*, following the terminology of X.509 certificates), which in turn issue certificates attesting to identities of individual users, as well as (potentially) to other certification authorities. This scheme, with some modifications, is still what powers the public key infrastructure used by TLS, the encryption layer of https secure Web requests.

There are several problems with this scheme. First, if a root certification authority is compromised, an attacker can cause an unbounded number of false sites to be accepted by the user's browser. Second, because of the centralized control and the need to take extensive security measures, the cost of acquiring a certificate is nontrivial. Thus, TLS adoption on the Web is for the most part limited to sites that are used directly for commerce. And, despite early promise, no public key infrastructure technology has emerged, which is usable for individuals.

Decentralized trust networks attempt to address these shortcomings. Ideally, instead of relying on a highly centralized authority, certifications of identity are issued by peers. From its launch in the early 1990s, PGP provided a mechnism for generating and validating these certificates using public key signature technology. The resulting network of certificates has been called the PGP "Web of Trust" and has been studied in some detail [5]. For the most part, validation of identities in the Web of Trust is a manual effort. Users download a set of relevant keys and certificates (usually from specialized search engines known as "keyservers," but potentially from other sources).

Several attempts sprung up to automatically evaluate whether a specific binding of an email address to a public key was valid. In conjunction with a keyserver, such a system would provide roughly the same functionality as a centralized, X.509 style PKI, but hopefully without the drawbacks of centralization.

Alas, it was not to be. From the assumptions underlying such a service, it is possible to derive an upper bound on the attack resistance, demonstrating that it is feasible for an attacker to get an unbounded number of key/name bindings accepted for the cost of a small number of attack edges.

The assumptions are as follows:

- A relatively small subgraph is available for evaluation.
- The metric is monotonic, in that additional certificates increase trust.
- The cost of establishing an identity must be low, specifically an indegree of no more than k certificates per node.
- A vast majority of "good" nodes should be accepted.

These assumptions derive from the fact that the keyserver itself is not trusted. If certificates assert negative reputation about an attacker, it is in the attacker's interest to simply withold those certificates. Similarly, if a single node has signed a very large number of certificates for other identities, then the attacker may withold evidence of that pattern as well.

The simplest metric (and one still at the heart of many X.509 style systems) is the existence of a path of length bounded by n edges. Note that this metric depends on the start node, that is, the node corresponding to the user making the evaluation (or at least a node which that user trusts). The attack is equally obvious: a false edge from a good node to a bad node yields acceptance of that node from all nodes within $n - 1$ hops. Since the system must accept a vast majority of good nodes, this means that a large majority of nodes will accept the bad node.

The early work in this field proposed several metrics for evaluating trust in these networks, but lacked rigorous analysis. Examples include Tarah and Huitema, 1992 [6], Beth et al. 1994 [2], and Maurer, 1996 [3]. Later papers, such as Reiter and Stubblebine [4], and Levien and Aiken 1998 [7] analyzed these sophisticated metrics and found them to be no more attack resistant than the simple distance metric.

Reiter and Stubblebine [8] also proposed a reasonably simple metric, which is in some ways an improvement over the shortest path length metric: a certificate is accepted if there exist k independent paths from the source to the target. Thus, an attack on only a single node will not be effective. (For the sake of completeness, the Reiter-Stubblebine metric combined both the requirement of k independent paths and a bound on the length of these paths. This makes the metric more difficult to evaluate—bounded independent paths is an NP-complete problem—and the impact on security is marginal.)

However, an attack on k nodes is just as catastrophic as much simpler metrics. As networks grow in size, the possibility of compromising a small number of nodes becomes more reasonable. At the scale of the Internet, such a scheme is obviously flawed. It is not practical to increase k because of the impact on the cost of legitimate certifications.

Given the above assumptions, it's not possible to do much better. Levien and Aiken [7] derive theoretical upper bounds, which are close to the performance of a proposed trust metric also based on network flow. Through careful manipulation of capacity constraints, it's possible to improve the number of edges required for successful attack to k^2, but even so the system becomes very vulnerable as it is scaled up.

It's clear that the fundamental problem is the limited view of the graph, to just a subset of the nodes. When this assumption is relaxed, and the evaluation is done over the entire graph, it becomes possible to tightly bound the number of accepted "bad" nodes.

5.3 Group Trust Metric

If the trust metric can only evaluate a small subset of the graph relevant to the target node, then there is no way to protect against accepting many, many similar target nodes once one is accepted. This attack is now known as the Sybil attack [9], named after a book about a person with multiple personality disorders. However, this pattern is quite apparent when evaluating the entire graph. It is practical to design a trust metric that bounds the number of such nodes accepted.

The "group trust metric" of Advogato is intended to be resistant to Sybil attacks. It takes as input the entire certification graph, and outputs a set of nodes that it accepts. The number of "bad" nodes accepted is bounded by the number of edges in the certification graph from good nodes to bad.

Let us introduce this trust metric with a motivating example. Suppose that a book publisher, wishing to promote a new book, wants to give copies of that book to all members of a loosely defined community such as free software developers. Assigning a person to manually determine membership in this group would be cost-prohibitive, and would very overlook legitimate members, especially because some may be difficult to identify.

At the other extreme, simply putting up a Web form inviting people to claim their own copies would be vulnerable to a large number of people receiving the book who are not members of the community. In fact, with a Sybil attack, one individual could obtain a large number of books, for example to resell for profit.

This motivating example is given as a concrete example of several more general properties:

- Most good nodes should be accepted, that is, the cost of rejecting a good node should be considered high.
- A small number of bad nodes can be accepted, but this number should be bounded.
- The exact set of nodes chosen need not be deterministic across runs.

Given these assumptions and a reasonably accurate social graph, the Advogato "group trust metric" can compute a set of accepted nodes. The "group" designation refers both to the evaluation of the members of a group and the fact that the metric computes the entire social graph as one group, as opposed to doing separate, independent evaluations of each of the certification paths as in previous scalar trust metrics.

The group trust metric is computed in three (conceptual) steps. First, a capacity is assigned to every node as a function of the shortest path distance from the seed to that node. Second, the graph is transformed into a graph with extra edges from each node to a special "supersink" node. Finally, a maximum network flow is computed for this modified graph. Each node that has flow across its corresponding edge to the supersink is accepted by the trust metric.

The exact values for the capacities at each distance are a tunable parameter, but in general, the capacity at the seed should be approximately the total number of good nodes in the graph, and the capacity at each subsequent hop should be approximately the previous level's capacity divided by the average outdegree. The capacities are integers, and of course the capacity must be at least one or there is no chance of the node being accepted.

The transformation of the graph is shown graphically in Fig. 5.1. Each node A with capacity c_A is split into two nodes: $A-$ and $A+$. The original inedges of A become inedges of $A-$. $A-$ gets two outedges: one of capacity $c_A - 1$ to $A+$, and one of capacity 1 to $A+$. The original outedges of A become outedges of $A+$.

The transformed graph has capacity constraints attached only to edges, not to nodes, so is suitable for evaluation by standard maximum network flow algorithms such as Ford-Fulkerson. In practice, we apply the additional heuristic that each path

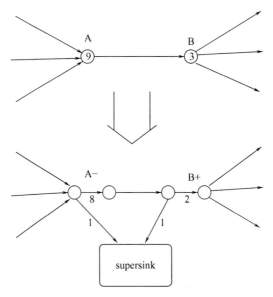

Fig. 5.1 Construction of edge-constrained network from node-constrained

chosen in the residual gr-aph for augmentation is a shortest path. Thus, an additional constraint is satisfied: for all nodes x, if there is flow from $x-$ to $x+$, then there is flow from $x-$ to the supersink.

An example of such a maximum flow and assignment is shown in Fig. 5.2. All nodes except for one (drawn with a dotted circle) have been accepted. For reference, each node is annotated with the flow into that node.

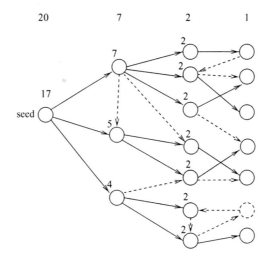

Fig. 5.2 Example of constrained flow through a trust network

Ironically, while the Advogato trust metric was never used to decide recipients of a giveaway such as described earlier, the idea of a "blog giveaway" has become popular recently. The blog owner gives away an item (often a handicraft) to a randomly chosen commenter. In the month of July 2007, the "Dog Days of Summer Bloggy Giveaway" recorded 506 such events [10]. When we ran an experimental trust metric over a social graph derived from blog comments, looking for potential spammers and Sybil attackers, a large number of these candidates turned out to be responses to the giveaway. A successful Sybil attack would result in a high probability of winning the prize, which would of course be unfair to the real readers of the blog. Thus, the group trust metric may find a real-world application similar to the thought-experiment that motivated its original design.

5.3.1 Proof of Attack Resistance

In this section, we prove the following theorem:

Theorem 1. *The number of bad nodes accepted by the above metric is bounded by* $\sum_{x \in S}(c_x - 1)$, *where S is the set of good nodes with edges to bad nodes.*

Proof outline. Consider the cut that includes all edges from good nodes to the supersink, and all edges from good nodes to bad nodes.

The flow from a good node x to a bad node cannot exceed $c_x - 1$, as the total flow into x is bounded by c_x and the above-mentioned constraint requires that there be unit flow from $x-$ to the supersink if there is any flow at all. Thus, the total number of bad nodes chosen is bounded by $\sum_{x \in S}(c_x - 1)$.

Note that the number of bad nodes accepted depends only on the number of edges from good nodes to bad nodes, not on the number of bad nodes. Thus, the trust metric is resistant to Sybil attacks.

5.4 Implementation in Advogato

To test the trust metric ideas, the Advogato Website was launched in 1999 with the network-flow based group trust metric at its heart. Advogato is primarily a community blog for free software developers, and also contains a wiki-like section for describing projects and the relationships between them.

These days, many elements of Advogato would be considered routine for community or social networking Websites, but were unusual or even controversial in late 1999 when the site was first launched. Most notably, users on Advogato were asked to input "peer certifications" through the site's UI. The site's social graph is constructed from these certifications. Advogato is an early instance of a *Social Network Site* [11], postdating the pioneering SixDegrees (1997), but coming before the current wave of social network sites such as Friendster (2002), Orkut (2004), and a huge number of newer sites.

The terminology for these social edges varies, with many sites following Friend-ster's lead designating them "friend" relationships, but other sites differ, such as LinkedIn, which calls them "connections". Advogato's choice of "certificate" derives from the literature of public key infrastructure, and may have been off-putting to early adopters, especially compared with the more affable terms adopted by other social network sites.

While the network flow trust metric is itself attack resistant, the implementation in Advogato was not. The trust metric evaluated whether users were members of the community, but then the result of this evaluation was used as simple access control. If an attacker were to become falsely accepted, they would be able to do unbounded damage, including posting spam, editing project descriptions, and so on. Even con-sidering only users who are members of the community, some users posted more than their share, often repetitive in nature. To address these, Advogato developed a second trust metric, described in detail in Section 5.5.3. This trust metric is a variant on eigenvector-based metrics, which will be discussed in the next section.

5.5 Eigenvector Trust Metrics

The original work on Advogato's trust metrics was strongly motivated by the desire to create a better public key infrastructure, as is reflected in the literature from the period. Meanwhile, other researchers focused on the problem of retrieving more relevant results from Web searching. The attack of trying to get spammy Web pages placed highly in search engine results is analogous to trying to get key/name bind-ings accepted in a public key infrastructure. Further, the link graph of the World Wide Web is analogous to a social graph.

In fact, PageRank [12] can be seen as another early example of an attack-resistant trust metric, although applied in a very different application domain. The HITS algorithm, used in the CLEVER search engine from IBM [13], was based on similar principles. Later, a number of other researchers saw the more general attack-resistance properties of eigenvector trust metrics, and applied them to other application domains such as P2P routing [14].

5.5.1 Stochastic Model of PageRank

The eigenvector formulation of PageRank is convenient for describing the algo-rithm, and for implementing it efficiently, but a simple stochastic model may be more intuitive for analysis, and for devising similar algorithms. A more detailed analysis based on Markov chains has also been published recently [15], and many of these results are also presented in an earlier academic paper [16].

The stochastic model for PageRank is as follows:

1. Begin with the token at the start node.
2. With probability 15%, stop.

3. Choose an outedge of the current node, and move the token along the edge.
4. Go to step 2.

The PageRank value assigned to each node is simply the probability that the experiment ends with the token on that node.

The algorithm generalizes easily enough to cases where start state is more than one node; it can be modeled either through the creation of a virtual start node with edges to all the real start nodes, or by choosing a start node at random from the set. There is another complication due to the fact that not all Web pages contain outedges, i.e. links to other pages. Different variants of PageRank use different approaches to deal with this issue. In the original publication of Brin et al. the graph was cleaned of these "dangling pages" before PageRank computation. However, a later presentation [17], using a stochastic model equivalent to that presented above, could include these dangling pages without difficulty.

The stochastic model also gives a more intuitive understanding of the 15% "restart probability". For each trial of the experiment, the token stops on a node at the end of a random walk of length k. With a stopping probability of 15, the distribution of k is simply a geometric distribution with an expected value of length 5.667. In general, this value should be the smallest possible that still covers most of the good pages on the Web, that is, that a random walk from the start node has a reasonably high probability of reaching the page. Obviously, determining this exact value requires empirical knowledge about the link graph, but it has been long held that six degrees of separation are sufficient to connect an entire global-scale network to a centrally located node, and the recent study of scale-free networks [18] makes these results more systematic.

5.5.2 Attack Resistance of PageRank

PageRank is indeed an attack-resistant trust metric, and fulfills the bottleneck property. A brief sketch establishing its attack resistance follows.

Assume for the sake of simplification that all Web pages have the same probability p_g that an outedge is a good page, that is, that the number of edges from good nodes to bad nodes is $(1 - p_g)/p_g$ times the number of edges from good nodes to other good nodes. In the real Web, of course, this distribution will be more heterogeneous, but this will not greatly affect the results; in fact, under the assumption that more "authoritative" Web sites are less likely to link to spam than a typical Website, and that these authoritative Websites are relatively more likely to appear in short walks from the start node, the actual performance will be better than this analysis.

Also assume that, in the worst case, all outedges from bad nodes point to other bad nodes. This is a reasonable assumption, because those edges are under the control of the attacker. Even if bad nodes contain edges to good nodes, this analysis is conservative, as such edges can only increase the probability that the token will land on a good node, and decrease the probability that it will land on a bad one.

Then, the probability $p[k]$ that a node is good at the end of a walk of length k is bad is straightforward to compute:

$$p[k] = p_g(1 - p[k-1])$$

In other words, the next hop in the walk is good if the previous hop was good and there is an edge from that good node to a another bad node (with probability p_g). Straightforward algebra yields (assuming that the start node is good, i.e. $p[0] = 1$):

$$p[k] = p_g^k$$

The total probability that the token will land on a node is a weighted sum over all path lengths. Thus, the probability that the token will end on a good node can be computed straightforwardly:

$$\begin{aligned}
p_{pr} &= \sum_k p_{stop} p[k](1 - p_{stop})^k \\
&= \sum k p_{stop}(p_g(1 - p_{stop}))^k \\
&= \frac{p_{stop}}{1 - p_g(1 - p_{stop})}
\end{aligned}$$

A direct result of this analysis is that the probability of the token landing on a good node scales roughly linearly with the stopping probability. Therefore, it makes sense to set this probability as high as possible while still ensuring that the distribution of walk lengths still ends up covering most of the good nodes in the graph.

Note that this analysis only establishes a bound on the sum of the PageRank values assigned to bad nodes. An attacker may be able to get a relatively large PageRank value attached to a single node by introducing many links to that node. Indeed, this is the technique used in the popular sport of "Googlebombing," to which ordinary PageRank is vulnerable. Google now implements a separate algorithmic defence against this attack [19].

5.5.3 Advogato's Eigenvector Metric

Advogato's first trust metric achieved its goals of identifying the members of the community reasonably accurately, but solving that problem did not lead directly to a good user experience. Sturgeon's Law applies even when restricted to community members. To address the problem of displaying only *interesting* blogs, Advogato implemented a second trust metric, based on eigenvectors, specifically for evaluating how interesting a blog is.

This trust metric could be used as a generic metadata engine, but as implemented, the only application was rating the quality of blogs. As in the analsysis of PageRank, a formulation in terms of a stochastic model is most intuitive.

The inputs to the trust metric consist of both a social graph and a set of *assertions*. An assertion is a triple consisting of the node id corresponding to the user making the assertion, a key, and a value. In the Advogato implementation, the key is simply the id of a blog, and the value is a quality evaluation on a 1–10 scale. In this implementation, the space of keys corresponds one to one with the node ids of the social graph, but this need not be the case. In a different application, the keys could just as easily represented songs, wines, or any other entity being evaluated.

The stochastic algorithm is as follows:

1. Begin with the token at the source node in the graph.
2. If the node contains an assertion matching the key, stop.
3. With probability 15%, stop.
4. Choose an outedge of the current node, and move the token along the edge.
5. Go to step 2.

The result is a probability distribution of values for the assertions matched. The probability that the token ends on any assertion can be interpreted as a *confidence value*, and the weighted mean of the values is the judgment of the trust metric. Other statistics on this probability distribution may also be computed. For example, the variance may be a measure of controversy.

The actual computation of this trust metric was done using a technique similar to the standard power method for computing eigenvectors in PageRank-style applications. Because the result of the trust metric varies depending on the start node, the amount of computation increases significantly as the system scales. Partly because of these limitations, the deployment was not very aggressive. In particular, only logged in users were able to retrieve an aggregated blog filtered by the trust metric's ratings.

Unfortunately, this trust metric has not yet been evaluated systematically, but anecdotally it seems to perform well. Characterizing this performance more formally would make an excellent topic for future research.

This algorithm is also similar in many respects to Golbeck's TidalTrust [20]. As in TidalTrust, short paths in the trust network have a much greater contribution to the computed trust values than longer paths. Golbeck confirms that algorithms implementing this heuristic are more likely to make accurate predictions: "TidalTrust strictly adheres to the observed characteristics of trust: shorter paths and higher trust values lead to better accuracy." However, TidalTrust is based on breadth-first graph traversal, rather than the eigenvector framework common to PageRank and Advogato's second metric.

References

1. Jacob L. Moreno and H. H. Jennings. *Who shall survive?: A New Appproach to the Problem of Human Interrelations.* Nervous and Mental Disease Publishing Co., 1934.
2. Thomas Beth, Malte Borcherding, and Birgit Klein. Valuation of trust in open networks. *Lecture Notes in Computer Science*, 875:3–18, 1994.

3. Ueli Maurer. Modelling a public-key infrastreucture. In E. Bertino, H. Kurth, G. Martella, and E. Montolivo, editors, *Computer Security-ESORICS '96*, number 1146 in LNCS, Springer Verlag, 1996.
4. Michael Reiter and Stuart Stubblebine. Toward acceptable metrics of authentication. In *Proceedings of the 1997 IEEE Symposium on Security and Privacy*, 1997.
5. Neal McBurnett. Pgp Web of trust statistics, 1996.
6. Anas Tarah and Christian Huitema. Associating metrics to certification paths. In *European Symposium on Research in Computer Security (ESORICS)*, pp. 175–192, 1992.
7. Raph Levien and Alexander Aiken. Attack resistant trust metrics for public key certification. In *7th USENIX Security Symposium*, San Antonio, Texas, January 1998.
8. Micheal Reiter and Stuart Stubblebine. Path independence for authentication in large-scale systems. In *Proceedings of the 4th ACM Conference on Computer and Communications Security*, 1997.
9. John R. Douceur. the Sybil attack. In *Proceedings of the 1st International Workshop on Peer-to-Peer Systems*, March 2002.
10. Rocks in My Dryer. Dog days of summer bloggy giveaway, July 2007.
11. danah m. boyd and Nicole B. Ellison. Social network sites: Definition, histroy, and scholarship. *Journal of Computer-Mediated Communication*, 13(1), 2007.
12. Lawrence Page, Sergey Brin, Rajeev Motwani, and Terry Winograd. The PageRank citation ranking: Bringing order to the Web. Technical report, Stanford University, 1998.
13. Jon M. Kleinberg. Authoritative sources in a hyperlinked environment. *Journal of the ACM*, 46(5):604–632, 1999.
14. Sepandar D. Kamcar, Mario T. Schlosser, and Hector Garcia-Molina. The EigenTrust algorithm for reputation management in P2P networks, 2003.
15. Amy N. Langville and Carl D. Meyer. *Google's PageRank and Beyond: The Science of Search Engine Rankings*. Princeton University Press, 2006.
16. Amy N. Langville and Carl D. Meyer. Deeper inside PageRank. *Internet Mathematics*, 1: 335–400, 2004.
17. Monica Bianchini, Marco Gori, and Franco Scarelli. Inside PageRank. *Lecture Notes in Computer Technology*, 5(1):92–128, February 2005.
18. Albert-László Barábasi. *Linked: How Everything is Connected to Everything Else and What It Means*. Perseus Books, 2002.
19. Matt Cutts, Ryan Moulton, and Kendra Carattini. A quick word about Googlebombs. Official GoogleWebmaster Central Blog, January 2007.
20. Jennifer Ann Golbeck. *Computing and applying trust in Web-based social networks*. PhD thesis, University of Maryland at College Park, College park, MD, USA, 2005. Chair-James Hendler.

Chapter 6
On Propagating Interpersonal Trust in Social Networks

Cai-Nicolas Ziegler

Abstract The age of information glut has fostered the proliferation of data and documents on the Web, created by man and machine alike. Hence, there is an enormous wealth of minable knowledge that is yet to be extracted, in particular, on the Semantic Web. However, besides understanding information stated by subjects, knowing about their credibility becomes equally crucial. Hence, trust and trust metrics, conceived as computational means to evaluate trust relationships between individuals, come into play. Our major contribution to Semantic Web trust management through this work is twofold. First, we introduce a classification scheme for trust metrics along various axes and discuss advantages and drawbacks of existing approaches for Semantic Web scenarios. Hereby, we devise an advocacy for local group trust metrics, guiding us to the second part, which presents Appleseed, our novel proposal for local group trust computation. Compelling in its simplicity, Appleseed borrows many ideas from spreading activation models in psychology and relates their concepts to trust evaluation in an intuitive fashion. Moreover, we provide extensions for the Appleseed nucleus that make our trust metric handle distrust statements.

6.1 Introduction

In our world of information overload and global connectivity leveraged through the Web and other types of media, social trust [34] between individuals becomes an invaluable and precious good. Hereby, trust exerts an enormous impact on decisions whether to believe or disbelieve information asserted by other peers. Belief should only be accorded to statements from people we deem trustworthy. Hence, trust assumes the role of an instrument for complexity reduction [30]. However, when supposing huge networks such as the Semantic Web, trust judgements based on personal experience and acquaintanceship become unfeasible. In general, we accord trust, concisely defined by Mui as the "subjective expectation an agent has about

C.-N. Ziegler (✉)
Siemens AG, Corporate Technology, Otto-Hahn-Ring 6, Geb. 31, Raum 260,
D-81730 München, Germany
e-mail: cai.ziegler@siemens.com

J. Golbeck (ed.), *Computing with Social Trust,* Human-Computer Interaction Series,
DOI 10.1007/978-1-84800-356-9_6 © Springer-Verlag London Limited 2009

another's future behavior based on the history of their encounters" [36], to only small numbers of people. These people, again, trust another limited set of people, and so forth. The network structure emanating from our very person, composed of trust statements linking individuals, constitutes the basis for trusting people we do not know personally. Playing an important role for the conception of Semantic Web trust infrastructure, the latter structure has been dubbed "Web of Trust" [13].

Its effectiveness has been underpinned through empirical evidence from social psychology and sociology, indicating that transitivity is an important characteristic of social networks [19, 39]. To the extent that communication between individuals becomes motivated through positive effect, drive towards transitivity can also be explained in terms of Heider's famous "balance theory" [18], that is, individuals are more prone to interact with friends of friends than unknown peers.

Hence, we might be tempted to adopt the policy of trusting all those people who are trusted by persons we trust, exploiting transitivity in social networks. Trust would thus propagate through the network and become accorded whenever two individuals can reach each other via at least one trust path. However, common sense tells us we should not rely upon this strategy. More complex metrics are needed in order to more sensibly evaluate trust between two persons. Among other features, these metrics must take into account subtle social and psychological aspects of trust and suffice criteria of computability and scalability, likewise.

The paper is organized as follows. In order to assess diverse properties of metrics, Section 6.2.1 briefly introduces existing trust metrics and classifies them according to our proposed classification scheme. An investigation of trust metric classes and their fitness for Semantic Web scenarios follows in Section 6.2.2, along with an overview of our asserted trust model. Besides, Section 6.2.2 exposes the urging need

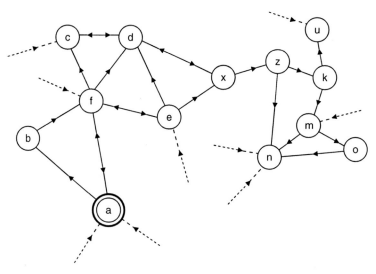

Fig. 6.1 Sample web of trust for agent *a*

for *local group* trust metrics and gives examples of possible application scenarios. Section 6.3 forms the second part of the paper and explicitly deals with these local group trust metrics. We briefly sketch the well-known Advogato trust metric and introduce our novel Appleseed trust metric in Section 6.3.2. Appleseed constitutes the major contribution of this paper and represents our own approach to local group trust computation. Many of its ideas and concepts borrow from spreading activation models, which simulate human semantic memory. Section 6.3.3 matches Appleseed and Advogato against each other, discussing advantages and drawbacks of either approach. Furthermore, results of experiments conducted to evaluate the behavior of Appleseed under diverse conditions are illustrated in Section 6.3.4. Section 6.3.5 indicates possible modifications and gives some implementation details, while Section 6.3.6 briefly presents the testbed we used to base all our experiments and comparisons upon. Eventually, in Section 6.4.1, semantics and implications of distrust are discussed, followed by the integration of distrust into the Appleseed framework in Section 6.4.2.

6.2 Trust in Social Networks

Trust represents an invaluable and precious good one should award deliberately. Trust metrics compute quantitative *estimates* of how much trust an agent a should accord to its peer b, taking into account trust ratings from other persons on the network. These metrics should also act "deliberately", not overly awarding trust to persons or agents whose trustworthiness is questionable.

6.2.1 Classification of Trust Metrics

Applications for trust metrics and trust management [5] are rife and not confined to the Semantic Web. First proposals for metrics date back to the early nineties, where trust metrics were deployed in various projects to support the Public Key Infrastructure [49]. Metrics proposed in [27, 41, 33, 4] count among the most popular ones for public key authentication and have initiated fruitful discussions. New areas and research fields apart from PKI have come to make trust metrics gain momentum. Peer-to-peer networks, ubiquitous and mobile computing, and rating systems for online communities, where maintenance of explicit certification authorities is not feasible anymore, have raised the research interest in trust. The whole plethora of available metrics can hereby be defined and characterized along various classification axes. We identify three principal dimensions with distinctive features. These axes are not orthogonal, though, for various features impose restrictions on the feature range of other dimensions. Mind that some of the below-mentioned categories have already been defined in prior work. For instance, Guha [15] differentiates between local and global trust, and distinctive features between scalar and group trust metrics are discussed in [26]. However, to our knowledge, no explicit

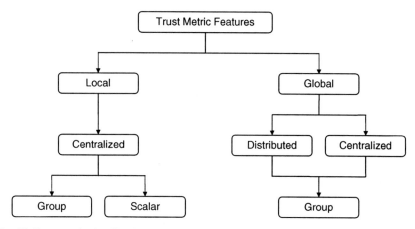

Fig. 6.2 Trust metric classification

categorization of trust metrics along various axes, supplemented with an analysis of axis interaction, exists. We therefore regard the classification scheme provided below as one major contribution of this paper. Its results are also summarized in Fig. 6.2.

6.2.1.1 Network Perspective

The first dimension influences semantics assigned to the values computed. Trust metrics may basically be subdivided into ones with *global* and ones with scope. Global trust metrics take into account *all* peers and trust links connecting them. Global trust ranks are assigned to an individual based upon complete trust graph information. Many global trust metrics, such as those presented in [23,15, 42] borrow their ideas from the renowned PageRank algorithm [37] to compute Web page reputation. The basic intuition behind the approach is that nodes should be ranked higher the better the rank of nodes pointing to them. Obviously, the latter approach works for trust and page reputation likewise.

Trust metrics with local scope, on the other hand, take into account personal bias. Interestingly, some researchers claim that only local trust metrics are "true" trust metrics, since global ones compute overall reputation rather than personalized trust[1] [36]. Local trust metrics take the agent for whom to compute trust as an additional input parameter and are able to operate on *partial* trust graph information. The rationale behind local trust metrics is that persons an agent *a* trusts may be completely different from the range of individuals that agent *b* deems trustworthy. Local trust metrics exploit structural information defined by personalized webs of trust. Hereby, the personal web of trust for individual *a* is given through the set of trust relationships emanating from *a* and passing through nodes it trusts either

---

[1] Recall the definition of trust given before, telling that trust is a "subjective expectation".

directly or indirectly, as well as the set of nodes reachable through these relationships. Merging all Webs of trust engenders the global trust graph. Local trust metrics comprise Levien's Advogato trust metric [28], metrics for modeling the Public Key Infrastructure [4, 33, 41] Golbeck's metrics for Semantic Web trust [13], and Sun Microsystems's Poblano architecture [7]. The latter work hereby strongly resembles Abdul-Rahman and Hailes [1].

6.2.1.2 Computation Locus

The second axis refers to the place where trust relationships between individuals are evaluated and quantified. Local[2] or centralized approaches perform all computations in one single machine and hence need to be granted full access to relevant trust information. The trust data itself may hereby be distributed over the network. Most of the before-mentioned metrics count among the class of centralized approaches.

Distributed metrics for the computation of trust and reputation, such as those described in [42, 23, 43], equally deploy the load of computation on every trust node in the network. Upon receiving trust information from its predecessor nodes in the trust graph, an agent a merges the data with its own trust assertions and propagates synthesized values to its successor nodes. The entire process of trust computation is necessarily asynchronous and its convergence depends on the eagerness or laziness of nodes to propagate information. Another characteristic feature of distributed trust metrics refers to the fact that they are inherently global. Though the individual computation load is decreased with respect to centralized computation approaches, nodes need to store trust information about *any other* node in the system.

6.2.1.3 Link Evaluation

The third dimension distinguishes scalar and group trust metrics. According to Levien [26], scalar metrics analyze trust assertions independently, while group trust metrics evaluate groups of assertions "in tandem". PageRank [37] and related approaches count among global group trust metrics, for the reputation of one page depends on the ranks of referring pages, thus entailing parallel evaluation of relevant nodes thanks to mutual dependencies. Advogato [28] represents an example for local group trust metrics. Most other trust metrics count among the category of scalar ones, tracking trust paths from sources to targets and not performing parallel evaluations of groups of trust assertions. Hence, another basic difference between scalar and group trust metrics refers to their functional design. In general, scalar metrics compute trust between two given individuals a and b taken from set V of all agents.

On the other hand, group trust metrics generally compute trust ranks for *sets* of individuals in V. Hereby, global group trust metrics assign trust ranks for every $a \in V$, while local ones may also return ranked subsets of V. Note that complete

---

[2] Mind that in this context, "local" refers to the *place of computation* and not network perspective.

trust graph information is only important for *global* group trust metrics, but not for *local* ones. Informally, local group trust metrics may be defined as metrics to compute *neighborhoods* of trusted peers for an individual a. As input parameters, these trust metrics take an individual $a \in V$ for which to compute the set of peers it should trust, as well as an amount of trust the latter wants to share among the most trustworthy agents. For instance, in [28], the amount of trust is said to correspond to the number of agents that a wants to trust. The output is hence given by a trusted subset of V.

Note that scalar trust metrics are inherently local, while group trust metrics do not impose any restrictions on features for other axes.

6.2.2 Semantic Web Trust

Most presented metrics and trust models have been proposed for scenarios other than the Semantic Web. In fact, research in trust infrastructure and metrics for the latter network of metadata still has to come of age and gain momentum. Before discussing specific requirements and fitness properties of trust metrics along those axes proposed before, we need to define one common trust model on which to rely upon for the Semantic Web. Some steps towards one such common model have already been taken and incorporated into the FOAF [8] project. FOAF is an abbreviation for "Friend of a Friend" and aims at enriching personal homepages with machine-readable content encoded in RDF statements. Besides various other information, these publicly accessible pages allow their owners to nominate all individuals part of the FOAF universe they know, thus weaving a "web of acquaintances" [13]. Golbeck has extended the FOAF schema to also contain *trust* assertions with values ranging from 1 to 9, where 1 denotes complete distrust and 9 absolute trust towards the individual for which the assertion has been issued [13]. Hereby, her assumption that trust and distrust represent symmetrically opposed concepts perfectly aligns with Abdul-Rahman and Hailes's work [2].

The model that we adopt is quite similar to FOAF and its extensions, but only captures the notion of trust and lack of trust, instead of trust and distrust. Note that zero trust and distrust are *not* the same [32] and may hence not be intermingled. Explicit modeling of distrust has some serious implications for trust metrics and will hence be discussed separately in Section 6.4. Mind that only few research endeavors investigated the implementation of distrust into trust models, for example, Jøsang et al. [21] and Guha [15, 16].

6.2.2.1 Trust Model

In this section, we present the constituents of our model for the Semantic Web trust infrastructure. As is the case for FOAF, we assume that all trust information is publicly accessible for any agent in the system through machine-readable personal homepages distributed over the network. This assumption may yield privacy concerns and will be discussed and justified later.

- **Agent set** $V = \{a_1, \ldots, a_n\}$. Similar to the FOAF approach, we assume agents $a \in V$ to be represented and uniquely identified by the URI of their machine-readable personal homepage.
- **Partial trust function set** $T = \{W_{a_1}, \ldots, W_{a_n}\}$. Every agent a is associated with one partial trust function $W_a : V \rightarrow [0, 1]^{\perp}$, which corresponds to the set of trust assertions that a has stated on its machine-readable homepage. In most cases, these functions will be very sparse as the number of individuals for which an agent is able to assign explicit trust ratings is much smaller than the total number n of agents on the Semantic Web:

$$W_{a_i}(a_j) = \begin{cases} p, & \text{if } \text{trust}(a_i, a_j) = p \\ \perp, & \text{if no rating for } a_j \text{ from } a_i \end{cases}$$

Note that the higher the value of $W_{a_i}(a_j)$, the more trustworthy a_i deems a_j. Conversely, $W_{a_i}(a_j) = 0$ means that a_i considers a_j to be not trustworthy at all. The assignment of trust through continuous values between 0 and 1 and their adopted semantics is in perfect accordance with [31], where possible stratifications of trust values are proposed. Our trust model defines one directed trust graph with nodes being represented by agents $a \in V$ and directed edges from nodes a_i to nodes a_j being trust statements with weight $W_{a_i}(a_j)$.

For convenience, we furthermore introduce the partial function $W : V \times V \rightarrow [0, 1]^{\perp}$, which we define as the union of all partial functions $W_a \in T$.

6.2.2.2 Trust Metrics for the Semantic Web

Trust and reputation ranking metrics have primarily been used for public key certification [40, 41, 27, 33, 4] rating and reputation systems part of online communities [15, 28, 26], peer-to-peer networks [23, 43, 25, 24, 3] and also mobile computing fields [9]. Each of these scenarios favors different trust metrics. For instance, reputation systems for online communities tend to make use of centralized trust servers that compute global trust values for all users on the system [15]. On the other hand, peer-to-peer networks of moderate size rely upon distributed approaches that are in most cases based upon PageRank [23, 43].

The Semantic Web, however, is expected to be made up of millions of nodes a representing agents. The fitness of *distributed* approaches to trust metric computation, such as depicted in [42] and [23], is hence limited by virtue of various reasons:

- **Trust data storage.** Each agent a needs to store trust information about any other agent b on the Semantic Web. Agent a uses this information in order to merge it with own trust beliefs and propagates the synthesized information to trusted agents. Even though we might expect the size of the Semantic Web to be several orders of magnitude smaller than the traditional Web, the number of agents which to keep trust information for will still exceed storage capabilities of "normal" agents.

- **Convergence.** The structure of the Semantic Web is diffuse and not subject to some higher ordering principle or hierarchy. Furthermore, the process of trust propagation is necessarily asynchronous. As the Semantic Web is huge in size with possibly numerous antagonist or idle agents, convergence of trust values might take a very long time.

The huge advantage of distributed approaches, on the other hand, is the immediate availability of computed trust information for any other agent in the system as well as the fact that agents have to disclose their trust assertions only to peers they trust [42]. For instance, suppose that a declares its trust in b to be 0.1, which is very low. Hence, a might want b not to know about that fact. As distributed metrics only propagate synthesized trust values from nodes to successor nodes in the trust graph, a would not have to disclose its trust statements to b.

As it comes to centralized, that is, locally computed, metrics, full trust information access is required for agents inferring trust. Hence, online communities based on trust require their users to disclose all trust information to the community server, but not necessarily to other peers [15]. Privacy is thus maintained. On the Semantic Web and in the area of ubiquitous and mobile computing, however, it is not only some central authority which computes trust. Any agent might want to do so. Our own trust model, as well as trust models proposed in [1, 9, 13], are hence based upon the assumption of publicly available trust information. Though privacy concerns may persist, this assumption is vital due to the mentioned deficiencies of distributed computation models. Moreover, centralized *global* metrics, such as depicted in [15, 37], also fail to fit the requirements imposed by the Semantic Web: due to the huge number of agents issuing trust statements, only dedicated server clusters could be able to manage the whole bulk of trust relationships. For small agents and applications roaming the Semantic Web, global trust computation is not feasible.

The traditional as well as the Semantic Web bear significant traits of small-world networks [13]. Small worlds theory has been investigated extensively by Stanley Milgram, social psychologist at Harvard University. His hypothesis, commonly referred to as "six degrees of separation", states that members of any large social network are connected to each other through short chains of intermediate acquaintances [14]. Relating his research results to trust on the Semantic Web, we come to conclude that average trust path lengths between any two individuals are small. Hence, locally computed *local* trust metrics considering trust paths from trust sources to trust targets, such as the ones proposed for PKI [4, 27, 33, 40, 41], may be expected to suitably lend themselves to the Semantic Web. In contrast to global metrics, no clustering of massive CPU power is required to compute trust.

Besides centrally computed *scalar* trust metrics taking into account personal bias, we advocate *local group* trust metrics for the Semantic Web. These metrics bear several welcome properties with respect to computability and complexity, which may be summarized as follows:

- **Partial trust graph exploration.** Global metrics require a priori full knowledge of the entire trust network. Distributed metrics store trust values for all agents in the system, thus implying massive data storage demands. On the other hand, when computing trusted *neighborhoods*, the trust network only needs to be explored partially: originating from the trust source, one only follows those trust edges that seem promising, that is, bearing high trust weights, and which are not too far away from the trust source. Inspection of personal, machine-readable homepages is thus performed in a just-in-time fashion. Hence, prefetching bulk trust information is not required.
- **Computational scalability.** Tightly intertwined with partial trust graph exploration is computational complexity. Local group trust metrics scale well to any social network size, as only tiny subsets of relatively constant size[3] are visited. This is not the case for global trust metrics.

By the time of this writing, local group trust metrics have been subject to comparatively sparse research interest and none, to our best knowledge, have been proposed for the Semantic Web. However, we believe that local group trust metrics will play an important role for trust-based communities on the Semantic Web. Application scenarios for group trust are rife. In order to not go beyond the scope of this article, we will give just one detailed example dealing with trust in metadata statements:

The Semantic Web basically consists of metadata assertions that machines can understand by virtue of ontology sharing. However, since the number of agents able to publish statements is vast, credibility in those statements should be limited. The issue of trust in Semantic Web content has already been addressed in [12]. Herein, the authors propose a centralized system which allows issuing statements and analyzing their reliability and credibility. Complementary to this work by Gil and Ratnakar, the W3C Annotea Project intends to provide an infrastructure for assigning annotations to statements [22]. These statements could also include statements about the credibility of certain metadata. Supposing such an environment and supposing an agent a who wants to reason about the credibility of an assertion s found on the Semantic Web, local group trust metrics could play an important role in its quest: not being able to judge the credibility of s on its own, a could refer to its personal Web of trust and compute its n most trusted peers. The latter trust neighborhood is now taking part in an opinion poll where a wants to know about the credibility its trusted peers assign to s. Technically, this could be achieved by searching Annotea servers for statements by a's peers about s. The eventual decision whether to believe s or not could then be made by averaging the credibility ratings of its trusted peers. Similar models with distributed reputation systems based on trust have been proposed in [25].

---

[3] Supposing identical parameterizations for the metrics in use, as well as similar network structures.

6.3 Local Group Trust Metrics

Local group trust metrics, in their function as means to compute trust neighbor-hoods, have not been subject to mainstream research until now. Actually, significant research has been limited to the work done by Levien [26, 27] having conceived the Advogato group trust metric. This section provides an overview of Advogato and introduces our own Appleseed trust metric, eventually comparing both approaches.

6.3.1 Outline of Advogato Maxflow

The Advogato maximum flow trust metric has been proposed by Levien [28] in order to discover which users are trusted by members of an online community and which are not. Hereby, trust is computed by a centralized community server and considered relative to a seed of users enjoying supreme trust. However, the metric is not only applicable to community servers, but also to *arbitrary* agents which may compute *personalized* lists of trusted peers and not one single global ranking for the whole community they belong to. In this case, the agent itself constitutes the singleton trust seed. The following paragraphs briefly introduce basic concepts. For more detailed information, refer to [26, 27, 28].

6.3.1.1 Trust Computation Steps

Local group trust metrics compute sets of agents trusted by those being part of the trust seed. In case of Advogato, its input is given by an integer number n, which is supposed to be equal to the number of members to trust [28], as well as the trust seed s, being a subset of the entire set of users V. The output is a characteristic function that maps each member to a boolean value indicating trustworthiness:

$$\text{Trust}_M : 2^V \times \mathbb{N}_0^+ \to (V \to \{\text{true, false}\})$$

The trust model underlying Advogato does *not* provide support for weighted trust relationships in its original version.[4] Hence, trust edges extending from individual x to y express blind, that is, full, trust of x in y. Metrics for PKI maintenance suppose similar models. Maximum integer network flow computation [10] was investigated by Reiter and Stubblebine [41, 40], in order to make trust metrics more reliable. Levien adopted and extended this approach for group trust in his Advogato metric:

Capacities $C_V : V \to \mathbb{N}$ are assigned to every community member $x \in V$ based upon the shortest-path distance from the seed to x. Hereby, the capacity of the seed itself is given by the input parameter n mentioned earlier, whereas the capacity of each successive distance level is equal to the capacity of the previous

---

[4] Though various levels of peer certification exist, their proposed interpretation does not corre-spond to weighted trust relationships.

level l divided by the average outdegree of trust edges $e \in E$ extending from l. The trust graph obtained hence contains one single source, which is the set of seed nodes considered one single "virtual" node, and multiple sinks, that is, all nodes other than those defining the seed. Capacities $C_V(x)$ constrain nodes. In order to apply Ford-Fulkerson maximum integer network flow [10], the underlying problem has to be formulated as single-source/single-sink, having capacities $C_E : E \rightarrow \mathbb{N}$ constrain edges instead of nodes. Hence, Algorithm 1 is applied to the old directed graph $G = (V, E, C_V)$, resulting in a new graph structure $G' = (V', E', C_{E'})$.

```
function transform (G = (V, E, C_V)) {
    set E' ← ∅, V' ← ∅;
    for all x ∈ V do
        add node x⁺ to V';
        add node x⁻ to V';
        if C_V(x) ≥ 1 then
            add edge (x⁻, x⁺) to E';
            set C_E'(x⁻, x⁺) ← C_V(x) − 1;
            for all (x, y) ∈ E do
                add edge (x⁺, y⁻) to E';
                set C_E'(x⁺, y⁻) ← ∞;
            end do
            add edge (x⁻, supersink) to E';
            set C_E'(x⁻, supersink) ← 1;
        end if
    end do
    return G' = (V', E', C_E');
}
```

Alg. 1. Trust graph conversion

Figure 6.3 depicts the outcome of converting node-constrained single-source/-multiple-sink graphs into single-source/single-sink ones with capacities constraining edges.

Conversion is followed by simple integer maximum network flow computation from the trust seed to the super-sink. Eventually, trusted agents x are exactly those peers for which there is flow from "negative" nodes x^- to the super-sink. An additional constraint needs to be introduced, requiring flow from x^- to the super-sink whenever there is flow from x^- to x^+. The latter constraint assures that node x does not only serve as an intermediate for the flow to pass through, but is actually added to the list of trusted agents when reached by network flow. However, the standard implementation of Ford-Fulkerson traces shortest paths to the sink first [10]. Therefore, the above constraint is satisfied implicitly already.

Example 1 (Advogato trust computation) Suppose the trust graph depicted in Fig. 6.3. The only seed node is a with initial capacity $C_V(a) = 5$. Hence, taking into account the outdegree of a, nodes at unit distance from the seed, that is, nodes

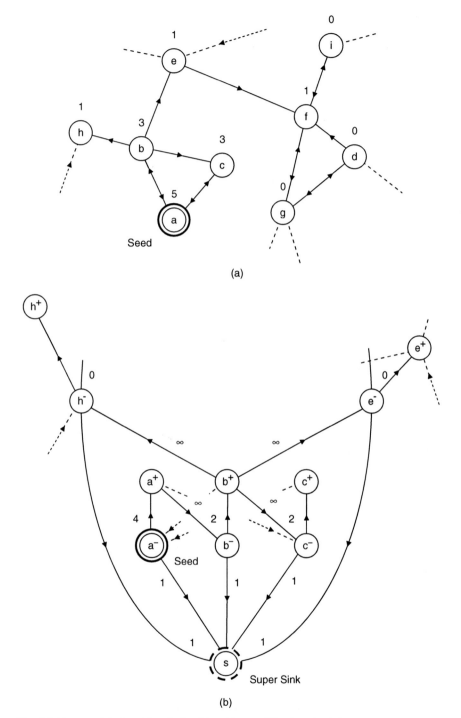

Fig. 6.3 Trust graph before (**a**) and after (**b**) making modifications for Advogato

b and c, are assigned capacities $C_V(b) = 3$ and $C_V(c) = 3$, respectively. The average outdegree of both nodes is 2.5 so that second level nodes e and h obtain unit capacity. When computing maximum integer network flow, agent a will accept itself, b, c, e, and h as trustworthy peers.

6.3.1.2 Attack-Resistance Properties

Advogato has been designed with resistance against massive attacks from malicious agents outside of the community in mind. Therefore, an upper bound for the number of "bad" peers chosen by the metric is provided in [28], along with an informal security proof to underpin its fitness. Resistance against malevolent users trying to break into the community may already be observed in the example depicted by Fig. 6.1, supposing node n to be "bad": though agent n is trusted by numerous persons, it is deemed less trustworthy than, for instance, x. While there are fewer agents trusting x, these agents enjoy higher trust reputation[5] than the numerous persons trusting n. Hence, it is not just the *number* of agents trusting an individual i, but also the trust *reputation* of these agents that exerts an impact on the trust assigned to i. PageRank [37] works in a similar fashion and has been claimed to possess similar properties of attack-resistance like the Advogato trust metric [26]. In order to make the concept of attack-resistance more tangible, Levien proposes the "bottleneck property" as common feature of attack-resistant trust metrics. Informally, this property states that the "trust quantity accorded to an edge $s \rightarrow t$ is not significantly affected by changes to the successors of t" [26]. Moreover, attack-resistance features of various trust metrics are discussed in detail in [27, 45].

6.3.2 Appleseed Trust Metric

The Appleseed trust metric constitutes the main contribution of this work and is our novel proposal for local group trust metrics. In contrast to Advogato, being inspired by maximum network flow computation, the basic intuition of Appleseed is motivated by spreading activation models. Spreading activation models have first been proposed by Quillian [38] in order to simulate human comprehension through semantic memory. They are commonly described as "models of retrieval from long-term memory in which activation subdivides among paths emanating from an activated mental representation" [44]. By the time of this writing, the seminal work of Quillian has been ported to a whole plethora of other disciplines, such as latent semantic indexing [6] and text illustration [17]. As an example, we will briefly introduce the spreading activation approach adopted in [6] for semantic search in contextual network graphs in order to then relate Appleseed to the former work.

---

[5] With respect to seed node a.

6.3.2.1 Searches in Contextual Network Graphs

The graph model underlying search strategies in contextual network graphs is almost identical in structure to the one presented in Section 6.2.2.1, that is, edges $(x, y) \in E \subseteq V \times V$ connecting nodes $x, y \in V$. Edges are assigned continuous weights through $W : E \rightarrow [0, 1]$. Source node s to start the search from is activated through an injection of energy e, which is then propagated to other nodes along edges according to some set of simple rules: all energy is fully divided among successor nodes with respect to their normalized local edge weight, that in, the higher the weight of an edge $(x, y) \in E$, the higher the portion of energy that flows along that edge. Furthermore, supposing average outdegrees greater than one, the closer node x to the injection source s, and the more paths leading from s to x, the higher the amount of energy flowing into x. To eliminate endless, marginal and negligible flow, energy streaming into node x must exceed threshold T in order not to run dry. The described approach is captured formally by Algorithm 2, which propagates energy recursively.

$$
\begin{aligned}
&\textbf{procedure } \text{energize} (e \in \mathbb{R}_0^+, s \in V) \; \{ \\
&\quad \text{energy}(s) \leftarrow \text{energy}(s) + e; \\
&\quad e' \leftarrow e \, / \, \textstyle\sum_{(s,n)\in E} W(s, n); \\
&\quad \textbf{if } e > T \textbf{ then} \\
&\quad\quad \forall (s, n) \in E : \text{energize} (e' \cdot W(s, n), n); \\
&\quad \textbf{end if} \\
&\}
\end{aligned}
$$

Alg. 2. Recursive energy propagation

6.3.2.2 Trust Propagation

Algorithm 2 shows the basic intuition behind spreading activation models. In order to tailor these models to trust computation, later to become the Appleseed trust metric, serious adaptations are necessary. For instance, procedure energize(e, s) registers *all* energy e that passed through node x, accumulated in energy(x). Hence, energy(x) represents the *rank* of x. Higher values indicate higher node rank. However, at the same time, all energy contributing to the rank of x is passed *without loss* to its successor nodes. Interpreting energy ranks as trust ranks thus implies numerous issues of semantic consistency as well as computability. Consider the graph depicted on the left-hand side of Fig. 6.4. Applying spreading activation according to [6], trust ranks of nodes b and d will be identical. However, common sense tells us that d should be accorded *less* trust than b, since its shortest-path distance to the trust seed is higher. Trust decay is commonly agreed upon [15, 21], for people tend to trust individuals trusted by immediate friends more than individuals trusted only by friends of friends. The right-hand side of Fig. 6.4 entails even more

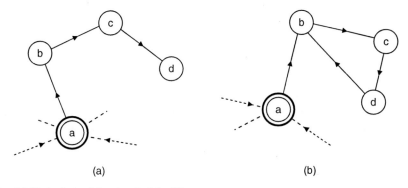

Fig. 6.4 Node chains (**a**) and rank sinks (**b**)

serious implications. All energy, or trust,[6] respectively, distributed along edge (a, b) becomes trapped in a cycle and will never be accorded to any other nodes but those being part of that cycle, that is., b, c, and d. These nodes will eventually acquire infinite trust rank. Obviously, the bottleneck property [26] does not hold. Similar issues occur with simplified versions of PageRank [37], where cycles accumulating infinite rank are dubbed "rank sinks".

6.3.2.3 Spreading Factor

We handle both issues, that is, trust decay in node chains and the elimination of rank sinks, by tailoring the algorithm to rely upon our global spreading factor d. Hereby, let in(x) denote the energy influx into node x. Parameter d then denotes the portion of energy $d \cdot$ in(x) that the latter node distributes among successors, while retaining $(1-d) \cdot$ in(x) for itself. For instance, suppose $d = 0.85$ and energy quantity in$(x) = 5.0$ flowing into node x. Then, the total energy distributed to successor nodes amounts to 4.25, while energy rank energy(x) of x increases by 0.75. Special treatment is necessary for nodes with zero outdegree. For simplicity, we assume all nodes to have an outdegree of at least one, which makes perfect sense, as will be shown later.

The spreading factor concept is very intuitive and, in fact, very close to real models of energy spreading through networks. Observe that the overall amount of energy in the network, after initial activation in^0, does not change over time. More formally, suppose that energy$(n) = 0$ for all $n \in V$ before injection in^0 into source s. Then the following equation holds in every computation step of our modified spreading algorithm, incorporating the concept of spreading factor d:

$$\sum_{x \in V} \text{energy}(x) = \text{in}^0 \qquad (6.1)$$

---

[6] The terms "energy" and "trust" are used interchangeably in this context.

Spreading factor d may also be seen as the ratio between *direct* trust in x and trust in the ability of x to *recommend* others as trustworthy peers. For instance, Beth et al. [4] and Maurer [33] explicitly differentiate between *direct* trust edges and *recommendation* edges.

We generally assume $d = 0.85$, though other values may also seem reasonable. For instance, having $d \leq 0.5$ allows agents to keep most of the trust they are granted for themselves and only pass small portions of trust to their peers. Observe that low values for d favor trust proximity to the source of trust injection, while high values allow trust to also reach nodes which are more distant. Furthermore, the introduction of spreading factor d is crucial for making Appleseed retain Levien's bottleneck property, as will be shown in later sections.

6.3.2.4 Rank Normalization

Algorithm 2 makes use of edge weight normalization, that is, the quantity $e_{x \to y}$ of energy distributed along (x, y) from x to successor node y depends on its *relative* weight, i.e., $W(x, y)$ compared to the sum of weights of all outgoing edges of x:

$$e_{x \to y} = d \cdot \text{in}(x) \cdot \frac{W(x, y)}{\sum_{(x,s) \in E} W(x, s)}$$

Normalization is common practice to many trust metrics, among those PageRank [37], EigenTrust [23], and AORank [15]. However, while normalized reputation or trust seem reasonable for models with plain, non weighted edges, serious interferences occur when edges are weighted, as is the case for our trust model adopted in Section 6.2.2.1.

For instance, refer to the left-hand side of Fig. 6.5 for unwanted effects: the amounts of energy that node a accords to successors b and d, that is, $e_{a \to b}$ and $e_{a \to d}$, respectively, are identical in value. Note that b has issued only *one* trust statement $W(b, c) = 0.25$, telling that its trust in c is rather weak. On the other hand, d assigns *full* trust to individuals e, f, and g. Nevertheless, the overall trust rank for d will be much higher than for any successor of d, for c is accorded $e_{a \to b} \cdot d$, while e, f, and g only obtain $e_{a \to d} \cdot d \cdot 1/3$ each. Hence, c will be trusted *three times* as much as e, f, and g, which is not reasonable at all.

6.3.2.5 Backward Trust Propagation

The above issue has already been discussed in [23], but no solution was proposed therein, arguing that "substantially good results" were achieved despite the drawbacks. We propose to alleviate the problem by making use of backward propagation of trust to the source: when computing the metric, additional "virtual" edges (x, s) from every node $x \in V \setminus \{s\}$ to the trust source s are created. These edges are assigned full trust $W(x, s) = 1$. Existing backward links (x, s), along with their

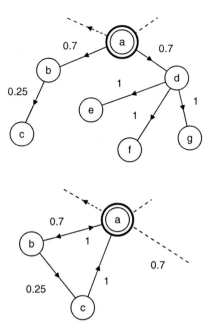

Fig. 6.5 Issues with trust normalization

weights, are "overwritten". Intuitively, every node is supposed to blindly trust the trust source s, see Fig. 6.5. The impacts of adding backward propagation links are threefold:

- **Mitigating relative trust.** Again, we refer to the left-hand graph in Fig. 6.5. Trust distribution in the underlying case becomes much fairer through backward propagation links, for c now only obtains $e_{a \to b} \cdot d \cdot (0.25/(1+0.25))$ from source s, while e, f, and g are accorded $e_{a \to d} \cdot d \cdot (1/4)$ each. Hence, trust ranks of both e, f, and g amount to 1.25 times the trust assigned to c.
- **Avoidance of dead ends.** Dead ends, that is, nodes x with zero outdegree, require special treatment in our computation scheme. Two distinct approaches may be adopted. First, the portion of incoming trust $d \cdot in(x)$ supposed to be passed to successor nodes is completely discarded, which contradicts our constraint of no energy leaving the system. Second, instead of retaining $(1 - d) \cdot in(x)$ of incoming trust, x keeps *all* trust for itself. The latter approach is also not sensible as it encourages users to not issue trust statements for their peers. Luckily, with backward propagation of trust, all nodes are implicitly linked to the trust source s, so that there are no more dead ends to consider.
- **Favoring trust proximity.** Backward links to the trust source s are favorable for nodes close to the source, as their eventual trust rank will increase. On the other hand, nodes further away from s are penalized.

Overly rewarding nodes close to the source is not beyond dispute and may pose some issues. In fact, it represents the tradeoff we have to pay for both welcome aspects of backward propagation.

6.3.2.6 Nonlinear Trust Normalization

In addition to backward propagation, an integral part of Appleseed, we propose supplementary measures to decrease the negative impact of trust distribution based on relative weights. Situations where nodes y with poor ratings from x are awarded high overall trust ranks, thanks to the low outdegree of x, have to be avoided (see Fig. 6.6). Taking the squares of local trust weights provides an appropriate solution:

$$e_{x \to y} = d \cdot \text{in}(x) \cdot \frac{W(x, y)^2}{\sum_{(x,s) \in E} W(x, s)^2}$$

As an example, refer to node b in Fig. 6.5. With squared normalization, the total amount of energy flowing backward to source a increases, while the amount of energy flowing to the poorly trusted node c decreases significantly. Accorded trust quantities $e_{b \to a}$ and $e_{b \to c}$ amount to $d \cdot \text{in}(b) \cdot (1/1.0625)$ and $d \cdot \text{in}(b) \cdot (0.0625/1.0625)$, respectively. More serious penalization of poor trust ratings can be achieved by selecting powers above two.

6.3.2.7 Algorithm Outline

Having identified modifications to apply to spreading activation models in order to tailor them for local group trust metrics, we are now able to formulate the core algorithm of Appleseed. Input and output are characterized as follows:

$$Trust_A : V \times \mathbb{R}_0^+ \times [0, 1] \times \mathbb{R}^+ \to (\text{Trust} : V \to \mathbb{R}_0^+)$$

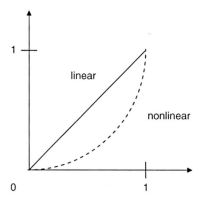

Fig. 6.6 Linear and nonlinear normalization

The first input parameter specifies trust seed s, the second trust injection e, parameter three identifies spreading factor $d \in [0, 1]$, and the fourth argument binds accuracy threshold T_c, which serves as one of two convergence criteria. Similar to Advogato, the output is an assignment function of trust with domain V. However, Appleseed allows *rankings* of agents with respect to the trust accorded. Advogato, on the other hand, only assigns boolean values, indicating presence or absence of trust.

Appleseed works with *partial* trust graph information. Nodes are accessed only when needed, that is, when reached by energy flow. Trust ranks trust(x), which correspond to energy(x) in Algorithm 2, are initialized to 0. Any unknown node u hence obtains trust(u) = 0. Likewise, virtual trust edges for backward propagation from node x to the source are added at the moment that x is discovered. In every iteration, for those nodes x reached by flow, the amount of incoming trust is computed as follows:

$$\text{in}(x) = d \cdot \sum_{(p,x) \in E} \left(\text{in}(p) \cdot \frac{W(p,x)}{\sum_{(p,s) \in E} W(p,s)} \right)$$

Incoming flow for x is hence determined by all flow that predecessors p distribute along edges (p, x). Note that the above equation makes use of linear normalization of relative trust weights. Replacement of linear by nonlinear normalization according to Section 6.3.2.6 is straight-forward, though. The trust rank of x is updated as follows:

$$\text{trust}(x) \leftarrow \text{trust}(x) + (1 - d) \cdot \text{in}(x)$$

However, trust networks generally contain cycles and thus allow no topological sorting of nodes. Hence, the computation of in(x) for reachable $x \in V$ is inherently recursive. Several iterations for all nodes are required in order to make computed information converge towards the least fixpoint. We give a criterion that has to be satisfied for convergence, relying upon accuracy threshold T_c briefly introduced before.

Definition 1 (Termination) Suppose that $V_i \subseteq V$ represents the set of nodes that were discovered until step i, and trust$_i(x)$ the current trust ranks for all $x \in V$. Then the algorithm terminates when the following condition is satisfied after step i:

$$\forall x \in V_i : \text{trust}_i(x) - \text{trust}_{i-1}(x) \leq T_c \tag{6.2}$$

Informally, Appleseed terminates when changes of trust ranks with respect to the prior iteration $i - 1$ are not greater than accuracy threshold T_c.

Moreover, when supposing spreading factor $d > 0$, accuracy threshold $T_c > 0$, and trust source s part of some connected component $G' \subseteq G$ containing at least two nodes, convergence, and thus termination, is guaranteed. The following paragraph gives an informal proof:

Proof 1 (Convergence of Appleseed) Assume that f_i denotes step i's quantity of energy flowing through the network, i.e., all the trust that has not been captured by some node x through function $trust_i(x)$. It follows from Equation 6.1 that in^0 constitutes the *upper boundary* of trust energy floating through the network, and f_i can be computed as below:

$$f_i = in^0 - \sum_{x \in V} trust_i(x)$$

Since $d > 0$ and $\exists (s, x) \in E, x \neq s$, the sum of current trust ranks $trust_i(x)$ of all $x \in V$ is *strictly increasing* for increasing i. Consequently, $\lim_{i \to \infty} f_i = 0$ holds. Moreover, since termination is defined by some fixed accuracy threshold $T_c > 0$, there exists some step k such that $\lim_{i \to k} f_i \leq T_c$.

```
function Trust_A (s ∈ V, in⁰ ∈ ℝ₀⁺, d ∈ [0, 1], T_c ∈ ℝ⁺) {
    set in₀(s) ← in⁰,  trust₀(s) ← 0,  i ← 0;
    set V₀ ← {s};
    repeat
        set i ← i + 1;
        set Vᵢ ← Vᵢ₋₁;
        ∀x ∈ Vᵢ₋₁ : set inᵢ(x) ← 0;
        for all x ∈ Vᵢ₋₁ do
            set trustᵢ(x) ← trustᵢ₋₁(x) + (1 − d) · inᵢ₋₁(x);
            for all (x, u) ∈ E do
                if u ∉ Vᵢ then
                    set Vᵢ ← Vᵢ ∪ {u};
                    set trustᵢ(u) ← 0, inᵢ(u) ← 0;
                    add edge (u, s), set W(u, s) ← 1;
                end if
                set w ← W(x, u) / ∑₍ₓ,ᵤ'₎∈E W(x, u');
                set inᵢ(u) ← inᵢ(u) + d · inᵢ₋₁(x) · w;
            end do
        end do
        set m = max_{y∈Vᵢ}{trustᵢ(y) − trustᵢ₋₁(y)};
    until (m ≤ T_c)
    return (trust : {(x, trustᵢ(x)) | x ∈ Vᵢ});
}
```

Alg. 3. Appleseed trust metric

6.3.3 Comparison of Advogato and Appleseed

Both Advogato and Appleseed are implementations of local group trust metrics. Advogato has already proven its efficiency in practical usage scenarios such as the Advogato online community, though lacking quantitative fitness information. Its success is mainly measured by indirect feedback, such as the amount of spam messages posted on Advogato, which has been claimed to be rather low. In order to evaluate the fitness of Appleseed as an appropriate approach to group trust computation, we intend to relate our novel approach to Advogato for comparison:

- **Attack-resistance.** This property defines the behavior of trust metrics in case of malicious nodes trying to invade into the system. For the evaluation of attack-resistance capabilities, we have briefly introduced the "bottleneck property" in Section 6.3.1.2, which holds for Advogato. In order to recapitulate, suppose that s and t are nodes and connected through trust edge (s, t). Node s is assumed good, while t is an attacking agent trying to make good nodes trust malevolent ones. In case the bottleneck property holds, manipulation "on the part of bad nodes does not affect the trust value" [26]. Clearly, Appleseed satisfies the bottleneck property, for nodes cannot raise their impact by modifying the structure of trust statements they issue. Bear in mind that the amount of trust accorded to agent t *only* depends on its predecessors and does not increase when t adds more nodes. Both spreading factor d and normalization of trust statements ensure that Appleseed becomes equally as attack-resistant as Advogato.
- **Trust weight normalization.** We have indicated before that issuing multiple trust statements dilutes trust accorded to successors. According to Guha [15], this does not comply with real-world observations, where statements of trust "do not decrease in value when the user trusts one more person [...]". The malady that Appleseed suffers from is common to many trust metrics, notably those based upon finding principal eigenvectors [37, 23, 42]. On the other hand, the approach pursued by Advogato does not penalize trust relationships asserted by eager trust dispensers, for node capacities do not depend on local information. Remember that capacities of nodes pertaining to level l are assigned based on the capacity of level $l - 1$ as well as the *overall* outdegree of nodes part of this level. Hence, Advogato encourages agents issuing numerous trust statements, while Appleseed penalizes overly abundant trust certificates.
- **Deterministic trust computation.** Appleseed is deterministic with respect to the assignment of trust rank to agents. Hence, for any arbitrary trust graph $G = (V, E, W)$ and for every node $x \in V$, linear equations allow to characterize the amount of trust assigned to x, as well as the quantity that x accords to its successor nodes. Advogato, however, is non deterministic. Though the *number* of trusted agents, and therefore the computed maximum flow size, is determined for given input parameters, the set of agents itself is not. Changing the order in which trust assertions are issued may yield different results. For example, suppose $C_V(s) = 1$ holds for trust seed s. Furthermore, assume s has issued trust certificates for two agents, b and c. The actual choice between b or c as trustworthy peer with maximum flow only depends on the order in which nodes are accessed.
- **Model and output type.** Basically, Advogato supports non weighted trust statements only. Appleseed is more versatile by virtue of its trust model based on weighted trust certificates. In addition, Advogato returns one set of trusted peers, whereas Appleseed assigns *ranks* to agents. These ranks allow to select

most trustworthy agents first and relate them to each other with respect to their accorded rank. Hereby, the definition of thresholds for trustworthiness is left to the user who can thus tailor relevant parameters to fit different application scenarios. For instance, raising the application-dependent threshold for the selection of trustworthy peers, which may be either an absolute or relative value, allows for enlarging the neighborhood of trusted peers. Appleseed is hence more adaptive and flexible than Advogato.

6.3.4 Parameterization and Experiments

Appleseed allows numerous parameterizations of its input variables. Discussions of parameter instantiations and caveats thus constitute indispensable complements to our contribution. Moreover, we provide experimental results exposing observed effects of parameter tuning. Note that all experiments have been conducted on data obtained from "real" social networks: several Web crawling tools were written to mine the Advogato community website and extract trust assertions stated by its more than 8,000 members. Hereafter, we converted all trust data to our trust model proposed in Section 6.2.2. Notice that the Advogato community server supports four different levels of peer certification, namely "Observer", "Apprentice", "Journeyer", and "Master". We mapped these qualitative certification levels to quantitative ones, assigning $W(x, y) = 0.25$ for x certifying y as "Observer", $W(x, y) = 0.5$ for an "Apprentice", and so forth. The Advogato community grows rapidly and our crawler extracted $3, 224, 101$ trust assertions. Heavy preprocessing and data cleansing was inevitable, eliminating reflexive trust statements $W(x, x)$ and shrinking trust certificates to reasonable sizes. Note that some eager Advogato members issued more than two thousand trust statements, yielding an overall average outdegree of 397.69 assertions per node. Common sense tell us that this figure is beyond dispute. Applying our set of extraction tools, we tailored the test data obtained from Advogato to our needs and extracted trust networks with specific average outdegree for the experimental analysis.

6.3.4.1 Trust Injection

Trust values trust(x) computed by the Appleseed metric for source s and node x may differ greatly from explicitly assigned trust weights $W(s, x)$. We have already mentioned earlier that computed trust ranks may *not* be interpreted as absolute values, but rather in comparison with ranks assigned to all other peers. In order to make assigned rank values more tangible, though, one might expect that tuning the trust injection in^0 to satisfy the following proposition will align computed ranks and explicit trust statements:

$$\forall(s, x) \in E : \text{Trust}(x) \in [W(s, x) - \epsilon, W(s, x) + \epsilon]$$

However, when assuming reasonably small ϵ, the approach does not succeed. Recall that *computed* trust values of successor nodes x to s do not only depend on assertions made by s, but also on trust ratings asserted by other peers. Hence, perfect alignment of explicit trust ratings with computed ones cannot be accomplished. However, we propose alignment heuristics, incorporated into Algorithm 4, which have proven to work remarkably well in diverse test scenarios. The basic idea is to add another node i and edge (s, i) with $W(s, i) = 1$ to the trust graph $G = (V, E, W)$, treating (s, i) as an indicator to tell whether trust injection in^0 is "good" or not. Consequently, parameter in^0 has to be adapted in order to make trust(i) converge towards $W(s, i)$. The trust metric computation is hence repeated with different values for
inj until convergence of explicit and computed trust value for i is achieved. Eventually, edge (s, i) and node i are removed and the metric computation is performed one more time. Experiments have shown that our imperfect alignment heuristics yield computed ranks trust(x) for direct successors x of trust source s, which come close to previously specified trust statements $W(s, x)$.

```
function Trust_heu (s ∈ V, d ∈ [0, 1], T_c ∈ ℝ⁺) {
    add node i, edge (s, i), set W(s, i) ← 1;
    set in⁰ ← 20, ε ← 0.1;
    repeat
        set trust ← Trust_A (s, in⁰, d, T_c);
        in⁰ ← adapt (W(s, i), trust(i), in⁰);
    until trust(i) ∈ [W(s, i) − ε, W(s, i) + ε]
    remove node i, remove edge (s, i);
    return Trust_A (s, in⁰, d, T_c);
}
```

Alg. 4. Adding weight alignment heuristics

6.3.4.2 Spreading Factor

Small values for d tend to overly reward nodes close to the trust source and penalize remote ones. Recall that low d allows nodes to retain most of the incoming trust quantity for themselves, while large d stresses the recommendation of trusted individuals and makes nodes distribute most of the assigned trust to their successor nodes:

Experiment 1 (Impact of factor d): We compare the distributions of computed rank values for three diverse instantiations of d, namely $d_1 = 0.1$, $d_2 = 0.5$, and $d_3 = 0.85$. Our setup is based upon a social network with an average outdegree of six trust assignments and 384 nodes reached by trust energy spreading from our designated trust source. We furthermore suppose $in^0 = 200$, $T_c = 0.01$, and linear weight normalization. Computed ranks are classified into 11 histogram cells with nonlinear cell width. Obtained output results are displayed in Fig. 6.7. Mind that we have chosen *logarithmic* scales for the vertical axis in order to render the diagram

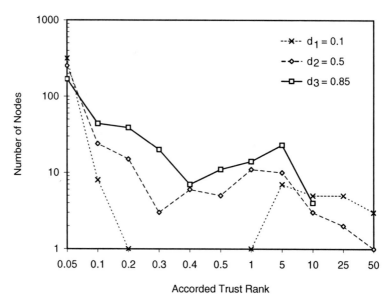

Fig. 6.7 Spreading factor impact

more legible. For d_1, we observe that this value engenders the highest amount of nodes x with ranks trust$(x) \geq 25$. On the other hand, virtually no ranks ranging from 0.2 to 1 are assigned, while the number of nodes with ranks smaller than 0.05 is again much higher for d_1 than for both d_2 and d_3. Instantiation $d_3 = 0.85$ constitutes the counterpart of d_1. No ranks with trust$(x) \geq 25$ are accorded, while interim ranks between 0.1 and 10 are much more likely for d_3 than for both other instantiations of spreading factor d. Consequently, the number of ranks below 0.05 is lowest for d_3.

The experiment demonstrates that high values for parameter d tend to distribute trust more evenly, neither overly rewarding nodes close to the source, nor penalizing remote ones too rigidly. On the other hand, low d assigns high trust ranks to very few nodes, namely those which are closest to the source, while the majority of nodes obtains very low trust rank. We propose to set $d = 0.85$ for general use.

6.3.4.3 Accuracy and Convergence Rate

We already mentioned earlier that the Appleseed algorithm is inherently recursive. Parameter T_c constitues the ultimate criterion for termination. We will show through an experiment that convergence is reached very fast, no matter how huge the number of nodes trust is flowing through, and no matter how large the initial trust injection:

Experiment(Convergence rate):The trust network we consider has an average outdegree of five trust assignments per node. The number of nodes for which trust ranks are assigned amounts to 572. We suppose $d = 0.85$, $T_c = 0.01$, and linear weight normalization. Two runs are computed, one with trust activation $in_1 = 200$, the other with initial energy $in_2 = 800$. Figure 6.8 demonstrates the

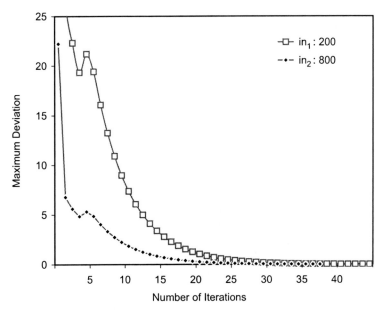

Fig. 6.8 Convergence of Appleseed

rapid convergence of both runs. Though the trust injection for the second run is four times as high as for the first, convergence is reached in only few more iterations: run one takes 38 iterations, run two terminates after 45 steps.

For both runs, we assumed accuracy threshold $T_c = 0.01$, which is extremely small and accurate beyond necessity already. However, experience taught us that convergence takes place rapidly even for very large networks and high amounts of trust injected, so that assuming the latter value for T_c imposes no scalability issues. In fact, the amount of nodes taken into account for trust rank assignment in the above example well exceeds practical usage scenarios: mind that the case at hand demands 572 documents to be fetched from the Web, complaisantly supposing that these pages containing personal trust information for each node are cached after their first access. Hence, we may well claim that the actual bottleneck of group trust computation is not the Appleseed metric itself, but downloads of trust resources from the network. This bottleneck might also be the reason for selecting thresholds T_c greater than 0.01, in order to make the algorithm terminate after fewer node accesses.

6.3.5 Implementation and Extensions

Appleseed was implemented in JAVA, based upon Algorithm 3. We applied moderate fine-tuning and supplemented our metric with an architectural cushion in order to access "real" machine-readable RDF homepages. Other notable modifications to the core algorithm are discussed briefly:

- **Maximum number of nodes.** We supplemented the set of input parameters by yet another argument M, which specifies the maximum number of nodes to unfold. This extension hinders trust energy from overly covering vast parts of the entire network. Note that accessing the personal, machine-readable homepages, which contain trust information required for the metric computation, represents the actual computation bottleneck. Hence, expanding as few nodes as possible is highly desirable. When choosing reasonably large M, for instance, twice the number of agents assumed trustworthy, we may expect to not miss any relevant nodes: mind that Appleseed proceeds breadth-first and thus considers close nodes first, which are more eligible for trust than distant ones.
- **Upper-bounded trust path lengths.** Another approach to sensibly restrict the number of nodes unfolded relies upon upper-bounded path lengths. The idea of constraining path lengths for trust computation has been adopted before by Reiter and Stubblebine [40] and within the X.509 protocol [40]. Depending on the overall trust network connectivity, we opt for maximum path lengths between three and six, well aware of Milgram's "six degress of separation" paradigm [35]. In fact, trust decay is inherent to Appleseed, thanks to spreading factor d and backward propagation. Stripping nodes at large distances from the seed therefore only marginally affects the trust metric computation results while providing major speed-ups at the same time.
- **Zero trust retention for the source.** Third, we modified Appleseed to hinder trust source s from accumulating trust energy, essentially introducing one novel spreading factor $d_s = 1.0$ for the seed only. Consequently, all trust is divided among peers of s and none retained, which is reasonable. Remember that s wants to discover trustworthy agents and not assign trust rank to itself. Convergence may accelerate, since $\text{trust}_{i+1}(x) - \text{trust}_i(x)$ used to be maximal for seed node s, thanks to backward propagation of trust. Furthermore, supposing the same trust quantity in^0 injected, assigned trust ranks become greater in value, also enlarging gaps between neighbors in trust rank.

6.3.6 Testbed for Local Group Trust Metrics

Trust metrics and models for trust propagation have to be intuitive, underpinning the need for the application of Occam's Razor. Humans must be able to comprehend *why* agent a was accorded higher trust rank than b and come to similar results when asked for a personal judgement. Consequently, we implemented our own testbed, which visually displays social networks, allows zooming of specific nodes, and layouts these appropriately, with minimum overlap. We made use of the yFiles [46] library to perform all sophisticated graph drawing. Moreover, our testbed permits to parameterize Appleseed through dialogs. Detailed output is provided, both graphical and textual. Graphical results comprise the highlighting of nodes with trust ranks above certain thresholds, while textual results return quantitative trust ranks of all accessed nodes, numbers of iterations, and so forth. We also implemented the Advogato trust metric and incorporated the latter into our testbed. Hereby, our implementation of Advogato does not require a priori complete trust graph information, but accesses nodes "just in time", similar to Appleseed. All experiments were conducted on top of the testbed application.

6.4 Distrust

Distrust is one of the most controversial topics and issues to cope with, especially when considering trust metrics and trust propagation. Most approaches completely ignore distrust and only consider full trust or degrees of trust [27, 36, 4, 40, 42]. Others, among those [1, 7, 3, 13], allow for distrust ratings, though, but do not consider the subtle semantic differences pertaining to the distinct notions of trust and distrust. Consequently, according to Gans et al. [11], "distrust is regarded as just the other side of the coin, that is, there is generally a symmetric scale with complete trust on one end and absolute distrust on the other." Furthermore, some researchers equate the notion of distrust with lack of trust information. Contrarily, in his seminal work on the essence of trust, Marsh [31] has already pointed out that those two concepts, that is, lack of trust and distrust, may not be intermingled. For instance, in absence of trustworthy agents, we might be more prone to accept recommendations from persons we do not trust, probably because of lack of prior experiences [32], than from persons we explicitly distrust, resulting from past bad experiences or deceit. However, even Marsh pays little attention to the specifics of distrust.

Gans et al. [11] were among the first to recognize the importance of distrust, stressing the fact that "distrust is an irreducible phenomenon that cannot be offset against any other social mechanisms", hence including trust. In their work [11], an explicit distinction between confidence, trust, and distrust is made. Moreover, the authors indicate that distrust might be highly relevant to social networks. Its impact is not inherently negative, but may also influence the network in an extremely positive fashion. However, the primary focus of the latter work is on methodology issues and planning, not considering trust assertion evaluations and propagation through appropriate metrics.

Guha [15, 16] eventually acknowledges the immense role of distrust with respect to trust propagation applications, arguing that "distrust statements are very useful for users to debug their Web of Trust". For example, suppose that agent a blindly trusts b, which again blindly trusts c, which blindly trusts d. However, a completely distrusts d. The latter distrust statement hence ensures that a will *not* accept beliefs and ratings from d, regardless of agent a trusting b trusting c trusting d.

6.4.1 Semantics of Distrust

The nonsymmetrical nature of distrust and trust, being two perfect dichotomies, has already been recognized by recent sociological research [29]. In this section, we investigate the differences between distrust and trust pertaining to possible inferences and the propagation of statements.

6.4.1.1 Distrust as Negated Trust

Interpreting distrust as the negation of trust was adopted by many trust metrics, among those trust metrics proposed in [1, 21, 2, 7]. Basically, these metrics compute trust values by analyzing *chains* of trust statements from source s to target t, eventually merging them to obtain an aggregate value. Each chain hereby becomes synthesized into one single number through *weighted multiplication* of trust values along trust paths. Serious implications resulting from assuming that trust concatenation relates to multiplication [42], and distrust to negated trust, manifest when agent a distrusts b, which distrusts c:[7]

$$\neg\text{trust}\,(a, b) \wedge \neg\text{trust}\,(b, c) \models \text{trust}\,(a, c)$$

Jøsang et al. [21] are well aware of this rather unwanted effect but do not deny its correctness, for the enemy of your enemy could well be your friend. Guha, on the other hand, indicates that two distrust statements cancelling out each other most often does not reflect desired behavior [15]. We adopt the opinion of Guha and claim that distrust may not be interpreted as negated trust.

6.4.1.2 Propagation of Distrust

The "conditional transitivity" [1] of trust is commonly agreed upon and constitutes the foundation and pivotal premiss that all trust metrics rely upon. However, no consensus in literature has been achieved as it comes to the *degree* of transitivity and the decay rate of trust. Many approaches therefore explicitly distinguish between recommendation trust and direct trust [21, 1, 33, 7] in order to keep apart the transitive fraction of trust from the nontransitive one. Hence, in these works, only the *ultimate* edge within the trust chain, that is, the one linking to the trust target, needs to be direct, while all others are supposed to be recommendations. For the Appleseed trust metric, this distinction is made through the introduction of the global spreading factor d. However, the conditional transitivity property of trust does not equally extend to distrust. The case of double negation through distrust propagation has already been considered. Now suppose, for instance, that a distrusts b, which trusts c. Supposing distrust to propagate through the network, we may come to make the following inference:

$$\text{distrust}(a, b) \wedge \text{trust}(b, c) \models \text{distrust}(a, c)$$

---

[7] By relying on predicate calculus expressions, we greatly simplify through supposing that trust, and hence distrust, is fully transitive.

This inference is more than questionable, for a penalizes c simply for being trusted by an agent that a distrusts. Obviously, this assumption is not sound and does not reflect expected real-world behavior. We assume that distrust does not allow to make direct inferences of any kind. This conservative assumption makes us stay on the "safe" side and is in perfect accordance with [15].

6.4.2 Incorporating Distrust into Appleseed

We compare our implementation of distrust with Guha's approach, who supposes an identical model of distrust. Guha computes trust by means of one global group trust metric, similar to PageRank [37]. For distrust, he proposes two candidate approaches. The first one directly integrates distrust into the iterative eigenvector computation and comes up with one single measure combining both trust and distrust. However, in networks dominated by distrust, the iteration might not converge. The second proposal first computes trust ranks by trying to find the dominant eigenvector, and then computes separate distrust ranks in one single step, based upon the iterative computation of trust ranks. Suppose that D_a is the set of agents who distrust a:

$$\text{DistrustRank}(a) = \frac{\sum_{b \in D_a} \text{TrustRank}(b)}{|D_a|}$$

The problem we perceive with this approach refers to *superimposing* the computation of distrust ranks *after* trust rank computation, which may yield some strange behavior: suppose an agent a which is highly controversial by engendering ambiguous sentiments, that is, on the one hand, there are numerous agents that trust a, and on the other hand, there are numerous agents which distrust a. With the approach proposed by Guha, a's impact through asserting distrust into other agents is huge, resulting from its immense positive trust rank. However, common sense tells us this should not be the case, for a is subject to tremendous distrust itself, thus levelling out its high trust rank.

Hence, for our own approach, we intend to directly incorporate distrust into the iterative process of the Appleseed trust metric computation, and not superimpose distrust afterwards. Several pitfalls have to be avoided, such as the risk of non-convergence in case of networks dominated by distrust [15]. Furthermore, in absence of distrust statements, we want the distrust-enhanced Appleseed algorithm, which we denote by trust_{A^-}, to yield results identical to those engendered by the original version trust_A.

6.4.2.1 Normalization and Distrust

First, the trust normalization procedure has to be adapted. We hereby suppose the more general case which does not necessarily assume linear normalization but normalization of weights to the power of q, as has been discussed in Section 6.3.2.6.

Let in(x), the trust influx for agent x, be positive. As usual, we denote the global spreading factor by d, and quantified trust statements from x towards y by $W(x, y)$. Function sign(x) returns the sign of value x. Note that from now on, we assume $W : E \rightarrow [-1, +1]$, for degrees of *distrust* need to be expressed as well. Then the trust quantity $e_{x \rightarrow y}$ distributed from x to successor node y is computed as follows:

$$e_{x \rightarrow y} = d \cdot \text{in}(x) \cdot \text{sign}(W(x, y)) \cdot w, \qquad (6.3)$$

where

$$w = \frac{|W(x, y)|^q}{\sum_{(x,s) \in E} |W(x, s)|^q}$$

The accorded quantity $e_{x \rightarrow y}$ becomes negative if $W(x, y)$ is negative, that is, if x distrusts y to a certain extent. For the relative weighting, the *absolute* values $|W(x, s)|$ of all weights are considered. Otherwise, the denominator could become negative, or positive trust statements could become boosted unduly. The latter would be the case if the sum of positive trust ratings slightly outweighed the sum of negative ones, making the denominator converge towards zero. An example demonstrates the computation process:

Example 2 (Distribution of Trust and Distrust) We assume the trust network as depicted in Fig. 6.9. Let the trust energy influx into node a be in$(a) = 2$, and global spreading factor $d = 0.85$. For simplicity reasons, backward propagation of trust to the source is not considered. Moreover, we suppose *linear* weight normalization, thus $q = 1$. Consequently, the denominator of the normalization equation is $|0.75| + |-0.5| + |0.25| + |1| = 2.5$. The trust energy that a distributes to b hence amounts to $e_{a \rightarrow b} = 0.51$, whereas the energy accorded to the distrusted node c is $e_{a \rightarrow c} = -0.34$. Furthermore, we have $e_{a \rightarrow d} = 0.17$ and $e_{a \rightarrow e} = 0.68$.

Observe that trust energy becomes lost during distribution, for the sum of energy accorded along outgoing edges of a amounts to 1.02, while 1.7 was provided for distribution. The effect results from the negative trust weight $W(a, c) = -0.5$.

6.4.2.2 Distrust Allocation and Propagation

We now analyze the case where the influx in(x) for agent x is *negative*. In this case, the trust allocated for x will also be negative, that is, in$(x) \cdot (1 - d) < 0$. Moreover, the energy in$(x) \cdot d$ that x may distribute among its successor nodes will naturally be negative as well. The implications are those which have been mentioned in Section 6.4.1, that is, distrust as negation of trust and propagation of distrust. For the first case, refer to node f in Fig. 6.9 and assume in$(c) = -0.34$, which is derived from Example 6.4.2.1. The trusted agent a distrusts c which distrusts f. Eventually, f would be accorded $d \cdot (-0.34) \cdot (-0.25)$, which is *positive*. For the second case, node g would be assigned a *negative* trust quantity $d \cdot (-0.34) \cdot (0.75)$, simply for

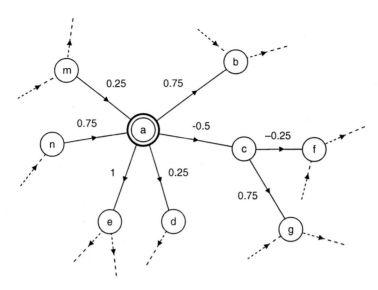

Fig. 6.9 Network augmented by distrust

being trusted by f, which is commonly distrusted. Both unwanted effects can be avoided by not allowing distrusted nodes to distribute any energy at all. Hence, more formally, we introduce a novel function $out(x)$:

$$out(x) = \begin{cases} d \cdot in(x), & \text{if } in(x) \geq 0 \\ 0, & \text{else} \end{cases} \qquad (6.4)$$

The function then has to replace $d \cdot in(x)$ when computing the energy distributed along edges from x to successor nodes y:

$$e_{x \to y} = out(x) \cdot sign(W(x, y)) \cdot w, \qquad (6.5)$$

where

$$w = \frac{|W(x, y)|^q}{\sum_{(x,s) \in E} |W(x, s)|^q}$$

This design decision perfectly aligns with our assumptions made in Section 6.4.1 and prevents the inference of unwanted side-effects mentioned earlier. Furthermore, one can see easily that the modifications introduced do not change the behavior with respect to Algorithm 3 when not considering relationships of distrust.

6.4.2.3 Convergence

Even in networks largely or entirely dominated by distrust, our enhanced version of Appleseed is guaranteed to converge. We therefore briefly outline an informal proof, knowing about the convergence of the core Appleseed algorithm, which has been shown before by Proof 6.3.2.7:

Proof 2 (Convergence in presence of distrust) Recall that only positive trust influx $in(x)$ becomes propagated, which has been indicated in Section 6.4.2.2. Hence, all we need to show is that the overall quantity of *positive* trust distributed in computation step i cannot be augmented through the presence of distrust statements. In other words, suppose that $G = (V, E, W)$ defines an arbitrary trust graph, containing quantified trust statements, but no distrust, that is, $W : E \rightarrow [0, 1]$. Now consider another trust graph $G' = (V, E \cup D, W')$ which contains additional edges D, and weight function $W' = W \cup (D \rightarrow [-1, 0])$. Hence, G' augments G by additional distrust edges between nodes taken from V. We now perform two parallel computations with enhanced Appleseed, one operating on G and the other on G'. In every step, and for every trust edge $(x, y) \in E$ for G, the distributed energy $e_{x \rightarrow y}$ is greater or equal than for its equivalent counterpart on G', for the denominator of the fraction given in Equation 6.5 can only become *greater* through additional distrust outedges. Second, for the computation performed on G', negative energy distributed along edge (x, y) can only *reduce* the trust influx for y and may hence even accelerate convergence. $\square$

However, as one might already have observed from the proof, there exists one serious implication arising from having distrust statements in the network. The overall accorded trust quantity does not equal the initially injected energy anymore. Moreover, in networks dominated by distrust, the overall trust energy sum may even be *negative*.

Experiment 3 (Network impact of distrust) We intend to analyze the number of iterations until convergence and the overall accorded trust rank of five networks. The structures of all these graphs are identical, being composed of 623 nodes with an average indegree and outdegree of 9. The only difference applies to the assigned weights, where the first graph contains no distrust statements at all, while 25% of all weights are negative for the second, 50% for the third, and 75% for the fourth. The fifth graph only contains distrust statements. Appleseed parameters are identical for all five runs, having backward propagation enabled, an initial trust injection $in^0 = 200$, spreading factor $d = 0.85$, convergence threshold $T_c = 0.01$, linear weight normalization, and no upper bound on the number of nodes to unfold. The left-hand side of Fig. 6.10 clearly demonstrates that the number of iterations until convergence, given on the vertical axis, decreases with the proportion of distrust increasing, observable along the horizontal axis. Likewise, the overall accorded trust rank, indicated on the vertical axis of the right-hand side of Fig. 6.10, decreases rapidly with increasing distrust, eventually dropping below zero. The same experiment was repeated for another network with 329 nodes, an average indegree and outdegree of 6, yielding similar results.

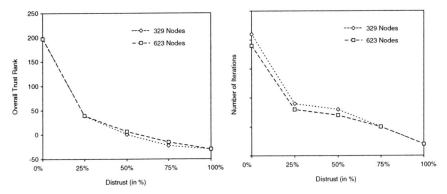

Fig. 6.10 Network impact of distrust

The effects observable in Experiment 3 only marginally affect the ranking itself, for trust ranks are interpreted *relative* to each other. Moreover, compensation for lost trust energy may be achieved by boosting the initial trust injection in^0.

6.5 Discussion

In this work, we have introduced various axes to classify trust metrics with respect to diverse criteria and features. Furthermore, we have advocated the need for local group trust metrics, eventually presenting Appleseed, our main contribution made. Through our proposed trust model, we have situated Appleseed within the Semantic Web universe. However, we believe that Appleseed suits other application scenarios likewise, such as group trust in online communities, open rating systems, ad-hoc and peer-to-peer networks.

For instance, Appleseed could support peer-to-peer-based file-sharing systems in reducing the spread of self-replicating inauthentic files by virtue of trust propagation [23]. In that case, explicit trust statements, resulting from direct interaction, reflect belief in someone's endeavor to provide authentic files.

Moreover, we have provided ample discussions of semantics and propagation models of distrust, owing to the fact that the latter concept has remained rather unattended by research. Details of its incorporation into the core Appleseed framework have also been provided.

However, several open issues for future research remain. Though having described ranking mechanisms and ways to align direct and indirect, that is, computed, trust relationships by means of heuristics, an actual policy for eventual *boolean* decision-taking with respect to which agents to grant trust and which to deny has not been considered. Note that possible criteria are application-dependent. For some, one might want to select the n most trustworthy agents. For others, all agents with ranks above given thresholds may be eligible.

We strongly believe that local group trust metrics, such as Advogato and Appleseed, will become subject to substantial research for diverse computing domains within the near future. For instance, the Appleseed core currently undergoes integration into our decentralized, Semantic Web-based recommender system [47, 48] playing an essential role in its overall conception.

At any rate, success or failure of Appleseed, Advogato, and other group trust metrics largely depend on the leverage that candidate application scenarios are able to unfold.

Acknowledgments We are very grateful to Lule Ahmedi, Nathan Dimmock, Kai Simon, and Paolo Massa for insightful comments and fruitful discussions, which helped us improve the quality of the paper.

References

1. Alfarez Abdul-Rahman and Stephen Hailes. A distributed trust model. In new Security Paradigms Workshop, pp. 48-60, Cumbria, UK, September 1997.
2. Alfarez Abdul-Rahman and Stephen Hailes. Supporting trust in virtual communities. In *Proceeding of the 33rd Hawali International Conference on System Sciences*, Mauti, HW, USA, January 2000.
3. Kari Aberter and Zoran Despotovic. managing trust in a peer-2-peer information system. In Henrique Paques,Ling Liu, and David Grossman,editors, it Proceeding of the Tenth International Conference Information and Knowledge Management, pp. 310–317. ACM Press, 2001.
4. Thomas Beth,Malte Borcherding, and Bright Klein. Valuation of trust in open networks. In *Proceeding of the 1994 European Symposium on Research in Computer Security*, pp. 3–18, 1994.
5. Matt Blaze, Joan Feigenbaum, and Jack Lacy. Decentralized trust management. In *Proceed-ing of the 17th Symposium on Security and Pricacy, pages* 164–173, IEEE Computer Society Prees, Oakland CA, USA, May 1996.
6. Maciej Ceglowski, Aaron Caburn, and John Cuadrado. Semantic search of unstructured data using contextural network graphs, June 2003.
7. Rita Chen and William Yeager. Poblano: A distributed trust model for peer-to-peer networks. Technical report, Sun Microsystems, Santa Clara, CA, USA, February 2003.
8. Edd Dumbill. Finding friends with XML and RDF, IBM's XML Watch, June 2002.
9. Laurent Eschenauer, Virigl Gligor, and John Baras. On trust establishment in mobile adhoc networks. Technical Report MS 2002-10, Imstitute for Systems Research, UniVeresity of Maryland, MD, USA, OCtober 2002.
10. Lester Ford and Ray Fulkerson. *Flows in Networks*. Princeton University Press, Princeton, NJ, USA, 1962.
11. Günter Gans, Mathias Jarks, Stefanie Kethers, and Gerhard Lakemeyer. Modeling the impact of trust and distrust in agent networks. In *Proceedings of the Third International Bi-Conference Workshop on Agent-oriented Information Systems*, Montreal, Canada, May 2001.
12. Yolanda Gil and Varun Ratnakar. Trusting information sources one citizen at a time. In *Proceedings of the First International Semantic Web Conference*, Sardinia, Italy, June 2002.
13. Jennifer Golbeck, Bijan Parsia, and James Hendler. Trust networks on the semantic web in. *Proceedings of Cooperative Intelligent Agents*, Helsinki, Finland, August 2003.
14. Elizabeth Gray, Jean-Marc Seigneur, Yong Chen, and Christian Jensen. Trust Propagation in small worlds. In Paddy Nixon and Sotirios Terzis, editors, *Proceedings of the First Interna-*

tional Conference on Trust Management, volume 2692 of *LNCS*, pp. 239–254. Springer-Verlag April 2003.

15. Ramanthan Guha. Open rating systems. Technical report, Sandford Knowledge Systems Laboratory, Sandford, CA, USA, 2003.

16. Ramanathan Guha, Ravi Kumar, Prabhakar Raghavan, and Andrew Tomkins. Propagation of turst and distrust. In *Proceedings of the Thirteenth International World Wide Web Conference*, ACM Press, New York, USA, May 2004.

17. Knut Hatmann and Thomas Strothotte. A speading activation approach to text illustration. In *Proceedings of the 2nd Interpersonal Symposium on Smart Graphics*, pp. 39–46, Hawthorne, NY, USA, ACM Press, 2002.

18. Fritz Heider. *The Psychology of Interpersonal Relations*. Wiley, New York, Ny, USA, 1958.

19. Paul Holland and Samuel Leinhardt. Some evidence on the transitivity of positive interpersonal sentiment. *American Journal of Sociology*, 77;1205–1209, 1972.

20. Richard Housely, William Ford, William Polk, and David Solo. Internet X.509 public key infrastucture, Internet Engineering Task Force RFC 2459, January 1999.

21. Audun Jøsang, Elizabeth Gray, and Michael Kinateder. Analysing topologies of transitive trust. In *proceedings of the Workshop of Formal Aspects of Security and Trust*, Pisa, Italy, September 2003.

22. Jose Kahan, Marja-Ritta Koivunen, Eric Prud' Hommeaux, and Ralph Swick. Annotea – an open RDF infrastrucute for shard web annotations. In *Proceedings of the Tenth International World Wide Web Conference*, pp. 623–632, Hong Kong, China, May 2001.

23. Speandar Kamamvar, Mario Schlosser, and Hector Garcia-Molina. The Eigen Trust algorithm for reputation management in P2P networks. In *Proceedings of the Twelfth International World Wide Web Conference*, Budapest, Hungary, May 2003.

24. Michael Kinateder and Siani Pearson. A privacy-enhanced peer-to-peer reputation system. In *proceedings of the 4th International Conference on Electronic Commerce and Web Technologies*, volume 2378 of *LNCS*, prague, Czech Republic, Springer-Verlag, September 2003.

25. Michael Kinateder and Kurt and Rothermel. Architecture and algorithms of a distributed reputation system. In Paddy Nixon and Sotirios Terzis, editors, *proceeding of the First International Conference on Trust Management*, volume 2692 of *LNCS*, pp. 1–16. Springer-Verlag, April 2003.

26. Raph Levien. *Attack Resistant Trust Metrics*. PhD thesis, UC Berkeley, CA, USA, 2003.

27. Raph Levien and Alexander Aiken. Attack-resistant trust for public key certification. In *Proceedings of the 7th USENIX Security Symposium*, San Antonio, TX, USA, January 1998.

28. Raph Levien and Alexander Aiken. An attack-resistant, scalable name service, 2000. Draft submission to the Fourth International Conference on Financial Cryptography, 2000.

29. Rot Lewicki, Daniel McAllister, and Robert Bies. Trust and distrust: New relationships and realities. *Academy of Management Review*, 23(12):438–458, 1998.

30. Niklas Luhmann. *Trust and Power*. Wiley, Chichester, UK, 1979.

31. Stephen Marsh. *Formalising Trust as a Computational Concept*. PhD thesis, Department of Mathematics and Computer Science, University of Stirling, Stirling, UK, 1994.

32. Stephen Marsh. Optimism and pessimism in trust. In Jose Ramirez, editor, *Proceedings of the Ibero-American Conference on Artificial Intelligence*, McGraw-Hill Caracas, Venezuela, 1994.

33. Ueh Maurer. Modelling a public key infrastructure. In Elisa Bertino, editor, *Proceedings of the 1996 European Symposium on Reserach in Computer Security*, Volume 1146 of *LNCS*, pp. 325–350. Springer-Verlag, 1996.

34. Harrison McKnight and Norman Chervany. The meaning of trust. Technical Report MISRC 96–04, Management Informations Systems Research Center, University of Minnesota, MN, USA, 1996.

35. Stanley Milgram. The small world problem. In John Sabini and Maury Sliver, editors, *The Individual in a Social World – Essays and Experiments*. McGraw-Hill, New York, NY, USA, 2nd edition, 1992.

36. Lik Mui, Mojdeh Mohtashemi, and Ari Halberstradt. A computational model of trust and reputation. In *Proceedings of the 35th Hawaii International Conference on System Sciences*, pp. 188–196, Big Island, HI, USA, January 2002.

37. Lawrence Page, Sergey Brin, RAjeev Motwani, and Terry Winograd. The pagerank citation ranking: Bringing order of the web. Technical report, Stanford Digital Library Technologies Project, 1998.

38. Ross Quillian. Semantic memory. In Marvin Minsky, editor, *Semantic Information Processing*, pp. 227–270. MIT Press, Boston, MA, USA, 1968.

39. Anatol Rapoport. Mathematical models of social interaction. In Duncan Luce, Robert Bush, and Eugene Galanter, editors, *Handbook of Mathematical Psychology*, Volume 2. Wiley, New York, NY, USA, 1963.

40. Michael Reiter and Stuart Stubblebine. Path independence for authentication in large scale systems. In *ACM Conference on Computer and Communications Security*, pp. 57–66, 1996.

41. Michael Reiter and Stuart Stubblebine. Toward acceptable metrices of authentication. In *Proceedings of the IEEE Symposium on Security and Privacy*, pp. 10–20, 1997.

42. Matthew Richardson, Rakesh Agrawal, and Pedro Domingos. Trust management for the semantic web. In *Proceedings of the Second International Semantic Web Conference*, Sanibel Island, FL, USA, September 2003.

43. Karthikeyan Sankaralingam, Simha Sethumadhavan, and James Browne. Distributed pagerank for P2P systems. In *Proceedings of the Twelfth International Symposium on High Performance Distributed Computing*, Seattle, WA, USA, June 2003.

44. Edward Smith, Susan Nolen-Hoeksema, Barbara Fredrickson, and Geoffrey Loftus. *Atkinson and Hilgards's Introduction to Psychology*. Thomson Learning, Boston, MA, USA, 2003.

45. Andrew Twigg and Nathan Dimmock. Attack-resistance of computational trust models. In *Proceedings of the Twelfth IEEE International Workshop on Enabling Technologies: Infrastructure for Collaborative Enterprises: Enterprise Security (Special Session on Trust Management)*, pp. 275–280, Linz, Austria, June 2003.

46. Roland Wiese, Markus Eiglsperger, and Michael Kaufmann. yfiles – visualization and automatic layout of graphs. In *Proceedings of the 9th International Symposium on Graph Drawing*, volume 2265 of *LNCS*, pp. 453–454, Springer-Verlag, Heidelberg, Germany, January 2001.

47. Cai-Nicolas Ziegler. Semantic web recommender systems. In Wolfgang Lindner and Andrea Perego, editors, *Proceedings of the Joint ICDE/EDBT Ph.D. Workshop 2004*, Crete University Press, Heraklion, Greece, March 2004.

48. Cai-Nicolas Ziegler and Georg Lausen. Analyzing correlation between trust and user similarity in online communities. In Christian Jensen, Stefan Poslad, and Theodosis Dimitrakos, editors, *Proceedings of the 2nd International Conference on Trust Management*, volume 2995 of *LNCS*, pp. 251–265, Springer-Verlag, Oxford, UK, March 2004.

49. Philip Zimmermann. *The Official PGP User's Guide*. MIT Press, Boston, MA, USA, 1995.

Chapter 7
The Ripple Effect: Change in Trust and Its Impact Over a Social Network

Jennifer Golbeck and Ugur Kuter

Abstract Computing trust between individuals in social networks is important for many intelligent systems that take advantage of reasoning in social situations. There have been many algorithms developed for inferring trust relationships in a variety of ways. These algorithms all work on a snapshot of the network; that is, they do not take into account changes in trust values over time. However, trust between people is always changing in realistic social networks and when changes happen, inferred trust values in the network will also change. Under these circumstances, the behavior the existing trust-inference algorithms is not yet very well understood. In this paper, we present an experimental study of several types of trust inference algorithms to answer the following questions on trust and change:

- How far does a single change propagate through the network?
- How large is the impact of that change?
- How does this relate to the type of inference algorithm?

Our experimental results provide insights into which algorithms are most suitable for certain applications.

7.1 Introduction

Trust is used in different ways in a variety of systems. *Social* trust, originating from social networks, is an important factor for many systems that seek to use social factors to improve functionality and performance. For example, when two individuals know each other, they know how much to trust one another. Two people who are not directly connected in a social network do not have a foundation for knowing about trust. However, the paths connecting them in the network contain information that can be used to infer how much they may trust one another.

J. Golbeck (✉)
College of Information Studies, 2118F Hornbake Building, University of Maryland, College Park, MD 20742, USA
e-mail: jgolbeck@umd.edu

J. Golbeck (ed.), *Computing with Social Trust,* Human-Computer Interaction Series, DOI 10.1007/978-1-84800-356-9_7 © Springer-Verlag London Limited 2009

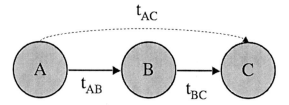

Fig. 7.1 An illustration of direct trust values between nodes A and B (t_{AB}), and between nodes B and C (t_{BC}). Using a trust inference algorithm, it is possible to compute a value to recommend how much A may trust C (t_{AC})

Consider that Alice trusts Bob, and Bob trusts Charlie. Although Alice does not know Charlie, she knows and trusts Bob who, in turn, has information about how trustworthy he believes Charlie is. Alice can use information from Bob and her own trust in Bob to infer how much she may trust Charlie. This is illustrated in Fig. 7.1.

There have been many algorithms developed for inferring trust in social networks. These algorithms differ from each other in the way they infer trust values and propagate those values over the network. Some of the algorithms are *global* [10, 4, 8]: they compute only a single trust value for a node in the network. The others are *local* [2, 5, 9]; their computations are based on network-flow techniques that allow them to propagate trust and do local inferences within the neighborhood of a node.

All existing work on trust inference has focused on developing algorithms in order to increase the accuracy of the inferred trust values in a social network. In this paper, we focused on a different aspect of trust inference. In particular, we investigated change in trust values in the social network and the impact of that change on the results of the existing algorithms. We designed an experimental study to understand the behavior of different trust inference algorithms with respect to the changes occur in the social network. The contributions of this study are as follows:

- *How far does a single change propagate through the network?* Our hypothesis was that the distance that a given trust value change propagages will vary among algorithms. In several algorithms, we saw the change propagate far through the network, affecting a significant number of inferences at every step.
- *How large is the impact of that change?* Our hypothesis was that the magnitude of the effect of the change in a given trust value will vary among algorithms. Our study demonstrated that in the trust-inference algorithms that searched through the network, the size of the changes remained relatively steady even as distance increased.
- *How does this relate to the type of inference algorithm?* Our hypothesis was that different types of algorithms would propagate the changes differently. We found this to be the case, and we present results on the features of each algorithm that impact its behavior.

7.2 Trust Inference Algorithms

There are many different approaches to computing trust inferences in social networks. Below, we present a summary of these algorithms where we have grouped types of trust inference algorithms into a taxonomy.

7.2.1 Local vs. Global

One of the major distinguishing characteristics of a trust inference algorithm is whether it considers personalization, and is a *local trust algorithm*, or if it computes a single trust value for each user, and is a *global trust algorithm*. The global approach is appropriate in applications where trust reflects behavior that is universally considered good or bad. For example, if trust is used in peer-to-peer systems, the reliability of a peer is a measure of its trustworthiness, since failed transactions are always bad. In other contexts, a local metric may be more appropriate. Local trust inference algorithms compute different values for the sink based on who the source is. When the application is one that is opinion-based, and there is no shared idea of good and bad or right and wrong, a local trust metric will compute a rating that most closely matches the preferences of the source.

7.2.2 Central Authority vs. Group vs. Individual

Global trust algorithms do not personalize the inference for the individual. Traditionally, these algorithms define some criteria for trustworthiness, and compute trust based on that criteria. As described earlier, in P2P systems, the trustworthiness of a peer is judged by how reliable it is. Each peer can keep track of the reliability of the peers with which it interacts, and the reliability information for different peers can be aggregated into a trust value. Essentially, a centralized authority dictates what constitutes trust and determines how well the nodes in the network meet that criteria.

One step more personalized than having a centralized authority is a group trust metric. These algorithms define a group of individuals in the network who serve as an authoritative "committee." Trust is computed from the perspective of the nodes on the committee. This model allows system users to determine trustworthiness, but prevents malicious attacks on the system by granting authority to users who have the system's best interest in mind. Advogato [8], at http://advogato.org, is one of the original examples where group trust metrics are used. The website serves as a community discussion board and resource for free software developers. A group trust metric is used to determine who is allowed to post and comment in different places, preventing spam postings and encouraging good behavior. Ziegler and Lausen [12] also propose a group trust metric, called Appleseed. Instead of using maximum flow as Advogato does, it employs spreading activation strategies to produce a trust ranking of individuals in the network.

Local trust algorithms compute trust from the perspective of the source node. These are appropriate in networks where trust is a function of opinion. For example, the FilmTrust website [3] has users rate how much they trust other users about movies. In this case, there is no universal right or wrong opinion about a film. A global or group trust metric would reflect the overall opinion of a user; however, this would not be useful to the individual. For example, if Bob highly trusts Alice's opinion, it does not matter if everyone else thinks Alice has terrible taste for movies – her opinions will still be useful to and trusted by Bob.

7.2.3 Computation Methods

Many of the algorithms for computing trust in P2P networks can be directly applied to social networks. In P2P systems, trust in a peer describes how well it can be expected to perform. Since performance generally does not vary based on which peer requests a file, global algorithms that compute a single trust value for each peer are appropriate. These algorithms usually employ matrix-representations for trust values and perform incremental matrix operations to infer trust until some convergence criteria has been reached.

A number of algorithms search for paths between the source and the sink in the network to infer trust. These algorithms are all local, or personalized; the trust computed for the sink varies depending on the source and the structure of the network. They infer trust by aggregating the trust of a node in the sink and in its immediate successors and propagating the aggregated value back to the parent of that node. For example, TidalTrust [2] and MoleTrust [9] both use a form of weighted average of trust values to compute a single trust value of a node in the sink.

7.3 Algorithms Studied

In this paper, our goal is not to identify the most accurate algorithms, but to show how changes in trust values affect inferred values. Thus, we have chosen a generic but a representative algorithm from each group of the taxonomy described to study the general differences in how changes in trust values affect inference.

7.3.1 Inference Algorithms Based on Matrix Arithmetic

One widely cited trust inference algorithm for P2P systems is EigenTrust [4]. It considers trust as a function of corrupt vs. valid files that the node provides. A peer maintains information about the trust it has in its peers with which it has interacted based on the proportion of good files it has received from that peer. For one peer to determine the trust it should have in another with which it has not interacted, it needs to gather information from the network and infer the trust. The EigenTrust algorithm calculates trust with a variation on the PageRank algorithm [10], used by Google for rating the relevance of web pages to a search. A peer creates a direct trust rating for another peer based on its historical performance. In its simple form, the algorithm uses a matrix representation of the trust values within the system and over a series of iterations it converges to a globally accepted trust rating of each peer. Because of safeguards built into the system, EigenTrust has been shown to be highly resistant to attack.

The traditional PageRank model cannot deal with very large Web graphs very efficiently. In [1], the authors address this issue by a method to incrementally compute PageRank for a large slowly evolving network so that the computation costs may be saved by not re-computing the scores for the unchanged portion. In particular, this approach partitions the network into two portions such that one of the subnetwork models the portion of the Web that is affected by some changes and the other portion is the part of the Web that is unaffected. Once the affected subnetwork portio, the PageRank of the unchanged vertices could be calculated by simply scaling the scores from the previous time instance. Since the percent of change in the structure is not high, the computation will include a smaller graph of the Web resulting in efficiency in many cases. Experimental results presented in [1] show significant speed up compared to the original PageRank algorithm.

The work by [6] focus on the cases on the Web, where the changes occur frequently and describes a way for updating the PageRank vector. The authors identify the need to update page rankings that occur in the web's structure as a potential bottleneck for the computation; in particular, when pages and links are added or deleted and the update is done by a brute force exploration as in the original PageRank algorithm. The paper describes a novel way to solve this issue by partitioning the state space into intervals of time such that the rank updates could be done independently in each partition and the ranking matrix for each update is a smaller approximation of the original one. The experiments demonstrate performance improvements for the updating algorithm compared to Google's full recomputation.

In their follow-up work [7], the authors provide a theoretical analysis that as the dumping constant increases, the PageRank vector becomes more sensitive to small changes. However, as the constant becomes smaller, the influence of the actual link structure in the web is decreased. The analysis shows that PageRank is robust and stable under perturbations, compared to other ranking algorithms; however, it also shows that a change in one outlink of a very low ranking page can turn the entire ranking upside down. The authors emphasize the need for updating the PageRank vector frequently. Pages that are larger in size are changed more often and more extensively than their smaller counterparts. Based on these analyses, the paper describes a new algorithm that provides a fast approximate PageRank for updates to the Web's link structure. The experimental results on this algorithm in comparison to the original PageRank are quite promising.

As a generalization of EigenTrust and other eigenvector-based trust inference algorithms, we have used a version of PageRank that considers weighted edges to study how changes in trust ratings propagate.

7.3.2 Network-Path Inference Algorithms

Richardson et al. [11] use social networks with trust to calculate the belief a user may have in a statement. This is done by finding paths (either through enumeration or probabilistic methods) from the source to any node, which represents an opinion of the statement in question, concatenating trust values along the paths to come up with the recommended belief in the statement for that path, and aggregating those values to come up with a final trust value for the statement. Their paper intentionally does not define a specific concatenation function for calculating trust between individuals, opting instead to present a general framework as their main result. To test their algorithms, they do choose a concatenation function (multiplication) and demonstrate the accuracy of their results using the Epinions network.

TidalTrust [2] is a trust algorithm that also uses trust values within the social network. It is a modified breadth-first search. The source's inferred trust rating for the sink ($t_{source,sink}$) is a weighted average if the source's neighbors' ratings of the sink. The source node begins a search for the sink. It will poll each of its neighbors to obtain their rating of the sink. If the neighbor has a direct rating of the sink, that value is returned. If the neighbor does not have a direct rating for the sink, it queries all of its neighbors for their ratings, computes the weighted average, and returns the result. Each neighbor repeats this process. Essentially, the nodes perform a breadth first search from the source to the sink. In this algorithm, nodes keep a running record of the search depth and the minimum trust value along each path. These are available to limit the information that is considered so that the result is as accurate as possible. TidalTrust was evaluated in two social networks and shown to predict trust values that were within approximately 10% of the known values.

MoleTrust [9] works in two steps. The first builds a directed acyclic graph from the source to all nodes within a fixed distance, known as the *Trust Propagation Horizon*. Cycles are removed by deleting edges from a node to another node that is equidistant or closer to the source. The second step uses this DAG to compute trust in the sink. MoleTrust first computes the trust score of all the users within one step of the sink, then of all the users within two steps, and so on. Once the trust values for the intermediate nodes are computed, they are used to compute the trust in the sink. That value is given by the average of the incoming trust values to the sink, weighted by the computed trust in the nodes that assigned those trust values. To improve accuracy, the algorithm ignores any information from nodes whose trust value is less than 0.6 on a 0–1 scale. Note that it is only possible to compute trust in the sink if it is within the trust propagation horizon of the source.

All these algorithms have optimizations that prune branches of the search, limit the depth of the search, or aggregate values differently. As a generalization, we developed an experimental algorithm that uses breadth-first search from source to sink to find paths. Nodes that know the sink pass their ratings to their parents in the search. Nodes that receive values compute a weighted average of their children's ratings of the sink, and pass the results to their parents. This closely resembles all three algorithms described earlier without any of the optimizations.

As mentioned earlier, Advogato is a website and a group trust metric [8]. Each user on the site has a single trust rating calculated from the perspective of designated seeds (authoritative nodes). Trust calculations are made using the maximum trust flow along a path from one of the authoritative seeds to the user. His metric composes certifications between members to determine the trust level of a person, and thus their membership within a group. Users can be certified at three levels: apprentice, journeyer, and master. Access to post and edit website information is controlled by these certifications. Like EigenTrust, the Advogato metric is quite resistant to attacks. By identifying individual nodes as "bad" and finding any nodes that certify the "bad" nodes, the metric cuts out an unreliable portion of the network. Calculations are based primarily on the good nodes, so the network as a whole remains secure. It is a global trust algorithm because the same seeds are used to make calculations for every user. Advogato is also a group trust metric because it uses groups to determine who can post messages. A common alteration to Advogato sets the user as the single seed, thus converting it to a local metric with personalized calculations.

7.4 Experimental Setup

The data set for our experiments was taken from the FilmTrust network (http://trust.mindswap.org). FilmTrust is a website with a social network where users rate how much they trust their friends about movies. There are approximately 1,500 members in the network. Many of those members do not have friends, however, and those singletons were excluded from our study. We used a total of 638 members in our study with 1,368 relationships between them.

To test the effect of a change in trust value, we began by selecting a pair of users with an edge between them in the network. To see the maximum impact of a change, we set the trust value between them to 1 (on a 0–1 scale). We then computed the inferred trust value between every pair of users in the network using our experimental algorithms. This gave us our initial set of trust values. We then changed the trust value for our selected pair of users from 1 to 0, and performed a second inference of trust between all pairs of users. The difference between the first and second executions was used to measure the spread and magnitude of the change.

Because we believe the structural attributes of a node influence the impact a change has, we also computed basic statistics for each node including degree, centrality (measured by average shortest path length), and clustering coefficient.

In our experiments, we used the following three trust inference algorithms: PageRank, Advogato, and TidalTrust. As we described earlier, both PageRank and Advogato are global trust-inference metrics, whereas TidalTrust is a local trust algorithm. We used two different versions of TidalTrust in these experiments. The original TidalTrust algorithm computes an inferred trust value from a source node to a sink based on the shortest path(s) between the two nodes, as described earlier.

We have also implemented a variant of TidalTrust, called TidalTrust++, in which the algorithm not only considers the shortest path between a source and a sink, but also all the other paths as well. The rationale behind this modified algorithm was to investigate how much a change in the network is propagated by TidalTrust—note that in the original TidalTrust algorithm, the propagated effect is expected to be minimal unless the change occurs directly on the shortest path between a source and a sink.

We designed and implemented the following experimental protocol in order to measure and analyze change in trust values and its impact on the network:

1. Choose a source node (the one assigning a rating)
2. Choose a sink node (the one being rated).
3. Set the source's rating of the sink to the highest possible trust rating.
4. Run the trust-inference algorithms in order to infer the trust that every other node has in the sink.
5. Infer the trust value from every node to every other node.
6. Change the value the source has for the sink from the highest rating as set in step 3 to the lowest possible value.
7. Repeat steps 4 and 5.

Based on this protocol, we have investigated the behavior and the outcomes of Advogato, PageRank, TidalTrust, and TidalTrust++ with several experimental parameters such as the amount of change propagated in the network, the overall magnitude of change during that propagation, and the influence of the network structure on the propagation of the change. The following section presents our results.

7.5 Results

7.5.1 Number and Distance of Changes

Given a change in the trust value between a given *source* and *sink* (we call these the "control source" and "control sink"), we began by investigating how far this change propagated through the networks, and the magnitude of those changes. For each node n with a path to the control sink, we computed the inferred trust value using each of the algorithms in our study. For each step away from the sink, we counted the number of nodes whose inferred trust value for the control sink changed, and measured the magnitude of that change.

For each control source–sink pair, we computed the fraction of nodes that saw a change in their inferred trust value for the control sink grouped by their distance from the control sink. We averaged these fractions over all control source–sink pairs, and these results are shown in Fig. 7.2. In PageRank, the average number of changes were always high (close to 100% in each case) due to the Eigenvector computations. Because the trust values are computed as the left principle eigenvector and must sum to one, any change will force the other values to normalize thus producing a change.

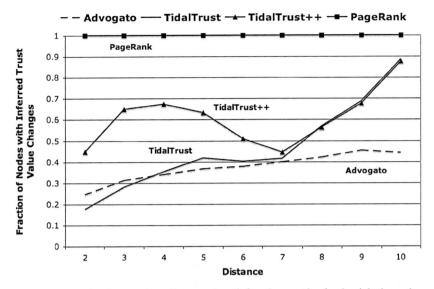

Fig. 7.2 Fraction of nodes at a given distance whose inferred trust value for the sink changed

In Advogato and TidalTrust, however, the average number of changes increases with the increasing distance as they both search through the network in our order to propagate and compute the trust values. The reason behind these results is that as the distance is increased between a node and its sink in the network, the likelihood that the change will occur in between those two nodes also increases. Since both TidalTrust and Advogato perform a breadth-first search between a node and a sink, they incorporate the change and propagate it in their inference more often in the network. The average size of the change propagated by TidalTrust is larger than that of Advogato since the latter performs it's search only from the designated seed nodes in the network to the outlier nodes, whereas the former performs a search between any two nodes in the network.

7.5.2 The Magnitude of Change

Next, we have studied the magnitude of the change propagated via our experimental algorithms throughout the network. Similar to the analysis above, for each control source–sink pair, we computed the average change in inferred trust values from all nodes to the control sink, grouped by distance. These values were averaged over all control source–sink pairs with results shown in Fig. 7.3.

In Advogato, TidalTrust, and TidalTrust++ when the inferred trust for the control sink, it changed significantly – between 30 and 70%. In PageRank, the change was very small. It is important to note that that PageRank is the only algorithm that does not output trust values in the same scale that they are assigned. Thus, we would not expect to see changes of the same magnitude as the other algorithms. The output

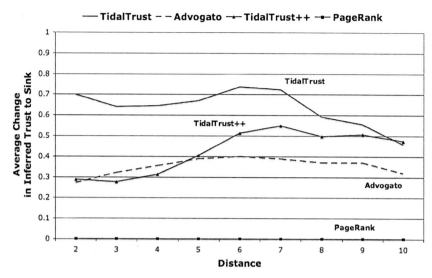

Fig. 7.3 Average magnitude of change in trust to the control sink as a function of the distance to that sink

of any eigenvector-based trust algorithm cannot be directly compared to algorithms like Advogato or TidalTrust.

The results were surprising. We initially expected that the size of the change to decrease with distance. As the distance to the sink increases, there are more paths available from a node to the sink. Thus, in both Advogato and the TidalTrust algorithms, there was opportunity for the change to be diminished as the paths that included the change were averaged with paths that did not include change. However, the fact that the magnitude of the change remains high as distance increases suggests that the change spreads somewhat evenly across all paths to the sink, so nodes three steps away encounter the approximately fraction of the time as nodes much further away.

For our main results, we computed the difference in inferred trust values when the value on a single edge changed from the maximum value to the minimum value. In practice, changes will likely be smaller than that. We also tested changes between the control sink of several smaller increments. The smaller changes had a proportional effect on the inferred values. The average magnitude of change in the inferred values had a direct linear relationship to the size of the change between the control source and control sink. This is expected, and it confirms that our experimental conclusions are applicable to the more common sized trust changes in real social networks.

7.5.3 Influence of the Network Structure

It seems obvious that the structural attributes of the nodes will affect how trust changes propagate through the network. For example, if a node on the edge of the network with no outgoing edges is the control sink, there should be no effect on inferences between other nodes. If only one person knows the control sink, and that trust value is changed, we would expect every inferred value to that sink to change. However, if many people know the control sink, we would expect different behavior.

In this study we performed a basic analysis looking for correlations between the structural attributes of the control nodes with the number and size of changes in inferred trust values. We were not able to discover any straightforward correlations. Most likely, there are more complex interactions between structure and trust inference than we were able to see in this initial analysis. Understanding this relationship is important future work.

7.5.4 Other Changes in Trust Inference

We have focused our analysis so far on changes in the inference to the control sink. However, a change in the value between the control source and sink can affect inferences between other nodes. Specifically, if an algorithm computing trust from A to B considers a path that includes the edge between the control source and control sink, the inferred trust for B may be affected.

In our experiments, we tracked the number and size of these changes. For both PageRank and Advogato, these changes would manifest as changes in the trust value for a given node that was not the control sink, since both algorithms are global. For TidalTrust and TidalTrust++, the changes would be measured as changes in the inferred value between a pair of nodes. To count the same way among all algorithms, we looked at the change based on pairs of nodes. For the global algorithms, if the trust value computed for a node A changed, then it would change in every pair considered. Table 7.1 shows these results.

Table 7.1 The average number of changes in trust inferences and the average size of changes between nodes other than the control source and control sink

Algorithm	Avg. # of Change	Avg. Change Size
PageRank:	1.0	1.0
Advogato:	0.001	0.174
TidalTrust:	0.0003	0.093
TidalTrust++:	0.001	0.056

7.6 Discussion and Conclusions

In social networks, trust between people, whether computed from data or asserted directly, is constantly changing. How does a single change impact trust inferences in the network? How far will that effect propagate and what will be the magnitude of its impact? In this study, we have analyzed several different types of trust inference algorithms to see answer these questions and relate the results to features of the algorithms themselves.

Using an eigenvector-based model, a network flow model, and a network search model, we found several results. Our experiment changed one value at a time and looked at the difference between inferred values computed when the control source changed its rating to the control sink from the maximum to minimum value. In all algorithms we found that a significant portion of nodes saw a change in their inferred value to the control sink. The faction of nodes whose inferred value changed was overall increasing. This is because the nodes further away had a higher change of encountering a path to the sink that went through the changed edge. We also saw that the magnitude of the change remained relatively constant over distance, illustrating that the impact of the change does not diminish with distance. Finally, we demonstrated that not only were trust inferences to the control sink impacted, but inferences between other nodes in the network, but inferred values between other pairs also changed.

The results here have implications for systems designed to use trust from social networks. Values can change frequently, and this study shows that a single change can lead to significant changes in inferred trust values throughout the network. Users of system that uses these values could, in turn, see significant changes in the behavior of the system as trust changes. With the general knowledge provided by this study, builders of intelligent systems with trust can consider ways to smooth the performance or adjust their computations to handle these changes in the network.

Acknowledgments Thanks to Sureyya Tarkan for her help in the initial stages of this research.

References

1. Prasanna Kumar Desikan, Nishith Pathak, Jaideep Srivastava, and Vipin Kumar. Invremental page rank computation on evolving graphs. In *WWW (Special interest tracks and posters)*, pages 1094–1095, 2005.
2. Jennifer Golbeck. *Computing and Applying Trust in Web-based Social Networks*. PhD thesis, University of Maryland, College Park, MD, April 2005.
3. Jennifer Golbeck. Generating predictive movie recommendations from trust in social networks. In *Proceedings of the Fourth International Conference on Trust Management*, 2006.
4. Sepandar D. Kamvar, Mario T. Schlosser, and Hector Garcia-Molina. The eigentrust algorithm for reputation management in p2p networks. In *WWW '03: Proceedings of the 12th international conference on World Wide Web*, pages 640–651, ACM Press, New York, NY, USA, 2003.
5. Ugur Kuter and Jennifer Golbeck: Sunny: A new algorithm for trust inference in social networks, using probabilistic confidence models. In *Proceedings of the National Conference on Artifical Intelligence (AAAI)*, 2007.
6. A. Langville and C. Meyer. Updating pagerank with iterative aggregation. In *Proceedings of the 13th World Wide Web Conference*, 2004.
7. Amy Nicole Langville and carl Dean Meyer. Survey: Deeper inside pagerank. *Internet Mathematics*, 1(3), 2003.
8. Raph Levien and Alex Aiken. Attack-resistant trust metrics for public key certification. In *7th USENIX Security Symposium*, pages 229–242, 1998.

9. P. Massa and P. Avesani. Trust-aware collaborative filtering for recommender systems. In *Proc. of Federated int. Conference On The Move to Meaningful Internet: CoopsIS, DOA, ODBASE*, 2004.

10. Lawrence Page, Sergey Brin, Rajeev Motwani, and Terry Winograd. The pagerank citation ranking: Bringing order to the Web. Technical report, Stanford Digital Library Technologies Project, 1998.

11. Matthew Richardson, R. Agrawal, and P. Domingos. Trust management for the semantic web. In *Proceedings of the Second International Semantic Web Conference*, 2003.

12. Cai-Nicolas Ziegler and Georg Lausen. Spreading activation models for trust propagation. In *Proceedings of the IEEE International Conference on e-Technology, e-Commerce, and e-service*. IEEE Computer Society Press, Taipei, Taiwan, March 2004.

Part III
Applications of Trust

Chapter 8
Eliciting Informative Feedback:
The Peer-Prediction Method

Nolan Miller, Paul Resnick, and Richard Zeckhauser

Abstract Many recommendation and decision processes depend on eliciting evaluations of opportunities, products, and vendors. A scoring system is devised that induces honest reporting of feedback. Each rater merely reports a signal, and the system applies proper scoring rules to the implied posterior beliefs about another rater's report. Honest reporting proves to be a Nash Equilibrium. The scoring schemes can be scaled to induce appropriate effort by raters and can be extended to handle sequential interaction and continuous signals. We also address a number of practical implementation issues that arise in settings such as academic reviewing and on-line recommender and reputation systems.

8.1 Introduction

Decision makers frequently draw on the experiences of multiple other individuals when making decisions. The process of eliciting others' information is sometimes informal, as when an executive consults underlings about a new business opportunity. In other contexts, the process is institutionalized, as when journal editors secure independent reviews of papers, or an admissions committee has multiple faculty readers for each file. The Internet has greatly enhanced the role of institutionalized feedback methods, since it can gather and disseminate information from vast numbers of individuals at minimal cost. To name just a few examples, eBay invites buyers and sellers to rate each other; NetFlix, Amazon, and ePinions invite ratings of movies, books, and so on a 1–5 scale; and Zagat Survey solicits restaurant ratings on a 1–30 scale on food, decor, and service.

Any system that solicits individual opinions must overcome two challenges. The first is underprovision. Forming and reporting an opinion requires time and effort, yet the information only benefits others. The second challenge is honesty. Raters' desire to be nice or fear of retaliation may cause them to withhold negative

N. Miller (✉)
Kennedy School of Government, Harvard University, Cambridge, MA, USA

J. Golbeck (ed.), *Computing with Social Trust,* Human-Computer Interaction Series, 185
DOI 10.1007/978-1-84800-356-9_8 © Springer-Verlag London Limited 2009

feedback.[1] On the other hand, conflicts of interest or a desire to improve others' perception of them may lead raters to report distorted versions of their true opinions.

An explicit reward system for honest rating and effort may help to overcome these challenges. When objective information will be publicly revealed at a future time, individuals' reports can be compared to that objective information. For example, evaluations of stocks can be compared to subsequent price movements, and weather forecasts can be compared to what actually occurs.

This analysis develops methods to elicit feedback effectively when independent, objective outcomes are not available. Examples include situations where no objective outcome exists (e.g., evaluations of a product's "quality"), and where the relevant information is objective but not public (e.g., a product's breakdown frequency, which is only available to others if the product's current owners reveal it).

In these situations, one solution is to compare raters' reports to their peers' reports and reward agreement.[2] However, if rewards are made part of the process, dangers arise. If a particular outcome is highly likely, such as a positive experience with a seller at eBay who has a stellar feedback history, then a rater who has a bad experience will still believe that the next rater is likely to have a good experience. If she will be rewarded simply for agreeing with her peers, she will not report her bad experience. This phenomenon is akin to the problems of herding or information cascades.

In this paper, we develop a formal mechanism to implement the process of comparing with peers. We label this mechanism the peer-prediction method. The scheme uses one rater's report to update a probability distribution for the report of someone else, whom we refer to as the reference rater. The first rater is then scored not on agreement between the ratings, but on a comparison between the *likelihood* assigned to the reference rater's possible ratings and the reference rater's actual rating. Raters need not perform any complex computations: so long as a rater trusts that the center will update appropriately, she will prefer to report honestly.

Scores can be converted to monetary incentives, either as direct payments or as discounts on future merchandise purchases. In many online systems, however, raters seem to be quite motivated by prestige or privileges within the system. For example, at Slashdot.org, users accumulate karma points for various actions and higher karma entitles users to rate others' postings and to have their own postings

---

[1] Dellarocas [9] shows that leniency in feedback can offer some advantages in deterring seller opportunism. The problem we are concerned with here is not systematic leniency, but the failure to report negative evaluations, whatever threshold is in use.

[2] Subjective evaluations of ratings could be elicited directly instead of relying on correlations between ratings. For example, the news and commentary site Slashdot.org allows meta-moderators to rate the ratings of comments given by regular moderators. Meta-evaluation incurs an obvious inefficiency, since the effort to rate evaluations could presumably be put to better use in rating comments or other products that are a site's primary product of interest. Moreover, meta-evaluation merely pushes the problem of motivating effort and honest reporting up one level, to ratings of evaluations. Thus, scoring evaluations in comparison to other evaluations is preferable.

begin with higher ratings [17] ; at ePinions.com, reviewers gain status and have their reviews highlighted if they accumulate points. Similarly, offline point systems that do not provide any tangible reward seem to motivate chess and bridge players to compete harder and more frequently.

The key insight that the correlation in agents' private information can be used to induce truthful revelation has been addressed, albeit in an abstract way, in the mechanism design literature. Seminal papers by d'Aspremont and Gérard-Varet [7, 8] and Crémer and McLean [5, 6] demonstrate that it is generally possible to use budget-balancing transfer payments to extract agents' private information. Adapting tools from statistical decision theory, Johnson, Pratt, and Zeckhauser [15] show how to construct budget-balancing transfer payments based on proper scoring rules. Johnson, Miller, Pratt, and Zeckhauser [14] extend those results to the case of multidimensional, continuous private information. Kandori and Matsushima ([16] Section 8.4.2) consider how to enforce cooperation in repeated games through correlated equilibria despite the lack of public information about stage game outcomes, and show how to apply a proper scoring rule to elicit truthful communication of private information about stage game outcomes.

This paper applies the *general* insights on the usefulness of proper scoring rules for eliciting correlated information to the *particular* problem of eliciting honest reviews of products, papers, and proposals. Our mechanism is well suited to Internet-based implementations, and it could potentially be applied to services such as NetFlix or Amazon.[3] Once ratings are collected and distributed electronically, it is relatively easy to compute posteriors and scores and keep track of payments.[4]

In Section 8.2 we construct payments based on proper scoring rules that allow the center to elicit the rater's private information and show how the payments can be adapted to address costly effort elicitation, and budget balance and voluntary participation requirements. Section 8.3 extends our approach to scenarios of sequential reporting and of discrete reporting based on continuous signals. In Section 8.4 we address practical issues that would arise in implementing proper scoring rules in real systems, including conflicts of interest, estimating the information the mechanism requires from historical reviewing data, and accommodating differences among raters in both tastes and in prior beliefs. We also discuss limitations of the mechanism. Section 8.5 concludes. Proofs and supporting materials are contained in two appendices.

---

[3] It could also be extended to eBay or Bizrate, which rate sellers rather than products. Rating sellers, however, complicates the analysis. For example, if sellers strategically vary the quality of service they provide over time, the correlation between one rater's evaluation and future raters' evaluations might be severed, disrupting our scoring mechanism.

[4] Drazen Prelec's Information Pump [24] exploits correlated information and proper scoring rules to elicit honest reports in a different setting, estimating the additional information provided by a sequence of true-false statements about an object.

8.2 A Mechanism for Eliciting Honest Feedback

A number of raters experience a product and then rate its quality. The product's quality product does not vary, but is observed with some idiosyncratic error. After experiencing the product, each rater sends a message to a common processing facility called the center. The center makes transfers to each rater, awarding or taking away points based on the raters' messages. The center has no independent information, so its scoring decisions can depend only on the information provided by other raters. As noted earlier above, points may be convertible to money, discounts or privileges within the system, or merely to prestige. We assume that raters' utilities are linear in points.[5] We refer to a product's quality as its type. We refer to a rater's perception of a product's type as her signal.

Suppose that the number of product types is finite, and let the types be indexed by $t = 1, ..., T$. Let $p(t)$ be the commonly held prior probability assigned to the product's being type t.[6] Assume that $p(t) > 0$ for all t and $\sum_{t=1}^{T} p(t) = 1$.

Let I be the set of raters, where $|I| \geq 3$. We allow for the possibility that I is (countably) infinite. Each rater privately observes a signal of the product's type.[7] Conditional on the product's type, raters' signals are independent and identically distributed. Let S^i denote the random signal received by rater i. Let $S = \{s_1, ..., s_M\}$ be the set of possible signals, and let $f(s_m|t) = \Pr(S^i = s_m|t)$, where $f(s_m|t) > 0$ for all s_m and t, and $\sum_{m=1}^{M} f(s_m|t) = 1$ for all t. We assume that $f(s_m|t)$ is common knowledge, and that the conditional distribution of signals is different for different values of t. Let $s^i \in S$ denote a generic realization of S^i. We use s_m^i to denote the event $S^i = s_m$. We assume that raters are risk neutral and seek to maximize expected wealth.

To illustrate throughout this section, we introduce a simple example. There are only two product types, H and L, with prior $p(H) = .5$, and two possible signals, h and l, with $f(h|H) = .85$ and $f(h|L) = .45$. Thus, $\Pr(h) = .5*.85 + .5*.45 = .65$.

In the mechanism we propose, the center asks each rater to announce her signal. After all signals are announced to the center, they are revealed to the other raters and the center computes transfers. We refer to this as the simultaneous reporting game. Let $a^i \in S$ denote one such announcement, and $a = (a^1, ..., a^I)$ denote a vector of announcements, one by each rater. Let $a_m^i \in S$ denote rater i's announcement when her signal is s_m, and $\bar{a}^i = (a_1^i, ..., a_M^i) \in S^M$ denote rater i's announcement strategy. Let $\bar{a} = (\bar{a}^1, ..., \bar{a}^I)$ denote a vector of announcement strategies. As is customary, let the superscript "$-i$" denote a vector without rater i's component.

Let $\tau_i(a)$ denote the transfer paid to rater i when the raters make announcements a, and let $\tau(a) = (\tau_1(a), ..., \tau_I(a))$ be the vector of transfers made to all agents. An announcement strategy $\bar{a}^i$ is a best response to $\bar{a}^{-i}$ for player i if for each m:

---

[5] We consider the impacts of risk aversion in Section 8.4.1.
[6] We briefly address the issue of non-common priors in Section 8.4.5.
[7] We refer to raters as female and to the center as male.

$$E_{S^{-i}}\left[\tau_i\left(\bar{a}_m^i, \bar{a}^{-i}\right) | s_m^i\right] \geq E_{S^{-i}}\left[\tau_i\left(\hat{a}^i, \bar{a}^{-i}\right) | s_m^i\right] \tag{8.1}$$

That is, a strategy is a best response if, conditional on receiving signal s_m, the announcement specified by the strategy maximizes that rater's expected transfer, where the expectation is taken with respect to the distribution of all other raters' signals conditional on $S^i = s_m$. Given transfer scheme $\tau(a)$, a vector of announcement strategies $\bar{a}$ is a Nash Equilibrium of the reporting game if (8.1) holds for $i = 1, ..., I$, and a strict Nash Equilibrium if the inequality in (8.1) is strict for all $i = 1, ..., I$.

Truthful revelation is a Nash Equilibrium of the reporting game if (8.1) holds for all i when $a_m^i = s_m$ for all i and all m, and is a strict Nash Equilibrium if the inequality is strict. That is, if all the other players announce truthfully, truthful announcement is a strict best response. Since raters receive no direct return from their announcement, if there were no transfers at all then any strategy vector, including truthful revelation, would be a Nash equilibrium. However, since players are indifferent among all strategies when there are no transfers, this Nash equilibrium is not strict.

8.2.1 The Base Case

Our base result defines transfers that make truthful revelation a strict Nash equilibrium. Because all raters experience the same product, it is natural to assume that their signals are dependent. Our results rely on a form of dependence which we call stochastic relevance.[8]

Definition: Random variable S^i is **stochastically relevant** for random variable S^j if and only if the distribution of S^j conditional on S^i is different for different realizations of S^i. That is, S^i is stochastically relevant for S^j if for any distinct realizations of S^i, call them s^i and $\hat{s}^i$, there exists at least one realization of S^j, call it s^j, such that $\Pr\left(s^j | s^i\right) \neq \Pr\left(s^j | \hat{s}^i\right)$.

Stochastic relevance is almost always satisfied when different types of products generate different signal distributions, as we assumed above, and so throughout the paper we assume that stochastic relevance holds for all S^i and S^j.[9]

Continuing the two-type, two-signal example, suppose that rater i receives the signal l. Recall that $p(H) = .5$, $f(h|H) = .85$, and $f(h|L) = .45$, so that $\Pr\left(s_l^i\right) = .35$. Given i's signal, the probability that rater j will receive a signal h is:

---

[8] The term "stochastic relevance" is introduced in Johnson, Miller, Pratt, and Zeckhauser [14]. It is the same as condition (A4) used in Kandori and Matsushima [16].
[9] In Miller, Resnick, and Zeckhauser [19], we show that stochastic relevance is generically satisfied in product-rating environments.

$$g\left(s_h^j|s_l^i\right) = f\left(h|H\right)\frac{f\left(l|H\right)p\left(H\right)}{\Pr\left(s_l^i\right)} + f\left(h|L\right)\frac{f\left(l|L\right)p\left(L\right)}{\Pr\left(s_l^i\right)}$$

$$= .85\frac{.15*.5}{.35} + .45\frac{.55*.5}{.35} \cong 0.54.$$

If i had instead observed h, then:

$$g\left(s_h^j|s_h^i\right) = f\left(h|H\right)\frac{f\left(h|H\right)p\left(H\right)}{\Pr\left(s_h^i\right)} + f\left(h|L\right)\frac{f\left(h|L\right)p\left(L\right)}{\Pr\left(s_h^i\right)}$$

$$= .85\frac{.85*.5}{.65} + .45\frac{.45*.5}{.65} \cong 0.71.$$

A scoring rule is a function $R\left(s^j|a^i\right)$ that, for each possible announcement a^i of S^i, assigns a score to each possible realization of S^j. A scoring rule is strictly proper if rater i uniquely maximizes her expected score by announcing the true realization of S^i.

The literature discusses a number of strictly proper scoring rules.[10] The three best known are:

1. Quadratic Scoring Rule: $R\left(s_n^j|a^i\right) = 2g\left(s_n^j|a^i\right) - \sum_{h=1}^{M}g\left(s_h^j|a^i\right)^2$.
2. Spherical Scoring Rule: $R\left(s_n^j|a^i\right) = \frac{g(s_n^j|a^i)}{\left(\sum_{h=1}^{M}g(s_h^j|a^i)^2\right)^{\frac{1}{2}}}$.
3. Logarithmic Scoring Rule: $R\left(s_n^j|a^i\right) = \ln g\left(s_n^j|a^i\right)$.

Further, if $R\left(\cdot|\cdot\right)$ is a strictly proper scoring rule, then a positive affine transformation of it, i.e., $\alpha R\left(\cdot|\cdot\right)+\beta, \alpha > 0$, is also a strictly proper scoring rule. The ability of the center to manipulate α and β is useful in inducing the raters to exert effort and satisfying their participation constraints (see Section 8.2.2). We will use $R\left(s_n^j|a^i\right)$ to denote a generic strictly proper scoring rule. At times we will illustrate our results using the logarithmic rule because of its intuitive appeal and notational simplicity. However, unless otherwise noted, all results hold for any strictly proper scoring rule.

Transfers based on a strictly proper scoring rule induce truthful revelation by agent i as long as her private information is stochastically relevant for some other publicly available signal. However, in our case each rater's signal is private information, and therefore we can only check players' announcements against other players' announcements, not their actual signals. For each rater, we will choose a reference rater $r(i)$, whose announcement i will be asked to predict. Let:

---

[10] See Cooke ([4], p. 139) for a discussion of strictly proper scoring rules. Selten [30] provides proofs that each of the three rules below is strictly proper and discusses other strictly proper scoring rules.

$$\tau_i^* \left(a^i, a^{r(i)} \right) = R \left(a^{r(i)} | a^i \right). \tag{8.2}$$

Proposition 1: *For any mapping r that that assigns to each rater i a reference rater* $r(i) \neq i$, *and for any proper scoring rule R, truthful reporting is a strict Nash equilibrium of the simultaneous reporting game with transfers* τ_i^*.

Proof. **(Proof of Proposition 1)** Assume that rater $r(i)$ reports honestly: $a^{r(i)}(s_m) = s_m$ for all m. Since S^i is stochastically relevant for $S^{r(i)}$, and $r(i)$ reports honestly, S^i is stochastically relevant for $r(i)$'s report as well. For any $S^i = s^*$, player i chooses $a^i \in S$ in order to maximize:

$$\sum_{n=1}^{M} R \left(s_n^{r(i)} | a^i \right) g \left(s_n^{r(i)} | s^* \right). \tag{8.3}$$

Since $R(\cdot|\cdot)$ is a strictly proper scoring rule, (8.3) is uniquely maximized by announcing $a^i = s^*$. Thus, given that rater $r(i)$ is truthful, rater i's best response is to be truthful as well.■

We illustrate Proposition 1 using the logarithmic scoring rule. Since $0 < g \left(s_m^j | s_n^i \right) < 1$, $\ln g \left(s_m^j | s_n^i \right) < 0$; we refer to τ_i^* as rater i's penalty since it is always negative in this case. Consider the simple example where rater i received the relatively unlikely signal l ($\Pr \left(s_l^i \right) = .35$). Even contingent on observing l it is unlikely that rater j will also receive an l signal ($g \left(s_l^j | s_l^i \right) = 1 - 0.54 = .46$). Thus, if rater i were rewarded merely for matching her report to that of rater j, she would prefer to report h. With the log scoring rule, an honest report of l leads to an expected payoff

$$\ln g \left(s_h^j | l \right) g \left(s_h^j | l \right) + \ln g \left(s_l^j | l \right) g \left(s_l^j | l \right) = \ln (.54).54 + \ln(.46).46 = -0.69.$$

If, instead, she reports h, rater i's expected score is:

$$\ln g \left(s_h^j | h \right) g \left(s_h^j | l \right) + \ln g \left(s_l^j | h \right) g \left(s_l^j | l \right) = \ln (.71).54 + \ln(.29).46 = -0.75.$$

As claimed, the expected score is maximized by honest reporting.

The key idea is that the scoring function is based on the updated beliefs about the reference rater's signal, given the rater's report. The updating takes into account both the priors and the reported signal, and thus reflects the initial rater's priors. Thus, she has no reason to shade her report toward the signal expected from the priors. Note also that she need not perform any complex Bayesian updating. She merely reports her signal. As long as she trusts the center to correctly perform the updating and believes other raters will report honestly, she can be confident that honest reporting is her best action.[11]

Note that while Proposition 1 establishes that there is a truthful equilibrium, it is not unique, and there may be nontruthful equilibria. To illustrate, in the example we have been considering two other equilibria are (8.1) report h all the time, and (8.2) report l all the time.[12] While such non-truthful equilibria exist, it is reasonable to think that the truthful equilibrium will be a focal point, especially when communication among raters is limited, or when some raters are known to have a strong ethical preference for honesty. In addition, the center can punish all the raters if it detects a completely uninformative equilibrium such as all h or all l.

8.2.2 Eliciting Effort and Deterring Bribes

Assuming costless evaluation and reporting allowed us to focus on the essence of the scoring-rule based mechanism. However, raters' willingness to exert effort will depend on the direct costs of effort as well as the opportunity cost of being an early evaluator rather than free riding off the evaluations of others. Avery, Resnick, and Zeckhauser [1] explore how market mechanisms can elicit costs and determine appropriate compensation levels, but the assumption that raters will exert effort once they accept compensation is problematic.[13] Here, we use a scoring rule to induce effort. We begin by assuming a fixed cost of rating. We then move on to consider how the center can induce raters to select an optimal effort level when additional costly effort leads to more precise signals.

Suppose there is a fixed cost, $c > 0$, of evaluating and reporting. To induce effort, the expected value of incurring effort and reporting honestly must exceed the expected value of reporting without a signal. As the proof of Proposition 1 makes clear, the truth-inducing incentives provided by scoring-rule based payments are unaffected by a positive rescaling of all transfers: if transfers $\tau_i^* \left(a^i, a^{r(i)} \right) = R \left(a^{r(i)} | a^i \right)$ induce truthful reporting, then $\tau_i^* \left(a^i, a^{r(i)} \right) = \alpha R \left(a^{r(i)} | a^i \right)$, where $\alpha > 0$, does as well. Since the rater is better-informed if she acquires a signal than if she doesn't, and better information always increases the expected value of a decision problem [28, 18], increasing the scaling factor increases the value of effort without affecting the incentives for honest reporting once effort is expended.

---

[11] In an experiment, Nelson and Bessler [21] show that, even when the center does not perform the updating for them, with training and feedback subjects learn that truthful revelation is a best response when rewards are based on a proper scoring rule.

[12] To verify the "always play h equilibrium," note that if the reference rater always reports high, the rater expects $\ln(.54)1 + \ln(.46)0 = -0.61619$ if she reports l, and $\ln(.71)1 + \ln(.29)0 = -0.34249$ if she reports h. Similar reasoning verifies the "always play l equilibrium".

[13] At the news and commentary site Slashdot, where users earn "karma" points for acting as moderators, staff have noticed that occasionally ratings are entered very quickly in succession, faster than someone could reasonably read and evaluate the comments. They call this "vote dumping."

Proposition 2: *Let $c > 0$ denote the cost of acquiring and reporting a signal. If other raters acquire and report their signals honestly, there exists a scalar $\alpha > 0$ such that when rater i is paid according to $\tau_i^* \left(a^i, a^{r(i)} \right) = \alpha R \left(a^{r(i)} | a^i \right)$, her best response is to acquire a signal and report it honestly.*[14]

Scaling can be used to induce raters to work harder to obtain better information. Without putting additional structure on the distributions under consideration, the natural notion of "better" information is to think about the rater's experience as being a random sample, with better information corresponding to greater sample size. If the cost of acquiring a sample is increasing and convex in its size, we can ask when and how the center can induce the raters to acquire samples of a particular size.

Because of space considerations, we relegate the technical presentation to Appendix B. However, the basic idea is straightforward.[15] For any sample size, stochastic relevance continues to hold. Thus, when the rater is paid according to a strictly proper scoring rule, she maximizes her expected score by truthfully announcing her information (if all other raters do as well). When a rater increases her sample size from, say, x to $x + 1$, the additional observation further partitions the outcome space. Using well-known results from decision theory [28, 18], this implies that the rater's optimized expected score increases in the sample size. Let $V^*(x)$ denote optimized expected score as a function of sample size. The question of whether the center can induce the rater to choose a particular sample size, x^*, then comes down to whether there exists a scaling factor, α^*, such that

$$x^* \in \arg\max_x \alpha^* V^*(x) - c(x).$$

If $V^*(x)$ is concave in x and $c(x)$ satisfies certain regularity conditions (i.e., $c'(0) = 0$, and $\lim_{x \to \infty} c'(x) = \infty$), it is possible to induce the agent to choose any desired sample size. We return to the question of eliciting effort in Section 8.3.2.1, where, due to assuming information is normally distributed, we are able to present the theory more parsimoniously.

Scaling can also be used to overwhelm individuals' outside preferences, including bribes that may be offered for positive ratings. For example, if a bribe has been offered for a positive rating, the constant c can be interpreted to include the potential opportunity cost of acquiring a negative signal and then reporting it.

8.2.3 Voluntary Participation and Budget Balance

In some cases, the expected payment from truthful reporting (and optimal effort) may be insufficient to induce the rater to participate in the mechanism in the first

---

[14] Proofs not included in the main text are in Appendix A.

[15] Clemen [3] undertakes a similar analysis in the context of a principal–agent problem.

place. This is most apparent when the logarithmic rule is employed, since the logarithmic score is always negative. However, this problem is easily addressed. Since adding a constant to all payments (i.e., letting the transfer be $\alpha_i R \left(a^{r(i)} | a^i\right) + k_i$) does not affect incentives for effort or honest reporting, the constant k_i can be chosen to satisfy either ex ante participation constraints (i.e., each agent must earn a non-negative expected return), interim participation constraints (i.e., each agent must earn a nonnegative expected return conditional on any observed signal), or ex post participation constraints (i.e., the agent must earn a non-negative expected return for each possible $\left(s^j, s^i\right)$ pair). To illustrate using the logarithmic case, let $\tau_0 = \min_{s_m, s_n \in S} (\alpha \ln g (s_m | s_n))$, and define $\tau^+ = \tau^* - \tau_0$. Transfers τ^+ will attract voluntary (ex post) participation while still inducing effort and honest reporting.

It is often desirable for the center to balance its budget. Clearly, this is important if scores are converted into monetary payments. Even if scores are merely points that the center can generate at will, uncontrolled inflation would make it hard for users to interpret point totals. If there are at least three raters, the center can balance the budget by reducing each rater's base transfer τ^* by some other rater's base transfer. Though all the transactions actually occur between raters and the center, this creates the effect of having the raters settle the transfers among each other.[16] Let $b(i)$ be the rater whose base transfer i settles (paying if τ^* is positive, and collecting if it is negative), and let $b(i)$ be a permutation such that $b(i) \neq i$ and $r(b(i)) \neq i$. Rater i's net transfer is:

$$\tau_i(a) = \tau_i^* \left(a^i, a^{r(i)}\right) - \tau_{b(i)}^* \left(a^{b(i)}, a^{r(b(i))}\right). \tag{8.4}$$

These transfers balance. The only raters whose reports can influence the second term are $b(i)$ and rater $b(i)$'s reference rater, $r(b(i))$, and by construction of $b(\cdot)$ they are both distinct from rater i. Since all reports are revealed simultaneously, rater i also cannot influence other players' reports through strategic choice of her own report. Thus, the second term in (8.4) does not adversely affect rater i's incentive to report honestly or put forth effort.

The balanced transfers in (8.4) do not guarantee voluntary participation. In some cases, a rater's net transfer may be negative. One way to assure ex-post voluntary participation is to collect bonds or entry fees in advance, and use the collected funds to ensure that all transfers are positive. For example, with the logarithmic scoring rule, $\min \tau \leq \min \tau^* = \tau_0$. If $-\tau_0$ is collected from each player in advance, and then returned with the transfer τ, each player will receive positive payments after the evaluations are reported. Some raters will still incur net losses, but their bonds prevent them from dropping out after they learn of their negative outcome.

---

[16] Since each player will receive her own base transfer and fund one other player's, the addition of τ_0 to each has no net effect, so we phrase the discussion in terms of the raw penalties τ^* rather than the net payments τ^+.

Alternatively, it may be sufficient to threaten to exclude a rater from future participation in the system if she is unwilling to act as a rater or settle her account after a negative outcome.

8.3 Extensions

We now consider two extensions to the base model. In the first, raters report sequentially rather than simultaneously. In the second, their types and signals are continuous rather than discrete.

8.3.1 Sequential Interaction

Sequential reporting may be desirable, since it allows later raters to make immediate use of the information provided by their predecessors. The mechanism adapts readily to sequential situations.[17] Rater i's transfer can be determined using any subsequent rater as a reference rater. To balance the budget, the transfer can be settled by any subsequent rater other than rater i's reference rater.

For example, suppose an infinite sequence of raters, indexed by $i = 1, 2, ...$, interacts with the product. Let rater $i + 1$ be rater i's reference rater, i.e., i's report is used to predict the distribution of rater $i + 1$'s report. Let $p(t)$ be the initial, commonly held prior distribution for the product's type. Let $p_1(t|s^1)$ denote the posterior distribution after rater 1 receives signal s^1. This can be computed using Bayes' Rule in the usual way. Rater 1's posterior belief about the probability that $S^2 = s^2$ when $S^1 = s^1$ is then given by $g(s^2|s^1) = \sum_{t=1}^{T} f(s^2|t) p_1(t|s^1)$. Using this distribution (and still assuming stochastic relevance), rater 1 can be induced to truthfully reveal s^1 using the scoring rule specified in Proposition 1. After rater 1 announces her signal, this information is made public and is used to update beliefs about the product's type.

This process can be iterated. When rater i is asked to announce her signal, the prior distribution over types takes into account all previous announcements. Incentives to rater i are constructed using a scoring rule that incorporates these updated beliefs, that is, rater i is scored using a strictly proper scoring rule applied to the distribution implied by rater i's announcement and the current beliefs about the product's type (which incorporates the announcements of the first $i - 1$ raters). To balance the budget, rater i's transfer could be paid by rater $i + 2$.

When a finite string of raters experience the product, the last rater has no incentive to lie, but also none to tell the truth, since there is no future signal upon which

---

[17] Hanson [12] applies a scoring-rule based approach in a model in which a number of experts are sequentially asked their belief about the distribution of a random event, whose realization is revealed after all experts have reported. In our model, the product's type is never revealed, and therefore, we must rely on other agents' reports to provide incentives.

to base her reward. Thus, there is a danger of the whole process unravelling. Fortunately, the center can solve this problem by grouping some raters together and treating group members as if they report simultaneously. For example, suppose there are 10 raters. Consider the last three: 8, 9, and 10. The center can score rater 8 based on 9 's announcement, 9 based on 10's, and 10 based on 8's. As long as the center can avoid revealing these three raters' announcements until all three have announced, effective incentives can be provided using our earlier techniques, and the chain will not unravel. Transfers can also be made within the ring in order to balance the budget for the ring.

8.3.2 Continuous Signals

Until now, we have considered discrete type and signal spaces. All of our results translate to the continuous case in a natural way (e.g., density functions replace discrete distributions, integrals replace sums, etc.). For example, if rater i reports signal s^i, the logarithmic score is computed as $\ln\left(g\left(s^j|s^i\right)\right)$, where $g\left(s^j|s^i\right)$ is now the posterior *density* of $S^j = s^j$ given $S^i = s^i$. Most importantly, the scoring rules we have discussed continue to be strictly proper in the continuous case.

In this section, we briefly consider two particularly interesting aspects of the problem with continuous signals and product-type spaces, a comparison of the three scoring rules when prior and sample information are normally distributed, and the problem of eliciting discrete information when signals are continuous.

8.3.2.1 Effort Elicitation with Normally Distributed Noise: A Comparison of Scoring Rules

Let q denote the unknown quality of the good, and suppose that raters have prior beliefs that q is normally distributed with mean μ and precision θ_q, where precision equals 1/variance. Suppose each rater observes a real-valued signal S^i of the object's quality that is normally distributed with mean q and precision θ_i. That is, each rater receives a noisy but unbiased signal of the object's quality. Conditional on observing $S^i = s^i$, the rater's posterior belief about q is that q is distributed normally with mean $\hat{\mu} = \frac{(\mu\theta_q + s^i\theta_i)}{(\theta_q + \theta_i)}$ and precision $\hat{\theta} = \theta_q + \theta_i$. [18]

Suppose that rater j observes signal S^j on the object's quality, where S^j is normally distributed with mean q and precision θ_j. Conditional on observing $S^i = s^i$, rater i's posterior belief about the distribution of S^j is that S^j is normally distributed with mean $\hat{\mu}$ and precision $\theta = \hat{\theta}\theta_j/\hat{\theta} + \theta_j$. [19]

---

[18] See Pratt, Raiffa, and Schlaifer [23].

[19] The variance of S^j conditional on S^i is the sum of the variance of the posterior belief about q, $1/\hat{\theta}$, and the variance of S^j conditional on q, $1/\theta_j$, which implies precision $\theta = \hat{\theta}\theta_j/\left(\hat{\theta} + \theta_j\right)$.

Since different observation-precision combinations lead to different posterior beliefs about the distribution of S^j, assuming stochastic relevance continues to be reasonable in the continuous case. If we make this assumption, then payments based on a proper scoring rule can induce effort and honest reporting. As before, rater i will prefer to be scored on her posterior for the reference rater j, and this is achieved by honestly reporting her observation and her precision, allowing the center to correctly compute her posterior.[20]

We assume that by exerting effort, raters can increase the precision of their signals. Let $c(\theta_i)$ represent the cost of acquiring a signal of precision $\theta_i \geq 0$, where $c'(\theta_i) > 0$, $c'(0) = 0$, $c'(\infty) = \infty$, and $c''(\theta_i) \geq 0$. To compare the logarithmic, quadratic, and spherical scoring rules, it is necessary to ensure that the rater is choosing the same signal precision under each rule. As suggested by our analysis in Section 8.2.2, the center can induce the rater to choose more or less effort by multiplying all transfers by a larger or smaller constant.

Let $f(x)$ be the probability density function of a normal random variable with mean μ and precision θ. Under the logarithmic scoring rule, the maximized expected utility as a function of precision (i.e., when the rater announces truthfully) is given by:

$$v_l(\theta_i) = \int \log(f(x)) f(x) dx = -\frac{1}{2} + \frac{1}{2} \log\left(\frac{\theta}{2\pi}\right).$$

It is straightforward to verify that $v_l(\theta_i)$ is increasing and concave in θ_i. Thus, as in the discrete case, by varying the multiplicative scaling factor, the center can induce the rater to choose any particular level of precision.

The scaling factor α that induces a particular θ_i is found by solving:

$$\max_{\theta_i} \alpha \left(-\frac{1}{2} + \frac{1}{2} \log\left(\frac{\theta}{2\pi}\right) \right) - c(\theta_i).$$

Setting the derivative of this expression equal to zero yields that choosing $\alpha = 2/\theta_j (\theta_q + \theta_i)(\theta_q + \theta_i + \theta_j) c'(\theta_i) \equiv \alpha_l$ induces precision θ_i under the logarithmic rule. Analogous calculations for the quadratic and spherical scoring rules find that to induce precision θ_i, $\alpha = 4\pi^{1/2}/\theta_j^{3/2} (\theta_q + \theta_i)^{1/2} (\theta_q + \theta_i + \theta_j)^{\frac{3}{2}} c'(\theta_i)$ and $\alpha = 4\sqrt{2}\pi^{1/4}/\theta_j^{5/4} (\theta_q + \theta_i)^{3/4} (\theta_q + \theta_i + \theta_j)^{5/4} c'(\theta_i)$ respectively.

Based on these choices for α, the variance and range of the transfers under each of the rules is:[21]

---

[20] Ottaviani and Sørensen [22] consider a related model, with normally distributed information of fixed precision for each rater. In their analysis, however, each rater attempts to convince the world of their expertise (i.e., that they have precise signals.) With that objective function, there is no equilibrium where signals are fully revealed. By contrast, we introduce an explicit scoring function that is not based solely on the inferred or reported precision of raters' signals, and full information revelation can be induced.

[21] Supporting computations for this table are available from the authors upon request.

Rule	Variance of transfers	Min	Max	Range
Log	$2A^2c'(\theta_i)^2$	$-\infty$	$A\log\left(\frac{\theta}{2\pi}\right)c'(\theta_i)$	∞
Quadratic	$\frac{16(2\sqrt{3}-3)}{3}A^2c'(\theta_i)^2$	$-2Ac'(\theta_i)$	$2\left(2\sqrt{2}-1\right)Ac'(\theta_i)$	$4\sqrt{2}Ac'(\theta_i)$
Spherical	$\frac{16(2\sqrt{3}-3)}{3}A^2c'(\theta_i)^2$	0	$4\sqrt{2}Ac'(\theta_i)$	$4\sqrt{2}Ac'(\theta_i)$

where $A = \frac{(\theta_i+\theta_q)(\theta_i+\theta_j+\theta_q)}{\theta_j}$.

Two notable features emerge from this analysis. First, the quadratic and spherical rules have the same variance and range of payments. This is because both rules specify scores that are linear in $f(x)$, and so, once scaled to induce the same precision, they differ only by an additive constant. Second, while the logarithmic rule has the smallest variance ($\frac{16}{3}\left(2\sqrt{3}-3\right) \simeq 2.4752$), its the range of payments is infinite because $\lim_{x\to0}\ln(x) = -\infty$. We refer to these results in Section 8.4.2, where we discuss how to choose among the scoring rules in particular application contexts.

8.3.2.2 Eliciting Coarse Reports

Raters' information is often highly nuanced. Yet, systems often employ coarser measures of quality, such as 1–5 stars. In this section, we consider situations where the center offers raters a choice between several "coarse" reports, and analyze whether it is possible to design payments that induce people to be as truthful as possible, i.e., to choose the admissible report closest to their true signal.

The problem of coarse reporting is both subtle and complex. Proper scoring rules induce people to truthfully announce their exact information. One might hope that in a sufficiently smooth environment, a rater offered a restricted set of admissible reports will choose the one that is "closest" to her true information. However, this intuition relies on two assumptions: that closeness in signals corresponds to closeness in posteriors over product types, and that close beliefs in product-type space correspond to close beliefs about the distribution of a reference rater's announcement. Although it remains an open question whether these assumptions hold in general, it is possible to show that they hold when there are only two types of products.

Suppose raters receive signals drawn from the unit interval and that there are only two types of objects, good (type G) and bad (type B). Their signal densities are $f(s|G)$ and $f(s|B)$. Let $p \in (0,1)$ denote the prior probability (commonly held) that the object is good. We assume that densities $f(s|G)$ and $f(s|B)$ satisfy the Monotone Likelihood Ratio Property (MLRP), that is, $\frac{f(s|G)}{f(s|B)}$ is strictly increasing in s.

MLRP implies the distribution for type G first-order stochastically dominates the distribution for B (see [11]). If rater i observes signal $S^i = s^i$, she assigns posterior probability $p\left(G|s^i\right) = \frac{pf(s^i|G)}{pf(s^i|G)+(1-p)f(s^i|B)}$ to the object's being good.

MLRP ensures that $p\left(G|s^i\right)$ is strictly increasing in s^i . Thus, MLRP embodies the idea that higher signals provide stronger evidence that the object is good.

We divide the signal space into a finite number of intervals, which we call bins, and construct a scoring rule such that rater i's best response is to announce the bin in which her signal lies, if she believes that all other raters will do the same. The construction of reporting bins and a scoring rule capitalizes on a special property of the quadratic scoring rule. Friedman [10] develops the notion of "effective" scoring rules. A scoring rule is effective with respect to a metric if the expected score from announcing a distribution increases as the announced distribution's distance from the rater's true distribution decreases. When distance between distributions is measured using the L_2-metric, the quadratic scoring rule has this property. Also, when there are only two types, the L_2-distance between two distributions of reference raters' announcements is proportional to the product type beliefs that generate them (if such beliefs exist).

Proposition 3: *Suppose there are two types of objects with signal densities that satisfy MLRP. Then, for any integer L, there exists a partition of signals into L intervals and a set of transfers that induce Nash Equilibrium truthful reporting when agents can report only in which interval their signal lies.*

The essence of the proof of Proposition 3, which appears in Appendix A, is as follows. After observing $S^i = s^i$, rater i's belief about the product's type (PT belief) is summarized by rater i's posterior probability that the product is good, $p\left(G|s^i\right)$. We begin by dividing the space of PT beliefs into L equal-sized bins. Since $p\left(G|s^i\right)$ is monotone, these PT-belief bins translate to intervals in the rater's signal space, which we refer to as signal bins. Signal bins can differ in size. A rater who announces her signal is in the lth bin of signals is treated as if she had announced beliefs about the product type at the midpoint of the lth PT bin, which implies some distribution for the reference rater's announcement (RRA). Each signal bin announcement thus maps to PT beliefs and then to an RRA distribution. The RRA distribution is scored using the quadratic rule.

Since the quadratic scoring rule is effective, given a choice among this restricted set of admissible RRA distributions the rater chooses the RRA distribution nearest (in the L_2 metric) to her true one. This turns out to be the one with PT belief nearest her true PT belief. If s^i is in the lth signal bin, the closest available PT belief is the midpoint of the lth PT bin. Thus, given coarse bins, the quadratic scoring rule induces truthful (albeit coarse) bin announcements.

Note that the bins are constructed by dividing the PT space rather than the signal space into equal-sized bins. While closeness of PT beliefs corresponds to closeness of RRA beliefs, close signals do not translate linearly to close PT beliefs. For example, suppose a rater observes signal $s^i = 0.5$, and that $p(G|0.5) = 0.3$. It is possible that $p(G|0.4) = 0.2$ while $p(G|0.6) = 0.35$. Thus, although the distance between signals 0.5 and 0.6 is the same as the distance between signals 0.5 and 0.4, the PT beliefs (and therefore the RRA beliefs) are closer for the first pair than for the second.

Even in the simple case of only two product types, it is somewhat complicated to show that raters will want to honestly reveal their coarse information. It remains an open question whether it is possible to elicit honest coarse reports in more complex environments.

8.4 Issues in Practical Application

The previous section provides a theoretical framework for inducing effort and honest reporting. Designers of practical systems will face many challenges in applying it. Many of these challenges can be overcome with adjustments in the transfer payment scheme, computation of parameters based on historical data, and careful choice of the dimensions on which raters are asked to report.

8.4.1 Risk Aversion

Until now, we have assumed that raters are risk neutral, that is, that maximizing the expected transfer is equivalent to maximizing expected utility. If raters are risk averse, then scoring-rule based transfers will not always induce truthful revelation. We present three ways to address risk aversion.

If the center knows the rater's utility function, the transfers can be easily adjusted to induce truthful reporting. If $U\,()$ is the rater's utility function and R is a proper scoring rule, then choosing transfers $\tau = U^{-1}\,(R)$ induces truthful reporting, since $U\left(U^{-1}\,(R)\right) \equiv R$ [33].

If the rater's utility function is not known, risk-neutral behavior can be induced by paying the rater in lottery tickets for a binary-outcome lottery instead of in money [29, 31]. In effect, the score assigned to a particular outcome gives the probability of winning a fixed prize. Since von-Neumann Morgenstern utility functions are linear in probabilities, an expected-utility maximizer will seek to maximize the expected probability of winning the lottery. Thus the lottery-ticket approach induces individuals with unknown non-linear utility functions to behave as if they are risk neutral. Experimental evidence suggests that, while not perfect, the binary-lottery procedure can be effective in controlling for risk aversion, especially when raters have a good understanding of how the procedure works. [22]

A third method of dealing with risk averse raters capitalizes on the fact that raters' risk aversion is likely to be less important when the variability in payments is small. Although we have presented our results for the case where each rater is scored against a single reference rater, the idiosyncratic noise in the rater's final payment (measured in terms of its variance) can be reduced by scoring the rater against multiple raters and paying her the average of those scores. By averaging the scores from a sufficiently large number of reference raters, the center can effectively eliminate

---

[22] See Roth [26], (pp. 81–83) and the references therein.

the idiosyncratic noise in the reference raters' signals. However, the systematic risk due to the object's type being unknown cannot be eliminated.

8.4.2 Choosing a Scoring Rule

Which of the three scoring rules we have discussed is best? Each rule has its relative strengths and weaknesses, and none emerges as clearly superior.

The logarithmic rule is the simplest, giving it a modest advantage in comprehension and computational ease. It is also "relevant" in the sense that it depends only on the likelihood of events that actually occur.[23] In addition, our results in Section 8.3.2.1 show that the payments needed to induce a particular effort level have lower variance under the logarithmic rule than under either of the other two rules, at least when information is normally distributed. If scores are used to evaluate the raters (for example, to decide whether to invite them back as reviewers in the future), this lower variance enables the logarithmic rule to provide a more reliable evaluation given the same number of trials.

On the other hand, the fact that $\log(x)$ goes to $-\infty$ as x decreases to zero renders the log rule unattractive when probabilities become small and raters' limited liability is a concern, or if the support of the raters' posterior distributions changes with their information. On a related note, under the log rule small changes in low-probability events can significantly affect a rater's expected score, which may be undesirable if raters have difficulty properly assessing low-probability events. A final disadvantage to the logarithmic score is that, in contrast to the quadratic rule, there is no metric with respect to which the logarithmic rule is effective [20]. That is, a rater's expected score from announcing a particular distribution need not increase as its distance (as measured by any valid metric) from the true distribution decreases.

As discussed above, the quadratic rule is effective with respect to the L_2-metric, which is what allowed us to solve the coarse reporting problem in Section 8.3.2.2. However, the quadratic rule is not relevant, so it can have the perverse property that, given two distributions, the quadratic score may be higher for the distribution that assigns lower probability to the event that actually occurs [34]. The spherical rule shares many properties with the quadratic rule (although its payments are always positive). As we saw in the normal-information case, once the spherical and quadratic rules are scaled to induce the same rating effort, they become identical up to an additive constant. The spherical rule is effective with respect to a renormalized L_2-metric (see [10]).

Jensen and Peterson [13] compare the three scoring rules in head-to-head experimental trials. They conclude that there is essentially no difference in the probabilities elicited from raters. They do note that subjects seem to have trouble understanding scoring rules involving both positive and negative payments; while

---

[23] Relevance is important in Bayesian models of comparing different probability assessors [32, 33], although this is not important for our application.

the quadratic rule has this property, it is easily addressed by adding a constant to all payments. Thus, except for situations where some events have low-probability or raters' information affects the set of possible events (i.e., moving support), factors that make the logarithmic score undesirable, there is no clear reason to prefer one scoring rule over the others.

8.4.3 Estimating Types, Priors, and Signal Distributions

In many situations, there will be sufficient rating history available for the center to estimate the prior probabilities of alternative types and signals so as to start the scoring process. One technique would define the product types in terms of the signal distributions they generate. For example, suppose that there are only two signals h and l. Products are of varying quality, which determines the percentage of users who submit h ratings for the product. The type space is continuous in principle, but in practice the site could approximately capture reality by defining a set of discrete types that partitions the space. For illustrative purposes, we define a fairly coarse partition of types, 1,..,9, with $f(h|i) = i/10$. That is, products of type 1 get rated h 10% of the time, and those of type 7 get rated h 70% of the time. The site would then estimate the prior distribution function $p(i)$ based on how many products in the past accumulated approximately $10i\%$ ratings.[24]

Table 8.1 illustrates updating of beliefs about the probability that a product is of any of the nine types. Note that the initial distribution is symmetric about type 5, implying that initial probability of h is .5. After receiving a report h, types that have higher frequencies of h signals become more likely, as shown in the second row of the table. After receiving two conflicting reports, h and l, the distribution is again symmetric about type 5, but the extreme types are now seen as less likely than they were initially.

8.4.4 Taste Differences Among Raters

Suppose that raters differ systematically in their tastes. For example, raters of type A might be generally harsher in their assessments than those of type B, so that,

Table 8.1 Initial and updated probabilities of nine types defined by their probability of yielding signal h

After signal	$p(1)$	$p(2)$	$p(3)$	$p(4)$	$p(5)$	$p(6)$	$p(7)$	$p(8)$	$p(9)$	$pr(h)$
	.05	.1	.1	.1	.3	.1	.1	.1	.05	.5
h	.01	.04	.06	.08	.3	.12	.14	.16	.09	.59
h, l	.02	.08	.1	.12	.36	.12	.1	.08	.02	.5

[24] Obviously, the partition could be finer, for example with types 1-99 defined by percentage of raters rating the product h. In addition, the partition need not be uniform: more types could be defined in the region that occur most often on a particular site.

with binary signals, they would be more likely to perceive goods of any particular type as being low quality, $f_A(l|t) > f_B(l|t)$. The same problems could arise if the differences among raters' perceptions covaried with the product types. For example, an action movie aficionado might perceive most action movies to be h and most romantic comedies to be l; perceptions would be reversed for fans of comedies.

When tastes differ systematically, the center will need to model rater types explicitly. As in the simpler case in Section 8.4.3, given a sufficient history the center can estimate the distribution of user types and for each type the signal distributions. An individual rater's history provides additional information for inferring the distribution from which her type is drawn.[25]

8.4.5 Non-Common Priors and Other Private Information

The incentives for effort and honest reporting depend critically on the center's ability to compute a posterior distribution for another rater's signal that the current rater would agree with, if only she had the information and computational ability available to the center. Problems may arise if raters have relevant private information beyond their own signals. Knowing that the center will not use that other private information, the rater will no longer be confident that an honest report of her signal will lead to scoring based on her true posterior beliefs about the distribution of another rater's signals. If she can intuit the correct direction, she may distort her reported signal so as to cause the center to score her based on posterior beliefs closer to what she would compute herself.

Fortunately, the mechanisms in this paper easily adapt if raters can report any private information they have about the distribution of product types, rater types, or signals contingent on product and rater types.[26] The center will use the reference rater's report to compute two scores. The first comes from the distribution implied by the reported private priors; the second is based on the posteriors computed from the priors and the reported signal. An honest report of priors maximizes the first score. The second is maximized when the center calculates accurate posteriors, and that occurs when both priors and signal are honestly reported. Thus, honest reports maximize either score.

---

[25] A variety of recommender systems or collaborative filtering algorithms rely on the past ratings of a set of users to make personalized predictions of how well each individual will like products they have not yet rated. See Breese, Heckerman, and Kadie [2] and Sarwar et al. [27] for reviews. Often these algorithms merely predict a scalar value for an individual's rating, but they could be extended to predict a distribution over signals for each rater for each product not yet rated. When an additional rating is added from rater i, the predicted distributions for each other rater for that product would be updated.

[26] Note that for peer-prediction scoring to work, we need to compare one rater's posterior to another rater's reported signal, so it is critical to elicit raters' signals separately from any other information that is also elicited from them.

In most practical situations, it will not be necessary to elicit all possible private information. Where the center has a sufficient history of past ratings, most raters will trust the center's inferences about the distribution of product types, rater types, and signals conditional on product and rater types. In those cases, raters need only report what they saw. However, when raters may have beliefs that diverge from the center's, it will be useful to offer raters an opportunity to report those beliefs, lest the unreported beliefs create incentives for distorting signal reports.

8.4.6 Other Potential Limitations

Other potential limitations could interfere with the smooth functioning of a scoring system based on the peer-prediction method. We mention three. First, while we have shown there is a Nash equilibrium involving effort and honest reporting, raters could collude to gain higher transfers. Of course, with balanced transfers it will not be possible for all of the raters to be better off through collusive actions, and it is unclear whether a subset of the raters could collude to gain at the expense of the remaining raters who exerted effort and reported honestly. For example, one rater can gain by knowing what a colluding reference rater will report, but it is not clear whether the gain would outweigh the losses for the colluding reference rater when she is scored against some other, honest rater. Even if such collusion were profitable, the center has two approaches available to deter it. The selection of who will serve as a reference rater for each rater can be randomized and delayed until after ratings are reported, which would make collusion harder to coordinate. In addition, the center may be able to detect suspicious rating patterns through statistical analysis, and then employ an outside expert to independently evaluate the product.[27]

A second potential limitation may arise when raters perceive multidimensional signals. Our scoring system can generalize easily to handle multiple dimensions by eliciting reports on several dimensions, such as food, decor, and service for restaurants. Scores can then be computed based on implied distributions for reports on one or all of the dimensions. If, however, some dimensions are not elicited, two problems emerge. First, information may not be captured that would be valuable to consumers. More troubling, in some situations the information not elicited from a rater may be useful in predicting the next report, in which case the rater may be tempted to manipulate the report that is requested.

Consider, for example, an interdisciplinary review panel. An economist with some knowledge of computer science may evaluate proposals as other economists do, but may perceive some additional signal about how computer scientists will perceive the proposals. Suppose she is asked to report only her perception of the proposal's quality. The center then computes an updated distribution of signals for the

---

[27] This would be analogous to a University Provost who normally accepts promotion and tenure recommendations with a minimal review, but may undertake the costly option of personally evaluating the portfolios of candidates from units whose recommendation patterns are suspicious, or employing an outside expert to evaluate those portfolios.

next rater, accounting for both raters' types as in Section 8.4.4. But the economist's secondary signal about how well computer scientists will like the proposal may allow her to compute a more accurate distribution than the center can, and thus she will sometimes want to report dishonestly in order to make the center more closely approximate her true beliefs.[28]

One solution to this problem would be to find a set of dimensions on which raters are asked to report such that any other signals the raters get are not relevant for predicting the next player's report. For example, if restaurant reviewers are asked to report separately on food, decor, and service, the transfer payments can induce honest reporting so long as any other independent signals that reviewers may receive (such as the number of people in the restaurant that night) are not useful in predicting how other raters will perceive food, decor, or service. On an interdisciplinary review panel, reviewers might be asked to separately report quality from the perspective of each of the disciplines involved. When scores are computed, they can be based on the probabilities for another player's report on any one dimension, or on all of them. Again, since honest reporting will cause the center to correctly compute the rater's beliefs about the reference rater's signal, honest reporting will be an equilibrium. Unfortunately, it may be difficult in practice to find a set of rating dimensions such that unreported signals for a rater are irrelevant to computing beliefs about reported signals for a reference rater.

Given the computational power and the information resources available to the center, it may not be necessary in practice to elicit from raters all of their weakly stochastically relevant signals. For example, suppose the center performs a complex collaborative filtering algorithm to predict the next rater's distribution, and the individual rater either lacks the computational resources or the history of everyone's previous ratings, or does not know in advance which rater she will be scored against. Although an additional private signal might make rater i think that, say, signal h is more likely for some raters than the center would otherwise compute, she will often be unable to determine which false report on the dimensions that the center elicits would raise her payoff.

A third potential limitation is trust in the system: people may not believe that effort and honest reporting are optimal strategies. In individual instances, raters who follow that strategy will have negative transfers, and they may incorrectly attribute such outcomes to their strategy rather than to the vagaries of chance. Few raters will be willing or able to verify the mathematical properties of the scoring system proven in this paper, so it will be necessary to rely on outside attestations to ensure public confidence. Professional experts could be invited to investigate the working of the systems, or independent auditors could be hired.

---

[28] Canice Prendergast's [25] model of Yes-Men is one example of this type of situation. In that model, the first rater receives one signal about the expected value of a business action and another signal about how well the next rater (the boss) will like that action. There is no scoring function that will elicit reports from which the center can infer just the rater's direct signal as opposed to her signal about the boss' signal. Thus, she will become, at least partially, a Yes-Man, who says what she thinks the boss will think.

8.5 Conclusion

Buyers derive immense value from drawing on the experience of others. However, they have the incentive to shirk from the collective endeavor of providing accurate information about products, be they microwave ovens or movies, academic papers or appliances. Peer-prediction methods, capitalizing on the stochastic relevance between the reports of different raters, in conjunction with appropriate rewards, can create incentives for effort and honest reporting.

Implementors of such systems will face a number of design choices, ranging from rating dimensions and procedures for selecting reviewers to technology platforms and user interfaces. This paper provides only a conceptual road map, not a detailed implementation plan, and only for those design decisions that involve incentives for effort and honest reporting. It is an important road map, however, because the most obvious approach to peer comparison, simply rewarding for agreement in reviews, offers inappropriate incentives.

The basic insight is to compare implied posteriors (rather than an actual report) to the report of a reference rater. A rater need not compute the implications of her own signal for the distribution of the reference rater, so long as she trusts the center to do a good job of computing those implications. There remain many pitfalls, limitations, and practical implementation issues, for which this paper provides conceptual design guidance.

Recommender and reputation systems require that ratings be widely collected and disseminated. To overcome incentive problems, raters must be rewarded. Whether those rewards are monetary or merely grades or points in some scoring system that the raters care about, intense computational methods are required to calibrate appropriate rewards. The upward march of information technology holds promise.

Acknowledgments Reprinted by permission, Miller, Nolan, Paul Resnick, Richard Zeckhauser. 2005. Eliciting informative feedback: The peer-prediction method. *Management Science* 51(9) 1359–1373. Copyright 2005, the Institute for Operations Research and the Management Sciences, 7240 Parkway Drive, Suite 310, Hanover, MD 21076 USA

Appendix A: Proofs

Proof of Proposition 2: Let $Z_i(0) = \arg\max_a \sum_{n=1}^{M} R\left(s_n^{r(i)}|a\right) f(a)$, so that the maximum expected value of any report made without acquiring a signal is $\alpha Z_i(0)$. Let

$$Z_i(1) = E_{s_m^i}\left(E_{s_n^{r(i)}} R\left(s_n^{r(i)}|s_m^i\right)\right) = \sum_{m=1}^{M} f\left(s_m^i\right) \sum_{n=1}^{M} g\left(s_n^{r(i)}|s_m^i\right) R\left(s_n^{r(i)}|s_m^i\right),$$

so that the expected value of getting a signal and reporting it is $\alpha Z_i(1)$. Savage's analysis of the partition problem (1954, Chapter 7) shows that acquiring the signal strictly increases the buyer's expected score whenever it changes the rater's posterior belief about the other raters' announcements (see also Lavalle (1968)). Thus $Z_i(1) > Z_i(0)$ when stochastic relevance holds.

Pick $\alpha > \frac{c}{Z_i(1)-Z_i(0)}$. Thus $\alpha Z_i(1) - \alpha Z_i(0) > c$, so the best response is to pay the cost c to acquire a signal and report it. ∎

Proof of Proposition 3: Divide the space of product type (PT) beliefs, which are just probabilities that the product is of the good type, into L equal-sized bins, with the lth bin being $B_l = (\frac{l-1}{L}, \frac{l}{L})$, and $B_L = [\frac{L-1}{L}, 1]$. Given these bins, the rater's PT belief induces a reference rater bin announcement (RRA) belief. Let $P_G^l = \int_{\frac{l-1}{L}}^{l} f(s|G)\,ds$ and $P_B^l = \int_{\frac{l-1}{L}}^{l} f(s|B)\,ds$, the probabilities assigned to the reference rater announcing the lth bin if the object is known to be good or bad, respectively. If the rater observes s^i, the likelihood of the reference rater's announcing the lth bin is:

$$P_{s^i}^l = \int_{\frac{l-1}{L}}^{l} p(G|s^i) f(s|G) + (1 - p(G|s^i)) f(s|B)\,ds$$
$$= p(G|s^i) P_G^l + (1 - p(G|s^i)) P_B^l,$$

Let $P_{s^i} = (P_{s^i}^1, ..., P_{s^i}^L)$ denote the RRA distribution of a rater who has observed s^i.

Since $p(G|s)$ is monotone in s, the inverse function $\pi(p)$ is well-defined. Let $\tilde{B}_l = [\pi(\frac{l-1}{L}), \pi(\frac{l}{L})]$ be the lth bin of signals and $\tilde{B}_L = [\pi(\frac{L-1}{L}), \pi(1)]$; i.e., raters observing signals in $\tilde{B}_l$ have PT beliefs in B_l. A rater who announces that her signal is in $\tilde{B}_l$ is paid using the quadratic scoring rule based on the RRA distribution for a rater who has PT belief $m_l = 2l - 1/2L$. Thus, if a rater always prefers to be scored on the PT bin that contains her true beliefs, she will report the signal bin that contains her true signal. The remainder of the proof is to show that it is optimal for a rater to be scored against the midpoint of the PT bin that contains her true posterior PT belief.

First, we show that closeness of PT beliefs corresponds to closeness of RRA beliefs. The distance between two PT beliefs p_1 and p_2 is simply their absolute difference, $|p_1 - p_2|$. For the distance between two RRA distributions, we use the L_2-metric. That is, if P and $\hat{P}$ denote two RRA distributions, the L_2-distance between them is given by $d(P, \hat{P}) = (\sum_l (P^l - \hat{P}^l)^2)^{1/2}$.

A rater who observes signal s^i assigns probability $P_{s^i}^l = p(G|s^i) P_G^l + (1 - p(G|s^i)) P_B^l$ to the reference rater announcing bin l. The distance between the posterior distributions of a rater observing s^i and a rater observing $\hat{s}^i$ is therefore given by:

$$d(P_{s^i}, P_{\hat{s}^i}) = \left(\sum_l (P_{s^i}^l - P_{\hat{s}^i}^l)^2\right)^{1/2} = |p(G|s^i) - p(G|\hat{s}^i)| \left(\sum_l (P_G^l - P_B^l)^2\right)^{1/2}.$$

$$(5)$$

Expression (5) establishes that the L_2-distance between two RRA distributions is proportional to the distance between the PTbeliefs that generate them.

The final step is to show that, given the choice between being scored based on the RRA distribution for $m_1, ..., m_L$, a rater observing s^i maximizes her expected quadratic score by choosing the m_l that is closest to $p\left(G|s^i\right)$, i.e., her true PTbeliefs. This follows from a result due to Friedman (1983, Proposition 1), who shows that the expected quadratic score of a rater with true RRA P is larger from reporting $\hat{P}$ than from reporting $\tilde{P}$ if and only if $d\left(\hat{P}, P\right) < d\left(\tilde{P}, P\right)$.[29] Thus Friedman's result, in conjunction with (5), establishes that if a rater believes the reference rater will truthfully announce her bin, then she maximizes her expected quadratic score by selecting the PTbin that contains her true beliefs.∎

Appendix B: Eliciting Effort

To consider the issue of effort elicitation, the rater's experience with the product is encoded not as a single outcome, but as a sequence of outcomes generated by random sampling from distribution $f\left(s_m|t\right)$. Greater effort corresponds to obtaining a larger sample. Let x_i denote the number of outcomes observed by rater i, i.e., her sample size. We require the rater to put forth effort to learn about her experience, letting $c_i\left(x_i\right)$ be the cost of observing a sample of size x_i, where $c_i\left(x_i\right)$ is strictly positive, strictly increasing, and strictly convex, and assumed to be known by the center.

For a rater who already observes a sample of size x, learning the $x + 1^{st}$ component further partitions the outcome space, i.e., larger samples correspond to better information. We begin by arguing that, holding fixed the agents' sample sizes, scoring-rule based payments can elicit this information. We then ask how the mechanism can be used to induce agents to acquire more information, even though such acquisition is costly.

For any fixed x_i, the information content of two possible x_i component sequences depends only on the frequencies of the various outcomes and not on the order in which they occur. Consequently, let $Y^i\left(x_i\right)$ be the M-dimensional random variable whose m^{th} component counts the number of times outcome s_m occurs in the first x_i components of the agent's information.[30] Let $y^i = \left(y_1^i, ..., y_M^i\right)$ denote a generic realization of $Y^i\left(x_i\right)$, where y_m^i is the number of times out of x_i that signal s_m is received, and note that $\sum_{m=1}^{M} y_M^i = x_i$. Rater i's observation of $Y^i\left(x_i\right)$ determines her posterior beliefs about the product's type, which are informative about the expected distribution of the other players' signals. Since different realizations of $Y^i\left(x_i\right)$ yield different posterior beliefs about the product's type, it is also natural to assume that $Y^i\left(x_i\right)$ is stochastically relevant for $Y^j\left(x_j\right)$, and we make

---

[29] Friedman (1983) calls metric-scoring rule pairs that have this property "effective."

[30] $Y^i\left(x_i\right)$ is a multinomial random variable with x_i trials and M possible outcomes. On any trial, the probability of the mth is $f\left(s_m|t\right)$, where t is the product's unknown type.

this assumption throughout this section. In the remainder of this section, we let $g\left(y^j\left(x_j\right)|y^i\left(x_i\right)\right)$ denote the distribution of $Y^j\left(x_j\right)$ conditional on $Y^i\left(x_i\right)$.

Lemma 1: *Consider distinct players i and j , and suppose $x_i, x_j \geq 0$ are commonly known. If agent i is asked to announce a realization of $Y^i\left(x_i\right)$ and is paid according to the realization of $Y^j\left(x_j\right)$ using a strictly proper scoring rule, i.e., $R\left(y^j\left(x_j\right)|y^i\left(x_i\right)\right)$, then the rater's expected payment is uniquely maximized by announcing the true realization of $Y^i\left(x_i\right)$.*

Proof: Follows from the definition of a strictly proper scoring rule.

Proposition 4 restates Proposition 1 in the case where the sizes of the raters' samples are fixed and possibly greater than 1, i.e., $x_i \geq 1$ for $i = 1,..., I$. It follows as an immediate consequence of Lemma 1.

Proposition 4: *Suppose rater i collects $x_i \geq 1$ signals. There exist transfers under which truthful reporting is a strict Nash Equilibrium of the reporting game.*

Proof of Proposition 4: The construction follows that in Proposition 1, using $Y^i\left(x_i\right)$ for the information received by rater i and constructing transfers as in (2) and (4). Under the equilibrium hypothesis, $j = r\left(i\right)$ announces truthfully. Let a^i denote rater i's announcement of the realization of $Y^i\left(x_i\right)$, and let transfers be given by:

$$\tau_i^*\left(y^j|a^i\right) = R\left(y^j|a^i\right). \tag{6}$$

Under these transfers, truthful announcement is a strict best response. ∎

Proposition 4 establishes that truthful reporting remains an equilibrium when raters can choose how much information to acquire. We next turn to the questions of how and whether the center can induce a rater to choose a particular x_i. Let j denote the rater whose signal player i is asked to predict (i.e., let $r\left(i\right) = j$), and suppose rater j has a sample of size x_j and that she truthfully reports the realization of $Y^j\left(x_j\right)$. For simplicity, we omit argument x_j in what follows. Further, suppose that rater i is paid according to the scoring-rule based scheme described in (6). Since x_i affects these transfers only through rater i's announcement, it is optimal for rater i to truthfully announce $Y^i\left(x_i\right)$ regardless of x_i.

Since x_i is chosen before observing any information, rater i's incentive to choose x_i depends on her ex ante expected payoff before learning her own signal. This expectation is written as $Z_i\left(x_i\right) = E_{Y^i}\left(E_{Y^j}R\left(Y^j|Y^i\left(x_i\right)\right)\right)$.

Lemma 2 establishes that raters benefit from better information, and is a restatement of the well-known result in decision theory that every decision maker benefits from a finer partition of the outcome space (Savage 1954).

Lemma 2: $Z_i\left(x_i\right)$ *is strictly increasing in x_i.*

Proof of Lemma 2: Fix x_i and let y^i be a generic realization of $Y^i\left(x_i\right)$. Conditional upon observing y^i, rater i maximizes her expected transfer by announcing distribution $g\left(Y^j|y^i\right)$ for rater j's information. Suppose rater i observes the $x_i + 1^{st}$ component of her information. By Lemma 1, i's expected transfer is now strictly maximized by announcing distribution $g\left(Y^j|\left(y^i, s_m\right)\right)$, and rater i increases her expected value by observing the additional information. Since this is true for every y^i, it is true in expectation, and $Z_i\left(x_i + 1\right) > Z_i\left(x_i\right)$. ∎

Lemma 2 establishes that as x_i increases, rater i's information becomes more informative regarding rater j's signal as x_i increases. Of course, the direct effect of rater i's gathering more information is to provide her with better information about the product, not about rater j. Nevertheless, as long as rater i's information is stochastically relevant for that of rater j, better information about the product translates into better information about rater j.

When transfers are given by (6), the expected net benefit to rater i from collecting a sample of size x_i and truthfully reporting her observation is $Z_i\left(x_i\right) - c\left(x_i\right)$. Hence, transfers (6) induce rater i to collect a sample of size $x_i^* \in \arg\max\left(Z_i\left(x_i\right) - cx_i\right)$.

Rater i's incentives to truthfully report are unaffected by a uniform scaling of all transfers in (6). Therefore, by a judicious rescaling of the payments to rater i, the center may be able to induce the agent to acquire more or less information. Expression (7) extends the transfers described in (6) to allow for multiple signals and a rescaling of all payments by multiplier $\alpha_i > 0$:

$$\tau_i^*\left(a^i, y^{r(i)}\right) = \alpha_i R\left(y^{r(i)}|a^i\right). \tag{7}$$

Under transfers (7), the maximal expected benefit from a sample of size x_i is $\alpha_i Z_i\left(x_i\right)$. Hence the center can induce rater i to select a particular sample size, $\hat{x}_i$, if and only if there is some multiplier $\hat{\alpha} > 0$ such that $\hat{x}_i \in \arg\max\hat{\alpha} Z_i\left(x_i\right) - c\left(x_i\right)$. The simplest case has $Z_i\left(x_i\right)$ concave, i.e., where $Z_i\left(x_i + 1\right) - Z_i\left(x_i\right)$ decreases in x_i.

Proposition 5: *If $Z_i\left(x_i + 1\right) - Z_i\left(x_i\right)$ decreases in x_i, then for any sample size $\hat{x}_i \geq 0$ there exists a scalar $\hat{\alpha}_i \geq 0$ such that when paid according to (7), rater i chooses sample size $\hat{x}_i$.*

Proof of Proposition 5: Since $Z_i\left(x\right)$ is concave, sample size $\hat{x}_i$ is optimal if there exists $\hat{\alpha}_i$ satisfying

$$\hat{\alpha}_i Z_i\left(\hat{x}_i\right) - c_i\left(\hat{x}_i\right) \geq \hat{\alpha}_i Z_i\left(\hat{x}_i + 1\right) - c_i\left(\hat{x}_i + 1\right), \text{ and}$$
$$\hat{\alpha}_i Z_i\left(\hat{x}_i\right) - c_i\left(\hat{x}_i\right) \geq \hat{\alpha}_i Z_i\left(\hat{x}_i - 1\right) - c_i\left(\hat{x}_i - 1\right).$$

Solving each condition for $\hat{\alpha}_i$ yields:

$$\frac{c_i\left(\hat{x}_i\right) - c_i\left(\hat{x}_i - 1\right)}{Z_i\left(\hat{x}_i\right) - Z_i\left(\hat{x}_i - 1\right)} \leq \hat{\alpha}_i \leq \frac{c_i\left(\hat{x}_i + 1\right) - c_i\left(\hat{x}_i\right)}{Z_i\left(\hat{x}_i + 1\right) - Z_i\left(\hat{x}_i\right)}.$$

Such an $\hat{\alpha}_i$ exists if and only if $\frac{Z_i(\hat{x}_i)-Z_i(\hat{x}_i-1)}{Z_i(\hat{x}_i+1)-Z_i(\hat{x}_i)} \geq \frac{c_i(\hat{x}_i)-c_i(\hat{x}_i-1)}{c_i(\hat{x}_i+1)-c_i(\hat{x}_i)}$. By our assumptions, this expression is always true. $\blacksquare$

If $Z_i(x_i+1) - Z_i(x_i)$ does not decrease in x_i, then there may be some sample sizes that are never optimal.[31] Nevertheless, increasing the scaling factor never decreases optimal sample size, and so while the center may not be able to perfectly control the raters' effort choices, it can always induce them to put forth greater effort if it wishes.

In practice, the center will not know each individual's cost of procuring additional information. However, the center may be able to estimate costs, and then pick a scaling factor that, in expectation, induces each rater to acquire an optimal-size sample.[32]

References

1. Avery, C., P. Resnick, and R. Zeckhauser, 1999. "The Market for Evaluations", *American Economic Review*, 89(3) 564–584.
2. Breese, J., D. Heckerman, C. Kadie. 1998. Empirical Analysis of Predictive Algorithms for Collaborative Filtering. *Proceedings of the Fourteenth Conference on Uncertainty in Artificial Intelligence*, Morgan Kaufmann Publisher, Madison, WI, July, 1998.
3. Clemen, R. 2002. Incentive Contracts and Strictly Proper Scoring Rules.*Test* 11(1) 195–217.
4. Cooke, R. M. 1991. *Experts in Uncertainty: Opinion and Subjective Probability in Science.* Oxford University Press, New York.
5. Crémer, J., R. McLean. 1985. Optimal Selling Strategies Under Uncertainty for a Discriminating Monopolist When Demands Are Interdependent. *Econometrica* 53(2) 345–361.
6. Crémer, J., R. Mc Lean. 1988. Full Extraction of Surplus in Bayesian and Dominant Strategy Auctions. *Econometrica* 56 (6) 1247–1257.
7. d'Aspremont, C., L.-A. Gérard-Varet. 1979. Incentives and Incomplete Information. *Journal of Public Economics* 11(1) 25–45.
8. d'Aspremont, C.A., L.-A. Gérard-Varet. 1982. Bayesian Incentive Compatible Beliefs. *Journal of Mathematical Economics* 10(1) 83–103.
9. Dellarocas, C. 2001. Analyzing the Economic Efficiency of eBay-like Online Reputation Reporting Mechanisms. *Proceedings of the 3rd ACM Conference on Electronic Commerce,* Tampa, FL, October 14–16, 2001.
10. Friedman, D. 1983. Effective Scoring Rules for Probabilistic Forecasts. *Management Science* 29(4) 447–454.
11. Gollier, C. 2001. *The Economics of Risk and Time.* MITPress, Cambridge, MA.
12. Hanson, R. 2002. Logarithmic Market Scoring Rules for Modular Combinatoral Information Aggregation. Working Paper, George Mason University Department of Economics, http://hanson.gmu.edu/mktscore.pdf.
13. Jensen, F., C. Peterson. 1973. Psychological Effects of Proper Scoring Rules.*Organizational Behavior and Human Performance* 9(2) 307–317.

---

[31] Clemen (2002) provides a number of examples of cases in which $Z_i(x_i+1) - Z_i(x_i)$ decreases in x_i

[32] The center chooses the scale that induces the optimal ex ante precision. Ex post, if raters know their costs, they will tend to choose lower precision if they are high cost and vice versa.

14. Johnson, S., N. Miller, J. Pratt, R. Zeckhauser. 2002. Efficient Design with Interdependent Valuations and an Informed Center. Kennedy School Working Paper, RWP02-025, http://ksgnotes1.harvard.edu/research/wpaper.nsf/rwp/RWP02-025.
15. Johnson, S., J. Pratt, R. Zeckhauser. 1990. Efficiency Despite Mutually Payoff-Relevant Private Information: The Finite Case. *Econometrica* **58**(4) 873–900.
16. Kandori, M., H. Matsushima. 1998. Private Observation, Communication and Collusion. *Econometrica* **66**(3) 627–652.
17. Lampe, C., P. Resnick. 2004. Slash(dot) and Burn: Distributed Moderation in a Large Online Conversation Space. CHI 2004, ACM Conference on Human Factors in Computing Systems, CHI Letters 6(1), 543–550.
18. Lavalle, I. 1968. On Cash Equivalents and Information Evaluation in Decisions Under Uncertainty: Part I: Basic Theory. *Journal of the American Statistical Association* **63**(321) 252–276.
19. Miller, N., P. Resnick, R. Zeckhauser. 2005. A sufficient condition for correlated information in mechanism design.mimeo, Harvard University, Cambridge, MA.
20. Nau, R. 1985. Should Scoring Rules Be Effective? *Management Science* **34**(5) 527–535.
21. Nelson, R., D. Bessler. 1989. Subjective Probabilities and Scoring Rules: Experimental Evidence.*American Journal of Agricultural Economics* **71**(2) 363–369.
22. Ottaviani, M., P. N. Sørensen. 2003. Professional Advice: The Theory of Reputational Cheap Talk.Working Paper, University of Copenhagen, http://www.econ.ku.dk/sorensen/Papers/pa.pdf.
23. Pratt, J., H. Raiffa, R. Schlaifer. 1965. *Introduction to Statistical Decision Theory.* McGraw-Hill, New York.
24. Prelec, D. 2001. A two-person scoring rule for subjective reports. Working Paper, Marketing Center, MITSloan School, http://mitsloan.mit.edu/vc/IPPacket.pdf.
25. Prendergast, C. 1993. A Theory of Yes Men.*American Economic Review* **83**(4) 757–770.
26. Roth, A. 1995. Introduction to Experimental Economics.J. Kagel, A. Roth, eds. *The Handbook of Experimental Economics,* Princeton University Press, Princeton, NJ, 3–110.
27. Sarwar, B. M., G. Karypis, J. A. Konstan, J. Riedl. 2000. Analysis of Recommender Algorithms for E-Commerce, Proceedings of the ACM E-Commerce 2000 Conference, Oct. 17–20, 2000, 158–167.
28. Savage, L. 1954. *Foundations of Statistics.* Dover Publications, New York.
29. Savage, L. 1971. Elicitation of Personal Probabilities and Expectations. *Journal of the American Statistical Association* **66**(336) 783–801.
30. Selten, R. 1998. Axiomatic Characterization of the Quadratic Scoring Rule. *Experimental Economics* **1**(1) 43–62.
31. Smith, C. 1961. Consistency in Statistical Inference and Decision.*Journal of the Royal Statistical Society, Series B (Methodological)* **23**(1) 1–37.
32. Staël von Holstein, C.-A. 1970. Measurement of Subjective Probability. *Acta Psychologica* **34**(1) 146–159.
33. Winkler, R. 1969. Scoring Rules and the Evaluation of Probability Assessors.*Journal of the American Statistical Association* **64**(327) 1073–1078.
34. Winkler, 1996. Scoring Rules and the Evaluation of Probabilities.*Test* **5**(1)1–60.

Chapter 9
Capturing Trust in Social Web Applications

John O'Donovan

Abstract The Social Web constitutes a shift in information flow from the traditional Web. Previously, content was provided by the owners of a website, for consumption by the end-user. Nowadays, these websites are being replaced by Social Web applications which are frameworks for the publication of user-provided content. Traditionally, Web content could be 'trusted' to some extent based on the site it originated from. Algorithms such as Google's PageRank were (and still are) used to compute the importance of a website, based on analysis of underlying link topology. In the Social Web, analysis of link topology merely tells us about the importance of the information *framework* which hosts the content. *Consumers* of information still need to know about the importance/reliability of the content they are reading, and therefore about the reliability of the *producers* of that content. Research into trust and reputation of the *producers* of information in the Social Web is still very much in its infancy. Every day, people are forced to make trusting decisions about strangers on the Web based on a very limited amount of information. For example, purchasing a product from an eBay seller with a 'reputation' of 99%, downloading a file from a peer-to-peer application such as Bit-Torrent, or allowing Amazon.com tell you what products you will like. Even something as simple as reading comments on a Web-blog requires the consumer to make a trusting decision about the quality of that information. In all of these example cases, and indeed throughout the Social Web, there is a pressing demand for increased information upon which we can make trusting decisions. This chapter examines the diversity of *sources* from which trust information can be harnessed within Social Web applications and discusses a high level classification of those sources. Three different techniques for harnessing and using trust from a range of sources are presented. These techniques are deployed in two sample Social Web applications—a recommender system and an online auction. In all cases, it is shown that harnessing an increased amount of information upon which to make trust decisions greatly enhances the user experience with the Social Web application.

J. O'Donovan (✉)
Department of Computer Science, University of California, Santa Barbara, California, USA
e-mail: jod@cs.ucsb.edu

J. Golbeck (ed.), *Computing with Social Trust,* Human-Computer Interaction Series, 213
DOI 10.1007/978-1-84800-356-9_9 © Springer-Verlag London Limited 2009

9.1 Introduction

Long before the World Wide Web, in the 1960s, Harvard professor Stanley Milgram proposed his Small World Experiments [14]. These consisted of a range of experiments designed to test Kochen and Pool's Small World Problem [4]: given a set N of people, what is the probability that each member of N is connected to another member via $k_1, k_2, k_3...k_n$ links?

Milgram's test examined the average path length for social networks of people in the United States by using parcel forwarding between source and target individuals via the US postal service. Milgram's experiments revealed that our society is a small world network with shorter-than-expected path lengths, so the probability of two random people knowing each other is less than the expected value. This concept has become more commonly known as the 'six degrees of separation' problem. There have been many protagonists and critics to Milgram's ideas since the 1960s, for example Malcolm Gladwell's popular book 'The Tipping Point' [5] proposes that connectivity in human social networks is largely dependent on a few extraordinary people, whom he calls 'connectors'. (Gladwell's research was based on findings from a range of articles originally published in The New Yorker.)

Of late, Social Web applications such as Wikis and social networking applications like MySpace and Facebook [10] are becoming hugely popular, making experiments such as Milgram's not only more feasible to perform, but also more relevant, since social connectedness can be harnessed and used to enhance the quality of a users experience in the online world.

In 2004 at the outset of my research in this area, a student at Harvard University, Mark Zuckerberg was developing a Social Web application to 'rate peoples looks'. Now in 2008 his application, Facebook, has become a social networking giant with a user base of 67 million. It is currently growing at a rate of 250,000 new users per day[1]. An interesting point of note is that this ubiquitous social networking application, which is bound to have a major impact on social networking research (and society in general), has its roots in the same place that Stanley Milgram performed his small world social networking experiments in the 1960s. A quick search on Facebook reveals many attempts to repeat Milgram's early experiments by getting massive numbers of users to join groups and perform simple tasks. The membership of these groups alone runs into millions of users. To put the growth of social networking into perspective, Milgram posted 296 letters to test his small worlds theory, and only a percentage of these got through to their destination. Facebook has a highly interconnected network of 67 million users who have expressed explicit trust statements about each other. This information has recently been made readily accessible through the Facebook API, which is sure to be a valuable resource for new research on trust within the Social Web.

One of todays foremost thinkers on the topic of network analysis is Alberto Barabási. Barabási hails the analysis of such networks as the 'true science of the

---

[1] http://www.facebook.com/press/info.php?statistics

future' [3]. In his popular book 'Linked' [2], he describes structural similarities between human social networks, Web topology, hierarchies of species in nature, and a range of other 'scale-free' networks. In 'Linked', the Web is classified as a scale free network because the degree distribution (i.e: the distribution of the number of links to each node) in the topological graph of the Web follows a mathematical 'power law'. A power law is a mathematical distribution usually characterised by a longer tail than a normal or gaussian distribution. Barabasi shows that a wealth of information can be uncovered by analysing the hubs and connectors in Web topology, examining how factors such as growth, node fitness and preferential attachment can define the structure of the Web. The explorations presented in this chapter are partly inspired by Barabasi's ideas but are applied not to the topology of nodes and links of the Web, but the topology of trust relations between the users within another scale free network: the Social Web.

In the Social Web, users are considered the important structure: the reliability of the user providing the information is as important as the information they provide. The notion of 'trust' for users of the Social Web can be viewed analogously to a PageRank in Web search. In a similar manner to each incoming link being considered as a 'vote' in the PageRank algorithm, a trust based algorithm must somehow compute an overall trust score for a user based on some combination of the individual 'units' of trust that the application has as input. Using eBay as an example, a trust algorithm might use the explicit vote given by both parties in a transaction as a unit of trust. The current eBay implementation simply takes the average of these values as the overall trust score. In this chapter we examine ways to gather individual units of trust in the Social Web and examine techniques to combine these values and reintegrate them to benefit users of the Social Web in some way. This work also addresses the issues involved in presentation of trust information to users on the Social Web, from the premise that trust information must be delivered at the right time, with minimal interference for the user.

9.2 Research on Trust in the Social Web

Of late there has been a lot of research attention towards issues of trust and reputation on the Social Web. [19, 23, 9, 1, 12]. This section examines the prominent related research from the perspective of trust modelling within our application domains of online auctions and recommender systems. Looking at the online auction eBay as a first example, Resnick [19] carried out a comprehensive analysis of eBay's trust and reputation system. This survey highlights some interesting findings regarding the nature of trust within the online auction, and the behaviour of its users. Five of Resnick's more salient findings from his work in [19 are listed below (with parenthesised addenda):

1. Despite incentives to free ride, feedback was provided more than half the time. (If people are generally willing to provide feedback most of the time, this means there will be raw data for a trust-modelling system to operate on.)

2. Well beyond reasonable expectation, the feedback was almost always positive. These 'false positives' in raw comment data may effect a trust value between users. The *AuctionRules* algorithm presented later shows how trust values mined from feedback comments can be used to compensate for the unnaturally positive discrete feedback ratings on eBay)

3. Reputation profiles were predictive of future performance. However, the net feedback scores that eBay displays encourages pollyanna assessments of reputations, and is far from the best predictor available.

4. Although sellers with better reputations were more likely to sell their items, they enjoyed no boost in price, at least for the two sets of items that we examined.

5. There was a high correlation between buyer and seller feedback, suggesting that the players reciprocate and retaliate. (It would be interesting to analyse the variance in feedback correlation between the current mechanism and a 'blind' feedback mechanism wherein a user knows the commentee will never see the feedback)

A similar survey to Resnick's was carried out in 2006 by Jøsang et al. in [7]. In this work, Jøsang describes the eBay reputation system as a *collaborative sanctioning system*, which naturally provides incentive for good behaviour of individuals thereby increasing performance of the market as a whole. Other relevant work by Jøsang et al. focuses on the transitive property of trust in online applications in [9, 8]. In their approach, a diverse set of dimensions was constructed to represent trust, and a mathematical notation was defined to manipulate trust values based on this simplification. The dimensions used in [8] are *trust origin*, *trust target* and *trust purpose*. Represented according to these dimensions, Jøsang et al. find that trust does have some properties of transitivity, based on their study of some basic trust topologies (Fig. 9.1).

Figure 9.1 shows two of the core ideas from Jøsang's 2003 work. Part (*a*.) depicts Jøsang's notion of parallel trust combination. In this figure, Alice can assess trust for a third party (David) by making decisions based on input from multiple sources (Bob and Claire). In this example, if Bob and Claire's recommended trust for David

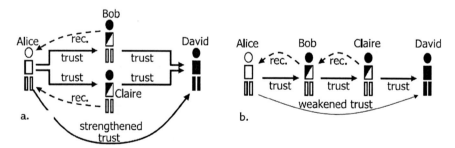

Fig. 9.1 Trust transitivity diagrams from Andun Jøsang's work in [8]. Part (**a**) shows recommendation from multiple sources and resultant parallel trust propagation. Part (**b**) shows basic recommendation and trust propagation across a chain of users

was highly correlated, it would stand to reinforce the derived trust that Alice has for David. Conversely, if Bob and Claire's recommendations about David were highly uncorrelated, it should lower the confidence level placed in the derived trust that Alice has for David. Jøsang deals in detail with various approaches to combine uncorrelated trust expressions of this form. An interesting perspective that was not discussed in [8] is that when Bob and Claire have uncorrelated trust statements for Alice about David, this tells us valuable information about Bob and Claire as recommenders. For example, if it manifests that David is highly trustworthy, and Bob has cautioned Alice that he is not trustworthy, then this misinformation should be remembered the next time Alice receives a recommendation from Bob. Essentially, the mistake should decrease Bobs overall trustworthiness as a recommender.

Figure 9.1 part (b.) shows the most basic form of trust transitivity defined in [8]. In this example, 'recommendations' are propagated from Claire, (who directly trusts the target David) through Bob to the source, Alice. As in a real world social or business situation, this results in a weaker trust (less confidence) than if Alice interacted with David directly. Note: In this example the term 'recommendations' is used to represent statements of the form 'I recommend that you should trust this person'.

Research in [22, 23] by Ziegler details the implementation of a propagation model for trust among users in the Social Web. Ziegler focused largely on use of semantic knowledge to achieve trust metrics. A classification scheme for trust metrics is developed in [22], and the benefits and drawbacks of this system are analysed in the context of several Semantic Web scenarios. Ziegler introduces the *Appleseed* system in [22] which is enabled to compute trust for local groups by borrowing ideas from spreading activation models in neuropsychology. According to Ziegler, trust metrics can be broadly categorised into *local* and *global*, where global metrics consider all peers/users and all the links between them. Global trust ranks are computed on the full trust graph, in a manner analogous to the Google PageRank algorithm. Local trust metrics on the other hand, only use partial trust graphs, and constitute *personalised* trust, based on the rational that the set of persons trusted highly by agent *a* may be different from those trusted by agent *b*.

9.3 Trust Sources on the Social Web

Figure 9.2 depicts the application area of this work within the context of the larger World Wide Web. Figure 9.2 also shows some of the application areas which rely heavily on the opinions and views of communities of users and some of the overlaps and interaction areas between these applications. In essence, we are saying that any application on the Social Web, which relies on the opinions, contributions or actions of communities of users, stands to benefit from analysis of the underlying trust relationships that exist in that community.

Trust is a difficult concept to define, and there are many, sometimes conflicting definitions from a range of disciplines. For the work presented in this chapter, we

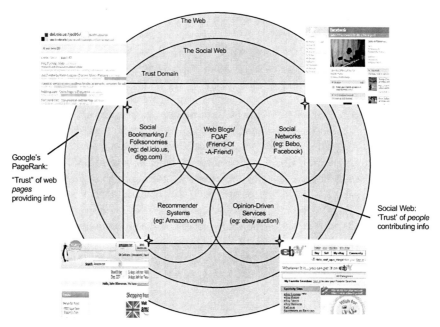

Fig. 9.2 Trust domain within the social Web

are mainly interested in trust in a *computational* sense, as explained by Marsh in [11], particularly, that trust can be viewed as a function of reputation, which can be computed over historical data.

Figure 9.3 provides an illustration of the general concept used in each of the three trust-based applications presented: Users interact with the Social Web application and provide information such as item ratings, product purchases, feedback comments about other users etc. Data-mining techniques can be applied to this data to compute models of trust between individual users. Information from these models can then be re-integrated into the existing mechanisms of the Social Web application to improve the user experience in some way. A high level classification of trust sources within Social Web applications is presented in Table 9.1. Two distinct types of trust are highlighted: *indirect-trust* is a value or set of values to represent trust, which has been computed using some proxy. Examples of such proxies include ratings, profile info, purchases and so on. *Direct-trust* is a value, opinion or comment expressed by one user directly about another during their interaction with the system, for example eBay feedback comments or facebook 'friends'. Research by Jøsang [7] discusses direct and indirect trust in the context of trust propagation between users on the Social Web, this is briefly discussed in the related work section. Jøsang's discussion focuses on the transitive properties of trust as it is passed from person to person. A distinction is drawn between Jøsang's concept and that illustrated in Fig. 9.3 where *indirect trust* uses items as a proxy for trust information between users. For instance, a rating of a movie or a purchased product.

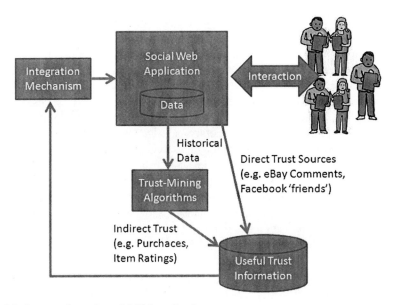

Fig. 9.3 Sources of trust in social Web applications

Table 9.1 Overview of three trust-based algorithms with application domain and classification of trust sources shown for each algorithm

Method	algorithm name	domain	Trust type	original input
1	tRec	ACF Systems	Indirect	Inattentive
2	AuctionRules	Feedback Systems, eg eBay	Direct	Attentive
3	PeerChooser	(Visual) ACF Systems	Both	Both

Table 9.1 expresses a high-level classification of trust sources within Social Web applications, and provides an overview of each of the three the techniques presented in this chapter, showing for each technique the trust type, source and domain. Source type indicates whether or not the initial indication of trust was *attentive* (e.g.: leaving a positive comment on eBay about a particular transaction partner) or implicit (e.g.: purchasing a product, following links etc.). For the purpose of our classification of trust sources, a source in which a user is not aware they are providing trust information is termed an *inattentive* trust source. In Table 9.1, trust type can be either *direct* or *indirect* and indicates whether the trust was expressed by one user directly about another, or computed using some proxy, as discussed above.

The first technique shown in Table 9.1 is a trust modelling algorithm for a collaborative (ACF) recommender system. In this technique, trust is computed over a historical dataset of ratings on movies. For the purpose of this discussion, we refer to these movie ratings as implicit- although the user has explicitly rated a movie, they have no knowledge that this information can be used to compute a trust value about them. This is also an indirect source of trust since the user is not directly making a trust statement about another user. The second technique presented takes an entirely different approach to harnessing trust information. The *AuctionRules* algorithm computes trust values between users by mining sentiment information from freetext comments on an online auction site. These types of trust can be considered as direct, since the original trust source is essentially a satisfaction statement made by one user directly about another. The source of trust in *Auction-Rules* is considered as *attentive*, since although the comments are processed by an NLP algorithm, a user has made an knowing effort to enter the original feedback comment and express a view about another user. The final trust source presented in this work can be viewed a combination of sources. *PeerChooser* is an interactive interface for an ACF recommender system in which users can view a personalised set of their neighbours trust values (computed by technique 1), and modify their values at recommendation time. This can help a user to express current mood and requirements for example. The trust sources used by the *PeerChooser* interface can be classified as a combination of both direct and indirect, since they are originally computed using item ratings, but then modified directly by the user in an interactive interface.

The remainder of this chapter presents the approach and evaluation of the three techniques used for sourcing trust in two Social Web applications, recommender systems and online auctions. This is followed by a comparative analysis of each technique with respect to the source of the trust information used.

9.4 Source 1: Modelling Trust from Ratings in ACF Recommender Systems

Recommender systems are a tool for tailoring large quantities of information to suit the needs of individual users. These systems are widely used on the Social Web, for instance Amazon.com recommends books to millions of users every day. In this section a technique is discussed for modelling trust from user ratings within an Automated Collaborative Filtering (ACF) recommender system. To date ACF systems have relied heavily on what might be termed the *similarity assumption*: that similar profiles (similar in terms of their ratings histories) make good recommendation partners. However, in the real world, a person seeking a recommendation would look further than just similarity with a potential recommender. For example, my friend Bob is a mechanic and is quite similar to me in many respects, but I happen to know from past experience that he has a limited knowledge of computer science, and because of this I would never seek a recommendation from him on anything related to computer science. However, I would trust him highly to recommend anything related to cars, as he has proven to be highly competent in this area in the past. We believe that similarity alone is not enough to base recommendations on in the online world. Trust is an important factor in deciding who to receive recommendations from in Social Web systems as well as in real world situations. Following is a description of the design, implementation and evaluation of a novel technique for modelling trust in ACF recommender systems.

A distinction is drawn between two types of profiles in the context of a given recommendation session or rating prediction. The *consumer* refers to the profile receiving the item rating, whereas the *producer* refers to the profile that has been selected as a recommendation partner for the consumer and that is participating in the recommendation session. So, to generate a predicted rating for item i for some consumer c, we will typically draw on the services of a number of producer profiles, combining their individual recommendations according to some suitable function, such as Resnick's formula, for example (see Eq. 9.1).

Our benchmark algorithm uses Resnick's standard prediction formula which operates by computing a weighted average of deviations from each neighbour's mean rating, and which is reproduced below as Eq. 9.1; see also [18]. In this formula $c(i)$ is the rating to be predicted for item i in consumer profile c and $p(i)$ is the rating for item i by a producer profile p who has rated i, $P(i)$. In addition, $\bar{c}$ and $\bar{p}$ refers to the mean ratings for c and p respectively. The weighting factor $sim(c, p)$ is a measure of the *similarity* between profiles c and p, which is traditionally calculated as Pearson's correlation coefficient.

$$c(i) = \bar{c} + \frac{\displaystyle\sum_{p \in P(i)} (p(i) - \bar{p})sim(c, p)}{\displaystyle\sum_{p \in P_i} |sim(c, p)|} \tag{9.1}$$

Item predictions are generated using benchmark correlation and prediction methods as it allows for ease of comparison with existing systems. As we have seen above Resnick's prediction formula discounts the contribution of a partner's prediction according to its degree of similarity with the target user so that more similar partners have a larger impact on the final ratings prediction.

The key to our technique is an assessment of the reliability of such partners profiles to deliver accurate recommendations in the future. This is achieved by assuming continuity and assessing the quality of each partner's contribution to recommendations in the past. Intuitively, if a profile has made lots of accurate predictions in the past, they can be viewed as more trustworthy that another profile that has made many poor predictions. In this section we define two models of trust and show how they can be readily incorporated into the mechanics of a standard collaborative filtering recommender system.

9.4.1 Combining Trust in ACF

Figure 9.4 shows a graphical overview of the trust-based recommendation process. In this figure, trust is integrated into a standard ACF algorithm. Initially, trust and similarity are calculated for every pair of users in the database in an offline process. There are a range of ways in which trust is computed, resulting in different models. These are discussed in detail in Section 9.4.2, for now the focus is on integration

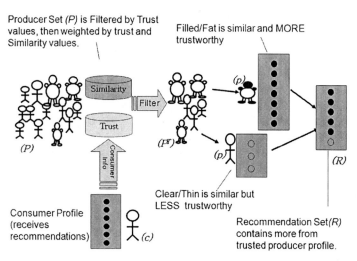

Producer Set *(P)* is Filtered by Trust values, then weighted by trust and Similarity values.

Filled/Fat is similar and MORE trustworthy

Clear/Thin is similar but LESS trustworthy

Consumer Profile (receives recommendations)

Recommendation Set*(R)* contains more from trusted producer profile.

Fig. 9.4 Integrating trust models into standard collaborative filtering

of trust into ACF. During the recommendation process, peer groups are firstly constructed based on a similarity function and then they are filtered based on trust. In Fig. 9.4, C is the active user (or 'consumer') who is seeking recommendations from the system. P is the set of potential recommendation partners (also known as the 'neighbourhood', 'peergroup' or 'recommendation producers') who are most highly correlated and therefore 'similar' to the active user. A personalised trust score is retrieved from a database for the consumer and each potential recommendation partner in turn. If this value is below a certain threshold, that potential producer is dropped from the candidate set. In this manner, only highly similar and highly trustworthy users from the final set of recommendation producers P_t.

Now that the set of producer profiles has been selected, the problem of combining their individual contributions must be addressed. To give a quick example, if I had two highly trusted friends who both were computer scientists, and I needed a recommendation on the quality of a new programming language, I would listen to both opinions, but most likely I would give more weight to the recommendation from person who had the better reputation in the field of programming languages. Accordingly, in Fig. 9.4 the contribution of each member of the trusted producer set P_t is weighted according to the associated trust value. In this manner, more trusted users (indicated as the fatter users in Fig. 9.4) have more influence over the final recommendation set R that is presented to the consumer. Section 9.4.3 provides a detailed description of the specific algorithms which have been developed to combine trust with similarity in the recommendation process.

9.4.2 Capturing Profile-Level & Item-Level Trust

Figure 9.5 shows a high-level overview of the computation described in this section. A ratings prediction for an item, i, by a producer p for a consumer c, is deemed

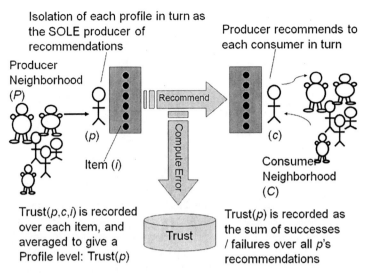

Isolation of each profile in turn as the SOLE producer of recommendations

Producer recommends to each consumer in turn

Producer Neighborhood (P)

(p)

Recommend

Compute Error

Item (i)

Trust

(c)

Consumer Neighborhood (C)

Trust(p,c,i) is recorded over each item, and averaged to give a Profile level: Trust(p)

Trust(p) is recorded as the sum of successes / failures over all p's recommendations

Fig. 9.5 Overview of the trust building process

correct if the predicted rating, $p(i)$, is within ϵ of c's actual rating $c(i)$; see Eq. 9.2. Of course normally when a producer is involved in the recommendation process they are participating with a number of other recommendation partners and it may not be possible to judge wether the final recommendation is correct as a result of p's contribution. Accordingly, when calculating the correctness of p's recommendation we separately perform the recommendation process by using p as c's sole recommendation partner. For example, a trust score for item $i1$ is generated for producer b by using the information in profile b *only* to generate predictions for each consumer profile. Equation 9.3 shows how a binary success/fail score is determined depending on whether or not the generated rating is within a distance of ϵ from the actual rating a particular consumer has for that item. In a real-time recommender system, trust values for producers could be easily created on the fly, by a comparison between our predicted rating (based only on one producer profile) and the actual rating which a user enters.

$$Correct(i, p, c) \Leftrightarrow |p(i) - c(i)| < \epsilon \tag{9.2}$$

$$T_p(i, c) = Correct(i, p, c) \tag{9.3}$$

From this we can define two basic trust metrics based on the relative number of correct recommendations that a given producer has made. The full set of recommendations that a given producer has been involved in, $RecSet(p)$, is given by Equation 9.4. And the subset of these that are correct, $CorrSet(p)$ is given by Equation 9.5.

$$RecSet(p) = \{(c_1, i_1), ..., (c_n, i_n)\} \tag{9.4}$$

$$CorrSet(p) = \{(c_k, i_k) \in RecSet(p) : Correct(i_k, p, c_k)\} \tag{9.5}$$

The *profile-level trust*, $Trust^P$ for a producer is the percentage of correct recommendations that this producer has contributed; see Equation 9.5. Obviously, profile-level trust is very coarse grained measure of trust as it applies to the profile as a whole.

$$Trust^P(p) = \frac{|CorrSet(p)|}{|RecSet(p)|} \tag{9.6}$$

Suppose a producer has been involved in 100 recommendations, that is they have served as a recommendation partner 100 times, and for 40 of these recommendations the producer was capable of predicting a correct rating, the profile level trust score for this user is 0.4. In reality, we might expect that a given producer profile may be more trustworthy when it comes to predicting ratings for certain items than for others. Accordingly we can define a more fine-grained item-level trust metric, $Trust^I$, as shown in Equation 9.7, which measures the percentage of recommendations for an item i that were correct.

$$Trust^I(p, i) = \frac{|\{(c_k, i_k) \in CorrSet(p) : i_k = i\}|}{|\{(c_k, i_k) \in RecSet(p) : i_k = i\}|} \tag{9.7}$$

9.4.3 Trust-Based Recommendation

Section 9.4.1 presented a high level graphical overview of the process by which trust is integrated into an ACF algorithm. Now we present details of three specific techniques for harnessing trust to achieve better recommendations. We will consider 2 distinct adaptations of a standard ACF technique: *trust-based weighting* and *trust-based filtering*, both of which can be used with either profile-level or item-level trust metrics. The third technique presented is a hybrid of the first two adaptations.

9.4.3.1 Trust-Based Weighting

Perhaps the simplest way to incorporate trust in to the recommendation process is to combine trust and similarity to produce a compound weighing that can be used by Resnick's formula; see Eq. 9.8.

$$c(i) = \bar{c} + \frac{\sum\limits_{p \in P(i)} (p(i) - \bar{p})w(c, p, i)}{\sum\limits_{p \in P(i)} |w(c, p, i)|} \tag{9.8}$$

$$w(c, p, i) = \frac{2(sim(c, p))(trust^{I}(p, i))}{sim(c, p) + trust^{I}(p, i)} \qquad (9.9)$$

For example, when predicting the rating for item i for consumer c we could compute the arithmetic mean of the trust value (profile-level or item-level) and the similarity value for each producer profile. A modification on this has been made by using the harmonic mean of trust and similarity; see Eq. 9.9 which combines profile similarity with item-level trust in this case. The advantage of using the harmonic mean is that it is robust to large differences between the inputs so that a high weighting will only be produced if both trust and similarity scores are high. Algorithm 1 is a pseudocode representation of the prediction process using trust-based weighing.

Input: Set of producer profiles P, trust model T, consumer profile c
Output: item recommendation for consumer profile
foreach *Producer Profile p* **do**
> **foreach** *CandidateItem i* **do**
> > w(c,p,i) = harmonicMean(sim(c,p), trust(p,i)) ;
> > sum = sum + (p(i)-p)w(c,p,i) ;
> > div = div + abs(sim(c,p)) ;
> **end**
> RecList(i) = ConsumersAverageRating + (sum/div) ;
end
return sortByValue(RecList)

           Algorithm 1: Prediction using trust-based weighting

9.4.3.2 Trust-Based Filtering

As an alternative to the trust-based weighting scheme above we can use trust as a means of filtering profiles prior to recommendation so that only the most trustworthy profiles participate in the prediction process. For example, Eq. 9.10 shows a modified version of Resnick's formula which only allows producer profiles to participate in the recommendation process if their trust values exceed some predefined threshold; see Eq. 9.11 which uses item-level trust ($Trust^{I}(p, i)$) but can be easily adapted to use profile-level trust. The standard Resnick method is thus only applied to the most trustworthy profiles. Pseudocode for the prediction process using trust-based filtering is shown in 9.10.

$$c(i) = \bar{c} + \frac{\sum_{p \in P^{T}(i)} (p(i) - \bar{p})sim(c, p)}{\sum_{p \in P^{T}(i)} |sim(c, p)|} \qquad (9.10)$$

$$P_{i}^{T} = \{p \in P(i) : Trust^{I}(p, i) > T\} \qquad (9.11)$$

Input: Set of producer profiles P, trust model T, consumer profile c
Output: item recommendation for consumer profile
foreach *Producer Profile p* **do**
   | **if** *Trust(i,p,c) $\geq$ threshold* **then**
   | | **foreach** *CandidateItem i* **do**
   | | | sum = sum + (p(i)-pAvg)sim(c,p) ;
   | | | div = div + abs(sim(c,p)) ;
   | | **end**
   | | RecList[i] = ConsumersAverageRating + (sum/div) ;
   | **end**
end
return sortByValue(RecList) ;

Algorithm 2: Prediction using trust-based filtering

9.4.3.3 Combining Trust-Based Weighting and Filtering

Of course, it is obviously straightforward to combine both of these schemes so that profiles are first filtered according to their trust values and the trust values of these highly trustworthy profiles are combined with profile similarity during prediction. For instance, Eq. 9.12 shows both approaches used in combination using item-level trust.

$$c(i) = \bar{c} + \frac{\displaystyle\sum_{p \in P^T(i)} (p(i) - \bar{p})w(c, p, i)}{\displaystyle\sum_{p \in P^T(i)} |w(c, p, i)|} \tag{9.12}$$

9.4.4 Evaluation

So far the argument has been that profile similarity alone may not be enough to guarantee high quality predictions and recommendations in collaborative filtering systems. Trust has been highlighted as an additional factor to consider in weighting the relative contributions of profiles during ratings prediction. In the discussion section all of the important practical benefits of incorporating models of trust into the recommendation process are analysed. Specifically, a set of experiments conducted to better understand how trust might improve recommendation accuracy and prediction error relative to more traditional collaborative filtering approaches is described.

This experiment uses the standard MovieLens dataset [18]. This set contains 943 profiles of movie ratings. Profile sizes vary from 18 to 706 with an average size of 105. We divide these profiles into two groups: 80% are used as the producer profiles and the remaining 20% are used as the consumer (test) profiles.

Before evaluating the accuracy of the new trust-based prediction techniques, trust values must firstly be build up for the producer profiles as described in the next section. It is worth noting that ordinarily these trust values would be built on-the-fly during the normal operation of the recommender system, but for the purpose of this experiment they have been constructed separately in an off-line process, but without reference to the test profiles. Having built the trust values, the effectiveness of our new techniques are evaluated by generating rating predictions for each item in each consumer profile by using the producer profiles as recommendation partners. This is done by using the following different recommendation strategies:

1. *Std* - The standard Resnick prediction method.
2. *WProfile* - Trust-based weighting using profile-level trust.
3. *WItem* - Trust-based weighting using item-level trust.
4. *FProfile* - Trust-based filtering using profile-level trust and with the mean profile-level trust across the producers used as a threshold..
5. *FItem* - Trust-based filtering using item-level trust and with the mean item-level trust value across the profiles used as a threshold.
6. *CProfile* - Combined trust-based filtering & weighting using profile-level trust.
7. *CItem* - Combined trust-based filtering & weighting using item-level trust.

9.4.5 Building Trust

Ordinarily the proposed trust-based recommendation strategies contemplate the calculation of relevant trust values on-the-fly as part of the normal recommendation process or during the training phase for new users. However, for the purpose of this study, trust values must be calculated in advance. This is done by running a standard *leave-one-out* training session over the producer profiles. In short, each producer temporarily serves as a consumer profile and rating predictions are generated for each of its items by using Resnick's prediction formula with each remaining producer as a lone recommendation partner; that is, each producer is used in isolation to make a prediction. By comparing the predicted rating to the known actual rating we can determine whether or not a given producer has made a correct recommendation – in the sense that the predicted rating is within a set threshold of the actual rating—and so build up the profile-level and item-level trust scores across the producer profiles.

This approach is used to build both profile-level trust values and item-level trust values. To get a sense of the type of trust values generated histograms of the profile-level and item-level values for the producer profiles in Fig. 9.6 and 9.7 are presented. In each case we find that the trust values are normally distributed but they differ in the degree of variation that is evident. Not surprisingly there is greater variability in the more numerous item-level trust values, which extend from as low as 0.5 to as high as 1. This variation is lost in the averaging process that is used to build the profile-level trust values from these item-level data. Most of the profile-level trust values range from about 0.3 to about 0.8. For example, in Fig. 9.7 approximately 13% of profiles have trust values less that 0.4 and 25% of profiles have trust values

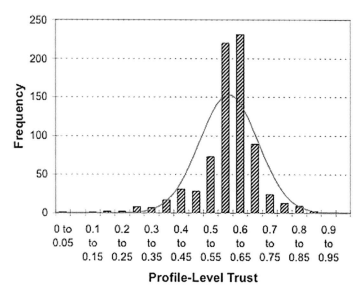

Fig. 9.6 The distribution of profile-level trust values among the producer profiles

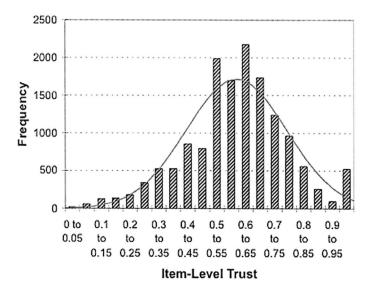

Fig. 9.7 The distribution of item-level trust values among the producer profiles

greater than 0.7. By comparison less than 4% of the profile-level trust values are less than 0.4 and less than 6% are greater than 0.7.

If there was little variation in trust then trust-based prediction strategies would not be expected to differ significantly from the standard Resnick method, but of course since there is much variation, especially in the item-level values, then significant differences between the predictions made by Resnick and the predictions made by our alternative strategies are expected. Of course whether the trust-based predictions are demonstrably better remains to be seen.

9.4.6 Recommendation Error

Ultimately, we are interested in exploring how the use of trust estimates can make recommendation and ratings predictions more reliable and accurate. In this experiment we focus on the mean recommendation error generated by each of the recommendation strategies over the items contained within the consumer profiles. That is, for each consumer profile, each of its rated items are temporarily removed and the producer profiles are used to generate a predicted rating for this target item according to one of the 7 recommendation strategies proposed above. It is worth pointing out that the rating error is calculated with reference to the item's known rating and an average error is calculated for each strategy.

The results are presented in Fig. 9.8 as a bar-chart of average error values for each of the 7 strategies. In addition, the line graph represents the relative error reduction enjoyed by each strategy, compared to the Resnick benchmark. A number of patterns emerge with respect to the errors. First, the trust-based methods all produce lower errors than the Resnick approach (and all of these reductions are statistically significant at the 95% confidence level) with the best performer being the combined

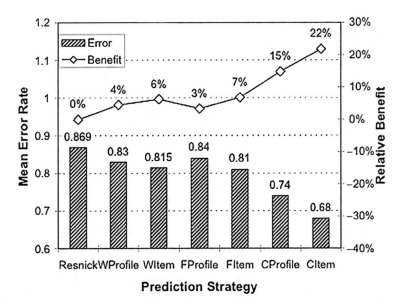

Fig. 9.8 Average prediction error and relative benefit (compared to resnick) for each of the trust-based recommendation strategies

item-level trust approach ($CItem$) with an average error of 0.68, a 22% reduction in the Resnick error.

It was found also that in general the item-level trust approaches perform better than the profile-level approaches. For example, $WItem$, $FItem$ and $CItem$ all out-perform their corresponding profile-level strategies ($WProfile$, $FProfile$ and $CProfile$). This is to be expected as the item-level trust values provide a far more fine-grained and accurate account of the reliability of a profile during recommendation and prediction. An individual profile may be very trustworthy when it comes to predicting the ratings of some of its items, but less so for others. This distinction is lost in the averaging process that is used to derive single profile-level trust values, which explains the difference in rating errors.

In addition, the combined strategies significantly out-perform their corresponding weighting and filtering strategies. Neither the filtering or weighting strategies on their own are sufficient to deliver the major benefits of the combination strategies. But together the combination of filtering out untrustworthy profiles and the use of trust values during the ratings prediction results in a significant reduction in error. For example, the combined item-level strategy achieves a further 16% error reduction compared to the weighted or filter-based item-level strategies, and the combined profile-level strategy achieves a further 11% error reduction compared to the weighted or filter-based profile-level approaches.

On average, over a large number of predictions, the trust-based predictions techniques achieve a lower overall error than Resnick. It is not clear, however, whether these lower errors arise out of a general improvement by the trust-based techniques over the majority of individual predictions, when compared to Resnick, or whether they arise because of a small number of very low error predictions that serve to mask less impressive performance at the level of individual predictions. To test this, the percentage of predictions where each of the trust-based methods wins over Resnick are examined here, in the sense that they achieve lower error predictions on a prediction by prediction basis.

These results are presented in Fig. 9.9 and they are revealing in a number of respects. For a start, even though the two weighting-based strategies ($WProfile$ and $WItem$) deliver an improved prediction error than Resnick, albeit a marginal improvement, they only win in 31.5% and 45.9% of the prediction trials, respectively. In other words, Resnick delivers a better prediction the majority of times. The filter-based ($FProfile$ and $FItem$) and combination strategies ($CProfile$ and $CItem$) offer much better performance. All of these strategies win on the majority of trials with $FProfile$ and $CItem$ winning in 70% and 67% of predictions, respectively.

Interestingly, the $FProfile$ strategy offers the best overall improvement in terms of its percentage wins over Resnick, even though on average it offers only a 3% mean error reduction compared to Resnick. So even though $FProfile$ delivers a lower error prediction than Resnick nearly 70% of the time, these improvements are relatively minor. In contrast, the $CItem$, which beats Resnick 67% of the time, does so on the basis of a much more impressive overall error reduction of 22%.

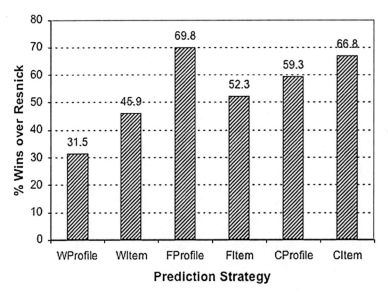

Fig. 9.9 The percentages of predictions where each of the trust-based techniques achieves a lower Error prediction than the Benchmark Resnick technique

9.4.7 Discussion

This concludes the implementation and evaluation of the first of the three techniques for sourcing trust in Social Web applications. The trust model presented used *indirect* trust, since it computes trust between users using their ratings on items as a proxy. The trust source in the model was *implicit*, since the users were not knowingly providing trust information while they were making their ratings. The following section presents the second technique for sourcing trust, this time in the domain of online auctions. In this technique, trust values are computed from negative sentiment which can be discovered from feedback comments existing in the system. This trust source can be classified as *direct*, since the users are expressing their views directly about other users in their comments. The trust values can be also considered as *attentive*, since users are knowingly expressing trust for other users as they enter feedback on the system.

9.5 Source 2: Extracting Trust From Online Auction Feedback Comments

Online auctions and marketplaces where users leave text based feedback comprise a significant percentage of Social Web applications. The second technique for modelling trust in Social Web focuses in this area. To address the problem of unnaturally high trust ratings on trading communities such as eBay, we look to the freetext comments and apply a classification algorithm tailored for capturing subtle indications of negativity in those comments. The situation arises frequently where users are afraid to leave a negative comment for fear of retaliatory feedback comments which could damage their own reputation [19]. In many of these cases, a positive feedback rating is made, but the commenter still voices some grievance in the freetext comment. This is the type of subtle but important information the *AuctionRules* algorithm attempts to extract.

9.5.1 The AuctionRules Algorithm

AuctionRules is a classification algorithm with the goal of correctly classifying online auction comments into positive or negative according to a threshold. *AuctionRules* capitalises on the restrictive nature of online markets: there are a limited number of salient factors that a user (buyer or seller) is concerned about. This is reflected in feedback comments. We define a set of seven core *feature sets* for which the algorithm will compute granular trust scores. The following sets have a coverage of 62% of the comments in our database. The algorithm can obtain semantic information from 62% of the comments at a fine grained level. It is shown in our experimental analysis how we can maintain over 90% coverage using this algorithm. The terms in brackets are contents of each feature set.

1. *Item* - The quality/condition of the product being bought or sold. (*item, product*)
2. *Person* - The person the user makes the transaction with. (*buyer, seller, eBayer, dealer*)
3. *Cost* - Cost of item, cost of shipping, hidden costs etc. (*expense, cost*)
4. *Shipping* - Delivery of the item, security, time etc. (*delivery, shipping*)
5. *Response* - Communication with the other party, emails, feedback comment responses. (*response, comment, email, communication*)
6. *Packaging* - The packaging quality/condition of the item (*packaging*)
7. *Payment* - how the payment will be made to the seller, or back to buyer for return (*payment*)
8. *Transaction* - the overall transaction quality (*service, transaction, business*)

This technique enables us not only to compute a personal trust score between individual users, but also to provide more granular information on a potential transactor. For example: 'User x is very trustworthy when it comes to payment, but shipping has been unsatisfactory in the past', This granular or *contextual* trust draws on the wealth of information in comments and can uncover hidden problems, which the current trust system on eBay might overlook. For example, if John in New York wants to order a crate of Italian wine from Lucia in Italy, it would be very beneficial for John to examine Lucia's history of shipping quality.

Figure 9.10 details *AuctionRules* working on a sample comment, which had a positive rating on eBay. (All of the explanation in this section refers to Fig. 9.10.)

comment 1: ***not a very fast shipper***,, high ***cost*** but still a nice ***item***

comment 2: *great **seller**, fast **shipping**, would buy from again*

comment n: ***nice*** *item!!! **product** delivered on time but very poorly **packaged**.*

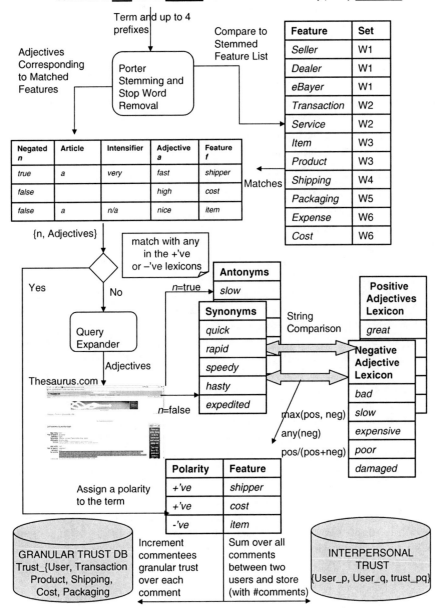

Fig. 9.10 The *AuctionRules* comment classification algorithm

Each term in a comment and up to four preceding terms are passed into an implementation of the Porter stemming algorithm [17]. The standard porter stemmer uses many rules for removing suffixes. For example, all of the terms in c are conflated to the root term *'connect'*. c = *connect, connected, connecting, connection, connections*. This reduces the number of terms and therefore the complexity of the data. The stemmer algorithm was modified to also stem characters not used by *Auction-Rules*, such as '?, !, *, (,)' for example.

Data dimension is reduced by removal of stop-words. Google's stop-word list[2] was used as the removal key. A future addition to the algorithm would put an automatic spelling corrector at this point. There were 11 different spelling occurrences of the word 'packaging' for example. Each stemmed term is compared against the stemmed terms from the feature list. If a match is found, the algorithm examines the preceding term types. This is shown graphically in Fig. 9.10. The algorithm recognises five term types:

- *nouns* the words contained in the feature sets.
- *adjectives* (e.g: 'nice', 'good') from a Web list of 150
- *intensifiers* (e.g 'very', 'more') list of 40.
- *articles* 'a' or 'the'
- *negators* (e.g. not, 'anything but') from a manually generated list (currently 17).

The table on the left in Fig. 9.10 shows the order in which these terms are analysed. From the five terms, two can provide semantic meaning about the feature: adjectives and negators. If an adjective is found without a negator, it is compared to an arrays 20 positive and an array of 20 negative adjectives. If a negator is found as the second or third preceding term, the process works with positive and negative arrays switched. If a match is found, the polarity for that feature is recorded.

If no match is found, *AuctionRules* uses query expansion, by calling an interface to an online thesaurus which returns an array of 20 synonyms. If a negator is present, the interface returns an array of 20 antonyms, and these lists are compared in a similar manner to our short lexicon of positive and negative adjectives. The matching results are recorded in three ways: (a) $max(pos, neg)$ (b) $any(neg)$ and (c) $neg/pos + neg$. In the case of (c) the polarity is recorded according to a configurable threshold α. Two separate trust databases are maintained: *granular* or *contextual* trust which is the trust computed for each feature for a user over all of the comments analysed. Equation 9.13 shows contextual trust t as a multi valued set of trust scores associated with each feature. Here, f denotes a particular feature and $t_f n$ is the associated trust score. The second trust database is *interpersonal* trust which is the average trust value recorded for all features on every comment made between two users.

$$t_{\text{granular}} \varepsilon \{t_{f1}, t_{f2}, ...t_{fn}\} \qquad (9.13)$$

---

[2] http://www.ranks.nl/tools/stopwords.html

Of course not every comment will contain words from the feature lists above. In cases where no features are found, the algorithm performs a straightforward count of positive and negative terms using the query expansion module where necessary. In this manner, coverage is maintained at over 90%, and many of the unclassifiable comments are foreign language or spelling mistakes. For example, from all the (10k) eBay comments stored by our crawler, 68 different misspellings of the word 'packaging' were found. It would be interesting as future work to analyse the effects of automatic spelling correction on our results.

One drawback with the current implementation is that negative sentiment which is represented in complicated grammatical expressions is often misinterpreted by the algorithm. For example, using the current implementation the sentence 'the item was anything but good, shipping was ok' gets misinterpreted to 'good shipping'. To overcome this more complex natural language processing rules need to be developed to account for more complex statements. However, the vast majority of comments crawled from eBay are expressed in simple grammar, so instances of the above problem are relatively few. There are several available 'black box' NLP classifiers, for example, the Stanford university NLP tools.[3] Future work on this algorithm should include a comparison between *AuctionRules* and these NLP classifiers.

9.6 Evaluation

We examine four factors in our evaluation of *AuctionRules*, including the *accuracy* of the *AuctionRules* classifier with respect to other techniques from machine learning. We also examine accuracy from a Mean Absolute Error perspective and by creating confusion matrices to examine performance with respect to false negative and positive classifications. As the system uses a very small amount of domain knowledge, and a limited number of features, we must examine the *coverage* of *AuctionRules* over our comments database. Finally, we make a comparison between the *scale* of trust achieved by *AuctionRules* against the current eBay scale.

9.6.1 Setup

Figure 9.11 explains the environment in which we test our algorithm. Data is crawled from the online auction site according to the crawler algorithm below. Importantly, unlike it's machine learning counterparts, *AuctionRules* requires *no* knowledge of the comment set it has to classify. The feature lists used by the algorithm are generic and should work on any set of online auction comments. Arguments have been made that *AuctionRules* relies heavily on domain knowledge and that this is very restrictive. The *AuctionRules* algorithm uses little domain knowledge in the form of lexicons of positive and negative words, intensifiers and so on.

---

[3] http://www-nlp.stanford.edu/software/index.shtml

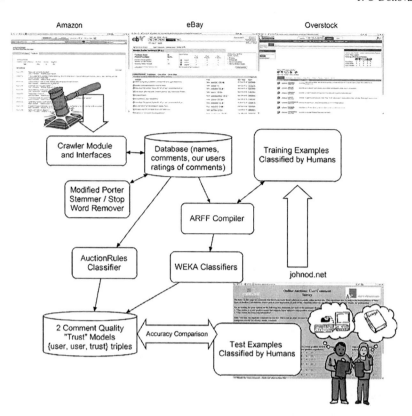

Fig. 9.11 Graphical overview of the trust-modelling process. (Current implementation only uses eBay as a source for ratings.)

AuctionRules will work on any system where users buy and sell from each other and leave textual feedback comments using no more domain knowledge than is used in the eBay system. Relative to the size of the application domain, the knowledge required by the algorithm is very minimal.

Algorithm 9.6.1: CRAWL(*String url_list, int maxbound*)

$$
\begin{aligned}
&\textbf{while } n < maxbound \\
&\textbf{for } i \leftarrow 1 \textbf{ to } \#Items\_on\_page \\
&\quad \textbf{do } \begin{cases} followSellerLink(); \\ \textbf{for } j \leftarrow 1 \textbf{ to } \#Comments\_on\_page \\ \quad \textbf{do } db.add(bId, sId, comment, sTrust, bTrust); \\ n \leftarrow n+1; \end{cases} \\
&\textbf{return };
\end{aligned}
$$

10,000 user comments were collected from the auction site using the crawler. As a social network visualisation was planned, data was collected from within a domain with highly interconnected and contained repeat-purchase users. After a manual analysis of a range of sub-domains of the auction site, Egyptian antiques was chosen as the data domain as it appeared to meet the prerequisites to a reasonable degree. Although a large number of comments were collected, only 1,000 were used in our experimental analysis.

9.6.1.1 User-Provided Training Data

In order to test any comment classification algorithm a benchmark set was required. 1,000 comments were compiled into an online survey[4] and rated by real users. In this survey, users were asked to rate the positiveness of each comment on a Likert scale of 1–5. 10 comments were presented to a user in each session. Each comment was made by different buyers about one seller. Users were required to answer the following:

- How positive is the comment (Average rating: 3.8442)
- How informative is the comment (Average rating: 3.1377)
- Would you buy from this seller (Average rating: 4.0819)

Figure 9.12 shows a screenshot of the comment classification pages where users provided ratings on each of the comments in our database. Currently, only results from the first question are used to develop and test *AuctionRules*. For future experiments we may incorporate results from the other questions. Permission was sought from eBay inc. to use the information from the eBay Web site in our experiments.

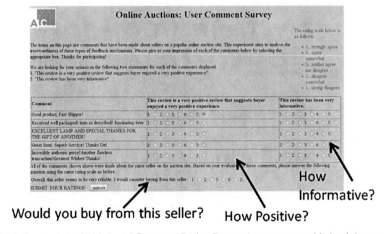

Fig. 9.12 Screenshot of Web-based Comment Rating Pages where users provided opinions on each crawled comment

---

[4] www.johnod.net/Surveyone.jsp

9.6.2 Comparing AuctionRules With Machine Learning Techniques

To examine classification accuracy of *AuctionRules*, it was tested against 7 popular algorithms. We chose three rule-based learners, *Zero-r, One-r, Decision Table*, one tree learner *C4.5 rules*, two Bayes learners, *Naive Bayes* and *BayesNet* and a lazy learning algorithm *K-Star*.

Figure 9.13 shows results of this experiment. For each algorithm we performed three runs. a 60:40 train-test split, an 80:20 split, and a 10-fold cross validation of the training set, which randomly selects a training set from the data over 10 runs of the classifier and averages the result. In the experiment, each algorithm made a prediction for every value in the test set, and this prediction was compared against the training set. *AuctionRules* beat all of the other classifiers in *every* test we performed, achieving over 90% accuracy in all of the evaluations, 97.5% in the 80:20 test, beating the worst performer *K-Star* by 17.5%, (relative 21.2%) and it's closest competitor *Naive Bayes* by 10.5%, giving a relative accuracy increase of 12.7%.

In addition to numerical accuracy, we examined where the high accuracy results were coming from more closely by assessing the confusion matrix output by the algorithms. This was necessary since prediction of false negatives would have an adverse effect on the resulting trust graph. This phenomenon has been discussed by Massa in [13] with respect to the *Moleskiing* application, and Golbeck in [6] with respect to the TrustMail application. Table 9.2 shows *AuctionRules* outperforming all of the other algorithms by predicting no false negatives. This is taken as a good result since in a propagation computation negative values should contain more weight because of their infrequency. When a value is presented to a user directly however, false positives are more damaging for an auction environment. *AuctionRules* also performs very well for false positives with a rate of 4.5%, half

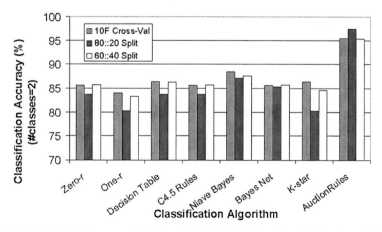

Fig. 9.13 Classification Accuracy [Classification Distribution from User Evaluations: 36% positive, 63% negative, using a threshold of 4 or higher for a positive comment.]

Table 9.2 Confusion matrices showing percentage true and false negatives and positives for four of the algorithms tested. [All of the other algorithms had similar results to the ones displayed.]

	AuctionRules		NaiveBayes		Decision Table		One-r	
	+'ve	-'ve	+'ve	-'ve	+'ve	-'ve	+'ve	-'ve
+'ve	91.4	0	84.1	1.2	84.6	1.2	77.3	8.1
-'ve	4.7	4.7	11.1	2.9	12.3	1.7	8.5	5.9

that of the closest competitor *One-r*. All of the algorithms displayed similar trend to the ones in Table 9.2, which shows results of the 80:20 classification experiment which had a test set of 234 comments. It was found during accuracy evaluations that there was a strong correlation between the number of feature terms recognised and the final accuracy of the classification. For our coverage experiments, we addressed the number of *hits* found with respect to coverage. This is detailed in the following section.

9.6.3 Coverage and Distribution Experiments

To assess the coverage of the *AuctionRules* feature-based trust calculator we examined the number of feature term hits that occur during classification. Coverage was tested in two modes. Firstly, the standard feature-based mode. In this case, 62% of the 1000 comments tested contained at least one hit from the feature list. This provides us with semantic knowledge about a large number of comments. However there is a sharp reduction in coverage when we look for comments with more than one hit. To increase coverage, *AuctionRules* uses simple term counting to supplement its feature-based approach in cases where it fails to find any terms. When

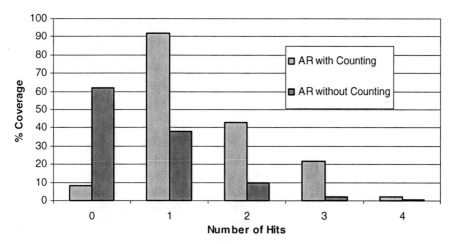

Fig. 9.14 Comparison of the coverage and hit ratio in *AuctionRules*

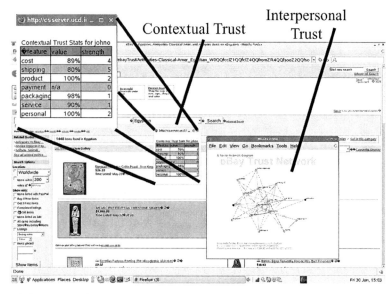

Fig. 9.15 Screenshot of the prototype auction interface showing contextual trust and interpersonal trust, mined from feedback comments

counting is applied the coverage is greatly increased with over 90% of the comments getting at least one hit. After manual examination, it is clear that majority of the other 8% can be attributed to misspellings, foreign language and other noise.

A distribution analysis was performed between the *AuctionRules* generated trust values and the current and found that the new trust values do capture some unseen negativity from feedback comments. This is manifested in a slightly more scaled distribution relative to the current eBay values. From 600 comments that were analyzed in the distribution experiment, 90 comments, which had been rated as 93–100 % positive, were taken out of that bracket by *AuctionRules*. This may seem like a small amount, but compared with the current system which has less than 1% negative ratings, *AuctionRules* produced 16%.

9.7 Discussion

The main contribution of this section is an algorithm for extracting *personalised* and *contextual* trust from the wealth of freetext comments on online auction sites. The algorithm operates on the assumption that online auction transactions can be categorised into a relatively small set of features. *AuctionRules* can extract context-specific and personal trust both retroactively and on the fly as new comments are added. There are a range of uses for the extracted trust scores. In this chapter we have shown one such use in a pop-up visualisation of the resulting trust network for a demonstration subset of the eBay marketplace. This visualisation also shows per-feature trust in a pop-up window for a buyer or seller. In our evaluations we show that even using a small lexicon of key features, coverage is still maintained above 90%. We show that the *AuctionRules* classifier beats seven popular learning algorithms at this classification task by up to 21% in accuracy tests using very minimal domain knowledge. *AuctionRules* has a favourable false negative rate for the classifier of 0% compared to up to 6% from benchmark algorithms and a false positive rate of 4.7% compared with 8.5–12.3% for the benchmark algorithms.

In the context of the classification of trust sources presented earlier, the trust values computed by *AuctionRules* are *direct* and *implicit* because a transactor is knowingly expressing trust information to the system about another specific user. The following section presents the implementation and analysis of the last technique for sourcing trust- asking the user directly at the moment a trust value is required. An interactive interface for collaborative filtering systems is presented which allows users to view pre-computed trust values, and make modifications to them as they receive recommendations from the system. With respect to the classification scheme, the trust sources in this system are a combination of several types and can be classified as both *direct* and *indirect* since trust values between a user seeking recommendations and each of his neighbours are displayed initially based on items which they both have rated. However, once a user manipulates this value through the interactive interface, they are providing a *direct* expression of trust.

9.8 Source 3: Extracting Trust through an Interactive Interface

The third application for computing and using trust information in the Social Web also focuses on ACF recommender systems, but from a very different perspective. In this technique, the focus is on extracting trust information directly from the end user at recommendation time. This is a form of *direct* and *attentive* trust as we are allowing an active user to knowingly provide trust information about other individuals. The idea behind recommender systems is to provide a user with a useful recommendation. Many recommender systems use item-based [20] or user-based [18] CF. CF models the social process of asking a friend for a recommendation. However, for people with no friends, or even bad friends, the social process obviously fails. In the CF literature, this failure has been termed the 'grey-sheep', 'sparsity' and 'early-rater' problems. In the real world it is difficult to choose who your peers will be, as modelled in most current CF systems. Imagine you want a movie recommendation and can choose a group of peers, in addition to your existing group. You might choose Stephen Spielberg, among others if your in the mood for a Sci-Fi flick. However, what if you told Mr Spielberg your top 10 movies, and he hated all of them. With this knowledge, would you still want his contributions?

In this technique, which follows from work in [16] we are interested in allowing a user to express trust values on a set of neighbours in order to allow them to benefit from improved recommendations that more accurately reflect their current preferences and mood. To achieve this the interface must convey meaningful

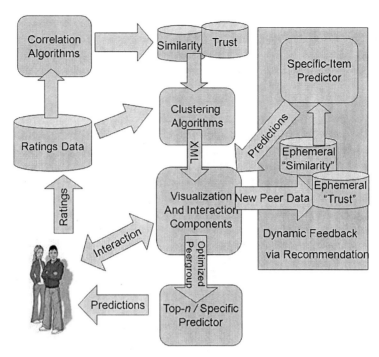

Fig. 9.16 Architecture of the PeerChooser visual interactive recommender system

information to the user about their neighbourhood structure and the interests of
their neighbours. This is a challenging problem as each neighbourhood represents
a high-dimensionality preference space which is difficult to render and even more
difficult for a user to interpret. To address this, while maintaining ease of use for the
end user, we have chosen to map the complex ratings data onto the space of movie
genres, which are presented as a set of user-connected *genre nodes* alongside their
neighbourhood representation; see Fig.9.17. An edge is created between a genre
node *g* and a user *u* if *u* displays an affinity for *g* in their ratings; in practice we use
a simple thresholding technique to identify affinities between users and genres if
more than 10% of the user's positive ratings reflect a given genre. These genre nodes
are also displayed using the force-directed graph layout algorithm, which causes
a natural clustering of users to genres as shown in Fig. 9.17; in this example we
allow each user to be connected to their two most dominant genres but in principle
each user can be connected to any number of genres, subject to presentation clarity
issues. *PeerChooser* provides highlighting functionality for nodes that are salient in
the CF process. The *k*-closest nodes to the active user are highlighted in red. Any
selected node is automatically scaled up to distinguish it from other nodes. Multiple
node selection is enabled for group manipulation of neighbours. When a node is
selected in *PeerChooser* the associated rating detail for that user is shown in a table.
Genre nodes in *PeerChooser* are linked to an icon database to represent each genre
clearly.

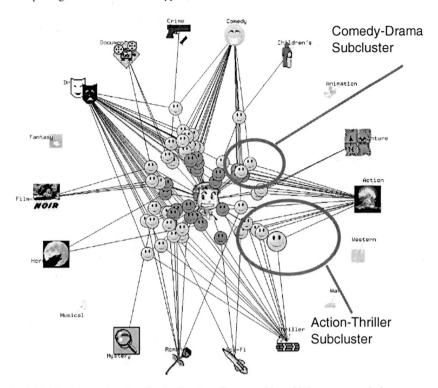

Fig. 9.17 MovieLens data visualised using *PeerChooser* with multiple genre associations

Labelling in *PeerChooser* is done on a per node basis. The label-positioning algorithm ensures that labels will not overlap on the graph and it attempts to place labels towards the outer edges of the graph wherever possible. Labels can be enabled or disabled on the basis of node type. For most of the visualisations in this paper we have displayed labels only on the genre nodes.

PeerChooser uses OpenGL technology on a Java platform, making it visually appealing to the end user. The layout algorithm is a force-directed graph which uses a standard spring model, with restrictions on the genre nodes. When the spring forces come to rest, the active user can interact with the graph by moving or deleting icons. Genre nodes are positioned around the outside of the graph and can be clicked on and moved freely. When this occurs, each connected neighbour node is moved by a relative distance in the same direction. This allows the user to make a bold statement about her current opinion on a particular genre. For example, if the comedy icon is moved towards the active user's avatar then all users who like comedy will be drawn closer and become 'more similar' to the active user for this session. We term this new value *ephemeral similarity*. Furthermore, users can make fine-grained statements by moving neighbour icons individually. On mouseover, nodes are highlighted and associated ratings are displayed in the right panel, shown in Fig. 9.18.

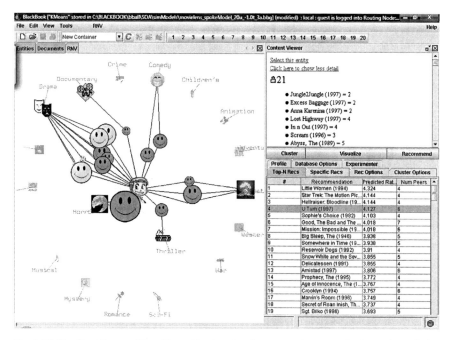

Fig. 9.18 The *PeerChooser* OpenGL application showing trust values as node size and correlation as edge length

9.8.1 Fair Representation of Genre Information

The genre distribution in the MovieLens data [citealpch09:bib15] has a massive bias towards three genres: Drama, Action, and Comedy. As a result, our initial clustered graphs tended to only show connections between non-active user nodes and nodes representing these three genres. To counter this problem and provide a more diverse set of neighbours we apply a scaling function to our edge drawing threshold based on number of occurrences of a genre in the database. Equation 9.14 shows how the system computes user to genre connectivity on a per-user basis. In Equation 9.14 G is the set of all genres, g represents one genre. Term $U_{\text{liked},g}$ indicates the number of items user U liked in genre g. U_{total} represents the total number of ratings by U; g_{total} is the number of movies in genre g and c is a scaling constant.

$$Max_{(g \in G)}\left(\frac{U_{\text{liked},g}}{U_{\text{total}}} + \frac{U_{\text{liked},g}}{g_{\text{total}}} \cdot c\right) \qquad (9.14)$$

Once our data has been clustered based on the algorithm described in the previous section, the graph is saved as an XML file. The advantage of using this format is that graphs can be saved and loaded repeatedly, meaning that the personalised recommendation graph is portable between different deployments of *PeerChooser*.

9.8.2 Visualising Trust Relations in PeerChooser

In addition to providing an explanation of the recommendation process to the end user, *PeerChooser* enables the user not only to visualise *correlation*, but also the *trust-space* generated from the underlying ratings data.

Following from the trust-mining experiments in Chapters 4 and 5, the trust matrix built on the MovieLens dataset was incorporated into the visualisation mechanism as a means to provide at-a-glance information to the end user on *trust* in conjunction with *similarity*. For this experiment, trust was computed using the algorithms from Chapter 4, and similarity was computed in the usual way, using Pearson's correlation over the raw rating data.

Figure 9.18 shows the *PeerChooser* application displaying trust and correlation in parallel. In this personalised graph, the active user is positioned at the centre with a personalised avatar. Non-active nodes are positioned around this, again with edge length fixed proportional to the Pearson correlation between the users. Node size is a function of the trust- smaller icons are less trustworthy and larger ones have higher trust. Using this graph the active user can easily discern the differences between similar users and trustworthy users. In this example, a highly trusted neighbour can be seen just below the active user's avatar. This neighbour is also highly correlated due to the close proximity to the active user node. Attached to the trusted peer is an icon representing the 'horror' genre. In the right panel the top-n recommendation list contains the slightly esoteric movie 'Hellraiser' in the top three, with a prediction of 4.1 from 5. This is most likely the influence of the trusted and correlated peer who likes horror movies.

9.8.3 Implementation

Three different attempts were made to produce an interactive visualisation for ACF, firstly a 2-dimensional graphing tool was used to plot our data, and secondly a 3-dimensional approach was used. The graphs produced from these attempts are shown in Fig. 9.19 However, in the layout algorithms in both of these approaches introduced too much noise to accurately base ACF predictions on the laid-out graph of the underlying data. The current *PeerChooser* interface, which we call Recommender Network Viewer (RNV) was developed to address the problem of noisy graph layouts for collaborative filtering visualisation. See for example Fig. 9.18. The layout of this graph in terms of node types, edges, and their respective roles in the visualisation has already been discussed. Now we provide some detail on the underlying implementation of the dynamic graph in RNV.

9.8.3.1 Distance Weighting

To incorporate user hints into the recommendation process we simply replace the standard similarity values (based on user-user ratings correlations) with a new similarity value that is based on the inverse *Euclidean distance* between the active user

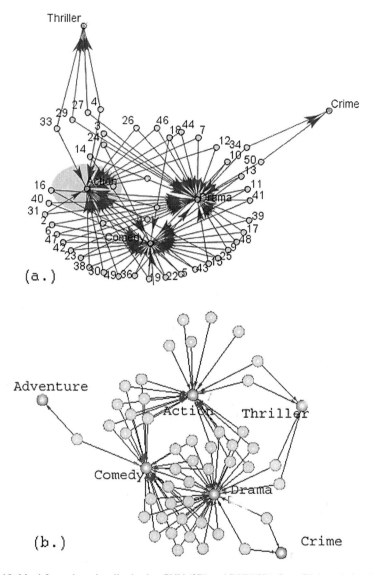

Fig. 9.19 MovieLens data visualised using SNV (2D) and DNV(3D) OpenGL-based visualisation tools

node and each of the k peer nodes that have been manipulated by the user. This is our *ephemeral similarity* value and is given by Equation 9.15. Here, Euclidean distance between pixels on the graph is normalised to the Pearson's correlation range of (-1, +1), max_dist is the maximum possible distance between the active user node and a peer node, while $node\_dist$ is the distance between the active node (i.e: the centre of the graph) and each peer node. Equation 9.16 shows the original Resnick prediction formula using ephemeral similarity in place of the standard Pearson correlation. The nomenclature is similar to that in Equation 9.1 with $c(i)$ being the predicted rating for an active user c on item i.

$$\text{eph\_sim}(c, p) = 2(1 - \frac{\text{node\_dist}}{\text{max\_dist}}) - 1) \tag{9.15}$$

$$c(i) = \bar{c} + \frac{\sum\limits_{p \in P(i)} (p(i) - \bar{p})eph\_sim(c, p)}{\sum\limits_{p \in P_i} eph\_sim(c, p)} \tag{9.16}$$

9.9 Evaluation

The majority of experiments involving recommender system algorithms are based on some form of automated testing, for example, predicting ratings for some 'hidden' subset of the rated data. This is only possible in absence of interactive components such as the ones of our *PeerChooser* system. Visualisation and interaction are additional 'tiers' to the process of collaborative filtering. The visualisation and interaction tiers bring many obvious advantages; however, it does prohibit the standard automated testing procedure since real people must explore and interact with the graph to attain results.

To evaluate the interactive visualisation components of the system, we performed controlled user trials. The objective of the trials was to ascertain as much information as possible about the users' overall experience using the visualisation techniques for profile generation and ratings prediction.

9.9.1 Experimental Data

For all of the evaluations in this chapter the small Movielens[5] [15] dataset was used. The base dataset consists of 100,000 ratings from 943 users on 1,682 items. The dataset has a sparsity of 93.7%.

The dataset contains no demographic information, but does contain genre information for each movie. Movies can be associated with multiple genres. Data is stored in a relational database and cached into memory where possible.

9.9.2 Rating Distributions

During user evaluations with our system two important comments were noted. Firstly, a 21 year old pointed out that he didn't know many of the movies in the

---

[5] http://movielens.umn.edu

dataset, and secondly, a 30 year old stated that there were a lot of 'classics' in the movie list he had to rate. These were worrying comments- it was feared that users might only remember the better, more popular movies, and accordingly produce an unnaturally high rating scale. To assess this possibility, we performed a comparative analysis between the distribution of dataset ratings and those from our user survey. Results from this analysis are presented in Fig. 9.20. There is a definite increase in the number of ratings in the top bin, but we were happy to find that the difference in the overall rating trend was not significant ($p < 0.01$).

9.9.3 Procedure

Our study involved 30 users, ranging in age between 21 and 30 years. Each trial took approximately 30 mins and consisted of three stages, a pre-study questionnaire in which participants provided general demographic information, and information relating to their experience using recommender systems and graph visualisations. We also asked the users to rank a list of movie genres according to their perceived popularity.

The second stage of the user trial required the participant to use the system to get recommendations.

Firstly, users were required to perform a familiarisation task. This involved users getting a recommendation for a movie from the list, interacting with the various user

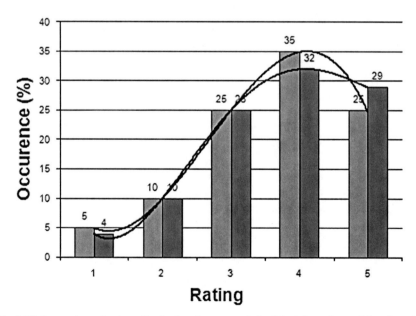

Fig. 9.20 Comparison of ratings distributions between existing MovieLens data and data from the user trials

nodes and genre nodes and manipulating the predicted rating to their taste. For the next task in the trial participants were required to use *PeerChooser's* manual rating window to generate a ratings profile via explicit ratings. Users were asked to rate 30 movies that they had watched on a scale of 1 (strong dislike) to 5 (strong like). Users then clicked on a submit button and the system correlated their ratings profile with the existing profiles.

To test the performance of our system we examined four techniques for generating recommendations, two with interaction and two without. For each approach we collected three values per item: the predicted rating, the actual rating, and the average rating in the whole database. The following list describes each approach:

1. *Average Layout* – The graph is laid out based on an 'average user'. We created this user by taking the average rating for the top 50 rated items. This technique was expected to yield the worst results as it contained no personalised information.
2. *Profile-Based Layout* – This is the benchmark CF algorithm. Correlations computed from a ratings profile are used to generate predictions.
3. *Profile-Based Layout with Manipulation* – Same as above but the user can manipulate the graph to provide information on current requirements.
4. *Profile-Based Layout with Manipulation and Feedback* – Same as above except the user receives dynamic recommendations on their salient items with each graph movement. We expected this to demonstrate the best performance.

For the *Average Layout* task users did not interact with the graph. They were simply shown a list of recommended items and asked to rate them (without showing them the predicted rating). Following from work by Swearingen et al. in [21] the predicted ratings were not displayed during this test as they could effect the users input. (Swearingen suggests that users tend to rate towards the machine-provided ratings.) Users then clicked on a submit button and the ratings were recorded.

A graph was then generated using our Pearson Clustering method described earlier. The cluster algorithm had a liked-item threshold of 3, meaning that the system only assumes an item is liked if the rating is 4 or 5. The number of neighbours to use in the computation was set to $k=30$ and the total number of users displayed on the graph was 400. The algorithm took the 400 most similar users from the entire database to display on the graph. The user then clicked on a button marked 'visualise' to show their personalised graph on the *PeerChooser* visualiser.

Users were then told to click on a button marked 'recommend' to a list of recommendations based on their personalised graph. Since the visualisation algorithm has zero effective noise for the collaborative filtering process, these recommendations are exactly equivalent to the benchmark Resnick CF algorithm from [18]. As with previous tasks, users rated 20 items and recorded their info. The penultimate recommendation task was similar to the above but with the addition of user manipulation on the graph.

In the final task the graph layout was as in the previous task. Users were asked to click checkboxes next to 5 movies they really liked and 5 that they hated. Users were

then told to click on a button marked 'specific predictions' and were provided with
the benchmark CF predictions on those items. Users were then told to take some
time to manipulate the graph to try and tweak the recommendations for their chosen
items to a value that most suited them. All users in the survey reported that they had
arrived at a satisfactory position within 2 mins without notification of a time constraint. At each movement users were provided with dynamic recommendations on
their 'salient' item-set according to the current neighbourhood configuration. This
allowed the users to dynamically assess the goodness of each movement performed.
Users were again presented with a list of recommended movies and asked to rate
them and store the information.

The concluding part of the user trial was the post-study questionnaire. This
contained the important questions regarding the users overall experience with the
interface. Results are shown in Fig. 9.22. Plotted are (as ratings between 1 and 5):
Subjective accuracy of the different methods as perceived by the user (not based on
actual prediction comparisons), the understandability of the used graph, user ratings
for the four techniques in Fig. 9.21. The next question is important: Would the user
prefer a visualisation-based approach over the standard active ratings-based technique in real life CF applications? The answer was a resounding 3.75 on average,
one of the highest values in the survey. Likewise high ratings were given for the
questions if the users gained knowledge through their interaction with the visualisation, the clarity of the labelling, informativeness of the right-hand information panel,
desirability of applying this technique in other domains, and usefulness of interaction (highest value of all). Only on the question of how much control the users felt
they had, and on the perceived accuracy did the survey yield ratings below average.

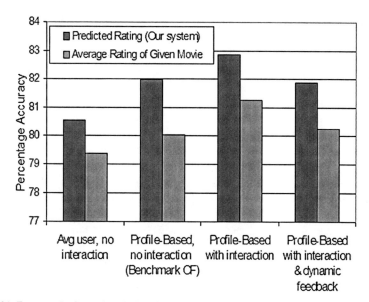

Fig. 9.21 Error results for each technique in the user trials

Table 9.3 Likert scale questions from the user survey

#	*Question Description*
S1	I am familiar with recommender systems
S2	I am familiar with interactive computer graphics
S3	I am familiar with graph visualizations
S4	Which did you think was the most accurate
S5	I found the graph easy to understand
S6	Look at the 4 graphs and rate each one
S7	Did you prefer the visualisation approach
S8	I gained knowledge about the underlying data from the visualization
S9	I felt that the labelling was appropriate
S10	I felt that the information in the right panel was helpful
S11	I felt that the *visualisation* system gave me more control of the recommendation algorithm
S12	Would you like to see this interface on other domains (e.g: Amazon.com)
S13	I felt that the icons communicated the genres appropriately
S14	I felt that the *visualisation* system gave me more control of the recommendation algorithm
S15	I felt that I benefitted from *interaction* with the system

Also, during this final questionnaire users were asked once more to rate a list of popular genres, as in the pre study to assess if there is any learning effect from use of the visualisation, which turned out to be the case. As but one example, on the post-study form, every user listed Drama, the most popular genre in the list of 5 most popular genres. On the pre-study form, only 8 out of 13 users had mentioned Drama.

9.9.4 Recommendation Accuracy

To evaluate the accuracy of the techniques, mean absolute error was computed between the predicted rating and the users actual rating for each of the methods. Results of our analysis are presented in Fig. 9.21 for four techniques. As expected, the average predictions– that is, predictions based on the average user described earlier, exhibited the worst performance, producing a an accuracy of 80.5%. Predictions based on an average user (column 1 in Fig. 9.21) have high accuracy, this is not surprising if we take a look at the rating distribution graph in Fig. 9.20. Users tended to rated only movies they liked, and the average user was constructed from a list of the most commonly rated movies, which as it turns out were generally the most highly rated movies. This may be attributed to the fact that the movies were not new and users tended to remember them in a good light. Our profile-based technique (column 3) with manipulation beats the benchmark (column 2) achieving a small relative increase of 1.05%. A single factor between groups ANOVA shows that these differences are significant in each case with $p = 0.006$, $F = 3.87$. This small increase is an important result because it indicates that manipulation does increase recommendation accuracy. Future work includes conducting this experiment over an extended time period to gain a better assessment of the performance of our technique compared with a CF system operating solely on historical rating data. We suspect that as data becomes more redundant, our method should become more accurate relative to standard techniques.

The most surprising result was that the dynamic feedback technique performed worse than the other profile-based techniques. After much analysis of the graphs it was determined that users tended to *over-tweak* the system to achieve desired results for their salient item sets. In doing this, many of the profile-based correlations were overwritten and the resulting layout was overfitted to the specific item sets. A solution to this may be to ensure diversity within the salient item sets.

To assess the effects of users interaction with the system a pre and post study questionnaire was answered by each participant. Table 9.1 lists each question from the survey and references the columns in Fig. 9.22. S1 to S3 indicate that all participants had experience with graphical interfaces, recommenders and visualisations. S4 tells us that, in contrast to our empirical accuracy tests, users felt that manual rating provided more accurate results. This was an interesting result which may indicate that users are more comfortable with familiar, manual rating systems. The four columns marked S6 represent participants' opinions on a range of different graph representations of the data, with column 8 being an exceptionally poor display. These are available for viewing at the URL above. S7 shows a clear preference for the visualisation approach, with 75% of users preferring *PeerChooser* over the traditional approach. The benefit of our technique as a recommendation *explanation* is shown by S8, where the majority of users felt they gained knowledge of the data from their interaction with the graphs. S9 and S10 indicate that users felt that labelling and node information were appropriate. S11 shows us that there were mixed views about the control that the interface provided on the CF algorithms. This response may be due to insufficient familiarisation time, since the technique does provide more access points to influence the CF process. S12 shows that more than 80% of participants agreed that they would like to see a *PeerChooser*-like interface

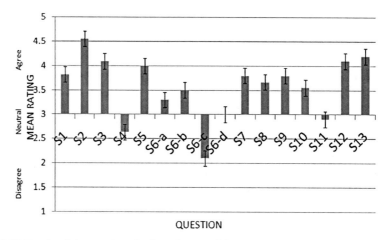

Fig. 9.22 Results of the questionnaire from the user trials

on other domains such as Amazon.com. This is an encouraging result, given that there is a broad scope of applications for our technique. More importantly, $S15$ shows that more than 80% of participants felt they benefitted overall from interacting with the system.

9.10 Comparison of Different Trust Sources

Trust information about users in the Social Web can be beneficial both to individuals and to the Social Web application as a whole. To illustrate the general benefits that are provided using each of the three trust-mining algorithms discussed in this chapter, a simple user-satisfaction trial was set up to ascertain the increase in user satisfaction, if any, created by integrating trust information from different sources back into each application. For this survey, 10 participants were asked to use each of the three applications twice. Once in normal operation, and once with the additional trust information added. For each application, participants overall satisfaction was elicited as follows:

1. *tRec*: Users rated 30 random items from the Movielens dataset. This information was used to compute recommendations using the item-level technique *CItem* to represent trust-based ACF. Users were also shown a list of 10 recommendations generated by the Resnick algorithm. (to represent normal ACF) Participants provided a percentage satisfaction with each recommendation and averages were taken for both modes.
2. *AuctionRules*: Users were asked to search for an item on a eBay-like interface. The first interface was similar to normal, showing sellers overall trust-ratings and feedback comments. The second interface, shown in Fig. 9.15 shows a trust-graph and contextual trust information mined from freetext comments for each seller in addition to the usual detail. For example, the general quality of packaging based on the information in the comments. For this experiment, users were simply asked to rate both presentation methods on a percentage scale. To account for the effects of ordering the interfaces were shown in varying orders. Averages were taken for both techniques.
3. *PeerChooser*: To analyse the effects of using trust information in the interactive recommender system on user satisfaction, participants were told to get 10 recommendations from the system, firstly using the visualisation technique but showing similarity values only, and secondly, showing both similarity and trust values. With trust as a function of node size and similarity as a function of edge length, as discussed earlier. Again, users rated their satisfaction with their recommended items on a percentage scale and an average value was taken for both modes.

Fig. 9.23 shows the results of this experiment for each of the three trust-mining algorithms presented. This graph plots the overall user satisfaction for each system,

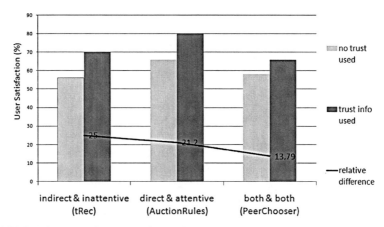

Fig. 9.23 Relative change in user satisfaction for each application operating with and without trust information

which harnessed its trust information from completely different sources. This graph is obviously not meant as a comparison between each technique, as comparison of user satisfaction across such heterogenous applications would not be viable. The important feature is the relative benefit score that is shown for each technique. This is the percentage increase in user satisfaction created by using trust data, over normal conditions (with no trust information) for each algorithm. For the *tRec* algorithm, which sourced trust information from *indirect* and *inattentive* data, (as discussed earlier), it is shown that using trust information can increase user satisfaction with predicted movie ratings by 30%, or a relative increase of 51%. It must be pointed out that this experiment is highly subjective and only computed over ten users. The motivation here is to show that an increase in user satisfaction can occur by using this trust source, more so than explicitly showing by how much.

For the *AuctionRules* algorithm, which sourced trust from freetext comments crawled from eBay, the average increase in satisfaction over the ten trials was 14%, or a relative increase of 21.2%. For *PeerChooser* the increase was 14%. Interestingly, the source of trust information for *AuctionRules* was both *direct* and *attentive*, meaning that users were expressing trust information directly about other users, and furthermore, they were aware that the they were expressing the information. Intuitively, this should have been the richest and most accurate source of trust information and probably should have resulted in more satisfied users than the other techniques, but it resulted in a smaller increase in user satisfaction, 3% less than the *tRec* algorithm, which used an *indirect* and *inattentive* trust source. *PeerChooser* uses both direct and indirect trust sources, since it uses the initial indirect values computed by tRec, then user-provided direct trust. This technique exhibited the smallest relative increase in user satisfaction with 13.9% However, there are a broad range of influencing factors and it is difficult to make an assumption as to why this was the case. What can be said about this data is that using additional trust information about interacting users in Social Web applications tends to produce increases in their overall satisfaction with the system.

9.11 Conclusions

The Social Web can be thought of as a *participation platform* in which users perform both social and business interactions. As such, it brings about a need to assess the trustworthiness of people who a user may interact with. The core argument in this chapter is that trust can be sourced in a variety of ways on Social Web applications. Three techniques for harnessing trust from different sources within Social Web applications have been presented, focusing on two main application areas, namely recommender systems and online auctions.

The first application presented a technique for modelling trust in recommender systems based on users' history of contributions to the recommendation process. Based on the earlier classification, the source of trust information in this instance is both *indirect* and *inattentive* since the user is not rating other users directly, and is not necessarily aware that they are providing trust information. This trust model can be used to improve the accuracy of collaborative filtering recommendations by up to 22% over the benchmark Resnick prediction algorithm.

The second technique sources trust information from online auction feedback comments. To analyse the potential in this source, the *AuctionRules* algorithm was developed. This is a trust-mining algorithm for online auctions which harnesses the wealth of information hidden in online auction feedback comments to provide new information about the reputations of potential transactors. The *AuctionRules* trust model is based on lightweight natural language processing over free text comments. Based on our classification, this trust source can be considered *direct* since the comment is targeted at another specific user, and *attentive* since the user is aware they are linking themselves to this other user. Analysis presented shows that *AuctionRules* extracts useful trust information from comments on eBay, which can enhance the overall user experience with the system.

The final source of trust analysed is a direct link with the user. To facilitate and test trust information provided on-the-fly by users interacting with a Social Web system, the *PeerChooser* interface was developed. This is an interface for an ACF recommender system which enables users to pick and choose a peergroup for collaborative filtering during the recommendation process. The *PeerChooser* interface affords the user the opportunity to manipulate a visualisation of similarity and trust of their neighbours in parallel. Users can adjust these values as they see fit to represent facets of their current mood or requirements.

Each trust source presented in this chapter has been analysed in its own right, with live user evaluations and automated testing. It is shown that each technique that uses trust yields an increase in general user-satisfaction with their use of the Social Web application, relative to normal, non-trust-based operating conditions of the system.

References

1. Paolo Avesani, Paolo Massa, and Roberto Tiella. A trust-enhanced recommander system application. Molesking. In *SAC '05: Proceedings of the 2005 ACM symposium onApplied computing*, pages 1589–1593 ACM Press, New York, NY, USA, 2005.
2. Albert-Laszlo Barabási. *Linked: How E verthing Is Connected to Everything Else and What It Means for Business, Science, and Everyday Life.* Plume Books, April 2003.
3. Terry Bossomaier. Linked: The new science of networks by albert-laszlo barabási. *Artif. Life,* 11(3):401–402, 2005.
4. deSola Pool and Manfred Kochen. Contacts and influence. *Social Networks,* 1(1):5–51, 1978.
5. Malcolm Galdwell. *The Tipping Point: How Little Things Can Make a Big Difference.* Time Warner Books UK, January 2002.
6. Jennifer Ann Golbeck. *Computing and applying trust in Web-based social networks.* PhD thesis, Univeristy of Maryland at College Park, College Park, MD, USa, 2005. Chair-James Hendler.
7. Andun Josang, Roslan Ismail, and Colin Boyd. A survey of trust and reputation systems for online service provision.
8. Audun Jøsang, Elizabeth Gray, and Michael Kinateder. Analysing Topologies of Transitive Trust. In Theo Dimitrakos and Fabio Matrinelli, editors, *Proceedings of the First International Workshop on Formal Aspects in Security and Trust (FAST2003),* pages 9-22, Pisa, Italy, September 2003.
9. Audan Jøsang, Elizabeth Gray, and Michael Kinanteder. *Simplification and Analysis of Transitive Trust Networks. Web Intelligence and Agent Systems: An International Journal,* pages 1-1, September 2005, ISBN ISSN: 1570-1263.
10. Cliff A.C. Lampe, Nicole Ellison, and Charles Steinfield. A familiar face(book): profile elements as signals in an online social network. In *CHI '07: Proceedings of the SIGCHI conference on Human factors in computing systems,* pages 435-444 ACM Press, New York, NY, USA, 2007.
11. S. Marsh. Formalising trust as a computational concept. *Ph.D. Thesis. Department of Mathematics and Computer Science,* University of Stirling, 1994.
12. Paolo Massa and Paolo Avesani. Trust-aware collaborative filtering for recommender systems. *Proceedings of International Conference on Cooperative Information Systems,* Agia Napa, Cyprus, 25 Oct 29, 2004.
13. Paolo Massa and Bobby Bhattacharjee. Using trust in recommender systems: an experimental analysis. *2nd International Conference on Trust Management, Oxford, England,* 2004.
14. S. Milgram. The small world problem. *Psychology Today,* 1:61-67, May 1967.
15. Bradley N. Miller, Istvan Albert, Shyong K. Lam, Joseph A. Konstan, and John Ridel. Movielens unplugged: experiences with an occasinally connected recommender systems. In *IUI '03: Proceedings of the 8th international conference on Intelligent user interfaces,* pages 263-266, ACM Press, New York, NY, USA, 2003.
16. John O'Donovan, Brynjar Gretatsson, Barry Symth, and Tobias Hollerer. Peerchooser: Visual interactive recommendation. *International Conference and Human Interaction (CHI'08),* 2008.
17. M. F. Porter. An algorithm for suffix stirpping. *Readings in information retrieval,* pages 313-316, 1997.
18. Paul Resnick, Neophytos Iacovou, Mitesh Suchak, Peter Bergstrom, and John Ridel. Grouplens: An open architecture for collaborative filtering of netnews. In *Procceddings of ACM CSCW'94 Conference on Computer-Supported Cooperative Work,* pages 175-186, 1994.
19. Paul Resnick and Richard Zeckhauser. Trust among strangers in internet transactions: Empirical analysis of ebay's reputation system. *The Economics of the Internet and E-Commerce. Volume 11 of Advances in Applied Microeconomics.,* December 2002.
20. Badrul M. Sarwar, George Karypis, Joseph A. Konstan, and John Reidl. Item-based collaborative filtering recommendation algorithms. In *World Wide Web,* pages 285-295, 2001.

21. Rashmi Sinha and Kirsten Swearingen. The role of transparency in recommender systems. In *CHI '02 extended abstracts on Human factors in computing systems*, pages 830-831. ACM Press, 2002.
22. Cai-Nicolas Ziegler and Georg Lausen. Propagation models for trust and distrust in social networks. *Information Systems Frontiers*, 7(4–5): 337-358, 2005.
23. Cai-Nicolas Ziegler and Michal Skubacz. Towards automated reputation and brand monitoring on the Web. In *Proceedings of the 2006 IEEE/WIC/ACM International Conference on Web Intleligence*, pages 1006-1070, IEEE Computer Society Press, Hong Kong, December 2006.

Chapter 10
Trust Metrics in Recommender Systems

Paolo Massa and Paolo Avesani

Abstract Recommender Systems based on Collaborative Filtering suggest to users items they might like, such as movies, songs, scientific papers, or jokes. Based on the ratings provided by users about items, they first find users similar to the users receiving the recommendations and then suggest to her items appreciated in past by those like-minded users. However, given the ratable items are many and the ratings provided by each users only a tiny fraction, the step of finding similar users often fails. We propose to replace this step with the use of a trust metric, an algorithm able to propagate trust over the trust network in order to find users that can be trusted by the active user. Items appreciated by these trustworthy users can then be recommended to the active user. An empirical evaluation on a large dataset crawled from Epinions.com shows that Recommender Systems that make use of trust information are the most effective in term of accuracy while preserving a good coverage. This is especially evident on users who provided few ratings, so that trust is able to alleviate the cold start problem and other weaknesses that beset Collaborative Filtering Recommender Systems.

10.1 Introduction

Recommender Systems (RS) [1] have the goal of suggesting to every user the items that might be of interest for her. In particular, RSs based on Collaborative Filtering (CF) [2] rely on the opinions expressed by the other users. In fact, CF tries to automatically find users similar to the active one and recommends to this active user the items liked by these similar users. This simple intuition is effective in generating recommendations and is widely used [1].

However, RSs based on CF suffer some inherent weaknesses that are intrinsic to the process of finding similar users. In fact, the process of comparing two users with the goal of computing their similarity involves comparing the ratings they provided for items. And in order to be comparable, it is necessary that the two users rated

P. Massa (✉)
Fondazione Bruno Kessler, Via Sommarive 18, Povo (TN), Italy
e-mail: massa@fbk.eu

J. Golbeck (ed.), *Computing with Social Trust,* Human-Computer Interaction Series, DOI 10.1007/978-1-84800-356-9_10 © Springer-Verlag London Limited 2009

at least some of the same items. However in a typical domain, for example in the domain of movies or books, the number of items is very large (in the order of the millions) while the number of items rated by every single user is in general small (in the order of dozens or less). This means that it is very unlikely two random users have rated any items in common and hence they are not comparable. Another important and underconsidered weakness is related to the fact that RS can easily be attacked by creating ad hoc user profiles with the goal of being considered as similar to the target user and influence the recommendations she gets. Other weaknesses refer to the fact that RSs are sometimes reported as difficult to understand and control and to the fact that most of the current real deployments of RSs have been as centralized servers, which are not under user control.

In order to overcome these weaknesses, we propose to exploit trust information explicitly expressed by the users. Users are allowed to state how much they consider trustworthy each other user. In the context of RSs, this judgement is related to how much they consider the ratings provided by a certain user as valuable and relevant. This additional information (trust statements) can be organized in a trust network and a trust metric can be used to predict the trustworthiness of other users as well (for example, friends of friends). The idea here is to not search for similar users as CF does but to search for trustable users by exploiting trust propagation over the trust network. The items appreciated by these users are then recommended to the active user. We call this technique a Trust-aware Recommender System.

The goal of this chapter is to present a complete evaluation of Trust-aware Recommender Systems, by comparing different algorithms, ranging from traditional CF ones to algorithms that utilise only trust information with different trust metrics, from algorithms that combine both trust and similarity to baseline algorithms. The empirical evaluation is carried out on a real world, large dataset. We have also evaluated the different algorithms against views over the dataset (for example only on users or items satisfying a certain condition) in order to hightlight the relative performances of the different algorithms.

The chapter is structured as follows. Section 10.2 presents the motivations for our work in greater detail while Section 10.3 describes our proposal, focusing on the concept of trust, introducing the architecture of Trust-aware Recommender Systems, and commenting on related works. Section 10.4 is devoted to the experiments in which we compared different algorithms and the experimental results are then summarized and discussed in Section 10.5. Section 10.6 concludes the chapter.

10.2 Motivations

Ours is an Information society. The quantity of new information created and made available every day (news, movies, scientific papers, songs, websites, ...) goes beyond our limited processing capabilities. This phenomenon has been named "information overload" and refers to the state of having too much information to make a decision or to remain informed about a topic. The term was coined in 1970 by Alvin Toffler in his book Future Shock [3].

Recommender Systems (RS) [1, 4] are tools designed to cope with information overload. Their task is to pick out of the huge amount of new items created every day only the few items that might be of interest for the specific user and that might be worthy of her attention. Unsurprisingly, systems that automate this facility have become popular on the internet. Online RS [1, 4], in fact, have been used to suggest movies, books, songs, jokes, etc. They have been an important research line because they promise to fulfill the e-commerce dream [4]: a different and personalized store for every single (potential) customer.

The most successful and studied technique for RSs is Collaborative Filtering [2] (CF). CF exploits a simple intuition: items appreciated by people similar to someone will also be appreciated by that person. While Content-based RSs require a description of the content of the items, Collaborative Filtering has the advantage of relying just on the opinions provided by the users expressing how much they like a certain item in the form of a rating. Based on these ratings, the CF system is able to find users with a similar rating pattern and then to recommend the items appreciated by these similar users. In this sense, it does not matter what the items are (movies, songs, scientific papers, jokes, ...) since the technique considers only ratings provided by the users and so CF can be applied in every domain and does not require editors to describe the content of the items.

The typical input of CF is represented as a matrix of ratings (see Table 10.1), in which the users are the rows, the items the column and the values in the cells represent user rating of an item. In Table 10.1 for example, ratings can range from 1 (minimum) to 5 (maximum).

The CF algorithm can be divided into two steps. The *first step* is the *similarity assessment* and consists of comparing the ratings provided by a pair of users (rows in the matrix) in order to compute their similarity. The most used and effective technique for the similarity assessment is to compute the Pearson correlation coefficient [2]. The first step produces a similarity weight $w_{a,i}$ for every active user a with respect to every other user i.

$$w_{a,u} = \frac{\sum_{i=1}^{m}(r_{a,i} - \bar{r}_a)(r_{u,i} - \bar{r}_u)}{\sqrt{\sum_{i=1}^{m}(r_{a,i} - \bar{r}_a)^2 \sum_{i=1}^{m}(r_{u,i} - \bar{r}_u)^2}} \tag{10.1}$$

The *second step* is the *actual rating prediction* and consists of predicting the rating the active user would give to a certain item. The predicted rating is the

Table 10.1 An example of a small users × items matrix of ratings

	Matrix reloaded	Lord of the rings 2	Titanic	La vita è bella
Alice	2	5		5
Bob	5		1	3
Carol		5		
Dave	2	5	5	4

weighted sum of the ratings given by other user to that item, where the weights are the similarity coefficient of the active user with the other users. In this way the rating expressed by a very similar user has a larger influence on the rating predicted for the active user. The formula for the second step is the following

$$p_{a,i} = \bar{r}_a + \frac{\sum_{u=1}^{k} w_{a,u}(r_{u,i} - \bar{r}_u)}{\sum_{u=1}^{k} w_{a,u}} \tag{10.2}$$

where $p_{a,i}$ represents the predicted rating that active user a would possibly provide for item i, r_u is the average of the rating provided by user u, $w_{a,u}$ is the user similarity weight of a and u as computed in step one, and k is the number of users whose ratings of item i are considered in the weighted sum (called neighbours).

However the Collaborative Filtering technique suffers from some key weaknesses we have identified and discuss in the following.

User similarity is often non computable. According to Equation 10.2, a user can be considered as neighbour for the active user only if it is possible to compute the similarity weight of her and the active user ($w_{a,u}$). In fact, in order to be able to create good quality recommendations, RSs must be able to compare the current user with every other user to the end of selecting the best neighbours with the more relevant item ratings. This step is mandatory and its accuracy affects the overall system accuracy: failing to find "good" neighbours will lead to poor quality recommendations. However, the rating matrix is usually very sparse because users tend to rate few of the available items (that can sum into the millions). Because of this *data sparsity*, it is often the case that two users don't share the minimum number of items rated in common required by user similarity metrics for computing similarity, and the system is not able to compute the similarity weight. As a consequence, the system is forced to choose neighbours from the small portion of comparable users and will miss other non-comparable but possibly relevant users. Moreover, even when two users share some commonly rated items, this number is usually very small and hence the computed user similarity is a very unreliable quantity: for example, deciding that two users are similar on the basis of the 3 movies they happened to both rate is not a very reliable measure. This problem is less serious for users who have already produced hundreds of ratings, but they are usually a small portion of the user base. Actually in most realistic settings most users have only provided a few or no ratings at all. They are called *cold start users* and it can be argued that they are the most important for RS since the system should be able to provide good recommendations, despite the small rating information available about them, in order to give them a reason to keep using the system and hence providing more ratings, which would allow better recommendation computation. However, they are the most challenging due to the small quantity of information available about them. Often, RSs fail on cold start users and are not able to produce recommendations for them with the consequence of driving them away. We believe that this is a serious weakness for RSs and that this aspect has been mainly neglected until now by the research efforts because the most used dataset for evaluating Recommender Systems didn't present these features. We will see in Section 10.4 how in real world datasets, both data sparsity and cold start users are the overwhelming reality.

Easy attacks by malicious insiders. Another weakness is related to attacks on Recommender Systems [5]. Recommender Systems are often used in e-commerce sites (for example, on Amazon.com). In these contexts, being able to influence recommendations could be very attractive: for example, an author may want to "force" Amazon.com to always recommend the book she wrote. And in fact, gaming standard CF techniques is very easy. While this important aspect has been neglected until recently, recently some recent studies have started to look at attacks of Recommender Systems [5, 6]. The simplest attack is the copy-profile attack: the attacker can copy the ratings of target users and fool the system into thinking that the attacker is in fact the most similar user to the target user. In this way every additional item the attacker rates highly will probably be recommended to the target user. Currently RSs are mainly centralized servers, and it should be noted that in general it is easy for a person to create countless fake identities, a problem that is also known as "cheap pseudonyms" [7]. E-commerce sites don't have incentives to disclose this phenomena and hence the impact of it on real systems is not known. Note however that there is at least one disclosed precedent. An occurrence of this behavior has been revealed publicly because of a computer "glitch" that occurred in February 2004 on the Canadian Amazon site. For several days this mistake revealed the real names of thousands of people who had posted customer reviews of books under pseudonyms [8]. By analyzing the real names, ti became evident that the author of a book had in fact created many different pseudonyms on the Amazon site and used all of them to write reviews about her book and rate it highly. The possibility seriously undermines the functioning of Recommender Systems sites, which rely on ratings provided by anonymous users.

Moreover, if the publishing of ratings and opinions becomes more decentralized, for example with Semantic Web formats such as hReview [9] (for items reviews) or FOAF [10] (for expressing trust statements about people), these types of attacks will increasingly become an issue. In fact, while registering on a centralized Recommender System site and providing ad-hoc attack ratings must generally be done by hand and is a time consuming activity, on the Semantic Web or in other decentralized architectures such as P2P networks this activity could easily be carried out with automatic programs (bots). Basically, creating such attacks will become as widespread as email spam is today, or at least as easy. We hence believe that coping with attacks is an important topic for the research community interested in Recommender Systems.

Current Recommender Systems are hard for users to understand and control. Another weakness is that RSs are mainly conceived and perceived as black boxes [11]: the user receives the recommendations but doesn't know how they were generated and has no control in the recommendation process. For example, in [12], the authors conducted a survey with real users and found that users want to see how recommendations are generated, how their neighbours are computed and how their neighbours rate items. Swearingen and Sinha [11] analyzed RSs from a Human Computer Interaction perspective and found that RSs are effective if, among other things, "the system logic is at least somewhat transparent". Moreover, it seems that, as long as RSs give good results, users are satisfied and use them, but, when they start recommending badly or strangely, it is very difficult for the user to understand the reason and to fix the problem; usually the user quits using the RS [13, 14]. Even if the RS exposes what it thinks of you (explicit or implicit past ratings on items) and allows the user to modify them, this is a complicated task, involving for example a re-examination of dozens of past ratings in order to correct the ones that are not correct [13]. It has been claimed that "few of the Amazon users revise their profiles" when the recommendations start becoming obviously wrong [14]. RSs use the step of finding similar users only in propedeutic ways for the task of recommending items, but they don't make the results of these computations visible to users, such as possibly similar unknown users: CF automates the process of recommending items but doesn't help in discovering like minded people for community forming.

RS are mainly deployed as centralized servers. Presently, the most used RSs are run as centralized servers where all the community ratings are stored and where the recommendations are computed for all users. This fact is a weakness for Recommender Systems for more than one reason.

One consequence is that users profiles are scattered in many different, not cooperating servers (for example, different subsets of a single user preferences about books of can be stored with Amazon, Barnes and Nobles, and many other online bookstores); every single server suffers even more sparseness and has problems in giving good quality recommendations. Moreover, this means users cannot move from one RS to another without losing their profiles (and consequently the possibility of receiving good recommendations and saving time). In essence, this situation is against competition and can easily lead to a global monopoly because it is almost impossible for new RSs to enter the market while, for consolidated RS owning much user information, it is even possible to enter new correlated markets. Clearly, companies prefer to not allow interoperability or publicity of this information because it is their company value. Anyway, as long as this useful information will remain confined in silos, it will not unveil all its potentially disruptive power. This lack of portability is a serious weakness of current Recommender Systems [15].

Moreover, the entity running the centralized RS is usually a commercial product vendor and its interests could be somehow different from giving the best recommendations to the user [16]. In general, users are not free to test for biases of the RSs or to know the algorithm used for generating the recommendations or to adapt it to their preferences or to run a completely different one.

While it is theoretically possible to run current RSs in a decentralized way, for example, on the small device under user control such as a mobile, in practice, Collaborative Filtering requires a large memory to store all the ratings and, mainly, a great computation power to perform all the operations on the possibly very huge ratings matrix.

We want also to point out how these centralized architectures are one of the reasons behind the lack of datasets and real testbeds on which to apply and test new research hypotheses related to RSs. It would be a totally different scenario if researchers could have access to all the rating information collected by centralized Recommender Systems such as Amazon and other online bookstore for instance. In fact, there were only few freely available datasets of ratings on items and they were used for offline testing but, in order to run online experiments, researchers had to invest a lot of time into creating their own RS and gathering enough users. However, this is not an easy task: Grouplens working group at the University of Minnesota[1] is a notable exception in this since it was able to get enough users for its online Recommender System, Movielens, and they were very kind in sharing it as a dataset usable by researchers.

In this section we have highlighted the weaknesses we believe beset current Recommender Systems. In the next section, we describe our proposal and how it alleviates these weaknesses.

10.3 Our Proposal: Trust-Aware Recommender Systems

In this section we summarize our proposal: Trust-aware Recommender Systems. We start by introducing basic concepts about trust networks and trust metrics. We then present the logical architecture of Trust-aware Recommender Systems. We conclude this section by comparing our proposal with related work in the literature.

10.3.1 Trust Networks and Trust Metrics

In decentralized environments where everyone is free to create content and there is no centralized quality control entity, evaluating the quality of this content becomes an important issue. This situation can be observed in online communities (for example, slashdot.org in which millions of users post news and comments daily), in peer-to-peer networks (where peers can enter corrupted items), or in marketplace sites (such as eBay.com, where users can create "fake" auctions) [17]. In these environments, it is often a good strategy to delegate the quality assessment task to the users themselves. The system can ask users to rate other users: in this way, users can express their level of trust in another users they have interacted with, i.e. issue a trust statement such as "I, Alice, trust Bob as 0.8 in [0,1]". The system can then aggregate all the trust statements in a single trust network representing the relationships between users. An example of a simple trust network can be seen in Fig. 10.1. As a consequence of the previously introduced properties of trust, such a network is a directed, weighted graph whose nodes are peers and whose edges are trust statements.

---

[1] Grouplens homepage is at www.cs.umn.edu/Research/GroupLens

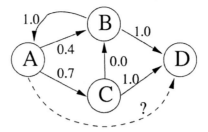

Fig. 10.1 Trust network. Nodes are users and edges are trust statements. The dotted edge is one of the undefined and predictable trust statements

Since in most settings, a user has a direct opinion (i.e. has issued a trust statement) only about a small portion of the other peers, some computational tools can be designed for predicting the trustworthiness of unknown peers. These tools are Trust Metrics and Reputation Systems. The main idea behind these techniques is trust propagation over the trust network: if peer A trusts peer B at a certain level and peer B trusts peer D at a certain level, something can be predicted about how much A should trust D.

These tools are starting to become more and more needed and useful because, thanks to the internet, it is more and more common to interact with unknown peers. Moreover, thanks to the internet, trust statements expressed by all peers can be published and made available to anyone so that aggregating them and reasoning on them is now becoming possible. This was not possible nor useful until a few years ago, and in fact, computational ways to exploit trust have begun to be proposed only very recently. In some sense, in order to get an idea of a certain peer's trustworthiness, we are relying on the judgments of other peers who have already interacted with them and shared their impression. There are many different proposed Trust Metrics [18, 10, 19, 20, 21].

An important distinction in Trust Metrics is in local and global [20]. Global Trust Metrics compute a single trust score for each peer of the trust network. This trust score is independent of the peer that is asking "How much should I trust this unknown peer?". Instead, Local Trust Metrics provide personalized scores. So a local Trust Metric might suggest to peer *Alice* to trust peer *Carol* and to peer *Bob* to distrust *Carol*. Global Trust Metrics compute a score for each peer that represents the average opinion of the whole community about that peer. Even if there is no agreement yet on definitions, in general, this global value is called "reputation" and "reputation systems" are what we called "global Trust Metrics". But the definitions are not that clear and very often the term "reputation" and "trust" are used synonymously just as "Reputation System" and "Trust Metric". PageRank [21], for example, is a global trust metric.

In the next section we will see how trust metrics can play a role in the context of Recommender Systems, essentially we propose them for replacing or integrating the users' similarity assessment of step 1.

10.3.2 An Architecture of Trust-Aware Recommender Systems

In this section we present the architecture of our proposed solution: Trust-aware Recommender Systems. Figure 10.2 shows the different modules (black boxes) as well as input and output matrices of each of them (white boxes). There are two input informations: the trust matrix (representing all the community trust statements) and the ratings matrix (representing all the ratings given by users to items). The output is a matrix of predicted ratings that users would assign to items. The difference with respect to traditional CF systems is the additional input matrix of trust statements. The two logical steps of CF remain the same. The first step finds neighbours and the second step predicts ratings based on a weighted sum of the ratings given by neighbours to items. The key difference is in how neighbours are identified and how their weights are computed. The weight $w_{a,i}$ in Equation 10.2 can be derived from the user similarity assessment (as in traditional CF) or with the use of a trust metric. In fact in our proposed architecture for the first step there are two possible modules able to produce these weights: a Trust Metric module or a Similarity Metric module. They respectively produce the Estimated Trust matrix and the User Similarity matrix: in both, row i contains the neighbours of user i and the cell of column j represents a weight in [0, 1] about how much user j is relevant for user i (trustable or similar). This is the weight $w_{a,i}$ in Eq. 10.2 and represents how much ratings by user i should be taken into account when predicting ratings for user a (second step). A more detailed explanation of the architecture can be found in [22]. In Section 10.4 we are going to present experiments we have run with different instantiations of the different modules. For the Trust Metric module we have tested a local and a global trust metric. As local trust metric we have chosen MoleTrust [20], a depth-first graph walking algorithm with a tunable trust propagation horizon that allows us to control the distance to which trust is propagated. As global trust metric we have chosen PageRank [21], probably the most used global trust metric. For the Similarity Metric module we have chosen the Pearson Correlation Coefficient since it is the one that is reported to be performed best in [2]. Regarding the Rating Predictor module (second step), we experimented with selecting only weights from

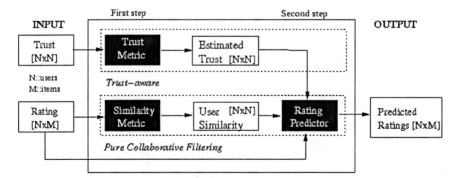

Fig. 10.2 Trust-aware recommender system architecture

the Estimated Trust matrix or the User Similarity matrix and with combining them. For the purpose of comparison, we have also run simple and baseline algorithms that we will describe in next section.

10.3.3 How Trust Alleviates RS Weaknesses

In the previous Section, we have presented our proposal for enhancing Recommender Systems by means of trust information.

In this section we discuss how Trust-aware Recommender Systems are able to alleviate the weaknesses besetting RSs that we have previously introduced. Section 10.4 will be devoted to empirical evidence confirming the claims, based on experiments run on a real world, large dataset.

The key new point of Trust-aware Decentralized Recommender Systems is to use trust propagation over the network constituted by trust statements in order to predict a trust score for unknown peers. This trust score can be used in the traditional Recommender System model in place of or in addition to the value of user similarity as a weight for the ratings of the specific peer.

The first weakness highlighted in Section 10.2 was that *often user similarity between two users is not computable* due to data sparsity. Instead, considering the trust statements expressed by all the peers, it is possible to predict a trust score for a larger portion of the user base. For example, by using a very simple global trust metric like the one used by eBay (see Section 10.4), it can be enough that a peer received at least one trust statement to be able to predict its trustworthiness. Even local trust metrics, which propagate trust starting from active users, are able to reach a large portion of the users in just a few propagation steps, considering that most social networks are highly connected and exhibit small world characteristics. Another important point related to the computability of user similarity that we mentioned when speaking about the weaknesses of current Recommender Systems is related to *cold start users*. Cold start users are the most critical users for standard CF techniques that are not able to generate any recommendation for them. Viceversa, they can benefit from the trust statements issued by other users. In particular, as soon as a cold start user provides at least one trust statement, it is possible to use a local trust metric. The local trust metric is able to propagate trust and predict trustworthiness for all reachable users, so that their ratings can be used in the rating prediction process. Issuing just one trust statement can be an effective mechanism for rapidly integrating new users, especially if compared with standard CF where users are usually required to rate at least 10 items before receiving a recommendation. A single trust statement can make the difference between an environment populated by users whose trustworthiness is totally uncertain to an environment in which it is possible to use a local trust metric and predict how much ratings provided by many other users can be taken into account.

With regard to *attacks on Recommender Systems*, considering trust information can be effective as well. For example, against shilling attacks [6] in which a user pretends to be similar to the user target of the attack. Trust-aware Recommender

Systems can be used to consider only ratings provided by users predicted as trust-worthy by the trust metric. Local Trust Metrics promise to be attack-resistant [18, 19], as long as there is no trust path from the active user to the users under control of the attacker. Essentially, while creating a fake identity is very easy and can be done by anyone [7], receiving a positive trust statement by a peer trusted by the user target of the attack is not as easy since it depends on judgments not under the control of the attacker. In our vision, exploiting of trust information allows being influenced only (or mainly) by "trustable" peers, either direct peers or indirect ones (friends of friends). This can reduce the user base used to find neighbors but surely keeps out malicious and fake peers. The sharing of opinions about peers is also a good way for detecting or spotting these attacks by virtue of a decentralized assessment process. In this way, malicious ratings provided by users under attacker control are not taken into consideration when generating recommendations for the active user, just as if they didn't exist.

The possibility of only or mainly considering ratings provided by users whose predicted trust score is above a certain threshold would help in alleviating the weakness related to the fact that traditional RSs are *computational expensiveness*. In fact, reducing the number of considered users a priori could allow the algorithm to scale even in a domain with millions of peers and to be run on less powerful devices. For example, the trust metric might be designed to analyze just peers at distance 1 (on which the active peer issued direct trust statements) and peers at distance 2 significantly reducing the number of considered peers.

We reported in Section 10.2 how traditional *RS are often seen by users as black boxes* [12, 11] and thought hard to understand and control [13, 14]. RSs are considered more effective by users if, among other things, "the system logic is at least somewhat transparent" [11]. We believe that the concept of direct trust is easier to understand for users than the concept of user similarity. User similarity is computed out of a formula, usually the Pearson Correlation coefficient, which is not too easy to understand for a normal user [12]. A possible interface could communicate the reasons behind a certain recommendation explicitly referring to ratings provided by trusted users, with a text message like the following "this movie was recommended to you because 3 of the users you trust (Alice, Bob, Charlie) rated it as 5 out of 5. You can see their user profiles and, in case the recommendation is not satisfying to you, you can possibly revise your connections with them" with links to these users' profiles [10]. In fact, Sinha and Swearingen have found that people prefer receiving recommendations from people they know and trust, i.e., friends and family-members, rather than from online Recommender Systems [23]. By showing explicitly the users trusted by the active user, RSs may let the user feel that the recommendations are in reality coming from friends and not from some obscure algorithms. However we didn't conduct Human Computer Interaction analysis and survey with real users about different recommendation explanation interfaces.

The last weakness we introduced in Section 10.2 is related to *centralized architectures* that are at the moment the most adopted for current RSs. We think Trust-aware Recommender Systems demand a decentralized environment where all users publish their information (trust and ratings) in some Semantic Web format and then every machine has the possibility of aggregating this information and computing recommendations on behalf of its users. In this way the rating prediction could be run locally on a device owned by the human user for whom ratings are predicted [15]. In this setting, the single peer can decide to retrieve and aggregate information from just a small portion of the peers, for example only ratings expressed by trusted peers. In this way, it is not necessary to build the complete ratings matrix or the complete trust network. This would reduce the computational power required for running the predictions and the bandwidth needed for aggregating the ratings. Trust-aware Decentralized Recommender Systems would not require very powerful computers, as is often the case for centralized service providers, but would work on many simple devices under the direct control of the human user.

In this section, we have argued how Trust-awareness alleviates some of the weaknesses of standard Recommender Systems. The next section discusses work related to our proposal.

10.3.4 Related Work

There have been some proposals to use trust information in the context of Recommender Systems. We will give an account of the most significant ones here.

In a paper entitled "Trust in recommender systems" [24], O'Donovan and Smyth propose algorithms for computing Profile Level Trust and Item Level Trust. Profile Level Trust is the percentage of correct recommendations that this producer has contributed. Item Level Trust is a profile level trust that depends on a specific item. As the reviewers note, this quantity represents more of a "competence" measure and in fact reflects a sort of global similarity value. While in their work trust values are derived from ratings (of the Movielens dataset), in our proposal trust statements are explicitly expressed by users.

The PhD thesis of Ziegler [19] concentrates on RSs from different points of research. Regarding the integration of trust, he proposes a solution very similar to ours, i.e neighbour formation by means of trust network analysis. He has designed a local trust metric, Appleseed [19], that computes the top-M nearest trust neighbours for every user. He has evaluated algorithms against a dataset derived from AllConsuming (http://allconsuming.net), a community of 3400 book readers, with 9300 ratings and 4300 trust statements. Only positive trust statements are available. Ziegler found that hybrid approaches (using taxonomies of books and hence based on content-based features of books) outperforms the trust-based one which outperforms the purely content-based one. Performances on users who provided few ratings were not studied in detail.

Golbeck's PhD thesis [10] focuses on trust in web-based social networks, how it can be computed, and how it can be used in applications. She deployed an online Recommender System, FilmTrust (http://trust.mindswap.org/filmTrust/) in which

users can rate films and write reviews and they can also express trust statements
in other users based on how much they trust their friends about movies ratings.
Trust statements in FilmTrust are weighted: users could express their trust in other
users on a ten level basis. Golbeck designed a trust metric called TidalTrust [10]
working in a breadth-first fashion similarly to MoleTrust [20]. We used MoleTrust
in our experiments because it has a tunable trust propagation horizon parameter that
lets us study how this parameter affects performances of the Recommender System.
It is interesting to note that Golbeck's findings are similar to ours and that will be
reported in the next section.

10.4 Empirical Validation

In this Section we present experiments we have conducted for evaluating the performances of Trust-aware Recommender Systems. In particular we compare different
instantiations of the modules of our proposed architecture (see Fig. 10.2), so that
the evaluated systems range from simple algorithms used as baselines to purely
Collaborative Filtering ones, from systems using only trust metrics, both global and
local, to systems that combine estimated trust and user similarity information. First
we describe the dataset used and introduce our evaluation strategy, then we present
the actual results of the experiments.

10.4.1 Dataset Used in Experiments: Epinions

The dataset we used in our experiments is derived from the Epinions.com web site.
Epinions is a consumers opinion site where users can review items (such as cars,
books, movies, software, …) and also assign numeric ratings to them in the range
from 1 (min) to 5 (max). Users can also express their Web of Trust, i.e. reviewers
whose reviews and ratings they have consistently found to be valuable and their
Block list, i.e. a list of authors whose reviews they find consistently offensive, inaccurate, or not valuable.[2] Inserting users in the Web of Trust is tantamount issuing
a trust statement of value 1, while inserting her in the Block List equals to issuing
a trust statement of value 0 in their regard. Intermediate values such as 0.7 are not
expressible on Epinions.

In order to collect the dataset, we wrote a crawler that recorded ratings and trust
statements issued by a user and then moved to users trusted by that users and recursively did the same. Note, however, that the block list is kept private in Epinions in
order to let users express themselves more freely, therefore it is not available in our
dataset.

The Epinions dataset represents the most meaningful and large example where
ratings on items and trust statements on users have been collected in a real world

---

[2] This definition is from the Epinions.com Web of Trust FAQ (http://www.epinions.com/help/faq/
?show=faq_wot)

environment. We released the crawled dataset so that other researchers can validate their hypotheses and proposals on it. The crawled dataset can be found at www.trustlet.org/wiki/epinions.

Our dataset consists of 49, 290 users who rated a total of 139, 738 different items at least once. The total number of reviews is 664, 824. The total number of issued trust statements is 487, 181. Rating matrix sparsity is defined as the percentage of empty cells in the matrix users × items and in the case of the collected dataset is 99.99135%. The mean number of created reviews is 13.49 with a standard deviation of 34.16. It is interesting to look at what we have called "cold start users". They are the large majority of users. For example, 26,037 users expressed less than 5 reviews and represent 52.82% of the population. The mean number of users in the Web of Trust (friends) is 9.88 with a standard deviation of 32.85. Another interesting point is the distribution of ratings. In our dataset, 45% of the ratings are 5 (best), 29% are 4, 11% are 3, 8% are 2 and 7% are 1 (worst). The mean rating is hence 3.99. Note that almost half of the ratings are a 5, that is, the maximum possible value.

The characteristics we briefly described are very different from those of the Movielens dataset,[3] the most commonly used dataset for RSs evaluation. In particular, in Movielens dataset all the users are guaranteed to have voted at least 20 items while in Epinions more than half of them have voted less than 5 items (cold start users). This also means that sparsity is much higher in Epinions and so finding overlapping on provided ratings between users and hence possible neighbours (step 1 of CF) is even harder. While on Epinions most of the rating values are 5 and 4, in Movielens all the different values are more balanced. This affects how different algorithms perform as we will see in the following sections.

10.4.2 New Evaluation Measures

The most used technique for evaluating Recommender Systems is based on *leave-one-out* [25]. Leave-one-out is an offline technique that can be run on a previously acquired dataset and involves hiding one rating and then trying to predict it with a certain algorithm. The predicted rating is then compared with the real rating and the difference in absolute value is the prediction error. The procedure is repeated for all the ratings and an average of all the errors is computed, the Mean Absolute Error (MAE) [25].

A first problem with MAE is that it weighs every error in the prediction of a rating in the same way. For example, let us suppose that our dataset contains only 101 users: one user provided 300 ratings while all the remaining 100 users provided just 3 ratings each. We call the first user a "heavy rater" and the other users "cold start users". In this way our dataset contains 600 ratings. The leave-one-out methodology consists in hiding these 600 ratings one by one and then trying to predict them.

---

[3] Distributed by Grouplens group at the University of Minnesota and available at http://www.cs.umn.edu/Research/GroupLens/

Typically, CF works well for users who have already provided numerous ratings and poorly on users who provided few ratings. A probable situation is that the error over the predictions of the heavy rater is small while the error over the predictions of the cold start users is high. However, in computing the Mean Absolute Error, the heavy raters weigh just as much as all the other users since they provided a very large number of ratings. This does not reflect the real situation in which there is actually one user who is probably satisfied with the prediction error (the heavy rater) and 300 users who are not satisfied (the cold start users). For this reason, the first additional measure we introduce is Mean Absolute User Error (MAUE). The idea is straightforward: we first compute the Mean Absolute Error for every single user independently and then we average all the Mean Absolute Errors related to every single user. In this way, every user has the same weight in the Mean Absolute User Error computation. This is very important since the Epinions dataset contains a large share of cold start users. In our experiments (see next section), this distinction was able to highlight different behaviours for different techniques that would otherwise have remained hidden inside the MAE value.

Another important measure that is often not reported and studied in evaluation of RSs is coverage. Herlocker et al. in their solid review of Recommender Systems evaluation techniques [25] underline how it is important to go "beyond accuracy" in evaluating RSs and count coverage as one step in this direction but also note how few works have investigated it. Coverage simply refers to the fraction of ratings for which, after being hidden, the RS algorithm is able to produce a predicted rating. It might in fact be the case that some RS techniques are not able to predict the rating a user would give to an item. Again we believe that coverage was understudied by many research efforts because in Movielens, the most used dataset for evaluation of RSs, the coverage over ratings tends to be close to 100%. This is due to the fact that all the users are guaranteed to have voted at least 20 items and that there are some items that are rated by almost every user. Instead on a very sparse dataset that contains a large portion of cold start users and of items rated just by one user, coverage becomes an important issue since many of the ratings become hardly predictable. While the percentage of predictable ratings (*ratings coverage*) is an important measure, it has the same problem we highlighted earlier for Mean Absolute Error, it weighs heavy raters more. Following the same argument as before, we introduce also the *users coverage*, defined as the portion of users for which the RS is able to predict at least one rating. In fact, it is often the case that a RS is successful in predicting all the ratings for a user who provides many ratings and performs poorly for a user who has rated few items. Going back to the example introduced earlier, it might be that for the heavy rater who rated 300 items, the RS is able to predict all of them, while it fails on all the ratings provided by the 100 cold start users. In this case, the ratings coverage would be $300/600 = 0.5$. Viceversa the users coverage would be $1/100 = 0.01$.

A possibility given by a very large dataset of ratings is to study performances of different RS techniques on different portions of the input data (called "views") that, given the large numbers, remain significant. It is possible for example to compute MAE only on users who satisfy a certain condition. For example, as we already mentioned, while it might be very easy to provide good quality recommendations to a user who already provided 100 ratings to the system (heavy rater) and hence has given a very detailed snapshot of her opinions, it might be much more difficult to provide good quality recommendations to a user who has just joined the system and, for example, has entered only 2 ratings. With this regard, it is possible to compute evaluation measures such as MAE or users coverage only on these portions in order to analyze how a certain technique works on a particular subset of the data.

Views can be defined over users, over items and over ratings depending on their characteristics. We have already implicitly introduced many times the view over users based on the number of ratings that they have provided: users who provided few ratings are called "cold start users" and users who provided many ratings are called "heavy raters". As acknowledged also by [26], evaluating the performances of RSs in "cold start" situations has not been extensively covered in the literature. Our evaluations will concentrate on the relative performances of different techniques on these different classes of users, such as cold start users, who provided from 1 to 4 ratings; heavy raters, who provided more than 10 ratings; opinionated users, who provided more than 4 ratings and whose standard deviation is greater than 1.5; black sheep, users who provided more than 4 ratings and for which the average distance of their rating on item i with respect to mean rating of item i is greater than 1.

Revealing views can be defined also over items. In this chapter we report evaluations performed on niche items, which received less than 5 ratings, and controversial items, which received ratings whose standard deviation is greater than 1.5. Making an error on a controversial item can be very serious and can mine the confidence the user places in the RS, for example, a user would be very unsatisfied to receive a recommendation for a movie about which she holds a clear and very negative opinion.

Additional views can be designed also on ratings. For example various measures can be computed only on ratings whose value is 1, in order to analyze how a certain technique performs on these ratings, or only on ratings whose value is greater or equal to 4.

We introduce these views because they better capture the relative merits of the different algorithms in different situations and better represent their weaknesses and strengths.

10.4.3 Results of the Experiments

Every different instantiation of the Trust-aware Recommender System architecture is evaluated with regard to the measures we have defined (MAE, MAUE, ratings coverage, users coverage), also focusing the analysis on the different views previously introduced, such as, for example, cold start users and controversial items. In the following we discuss the results of the experiments condensed in Tables 10.2 and 10.3. Figs. 10.4 and 10.5 graphically present just one of the measures reported

Table 10.2 Accuracy and coverage measures on ratings, for different RS algorithms on different views

Mean absolute error / Ratings coverage

	Algorithms				
Views	CF	MT1	MT2	MT3	TrustAll
All	0.843 51.28%	0.832 28.33%	0.846 60.47%	0.829 74.37%	0.821 88.20%
Cold users	1.094 3.22%	0.674 11.05%	0.833 25.02%	0.854 41.74%	0.856 92.92%
Heavy raters	0.850 57.45%	0.873 30.85%	0.869 64.82%	0.846 77.81%	0.845 92.92%
Contr. items	1.515 45.42%	1.425 25.09%	1.618 60.64%	1.687 81.01%	1.741 100.0%
Niche items	0.822 12.18%	0.734 8.32%	0.806 24.32%	0.828 20.43%	0.829 55.39%
Opin. users	1.200 50%	1.020 23.32%	1.102 57.31%	1.096 74.24%	1.105 92.80%
Black sheep	1.235 55.74%	1.152 23.66%	1.238 59.21%	1.242 76.32%	1.255 97.03%

Table 10.3 Accuracy and coverage measures on users, for different RS algorithms on different views

Mean Absolute User Error / Users Coverage

	Algorithms				
Views	CF	MT1	MT2	MT3	TrustAll
All	0.938 40.78%	0.790 46.64%	0.856 59.75%	0.844 66.31%	0.843 98.57%
Cold users	1.173 2.89%	0.674 17.49%	0.820 30.61%	0.854 42.49%	0.872 96.63%
Heavy raters	0.903 86.08%	0.834 79.78%	0.861 88.42%	0.834 89.42%	0.820 100.00%
Contr. items	1.503 15.76%	1.326 11.74%	1.571 21.66%	1.650 27.85%	1.727 37.16%
Niche items	0.854 10.77%	0.671 10.27%	0.808 20.73%	0.843 32.83%	0.848 52.04%
Opin. users	1.316 61.20%	0.938 60.74%	1.090 76.51%	1.092 79.85%	1.107 100.00%
Black sheep	1.407 67.78%	1.075 60.83%	1.258 75.34%	1.285 77.70%	1.300 100.00%

in the tables, precisely the row labeled "Cold users" (i.e., MAE and ratings coverage on predictions for cold start users and MAUE and users coverage) in order to give the reader a visual grasp of the relative benefits of the different techniques.

10.4.3.1 Trivial Algorithms Seem Very Effective

As a first step in our analysis we tested a very simple algorithm that always returns 5 as the predicted rating a user would give to an item. We call this algorithm *Always5*.

$$prediction_{\text{Always5}}(a, i) = 5$$

This trivial algorithm is not meaningful from a RS point of view since, for instance, it does not allow to differentiate and prioritize the different items. However, it allowed us to start exploring which MAE a simple algorithm would achieve. The MAE over all the ratings is 1.008. This result is not too bad, especially if we compare it with more complex algorithms as we will do in the following.

Another trivial algorithm is the one we call *UserMean*. The idea of UserMean is simply to return the mean of the ratings provided by one user. Remember that we use leave-one-out as evaluation technique so we remove every single rating before computing the prediction.

$$prediction_{UserMean}(a, i) = \frac{\sum_{j=1}^{m}(r_{a,j})}{m}$$

where m is the number of items rated by user a.

The reason for such good performances is that in our dataset most of the rating values are in fact 5 and this is a notable difference with respect to other datasets, for instance MovieLens, on which these trivial algorithms work very badly. But in our case we have two very simple and not personalized algorithms that seem to perform well enough. This fact suggested to us that just presenting the Mean Absolute Error over all the ratings is not a useful way to compare different algorithms. We introduced the evaluation views explained in Section 10.4.2 in order to have an evaluation technique better able to capture the relative merits of the different algorithms in different situations and to better represent their weaknesses and strengths. In fact, on the controversial items view for instance, these trivial algorithms perform very badly.

10.4.3.2 Simple Average Better than Collaborative Filtering

Another trivial algorithm is the one that predicts – as a rating for a certain item – the unweighted average of all the ratings given to that item by all the users but the active user. It is a non-personalized technique that is like assigning 1 as similarity or trust weight to all the users in the second step of CF (Equation. 10.2 with $w_{a,i}$ always equal to 1) For this reason we call it *TrustAll*.

$$prediction_{TrustAll}(a, i) = \bar{r}_a + \frac{\sum_{u=1}^{k}(r_{u,i} - \bar{r}_u)}{k} \tag{10.3}$$

To our surprise, TrustAll outperformed standard Collaborative Filtering algorithms, achieving a MAE of 0.821 (against 0.843 of standard *CF*). On the other hand, on MovieLens dataset, we observe the expected result: MAE of CF is 0.730 while MAE of TrustAll is 0.815. Moreover, the number of predictable Epinions ratings (the coverage) is 51.28% for CF and 88.20% for TrustAll, while on Movielens ratings they are both close to 100%. The reason for these important differences is in the datasets. The Epinions dataset contains mostly 5 as rating value and most of the users provided few ratings (cold start users). We believe these facts, not observed in other RS datasets, allowed us to study certain characteristics of RS algorithms that were previously unexplored. The problem with CF in our dataset is that the Pearson correlation coefficient (similarity weight output of the first step of CF) is often not computable because of data sparsity and hence only the ratings of a small percentage of the other users can be utilized when generating a recommendation for the active user. Since there is not too much variance in rating values (most of them are 5), an unweighted average is usually close to the real value. On cold start users, the balance is even more for TrustAll. The coverage of CF on cold start users is only 3.22% while the coverage of TrustAll is 92.92% and the MAE of CF is 1.094 while the MAE of TrustAll in 0.856. Note that in the real-world Epinions dataset, cold start users make up more than 50% of total users. In fact, for a cold start user the first step of CF almost always fails since it is very unlikely to find other users which have rated the same few items and hence the similarity weight is not computable. However, these results are not totally dismissive of CF, in fact, on controversial items CF outperforms TrustAll (MAE of 1.515 against 1.741). In this case, CF is able to just consider the opinions of like minded users and hence to overcome the performances of TrustAll, a technique that – not being personalized – performs more poorly. This means that when it is really important to find like-minded neighbours CF is needed and effective. Also note that the error over ratings received by controversial items is greater than the error over all the ratings, meaning that it is harder to predict the correct ratings for these items.

10.4.3.3 Trusted Users are Good Predictors

In this subsection we start comparing performances of RS algorithms that use only trust information (top box in Fig. 10.2) with standard CF (bottom box). We start by using only the users explictly trusted by the active user, i.e. not propatagating trust or setting the propagation horizon at 1 for the local Trust Metric MoleTrust. We call this algorithm *MT1*.

The Formula is very similar to Formula 10.2, the only difference being that users weights are derived from the direct trust statements.

$$prediction_{\text{MT1}}(a, i) = \bar{r}_a + \frac{\sum_{u=1}^{k} trust_{a,u}(r_{u,i} - \bar{r}_u)}{\sum_{u=1}^{k} trust_{a,u}} \qquad (10.4)$$

where k is the number of users in which user u expressed a trust statement and $trust_{a,u}$ is the value of the trust statement explicitly issued by user a about user u. In the case of the analyzed dataset, k is the number of users in the Web of Trust (friends) and $trust_{a,u}$ has value 1.

In general, RSs based on trust propagation work better with cold start users. They don't use the (little) rating information for deriving a similarity measure to be used as weight for that user, but use the trust information explicitly provided by the user. In this way, even for a user with just one friend, it is possible that that friend has rated the same items and hence evaluating the accuracy of a prediction becomes possible. It is also possibly the case that that friend has very similar tastes to the current user and hence the error is small. In fact, the MAE of MT1 over cold start users is 0.674 while the MAE of CF is, as already discussed, 1.094. The difference in error is very high and particulary relevant since it is important for RSs to provide personalized recommendations as soon as possible to users who have not yet provided many ratings so that these users appreciate the system and keep using it, providing more ratings. Moreover, cold start users are a very large portion of the users in our dataset.

Let us now compare performances of CF and MT1 over all the ratings. The MAUE achieved by MT1 and CF is respectively 0.790 and 0.938. Regarding prediction coverage, while CF is able to predict more ratings than MT1 (ratings coverage is 51.28% vs. 28.33%), MT1 is able to generate at least a prediction for more users (users coverage is 46.64% vs. 40.78%). Summarizing, MT1 is able to predict fewer ratings than CF but the predictions are spread more equally over all users (which can then be at least partially satisfied) and, regarding errors, CF performs much worse than MT1 when we consider the error achieved over every single user in the same way and not depending on the ratings provided. These facts have the following reason: CF works well - both in terms of coverage and in terms of error - for heavy raters (users who already provided a lot of ratings) while it performs very poorly on cold start users. On many important views such as controversial items and opinionated users MT1 outperforms both CF and TrustAll.

10.4.3.4 Propagating Trust with a Local Trust Metric

In the previous section we analyzed performances of RS algorithms that consider only trust information but don't propagate trust.

One of the weaknesses we highlighted in Section 10.2 was the fact that user similarity is often non computable and in this way the number of neighbours whose ratings can be considered in Formula 10.2 is small. We claimed this was especially the case for cold start users. We also claimed that, by using explicit trust statements and trust propagation, it was possible to predict a trust score for many more users and use this quantity in place of (or in combination with) the user similarity weight.

Here we analyze and compare the number of users for which it is possible to compute a user similarity value and a predicted trust one.

In Fig. 10.3 we plot the number of comparable users averaged over all the users who created a certain number of reviews. We define 2 users comparable if they have rated at least 2 items in common. On every comparable user it is possible to compute the Pearson correlation coefficient and to use it as a weight for that user. Unsurprisingly, the users who created many reviews have a higher number of users against which Pearson is computable. However, the plot shows that even for those users the coverage over user base is very limited: for example, the 54 users who created 60 reviews have a mean number of users against which Pearson is computable of 772.44 that is only the 1.57% of the entire user base.

Figure 10.3 shows only a portion of the total graph, in fact the y axis can go up to 49,290 users and the x axis up to 1,023 items. In an ideal system, it would be possible to compare each user against every other user; in this case the mean number of users would have been $49, 289$ independently of the number of written reviews. Instead, Fig. 10.3 makes evident how on the Epinions dataset the technique is far from ideal.

Let us now concentrate on "cold start users". For users who expressed less than 5 ratings (who are more than 50% of the users) Pearson Correlation Coefficient is

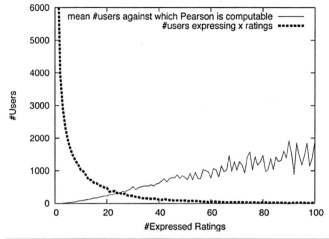

User base	No. of Users	Frac. of Total	Mean No. of Comp. Users
All	49,290	100.00%	160.73
5−	26037	52.82%	2.74
10−	33504	67.97%	11.27
20−	40597	82.36%	33.53
50+	2661	5.40%	1447.88
100+	882	1.79%	2162.52

Fig. 10.3 The thick line plots the number of users who have expressed a specific number of ratings. For each of these users, the thin line plots how many *comparable* users exist in the system on average. (By comparable we mean that the 2 users have rated at least 2 items in common). The table groups results for class of users depending on number of expressed ratings

computable on average only against 2.74 users over 49,290 (as shown in the row labeled "5-" of Fig. 10.3) and also only 1,413 of the 26,037 cold start users have at least 10 users against which Pearson is computable. It is worth noting that, even for the most overlapping user, Pearson correlation coefficient is computable only against 9,773 users that is just 19.83% of the entire population.

This plot is a stray evidence of how Pearson correlation coefficient is often not computable and hence ineffective.

Let us now analyze the computability of predicted trust and compare it with computatibilty of user similarity. We compute the number of users in which it is possible to predict trust starting from a certain user as the number of users at a certain distance from that user. In Table. 10.4 we report the mean number of users reachable by propagating trust at different distances and the mean number of users for which user similarity weight is computable. The standard CF technique (Pearson correlation coefficient) on average allows computing user similarity only on a small portion of the user base, precisely 160.73 over 49,290 (less than 1%!). On the other hand, by propagating trust it could be possible to infer trust in the other users and use this value as an alternative weight when creating a recommendation. For the average user, in one trust step it is possible to cover 9.88 users (direct

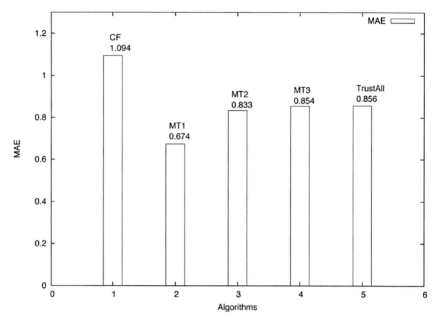

Fig. 10.4 MAE on cold start users for some representative algorithms

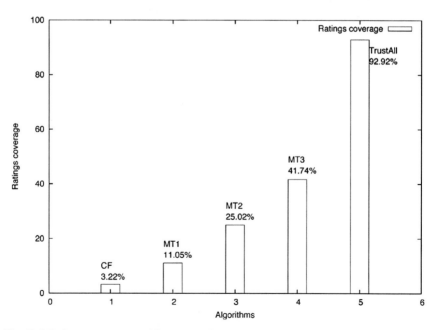

Fig. 10.5 Ratings coverage on cold start users for some representative algorithms

Table 10.4 Mean number of comparable users with different methods: Trust and Pearson correlation coefficient. Mean number of comparable users with different methods: Trust and Pearson correlation coefficient. For trust, we indicate the mean number of users reachable through some trust chain in at most x steps. For Pearson, we indicate the mean number of users against which Pearson coefficient is computable (i.e. overlap of at least 2 items). Both are computed over every user (even the ones with 0 ratings or 0 friends)

Userbase	Propagating trust (up to distance)				Using pearson
	1	2	3	4	
All users	9.88	400	4386	16334	161
Cold start users	2.14	**94.54**	1675	9121	**2.74**

friends), in 2 steps 399.89 users (friends of friends), in 3 steps 4386.32 users, and in 4 steps 16,333.94 users. In computing these values we also considered the users who were not able to reach all the other users, for example the users who provided 0 friends.

The previous difference in coverage of the user base with the two techniques is even exacerbated in the case of "cold start users", users who expressed less than 5 ratings. The mean number of users against which Pearson is computable for this class of users is only 2.74 (0.0056% of the users). Instead, by propagating trust, it is possible to reach 94.54 users in just 2 steps and 9,120.78 in 4 steps (see Table. 10.4).

This table tells that on a dataset of real users (Epinions), trust propagation is potentially able to predict a trust score in many more users than the traditional RS technique of computing user similarity over the ratings matrix using the Pearson Correlation Coefficient. Note also that, because of the sparsity of the rating data, the Pearson Correlation Coefficient is usually computed only based on a small number of overlapping items, producing a noisy and unreliable value. This difference in the number of users in which it is possible to compute similarity and trust is even exacerbated for cold start users. These users are usually the largest portion of users and also the ones to benefit most from good quality recommendations.

Since by propagating trust it is possible to reach more users and hence to compute a predicted trust score in them and to count them as neighbours, the prediction coverage of the RS algorithm increases. In fact the larger the trust propagation horizon, the greater the coverage (see columns MT1, MT2 and MT3 of Table 10.2 and 10.3). For instance, on all ratings, the ratings coverage increases from 28.33% for MT1, to 60.47% for MT2, to 74.37% for MT3. By continuing to propagate trust (i.e. expanding the trust propagation horizon) it is possible to consider more and more users as possible neighbours and hence to arrive at 88.20%, the ratings coverage of TrustAll which considers every user who provided a rating. The downside of this is that the error increases as well. For example, on cold start users, the MAUE is 0.674 for MT1, 0.820 for MT2 and 0.854 for MT3. These results say that by propagating trust it is possible to increase the coverage (generate more recommendations) but that it also considers users who are worse predictors for the current user so that the prediction error increases as well. The trust propagation horizon basically represents a tradeoff between accuracy and coverage.

10.4.3.5 Global Trust Metrics not Appropriate for Recommender Systems

An additional experiment we performed is about testing the performance of global Trust Metrics as algorithms for predicting the trust score of unknown users. A global trust metric predicts the same trust scores in other users for every user. This technique, like TrustAll, is hence not personalized. We have chosen to run PageRank [21] as global trust metric and to normalize the output value in [0,1]. We call the Recommender System that uses PageRank for its Trust Metric module, *PR*. PR performs similarly to TrustAll, even slightly worse (MAE of 0.847 and 0.821 respectively). This means that a global Trust Metric is not suited for Recommender Systems whose task is to leverage individual different opinions and not to merge all of them into a global average. We also tried to restrict the neighbours to just the first 100 users as ranked by PageRank but this algorithm (called *PR100*) – while of course reducing the coverage - reports even larger errors (MAE of 0.973). The reason behind these bad performances is that globally trusted users (as found by PageRank) tend to be peculiar in their rating patterns and provide more varied ratings so that averaging them generates larger errors. In contexts such as understanding which is the most relevant web page about a certain topic or the most relevant scientific paper, global trust metrics such as PageRank can be highly effective. However global trust metrics are not suited for finding good neighbours, especially because the task of RSs is to provide personalized recommendations while global trust metrics are unpersonalized. We also showed in [20] that also in social contexts local trust metric performs better. This is especially true for controversial users, for which a common agreement cannot exist. We suggested how it might be important for the healthiness of a society to favor diversity of opinons and not to force everyone to suffer from the tyranny of the majority [20] and hence to adopt local trust metrics.

10.4.3.6 Combining Estimated Trust and User Similarity

In the architecture of Trust-aware Recommender Systems (Figure 10.2), the "rating predictor" module takes as input both the Estimated Trust matrix and the User Similarity matrix. The idea is that the weight of a neighbour used in Equation 10.2 can be derived both from the user similarity value computed by the Similarity Metric (Pearson Correlation Coefficient in our case) and the predicted trust value computed by a Trust Metric. We have already commented on the number of users for which it is possible to compute a similarity weight or a predicted trust in the previous subsection [22]. However, in order to devise a way of combining these two matrices, it is interesting to analyze how much they overlap. As previously reported, the number of users reachable in one step (the ones used by MT1) are on average 9.88 and the number of users in which a user similarity coefficient is computable are on average 160.73. The two matrix rows overlap only on 1.91 users on average, that is only for 1.91 users we have both a predicted trust and a user similarity. The number of users reachable propagating trust up to distance 2 is 399.89. Comparing it again with the number of users in which a similarity coefficient is computable (160.73), the average number of users present in both lists is 28.84. These numbers show how

Pearson Correlation coefficient and MoleTrust address different portions of the user base in which they are able to compute a weight. So, in order to combine these weights, we tested the simple technique of computing a weighted average when there are two weights available and, in case only one is available, of using that. We call this technique *CF+MTx*: for example the system that combine CF and MT1 is called CF+MT1. The results are not very good. When comparing CF+MT1 with CF and MT1 for example, we see that the coverage is greater than the coverage of the two techniques. This is of course to be expected since CF+MT1 considers both the users for which it is possible to predict a trust score (as MT1 does) and the users for which it is possible to compute a user similarity (as CF does). However, the error of CF+MTx generally lies in between of CF and MTx, that is worse than MTx and better than CF. The problem is that, as we reported earlier, CF is almost never able to find good neighbours and hence making an average of the users who are similar and of the users that are trusted produces worse results than just considering trusted users. Since techniques that used only trust were superior in previous tests to CF-based ones, we also try to just use the predicted trust score when both the weights were available but the results are very similar.

10.5 Discussion of Results

In this section we summarize and discuss the most important results of the presented experiments. The first important result it that considering only the ratings of directly trusted users is the technique that, in general, achieves the smallest error with an acceptable coverage. The comparative improvement over the other techniques is particularly evident with regard to controversial items and black sheep, two of the most important and challenging views. With regard to cold start users, standard CF techniques totally fail and are not able to generate any recommendation. Instead, by considering ratings of trusted users we achieve a very small error and are able to produce a recommendation for almost 17% of the users. We can therefore state that providing a single trust statement is an easy, effective and reliable way of bootstrapping the Recommender System for a new user. It is important to underline that the evidence is based on experiments carried out on a real world, large dataset. In particular the Epinions datasets allowed us to explore topics which were not addressed before in research papers, such as cold start users and other views. Using our local Trust Metric MoleTrust in order to propagate trust allows users trusted by trusted users (at distance 2 from active user in the directed trust network), or even further away users, to be considered as possible neighbours. In this way, the coverage increases significantly, but the error increases as well. This means that ratings of users at distance 2 (or more) are less precise and less useful than ratings of users at distance 1, i.e. directly trusted by the active user. However it is an open issue to see if different local trust metrics are able to extract just some of the other users such that their ratings are really effective in improving the recommendation accuracy. In fact, this method can be used to evaluate the quality of different trust metrics, that is, a better trust metric is the one that is able to find the best neighbours and hence to reduce the prediction error. As a last point we would like to highlight how Collaborative Filtering, the state of the art technique, performed badly in our experiments, especially on cold start users (which in fact are more than 50% in our dataset). The reason for this lies in the characteristics of the datasets used for evaluation. In previous research evaluations the most used dataset was MovieLens, while we used a dataset derived from the online community of Epinions.com. As we have already explained they present very different characteristics. It is still an open point to understand how much the different datasets influence the evaluation of different algorithms' performances. In order to help this process, we released the dataset we crawled from Epinions. The dataset is downloadable at http://www.trustlet.org/wiki/epinions.

10.6 Conclusions

In this chapter we have presented our proposal for enhancing Recommender Systems by use of trust information: Trust-aware Recommender Systems. We have presented a deep empirical evaluation on a real world, large dataset of the performances of different algorithms ranging from standard CF to algorithms powered with local or global trust metrics, from the combination of these to baseline algorithms. We have also segmented the evaluation only on certain views (cold start users, controversial items, etc.) over the dataset in order to better highlight the relative merits of the different algorithms. The empirical results indicate that trust is very effective in alleviating weaknesses inherent to RSs. In particular, the algorithms powered with MoleTrust local trust metric are always more effective than CF algorithm, which surprisingly performs even worse than simple averages when evaluated on all the ratings. This difference is especially large when considering cold start users, for which CF is totally ineffective. The trust propagation horizon represents a tradeoff between accuracy and coverage, that is, by increasing the distance to which trust is propagated by the local trust metric the prediction coverage increases but the error increases as well. Results also indicate that global trust metrics are not appropriate in the context of RSs. Given that the user similarity assessment of standard CF is not effective in finding good neighbours, the algorithms that combine both user similarity weight and predicted trust weights are not able to perform better than algorithms that just utilize trust information.

References

1. P. Resnick and H. Varian. Recommender systems. *Communications of the ACM*, 40(3):56–58, 1997.
2. J. Breese, D. Heckerman, and C. Kadie. Empirical analysis of predictive algorithms for collaborative filtering. In *Proceedings of the Fourteenth Conference on Uncertainty in Artificial Intelligence*, Madison, WI, July 1998. Morgan Kaufmann.
3. A. Toffler. Future shock, 1970. Random House, New York.

4. J.B. Schafer, J. Konstan and J. Riedl. *Recommender Systems in E-Commerce*. Proceeding of the ACM Conference on Electronic Commerce, Pittsburgh, PA, USA, 1999

5. M. P. O'Mahony, N. J. Hurley, and G. C. M. Silvestre. Recommender systems: Attack types and strategies. In *Proceedings of the 20th National Conference on Artificial Intelligence (AAAI-05)*, Pittsburgh, Pennsylvania, USA, 9–13, Jul 2005. AAAI Press.

6. S. K. Lam and J. Riedl. Shilling recommender systems for fun and profit. In *Proceedings of WWW04*, 2004.

7. E. J. Friedman and P. Resnick (2001). The Social Cost of Cheap Pseudonyms. *Journal of Economics and Management Strategy*, 10(2):173–199.

8. Ctv.ca (2004). Amazon glitch outs authors reviewing own books. Retrieved December 28, 2007, from http://www.ctv.ca/servlet/ArticleNews/story/CTVNews/1076990577460_35.

9. Microformats.org. hreview. Retrieved December 28, 2007, from http://microformats.org/wiki/hreview.

10. J. Golbeck. *Computing and Applying Trust in Web-based Social Networks*. PhD thesis, University of Maryland, 2005.

11. K. Swearingen and R. Sinha. Beyond algorithms: An HCI perspective on recommender systems. in ACM SIGIR 2001 Workshop on Recommender Systems, New Orleans, Lousiana, 2001.

12. J.L. Herlocker, J.A. Konstan, and J. Riedl. Explaining Collaborative Filtering Recommendations. In *Proc. of CSCW 2000.*, 2000.

13. J. Zaslow. If TiVo Thinks You Are Gay, Here's How to Set It Straight. The Wall Street Journal, 26 November 2002

14. L. Guernsey. Making Intelligence a Bit Less Artificial. New York Times, 5 January 2003.

15. B. N. Miller, J. A. Konstan, and J. Riedl. Pocketlens: Toward a personal recommender system. *ACM Trans. Inf. Syst.*, 22(3):437–476, 2004.

16. N. Wingfield and J. Pereira. Amazon uses faux suggestions to promote new clothing store, December 2002. Wall Street Journal.

17. P. Massa. A survey of trust use and modeling in current real systems, 2006. Chapter in "Trust in E-Services: Technologies, Practices and Challenges", Idea Group, Inc.

18. R. Levien. *Advogato Trust Metric*. PhD thesis, UC Berkeley, USA, 2003.

19. C.-N. Ziegler. *Towards Decentralized Recommender Systems*. PhD thesis, Albert-Ludwigs-Universität Freiburg, Freiburg i.Br., Germany, June 2005.

20. P. Massa and P. Avesani. Trust metrics on controversial users: balancing between tyranny of the majority and echo chambers, 2007. International Journal on Semantic Web and Information Systems.

21. L. Page, S. Brin, R. Motwani, and T. Winograd. The pagerank citation ranking: Bringing order to the web. Technical report, Stanford, USA, 1998.

22. P. Massa and P. Avesani. Trust-aware collaborative filtering for recommender systems. In *Proc. of Federated Int. Conference On The Move to Meaningful Internet: CoopIS, DOA, ODBASE*, 2004.

23. R. Sinha and K. Swearingen. Comparing recommendations made by online systems and friends, 2001. In Proceedings of the DELOS-NSF Workshop on Personalization and Recommender Systems in Digital Libraries. Dublin, Ireland.

24. J. O'Donovan and B. Smyth. Trust in recommender systems. In *IUI '05: Proceedings of the 10th international conference on Intelligent user interfaces*, pages 167–174, New York, NY, USA, 2005. ACM Press.

25. J. L. Herlocker, J. A. Konstan, L. G. Terveen, and J. T. Riedl. Evaluating collaborative filtering recommender systems. *ACM Trans. Inf. Syst.*, 22(1):5–53, 2004.

26. J. Herlocker, J. Konstan J., A. Borchers, and J. Riedl. An Algorithmic Framework for Performing Collaborative Filtering. In *Proceedings of the 1999 Conference on Research and Development in Information Retrieval*, 1999.

Chapter 11
Trust and Online Reputation Systems

Ming Kwan and Deepak Ramachandran

Abstract Web 2.0 technologies provide organizations with unprecedented opportunities to expand and solidify relationships with their customers, partners, and employees—while empowering firms to define entirely new business models focused on sharing information in online collaborative environments. Yet, in and of themselves, these technologies cannot ensure productive online interactions. Leading enterprises that are experimenting with social networks and online communities are already discovering this fact and along with it, the importance of establishing trust as the foundation for online collaboration and transactions. Just as today's consumers must feel secure to bank, exchange personal information and purchase products and services online; participants in Web 2.0 initiatives will only accept the higher levels of risk and exposure inherent in e-commerce and Web collaboration in an environment of trust. Indeed, only by attending to the need to cultivate online trust with customers, partners and employees will enterprises ever fully exploit the expanded business potential posed by Web 2.0. But developing online trust is no easy feat. While various preliminary attempts have occurred, no definitive model for establishing or measuring it has yet been established. To that end, nGenera has identified three, distinct dimensions of online trust: reputation (quantitative-based); relationship (qualitative-based) and process (system-based). When considered together, they form a valuable model for understanding online trust and a toolbox for cultivating it to support Web 2.0 initiatives.

11.1 Introduction

To capture the hearts and minds of a digital generation, businesses need to redefine their communication approaches. Today's leading organizations are harnessing the power of mass collaboration, community, and technology to engage customers in a new continuum of participation that sees them acting as both final consumers and co-producers of goods and services. But knowing how to utilize Web 2.0 tools is

M. Kwan (✉)
nGenera (Formerly New Paradigm) 145 King St. East, Toronto, Ontario, Canada M5C 2Y7
e-mail: mkwan@ngenera.com

J. Golbeck (ed.), *Computing with Social Trust*, Human-Computer Interaction Series, DOI 10.1007/978-1-84800-356-9_11 © Springer-Verlag London Limited 2009

only part of this process. Determining which communication approaches are best suited to a particular business, its customers, and the image and reputation it wants to build, is crucial.

Since the *raison d'être* of Web 2.0 is collaboration—often with strangers—trust is the linchpin of this new continuum of participation. To succeed, users must trust one another and companies must foster the requisite level of trust to incent user participation. Web pundits make it seem simple: start a Facebook group, start blogging, create a community. However, a much more in-depth understanding of how trust is established, maintained and nurtured is needed before user engagement can be cultivated in today's online reality.

This report presents a model for understanding and building online trust based on:

- a quantitative measure of reputation;
- a qualitative measure of relationships; and
- a systems-based approach to establishing trust in an organization or its processes.

This model will be especially helpful to those establishing and using social media sites, online communities and other Web 2.0 applications—for employees, partners, and consumers alike.

However, one important caveat must be noted. Trust is *contextual* and depends entirely on the situation, time and purpose of an individual's engagement with a particular organization. What works for one enterprise at one time may not work for the next. Therefore, what is required is a dynamic, customized methodology for building online trust. Dr. Luca de Alfaro, associate professor of Computer Engineering at the University of California, Santa Cruz and lead of UCSC's Wiki Lab, describes the challenge: *"The more you open, ... and with the multiplication of sources of information, the issue of trust will be ever more important"* [25].

11.1.1 What Is Trust?

The concept of trust is still open territory; particularly when it comes to characterizing it for the online environment. Many definitions have been developed by strategists and academics but no one definitive model has prevailed.

For the purpose of this paper, we offer the following observations. Trust is the expectation that others have (1) *good intentions*; and (2) *the competence to see those intentions through*. Trust is *non-transitive*: though I trust you, I may not trust the people you trust. And trust is highly situation-specific: though I might trust you for a given purpose (e.g., to fix my car), I may not trust you for a different purpose or at a different time (e.g., to babysit my daughter).

11.2 The Complex World of Online Trust

Online transactions take place in an entirely virtual realm where it is nearly impossible to receive the traditional cues that are apparent in the physical world.

Considerations such as body language, tone of voice, facial expressions and other important sensory data that inform people's perception of trust offline are missing in the virtual world. Today, new and more objective cues are being developed to help users gauge trustworthiness online. Enterprises must become fluent in the use of these digital cues, which, in many cases, are better indicators of user intention, competence, and reputation, than the mere sensory information we depend upon offline.

11.2.1 Learning to Gauge Intention

As Don Tapscott puts it in his book, *The Naked Corporation*, trust includes "*the expectation that others will be honest, accountable, considerate and open*" [36]. Online community members want reassurance that other participants possess similar aims and will observe social norms. Thanks to the transparent nature of these organizations, concerned members can witness for themselves whether a given individual has joined the community to be an active contributor and add value or pursue ulterior motives. Dr. Jennifer Golbeck, an assistant professor at the College of Information Studies at the University of Maryland puts it nicely, "If you can give them [members] more insight into what's going on and make it transparent, people will trust it more and especially if you're using social relationships. . ." [23]

11.2.2 Evaluating and Validating Competence

New methods for evaluating and validating user competence online have also been instituted. Approaches vary depending on the type of community but successful communities and platforms provide ways for enterprises to validate users, such as by investigating their activity histories or screening their past contributions.

11.2.2.1 Treating Online "Friends of Friends" with a Degree of Skepticism

Trust cannot be easily transferred (non-transitive nature). Although mapping out relationships and figuring out how individuals are connected within a network is simpler on the Web, this information doesn't make knowing *who* to trust that much easier to determine. And while the ancient proverb, "The enemy of my friend is my enemy," may still form the basis of foreign policy doctrine, its antithesis, "The friend of my friend is my friend," doesn't necessarily hold true—particularly online.

11.2.2.2 Tying It all Together to Provide Context

A given individual may behave in a trustworthy manner in one situation and not in another. The common thread connecting the three previously described characteristics: intention, competence and non-transitive nature, is that they are all situation-specific; they depend on purpose and time. Accordingly, trust varies by situation on a case-by-case basis. Therefore, each online interaction should be evaluated individually to make the best determination, while keeping these three characteristics in mind to direct judgment.

Businesses, administrators, and creators of Web 2.0 tools are responsible for providing the necessary provisions to gain user confidence. Since face-to-face interactions are absent from Web encounters, the usual process of validation and authentication which traditionally informs our perceptions of trust is missing. So, how does one ascertain whether a person is really who they say they are? Web 2.0 tools are changing the game by providing new types of cues that are more relevant to the virtual realm. Forward-thinking enterprises have a strategic opportunity to become proficient at generating the requisite cues to engender high levels of trust with consumers, partners and employees so as to reap the rewards of these more profound business relationships.

As Shawn Broderick, founder and CEO of TrustPlus, a reputation-building and tracking service for the Web notes, "If we're not trustworthy, then there's no reason to pay any attention to us" [27].

11.3 Web 1.0 vs. Web 2.0

Where Web 1.0 employed a broadcast model in which enterprises disseminated information to users who were required to determine its validity; the model for Web 2.0 is a conversation between engaged participants who can self-organize and where transparency is achieved through broader access to information. "We've gone from broadcast to conversation and who's talking in that conversation has become more important because of it," [28] says Will Shaver, the developer of trust gradients [33] for distinguishing between new and vetted information on Wikipedia. Companies, news agencies and broadcasters no longer have the lock on influence that they held under Web 1.0. Today's enterprises must learn how to deal with this shift in power and influence online and consumers must adapt to this new environment.

With Web 1.0, consumers were used to reading a monologue of certified information; whereas, Web 2.0, is about collaboration and trusting the people on the other side of the conversation. Users now have the power to discuss information, debate it among themselves and express their opinions. The catch is that they need to learn how to filter out the noise now that everyone has a voice.

11.3.1 How Can It Help Me?

Customers, employees and prospects are already using the Web to interact with each other and build communities; complex relationships are being developed, models of trust are maturing and social norms have already been established. As enterprises join these communities and try to extend their brands online, it is important that they understand this landscape and are familiar with the different elements of trust.

Companies that are trusted can become online community leaders and respected sources of information, as well as garnering support for their brands from evangelists.

There are three, distinct key influencers of trust that can help enterprises take advantage of the opportunity and change ushered in by Web 2.0. They are not mutually exclusive. In fact, they are closely related. The most successful companies use the three of them to form a customized approach to building trust.

11.4 The New Model of Online Trust

Three new approaches to understanding and building trust are emerging (Fig. 11.1):

1. **Reputation Based** (Quantitative)
2. **Relationship Based** (Qualitative)
3. **Process Driven** (System)

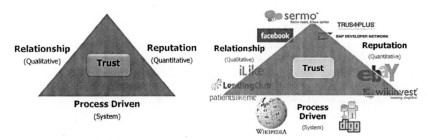

Fig. 11.1 Model of online trust (Source: nGenera Insight 2008)

This model highlights the elements that need to be present when establishing trust with employees, partners and/or consumers (an important consideration for online communities). It also provides a comprehensive reference point for developing applications and platforms that users will find reliable and trustworthy.

11.5 Reputation

Systems that measure reputation allocate a score to the trust object (trustee) for a particular event, transaction, or individual. These scores provide a quantitative metric for others to adjudicate and form opinions about. Rating systems are the most common method for establishing reputation. The most obvious example of an organization that successfully measures reputation to build trust is eBay – arguably the first Web 1.0 company to popularize the concept. Much of eBay's success is due to its feedback system. Buyers and sellers are used to the idea of reputation scores and consider them a reasonable indicator of a person's relative trustworthiness and reliability.

Scores can also be provided in the form of a title or designation rather than as ratings. However, for such designations to be effective, they must be valued and difficult to achieve, otherwise they will be perceived as useless. Microsoft's developers' communities have done this well. They encourage users to contribute consistently and with high quality through Microsoft's Most Valuable Professional program (MVP) which is recognized and valued throughout the developer community. The program is not limited to Microsoft networks; it is applicable to all developer communities related to Microsoft services [17].

The MVP program has an aura of esteem, especially since only 3,500 people have earned the designation worldwide, out of more than 100 million participants [7]. Not only is it a prestigious designation, Microsoft also offers MVP awardees benefits that act as strong positive reinforcements for developers to add value to the communities in which they participate. Natty Gur, an enterprise architect, MVP and SAP Developer Network (SDN) top contributor, puts it this way,

> ... As an MVP, you are very connected to developers and teams internally at Microsoft and you have the ability to, if not influence, to be aware of their directions right now.... you get benefits that others don't have, so it puts you in a better position [26].

Gur contrasts Microsoft's MVP program with the SAP Developer Network (SDN):

> In the SAP area ...you can contribute as much as you want, you don't have any mechanism at all to connect mentors to internal teams inside SAP... Those guys we talked to at Microsoft were very enthusiastic about it [MVP], because we have direct impact on the things they are doing and they can use it as valuable assets to finding solutions. At SAP, it's missing. SAP teams and developers are detached from the field [26].

11.5.1 Trouble in Paradise—The SAP Developer Network

SDN is an example of a community struggling with the problems of incentives and gaming. Although SDN has experienced significant success, its poorly designed reputation system requires significant modification. Scale has also affected the community's dynamics. Eric Johnson, a consultant and top SDN contributor observes:

> I think there're still a lot of really good ideas and a lot of really smart people [at SDN]... but now, there are so many average answers to go through. I used to post a question and get two really, really good answers and one average answer. Now, it's gone the other way, where it's ten or 15 people who just link to other threads... [20]

Active contributors to SDN remark that the overall quality of contributions was much higher at the community's outset largely because users were able to keep track of contributors. Top contributors knew each other and users felt pressured to contribute relevant, value-added input since it was an indication of their competence. Now that the user base has exploded to over 1 million users [32], the community has outgrown the tools SAP provides, and is no longer successfully managing itself. One key reason for this is that SAP's reputation tool is so one-dimensional.

The root of the problem is that SDN allows users to accumulate points simply for answering questions, no matter how good or bad the quality of the answer. According to insiders, many SDN users are now participating for reasons other than acting as a resource to others, thereby increasing the "noise" in the community. Johnson affirms, "A lot of people are just on there [SDN] for the points... it's starting to erode the spirit of the point system" [20]. Multiple incentives encourage users to participate, such as developing a high point count (which builds the perception that one is a reputable contributor) being recognized on the Top Contributors chart, or even, receiving tangible rewards, such as iPod giveaways. "Unfortunately, none of these are the 'right' reasons to be contributing," says Anton Wenzelhuemer, T-Systems and SDN top contributor.

> In general, the material on SDN is quite trustworthy.... But lately, there is unfortunately, more and more material contributed which is just trivial (not to say useless). This seems to be a problem of scale as well as SDN's recognition system which encourages people to cheat the system, which, in turn, decreases the quality and trustworthiness of the whole content [19].

Critics of SDN claim that there has been a significant increase in average to below average contributions, all of which are made simply to gain points. To address this problem, SAP recently introduced the SAP Mentor Program which is loosely based on Microsoft's MVP concept. It's a step in the right direction but some issues still need to be addressed. Although SAP mentors are nominated and undergo a review process, the main determinant in being accepted is still the number of acquired points rather than the quality of contributions. According to Natty Gur:

> The SDN community just goes by the number of posts that I've done and the points for each post and that's all, they don't count the quality, just the quantity. And it [the contributions] must be over the SDN, if I have my own Website and I'm writing tons of things on implementation in the SAP area, they don't care about it. For them, it's a way to keep the trusted contributors on the SDN. With Microsoft, it's "You guys are helping our customers and we know it and we want to thank you and we will give you some kind of prize that you will be attributed with and we will connect you internally to the right teams because you will benefit from it and we will benefit from it." It's a completely different attitude [26].

11.5.2 When to Use Reputation as the Basis for Trust

Although a reputation-driven (quantitative) system provides an easy and objective way to measure reputation within large groups, these can be inflexible and must be carefully designed. Otherwise, they can easily be abused and gamed for their perceived benefits. Reputation systems are excellent for evaluating commercial peer-to-peer *transactions* and creating content or knowledge. Using an objective authentication process to supplement a reputation system further augments trust by reassuring users that they are among verified community members.

A properly designed reputation system creates incentives for users to behave honestly and reputably. Therefore, it is important to build algorithms and measure feedback quantitatively to promote positive behavior and discourage gaming. When users are not held accountable for the content, feedback, and ratings they contribute, there is no incentive for them to behave honestly. This increases the risk of gaming and decreases quality. Anonymity (in the context where an individual user is not attached to an identifying screen name or pseudonym) is not encouraged for reputation systems since reputation is built on the ability to authenticate users and hold them accountable for their actions.

11.6 Relationship

Another dimension of online trust, relationship, relies on *qualitative* assessments based on connections found in social networks and online communities. Here, the end user must make a decision with heavy reliance on the context of the situation and the available data. Users employ sources of rich information—contributed often by other users—to make educated decisions and judgments about situations and people.

Although online trust is not perfectly transitive, viewing information about a person's extended relationships is useful when making inferences about other people's trustworthiness. For example, knowing that user "Y" is a friend of your friend "X," makes user "Y" slightly more credible. To that end, most social networks have some form of "common friends" or degrees-of-separation function that represents these extended relationships.

Communities naturally exploit the relationship dimension of online trust since it is an extension of people's need to interact. Members tend to bring relationships into an online community and manage them with or without official endorsement. Self-organizing end users call their own shots and make decisions based on their preferences. When users express relationships explicitly (by creating a list of "friends") it makes communities incredibly easy to segment, since users often cluster in groups of like-minded individuals that share common interests, habits and preferences. Often in these types of networks, consumers will seek out corporate groups or companies that interest them—these are the most loyal and attentive audiences.

11.6.1 Social Networking

Facebook is an ideal illustration of the power of relationships. It has quickly become the second most popular social network (behind MySpace) based on hours spent (ComScore, August 2007 [8]), with 85 percent of the four-year university student market [6] and expanding high school and working professional populations (more than half of Facebook users are outside of college [6]) (Fig. 11.2).

All Facebook users complete a basic profile where they have the option to fill in personal information. A typical profile may include, but is not limited to, facts about the individual's education, interests, favorite movies, books, TV shows and quotes, as well as contact information (such as e-mail, phone number, address). Thousands of additional applications allow users to share photos, videos, travel experiences, surveys, blog posts and virtually any other information imaginable, and the ability to create public and private groups and events.

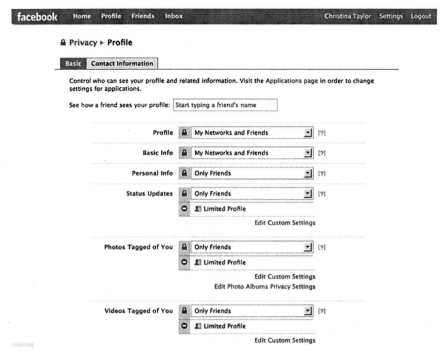

Fig. 11.2 Privacy settings in Facebook (Source: Facebook.com)

User profiles contain a plethora of rich, searchable information—a lot of which is created automatically, based on your activity. For instance, one of the richest, most informative elements of a user's profile is a simple "newsfeed" of recent actions such as adding friends, posting photos, or joining groups (Fig. 11.3). Another informative element, out of any specific user's control, is the "wall posts", or comments left by friends for everyone to see. These two kinds of rich information (and others, such as favourite videos, music, etc.) make it is easy for users to find others with similar interests. Facebook is organized on networks based on school, geographical area and/or place of employment. By default, any member of a user's network has access to his or her profile, but users have control over privacy settings that manage who may view their profile, message them etc. and these settings can be network specific.

Joining Facebook doesn't automatically allow one to see everyone's profile. Instead, there is tiered system. Some users have open profiles that permit anyone within their network to view their page; others have completely closed profiles that can only be accessed by their friends. Accessing a closed profile requires an additional layer of authentication based on a "friend request."

Certain features provide readily accessible information about a user's activity. For example, the "newsfeed" feature updates each time a user performs any task on Facebook (if they didn't adjust privacy settings). These features inform every

Fig. 11.3 A facebook news feed (Source: Facebook.com)

friend in the user's network about everything from new pictures added or tagged, to planned events, to messages posted to others' profiles, and even relationship status. As 22-year- old Katherine Kimmel notes, "You're not really dating until you put it on Facebook" [31].

Users can employ this wealth of information to make better informed decisions based on specific trust cues; particularly since context is all important. For example, one seeks different characteristics in a party guest than in a potential tenant. The "party host" user has the option of relying on other users' friends list, music preferences, party pictures, and relationship status to select a guest. Likewise, cues about employment status, family pictures, and friends' comments could be used to inform a decision regarding the selection of an appropriate tenant. The information users display in their profiles contributes to the kind of opinions viewers form of them; including their level of "trustworthiness."

11.6.2 Opening Up APIs

To exploit the countless opportunities presented by the relationships on its network, Facebook opened its Application Programming Interfaces (APIs) thereby allowing third-party applications to be developed. This open platform provides an opportunity for businesses to leverage existing relationships and pre-established trust. Trust levels on the network tend to be high since many Facebook relationships stem from real, in-person relationships. Businesses such as Lending Club (a peer-to-peer lending service), Faceforce (a customer relationship management CRM plug-in), WorkLight (a secure enterprise overlay for Facebook), and iLike (a clever music sharing application) have thrived in this manner.

11.6.3 Exploiting the Value of Social Networks

Faceforce is a mash up of a popular Web-based customer relationship management (CRM) software, Salesforce.com, and Facebook (Fig. 11.4). Faceforce was developed by Clara Shih, AppExchange product manager at Salesforce.com and Todd Perry, a software engineer at Facebook. As such, Faceforce isn't affiliated with either company [29] (Fig. 11.5).

Although initially, people questioned the value of integrating the two platforms, Faceforce soon proved its worth by empowering users to build deeper relationships with their customers and prospects. Faceforce opens a new world of opportunity by

Fig. 11.4 Faceforce is a mashup of Facebook and Salesforce.com

Faceforce is a connection utility that **unleashes the power of your social network** for building **better customer relationships**.

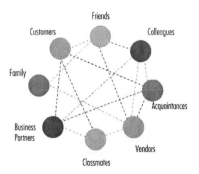

Fig. 11.5 Faceforce flash demo, created by Clara Shih, the application's developer [34]

Fig. 11.6 Screenshot of Faceforce interface [34]

bringing the power of relationships to contact management and cold calling. Today, users of both platforms can access rich data that connects relationships on Facebook to potential business contacts and leads from Salesforce. The mash up also allows users to perform typical Facebook actions, such as messaging, writing on a wall, sending a gift, poking, and viewing a full profile (if the user appears on the contact's "friends list") (Fig. 11.6).

11.6.3.1 WorkLight WorkBook

Unlike Faceforce which is free, WorkBook is a subscription-based security overlay for Facebook that enterprises can purchase for $10 per user per month. Developed by WorkLight, WorkBook is a secure Enterprise 2.0 solutions provider [13]. This application allows employees to interact securely with peers through Facebook. "WorkBook combines all the capabilities of Facebook with all the controls of a corporate environment, including integration with existing enterprise security services and information sources" [37] (Fig. 11.7).

Fig. 11.7 WorkLight has developed WorkBook, a secure Enterprise 2.0 solutions provider (Source: myworklight.com)

WorkBook addresses the typical security concerns that arise when employees use public sites to post potentially private company information; the overlay works within company firewalls and integrates the collaboration and communication capabilities of Facebook with the needs of the workplace. Employees are able to search for colleagues with similar interests or required skills by name, location, and area of expertise, as well as publish and receive company-related news, create bookmarks to enterprise application data, share information securely with authorized colleagues, and update their status [37]. By making it relevant to the enterprise and leveraging users' familiarity with the popular Facebook product, this application is helping companies warm up to the idea of using social networking within a business context.

WorkLight also provides secure integration of enterprise applications for 13 other consumer technologies: MySpace, Facebook, iGoogle, Netvibes, Microsoft Live, Yahoo widgets, Apple Dashboard, Google Desktop, Windows Vista Sidebar, del.icio.us, RSS, Google Gears and Adobe AIR [30].

11.6.3.2 Social Graphs Anchor Relationship-Based Trust

WorkBook and Faceforce aptly depict the concept of *social graphs* as models for contextual relationship-based trust (Fig. 11.8). A social graph is a set of relationships, appropriate to a given purpose—for instance, my social graph for work colleagues (or even a particular work project) is different than my social graph for friends (or a party). To accommodate different social graphs, companies such as Facebook are exploring allowing users to present different profiles of themselves for different purposes (though this is not available at press time). For example, users would typically want to share different information and different elements of their online profiles with different groups (e.g., work colleagues, family, friends). The best relationship-based trust systems will allow users to create different social

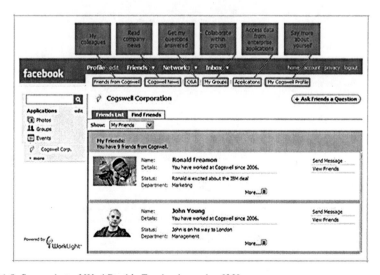

Fig. 11.8 Screenshot of WorkBook's Facebook overlay [30]

graphs and leverage these differences to offer situation specific features and functionality. A planning space for a business meeting and a Friday-night party would
naturally require different elements. A system that can allow for these types of distinctions will ultimately flourish.

11.6.4 iLike... to Share... and Lend

Increasingly, companies are finding that they can achieve phenomenal growth by
incorporating social networking applications into their business models. A social
music discovery company, iLike, developed a complementary Facebook application
that has achieved viral success by leveraging existing friendships and connections.
The application exploits established relationships and young peoples' desire to share
music with their friends (Fig. 11.9).

   ILike CEO Ali Partovi provides some insight into why the company is thriving:
"...Our system was always tied to friendships, [so] it became naturally viral.... On
Facebook, we built this application that really took advantage of and depended on
friend relationships as a core part of the discovery. The relationships were already
present and an intrinsic form of trust was there already" [12]. Simply put, users were
willing to add the application to their Facebook profiles because their friends were
adding it. Within one year, iLike has amassed over 21 million users [18] and is still
growing according to a company representative. When iLike first integrated with
Facebook, it grew at a rate of approximately 300,000 new users per day for the first
two weeks [10].

Fig. 11.9 Monthly growth of social networking sites since launch (Source: Tim Draper
Presentation on Viral Distribution, via Like blog 2007)

Partovi further explains:

> It's really an exciting time to be an entrepreneur because [Facebook] made possible things that just would not have been possible to build five years ago or two years ago... There are so many new things someone can create today as a start-up that just wouldn't have been really feasible before the Facebook platform because of the way it lets you take advantage of friend relationships and because of the viral growth that it enables. It exposes a lot of personalized data about a user that you can use to create really neat things [12].

The use of relationship data extends to other industries as well. Consider the credit industry, which now has the ability to extend its traditional reputation-based trust system (i.e. only considering numeric credit ratings). New finance-based entrepreneurial ventures are looking to harness the power of Web 2.0 and its ability to incorporate relationships and processes to add value for consumers. Prosper.com is one of the most successful peer-to-peer (P2P) lending sites to date, with more than 600,000 members and $122,000,000 in loans. From a company spokesperson, "Our system uses a powerful algorithm called LendingMatch, which finds relationships between borrowers and lenders based on geography, education, profession, or connectedness within a given social network and then presents lenders with diversified loan portfolios reflecting these relationships, as well as the lender's individual risk preferences" [5].

It is estimated that $267 million [2] worth of loans were made in 2007 through social lending, making it one of the faster areas of growth in financial services. According to the Gartner Group, "By 2010, social banking platforms will have captured ten percent of the available market for retail lending and financial planning" [7]. Zopa, another P2P lending service whose initial success was in the UK, now has approximately 185,000 members (although not all of them have transacted on the site) and has had about £20 million borrowed since its launch in March 2005 [35]. Since then, it has also launched operations in the US and Italy. Zopa's managing director Giles Andrews weighs in on the issue:

> Banks are the worst offenders in this homogenous sort of way, certainly in the UK and probably in the USA. Banks have become extremely efficient in manufacturing new products. They make products that aren't needed to be made and aren't particularly relevant to consumers. That also applies on the investment side, they [banks] don't seem to have an understanding of the investment products that are being pushed and so you begin to think "well there must be an opportunity to create a market place." [22]

Social lending provides an avenue for users to customize their own deals in as transparent a model as possible—thereby catering to a growing group of self-reliant customers.

Another similar organization, Lending Club, is a new peer-to-peer lending service, which has developed a Facebook application. John Donovan, Lending Club co-founder & COO, explains,

> We wanted to leverage the trust which exists within many social communities [like those on Facebook] and we knew that our platform provided value to the entire community, not just those who needed to borrow money. Leveraging and fostering trust was critical to establishing connectivity between members of various online social communities [24].

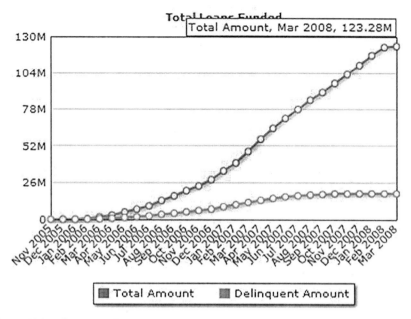

Fig. 11.10 Lending stats—Total Loans Funded [15]

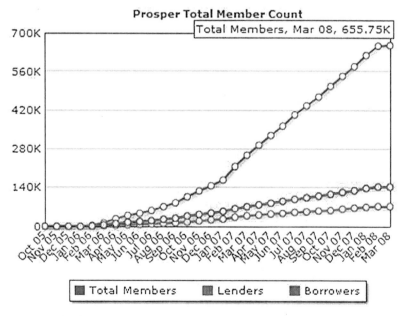

Fig. 11.11 Lending Stats—Prosper Total Member Count [16]

This strategy appears to have worked. From May 24, 2007 to February 29, 2008, LendingClub has issued 1,214 loans worth $10,645,025, with a zero percent default rate [14] (Figs. 11.10 and 11.11).

11.6.5 Sponsored Groups

In addition to applications, companies have also created sponsored groups on Facebook (and occasionally, Facebook members create unauthorized versions of them; either because they love or hate the company). The content of these pages is not entirely company controlled. Although it can be moderated, companies must be careful about editing content because Facebook is transparent and people will talk about the company's actions. If users believe that an enterprise is censoring negative content, then they will take issue with it publicly.

Companies hoping to connect with customers should make use of Facebook groups where consumers seek out the groups that interest them. This provides organizations with a forum for gathering valuable information about the target audience and brand perceptions from both online interactions and user group contributions (if discussion and wall functions are enabled). A 2007 study by Britain's Information Commissioner's Office illustrates the wealth of information available on Facebook—reporting that 60 percent of users post their date of birth, ten percent post their address, 33 percent never read privacy policies, 60 percent have never considered that what they put online might be permanent and 70 percent don't care that their personal profiles can be publicly viewed [11].

11.6.6 When to Use Relationship as the Basis of Trust

Building online trust using information derived from relationships has its drawbacks. Due to trust's contextual nature, every situation must be considered individually. Moreover, because trust is non-transitive and highly personalized, such judgments are very subjective; placing greater emphasis on transparency. Right or wrong, a clear, objective view of the information flow and connections within a user's personal network increases the perception that their trustworthiness can be predicted.

Online communities and social networks are natural environments for building trust based on relationships. However, since relationship-inferred trust is based mainly on available information, the potential for bias or one-sided views of situations is always present. Relationship-based trust must be reinforced if trust is to be maintained.

In these communities, verification and authentication are vital. They ensure that the platform upon which the relationship is based (identity) is not compromised. If a social network opts away from verification, there is the potential for people to be wary of other users—a scenario that developed at MySpace when it was discovered that several convicted sex offenders were part of the community under pseudonyms, posing a threat to that platform's large youth population. Allowing anonymous users to become members removes the checks and balances that discourage gaming. Users may not be held accountable for their actions, affecting both credibility and reliability.

11.7 Process

Sometimes, issues of trust relate to a system, procedure, or end-product rather than a person. This is called *process-driven trust*. For an online product or service to be considered trustworthy, a robust process and reliable system that provides a sense of control and accountability are mandatory.

A strong process allows applications to harness the wisdom of crowds and individual contributions and use it to create value in a community. Properly implemented, such a process decreases the need for additional measures to ensure community members and information found within the community are trustworthy.

The most obvious example of a process-based system is Wikipedia, the world's largest, free, online encyclopedia. Much of Wikipedia's success is due to the powerful process behind it; users know that a strong system of governance generates content that is, for the most part, reliable. With Wikipedia, a reader doesn't need to trust so much the last editor of an article (a person); rather, she can trust the transparent system of checks and balances (the process) that ensures any recent edit is relatively impartial and likely to be true.

Key features of Wikipedia's editing process are transparency and ease of use. All individual activities involving edits to page content are tracked. The edit history follows contributors/editors for a lifetime so "background checks" on particular editors are made easy by clicking on their profile for a full list of past edits, topics contributed to most frequently and the type of changes made. The ease of restoring previous versions of content if the latest one is vandalized is another key to Wikipedia's success. These simple, easy to use and transparent processes allow people to trust the online encyclopedia's content.

11.7.1 Caught in the Act—Reinforcing Process

Wikipedia has a group of dedicated volunteers that behaves as a governing body. Although these individuals occupy different roles, they all police Wikipedia—searching for vandals, identifying inaccurate information and retrofitting erroneous entries to ensure accurate and trustworthy content. Erik Moeller, a former member of the Board of Trustees of the Wikimedia Foundation, and the Foundation's current Deputy Director, notes:

> A challenge is determining when to confer trust on people; to make sure that people who ascend into the inner circle of Wikipedia are not those people [gamers] but rather people who want to contribute to the mission of Wikipedia... The process is already reasonably strong in ensuring the integrity of the end result, at least when it comes to articles that are primarily edited by members of the trusted core community [21].

Yet, critics of Wikipedia remain concerned about the reliability of content; they feel that Wikipedia's standalone process isn't enough to deter destructive behavior. To remedy this situation, external third parties are working to make Wikipedia more trustworthy by creating complementary algorithms to help users infer trustworthiness. To date, developers at the University of California, Santa Cruz (UCSC) have made the greatest headway and have established a partnership with the Wikimedia Foundation.

The UCSC Wiki Lab, led by Professor Luca de Alfaro, is developing an algorithm that provides a visual representation for users to immediately gauge the trustworthiness of a sentence Figure 11.12. This method is arguably the most objective approach, since it pulls raw data from the edit history of an article, taking into account the number of edits the text has survived. The longer a word remains unedited, the more "trustworthy" it becomes. The algorithm also has the ability to link editing records back to the original author—thereby providing a way for determining an author's relative trustworthiness based on their personal edit history and the length of time their edits remain untouched.

The most suspect content is highlighted in bright red, while the most reliable content has no highlighting. Alfaro has dubbed this particular system for determining reputation a "content-driven reputation system," since the end product (the content) drives the process.

Another initiative to help make the content on Wikipedia more trustworthy is Wiki Scanner, developed by Caltech graduate student, Virgil Griffith. Wiki Scanner has the ability to link back anonymous edits to specific IP addresses. In turn, these IP addresses can be associated with specific corporations and organizations. Some common vandalism and abuse of the Wikipedia system as identified by Griffith are [9]:

1. *Wholesale removal of entire paragraphs of critical information. (This commonly happens to content about political figures and corporations.)*
2. *White-washing or replacing negative/neutral adjectives with positive adjectives that mean something similar. (This commonly happens to content about political figures.)*
3. *Adding negative information to a competitor's page. (This commonly happens to content about corporations.)*

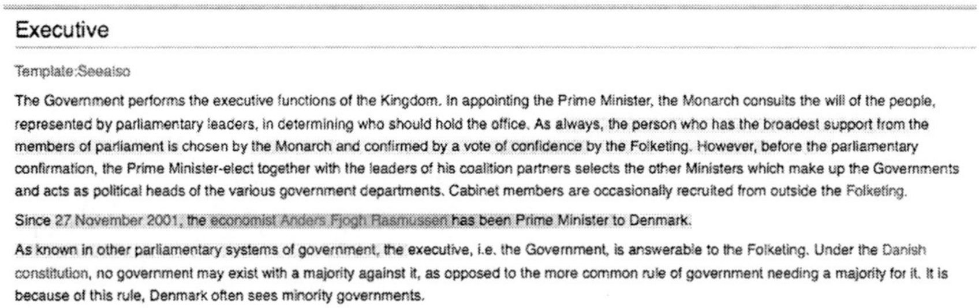

Executive

Template:Seealso

The Government performs the executive functions of the Kingdom. In appointing the Prime Minister, the Monarch consults the will of the people, represented by parliamentary leaders, in determining who should hold the office. As always, the person who has the broadest support from the members of parliament is chosen by the Monarch and confirmed by a vote of confidence by the Folketing. However, before the parliamentary confirmation, the Prime Minister-elect together with the leaders of his coalition partners selects the other Ministers which make up the Governments and acts as political heads of the various government departments. Cabinet members are occasionally recruited from outside the Folketing.

Since 27 November 2001, the economist Anders Fjogh Rasmussen has been Prime Minister to Denmark.

As known in other parliamentary systems of government, the executive, i.e. the Government, is answerable to the Folketing. Under the Danish constitution, no government may exist with a majority against it, as opposed to the more common rule of government needing a majority for it. It is because of this rule, Denmark often sees minority governments.

Fig. 11.12 UCSC Wiki Lab demo [3]

This new application has embarrassed several government organizations and corporations. For example, ATM and security system provider Diebold has been caught editing Wikipedia on several occasions. In one case, it was caught deleting entries related to criticisms and controversy surrounding the company [4] (Fig. 11.13).

Similarly, Chevron was caught deleting an entry regarding the fine it had to pay for violating Iraq oil sanctions [1] (Fig. 11.14).

11.7.2 So What?

People recognize the value that a system like Wikipedia brings to the Web and ordinary citizens are working to improve it by closing gaps where the system can be

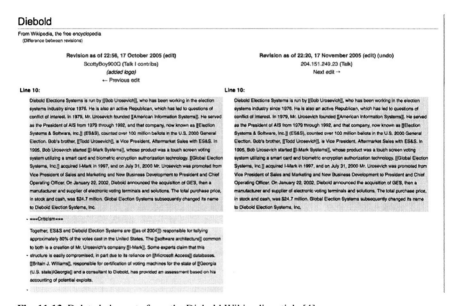

Fig. 11.13 Deleted elements from the Diebold Wikipedia article [4]

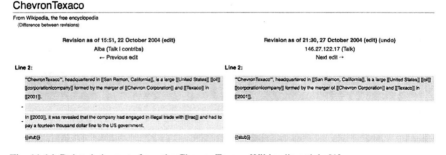

Fig. 11.14 Deleted elements from the ChevronTexaco Wikipedia article [1]

exploited or compromised. These individuals are developing mechanisms to provide transparency and accountability, and in so doing, are incorporating both the relationship and process dimensions of trust. The ability to link back anonymous edits to assigned IP addresses, especially those of known organizations, removes the element of anonymity. This, in turn, facilitates users' ability to search for trusted content and make better informed decisions.

According to the Wiki Scanner Website, there have been 34,417,493 edits in the English Wiki Scanner database from February 7th, 2002 to August 4th, 2007, and 187,529 distinct organizations that have made edits to English Wikipedia [9].

The ingenious manner in which Wikipedia incorporates relationship into its community is intimately related to its editing process which, in turn, helps users infer reputation. Each Wikipedia entry is associated with either an IP address or user account, through which all edits and contributions are tracked. Additionally, anyone using Wikipedia has the ability to click on a user's profile and view that individual's personal activity within Wikipedia. Inquiring minds are able to view what topics a user makes frequent contributions to and the specific edits made. It then becomes extremely easy for anyone to learn about the user and determine whether he is a productive member of the community, or a promoter of a hidden agenda.

11.7.3 When to Use Process as the Basis for Trust

The process-driven approach works well for items in "the commons" that need a strong infrastructure and system to guide users towards a specific goal or benefit. Having a strong process creates a natural incentive system for people to contribute positively. This dimension of trust requires the most involvement from administrators and designers, but it also represents the most value to users since it alleviates the burden of relying solely on reputation or relationship. Process-based trust also tends to be more scalable; making it appropriate for large groups of diverse users with unrelated motivations.

To reinforce user trust, various complementary features can be implemented. Important considerations include: keeping the process simple, transparent and easy to understand; employing an authentication/verification process to reassure users that community members have been screened; and ensuring all users are tied to one identifying factor so that activity can be tracked back.

Administrators should have faith that their system is built well enough to deter negative behavior, or at least be able to identify and retrofit it. Therefore, it is important to let the process play out the way it is meant to function, even when a "gamer" is identified. Erik Moeller explains how Wikipedia's underlying process is self-reinforcing:

> There is a temptation to say... "They're just causing trouble, let's just get rid of them." But if you do that, they come back again under a different name, or they go away mad and bring more people back with them... What we have learned is [that] basically a very gentle approach works. You let them edit and you change things back after they make them a mess [21].

Employing a different process would not only aggravate potential vandals, it would also give the impression that even administrators do not trust the ability of the regular process to deal with detrimental behavior.

11.8 A Recipe for Online Trust Based on Three Ingredients

As organizations launch collaborative initiatives and participate in (or create) online communities, they must adapt their policies and practices to a radically different business landscape. They face important questions about how their relationship management, information sharing and behavioral practices will change. Central to these decisions is the foundational issue of trust. While the consequences of an absence of trust are very clear (take the crash of Wall Street in 1929 for example), it's far less obvious how to design and embed trust into the fabric of an online product, service, or community. nGenera's trust model, based on the dimensions of reputation, relationships and process, offers an excellent starting point. But how can that model be put to use in practice and what courses of action does it suggest for those seeking to engender trust online?

First, it's important that all three dimensions of trust work in concert. The best and most successful companies, whether purposely or inadvertently, often rely on a combination of reputation, relationship and process. This allows the various dimensions to reinforce each another, resulting in a stronger overall impact. For example, eBay's latest rating system adds qualitative *relationship* data (free-form comments from customers; plus some information about recent activity) to the traditional quantitative *reputation* elements (numerical ratings). This provides more depth to a potential customer, trying to distinguish between two potential vendors with similar quantitative scores—and it also helps ensure those quantitative scores are driven by more-calibrated input between different customers. In addition, all the famous eBay efforts to reduce gaming and fraud (including money-back guarantees through PayPal, for instance) improve the *process* element, the trust in the system itself.

In hindsight, such solutions can seem obvious and easy to implement, but in practice these systems are often designed with the utmost care and are deliberately structured to account for specific community needs. In the best case, an ill conceived or "cookie-cutter" approach to trust will simply be ignored and, in the worst case, it can lead to the demise of an entire community. The good news is that any organization can experiment with some relatively simple and risk-free approaches to enhancing trust. Thereafter, it will be easier for enterprises to envision, develop and implement the kind of complex approaches to trust-building that confer significant strategic advantages. The most successful approaches, like eBay's, evolve over time as participants identify successful elements and risk areas.

The following advice will prove helpful to forward thinking organizations seeking to use the previously described dimensions to cultivate online trust.

Reputation

1. **Incorporate provisions that make users accountable for their actions and encourage responsible behaviors.** If these measures aren't established, then there will be no incentive for users to act responsibly. A reputation system needs to be designed so that it isn't open to gaming, otherwise it will lose credibility and ultimately, fall into disuse.
2. **Build a system where reputation is hard to achieve and valued.** Reputation systems help anchor trust more permanently within a community. Users may be more reluctant to leave your network if there is value in the rating and reputation they have established.
3. **Provide the requisite tools for users to validate and authenticate.** These measures provide an additional layer of security; people want to know that the person they're speaking with knows what they're talking about and is who they say they are.

Relationship

1. **Offer transparency and privacy controls.** Transparency allows users to cultivate open relationships, while privacy controls offer the ability to manage the disclosure of information and level of interaction with others. To leverage this grass-roots source of trust, a community must simply support these pre-existing behaviors.
2. **Reinforce trust by supplementing relationship information (which can be fleeting) with input derived from reputation and/or process-driven systems.** While trusted relationships can make for a stronger community, when community members move, the trust leaves with them.
3. **Use consistent behaviors.** Behaviors need to align with what the company is saying and portraying: this is not just a PR exercise. If users feel that a company is being insincere, they will take issue with it publicly. If you do something wrong, don't apologize unless you mean it and can take immediate action that produces tangible results.

Process

1. **Be open, transparent and honest. Keep the process simple and easy to use and understand.** If a process is too complicated, it won't be used. It's also important that users understand how the system is governed—transparency creates trust by allowing users to understand how the enterprise operates and infer its intentions.
2. **Constantly improve the system to make it more robust.** Small changes may have huge effects and wherever there are gaps, people will be looking to take advantage of them. With process-based trust, architecture concerns and incentives for successful gaming rise to an entirely different level. The most successful

processes are those in which the issue of trust doesn't cross users' minds. They simply use the system based on an understanding that it is robust enough to withstand harmful behaviors.

3. **Use a "laissez faire" strategy if it suits your goals and needs.** Sometimes it's best to create the community and let it develop on its own. Good trust systems are self-governing and offer little intervention from the company itself.

Acknowledgments We are grateful to Nauman Haque and Alan Majer, our colleagues at nGenera for their helpful insights and contributions in helping complete the paper.

References

1. Chevron Texaco Different between revisions. (2004). http://en.wikipedia.org/w/index.php?diff=prev&oldid=6911356.
2. Chu, Kathy. (2007). Alternative lending sties often have good deals. USA Today. http://www.usatoday.com/money/perfi/credit/2007-12-25-peerlending-pers_N.htm.
3. De Alfaro, Luca. (2007) Wikipedia Trust Coloring Demo. http://wiki-trust.cse.ucsc.edu/index.php?title=Politics_of_Denmark&direction=next&oldid=77697234.
4. Diebold Difference between revisions. (2005). http://en.wikipedia.org/w/index.php?diff=prev&oldid=28623375.
5. Donovan, John. (2007). LendingMatch: Our secret Sauce. LendingClub Blog. http://blog.lendingclub.com/2007/06/02/lendingmatch%e2%84%a2-our-secret-sauce/.
6. Facebook Press Room. http://www.Facebook.com/press/info.php?statistics.
7. Finextra.com. (2008). Banks facing increasing competition from social networks - Gartner. http://www.finextra.com/fullstory.asp?id=18049.
8. Fulgoni, Gian. (2007). Consumer Trends in Social Networking. http://www.comscore.com/blog/2007/10/consumer_trends_in_social_netw.html. Accessed October 30, 2007.
9. Griffith, Virgil. (2007). WikiScanner FAQ. http://virgil.gr/31.html.
10. iLike blog. (2007). Holy cow… 6mm users and growing 300k/day. http://blog.ilike.com/ilike_team_blog/2007/06/holy_cow_6mm_us.html.
11. Information Commisioner's Office. (2007). Social Networking Press Release. http://www.ico.gov.uk/upload/documents/pressreleases/2007/social_networking_press_release.pdf.
12. Intruders TV interview. (2007) Interview with Ali Partovi, founder of iLike: the most popular application on Facebook. http://ie.intruders.tv/Interview-with-Ali-Partovi,-founder-of-iLike-the-most-popular-application-on-Facebook_a134.html.
13. Ives, Bill. (2007). Worklight Enters the Enterprise Facebook Market. The FASTforward blog. http://www.fastforwardblog.com/2007/12/20/worklight-enters-the-enterprise-facebook-market/.
14. Lending Club website. www.lendingclub.com.
15. LendingStats, Prosper Loans Funded. http://www.lendingstats.com/loansFunded.
16. LendingStats, Prosper Membership Growth. http://www.lendingstats.com/membership-Growth.
17. Microsoft Most Valuable Professional, Frequently Asked Questions. http://mvp.support.microsoft.com/gp/mvpfaqs.
18. New Paradigm e-mail interview with Ali Partovi, iLike founder and CEO. January 25, 2008.
19. New Paradigm e-mail interview with Anton Wenzelheumer, SDN Top contributor – T-Systems, November 21, 2007.
20. New Paradigm interview with Eric Johnson, SDN Top contributor – Capgemini Consultant, November 6, 2007.

21. New Paradigm interview with Erik Moeller, Deputy Director, Wikimedia foundation, October 24, 2007.
22. New Paradigm interview with Giles Andrews, Managing Director, Zopa UK, October 24, 2007.
23. New Paradigm interview with Jennifer Golbeck, September 21, 2007.
24. New Paradigm interview with John Donovan, Founder & CEO of Lending Club, October 19, 2007.
25. New Paradigm interview with Luca de Alfaro, UCSC Wiki Lab, September 21, 2007.
26. New Paradigm interview with Natty Gur, SDN top contributor, November 9, 2007.
27. New Paradigm interview with Shawn Broderick, CEO Trust Plus, October 3, 2007.
28. New Paradigm interview with Will Shaver, Trust Gradients, September 18, 2007.
29. Ostrow, Adam. (2007). Salesforce.com Application for Facebook. http://mashable.com/2007/09/13/facebook-salesforce/.
30. Perez, Sarah. Social Tools Go to Work... Facebook, MySpace, Netvibes, iGoogle, and More in the Enterprise. Read Write Web. http://www.readwriteweb.com/archives/social_tools_go_to_work_in_the_enterprise.php.
31. Rosenbloom, Stephanie. (2007). On Facebook, Scholars Link Up with Data. The New York Times. http://www.nytimes.com/2007/12/17/style/17facebook.html?pagewanted=print.
32. SDN email update.
33. Shaver, Will. (2007). Wikipedia Trust Gradients. http://primedigit.com/wikifix/.
34. Shih, Clara. (2007). Faceforce flash demo. http://www.thefaceforce.com/demo/Faceforce%20-Demo.swf.
35. Walker, Tim. (2008). The Googles of tomorrow. Independent.co.uk. http://www.independent.co.uk/life-style/gadgets-and-tech/features/the-googles-of-tomorrow-787804.html.
36. Tapscott, Don and Ticoll, David, *The Naked Corporation How the Age of Transparency Will Revolutionize Business*, (Toronto: 2003).
37. WorkLight Solutions. (2007). WorkBook: A Secure Corporate Overlay for Facebook. http://www.myworklight.com/currentPage.aspx?catid=69&pageid=93.

Chapter 12
Internet-Based Community Networks: Finding the Social in Social Networks

K. Faith Lawrence

Abstract In this chapter we explore the concept of community within social networks and the effect that this primarily social construct can have on the way in which we understand trust within an online network. To do this we analyse and compare a number of the definitions that are both traditionally used to identify online communities and which have developed with the advent of semantically described social networks. Taking these definitions we apply them to a number of groups within a visualisation of a social network and, using this case study, consider the differences that are apparent between the types of groups. Finally, we discuss how the social implications inherent within the definition of community interact with the trust and reputation systems that exist in such networks. In doing so, we focus on the social aspect of the social network and the ways in which the social and technical worlds entwine.

12.1 Introduction

In much the same way that the rise of the Internet resulted in the re-examination of many ideas that had existed within the offline world, so the advent of the semantic web has lead to another reinvention of many of these same concepts. In this chapter, we consider the idea of community as it has evolved with the development of new technology and the role it plays within the human element of the social network.

While often associated with the user-driven Web 2.0 phenomenon, social networks represent one of the most successful and accessible examples of metadata-linked data systems to date. They also represent one in which the user is a vital component within that system. It therefore behoves us to look back on those communal constructs and definitions that already exist, both off and online, and which remain applicable within our new semantically defined world. Having done so, we create a new context within which to examine the calculation and importance of related aspects of network interaction such as trust and reputation.

K.F. Lawrence (✉)
University of Southampton, Southampton, UK
e-mail: kf03r@ecs.soton.ac.uk

J. Golbeck (ed.), *Computing with Social Trust,* Human-Computer Interaction Series,   313
DOI 10.1007/978-1-84800-356-9_12 © Springer-Verlag London Limited 2009

12.2 Defining Community in the Age of Social Networks

The concept of an online or virtual community was a matter of some debate among early researchers in the field as previous theories on community had required a real-world spatial component. The 1996 Computer Supported Cooperative Work conference "settled on an approach of defining the concept by 'prototypical attributes', so that communities with more of these attributes were clearer examples of communities than those that had fewer." [32]. While not fully resolving the debate, the resulting definition was deliberately context neutral so that it could be applied to both on and offline communities. Whether doubt remained as to their existence or not, research into virtual communities became accepted. Preece [25] defined an online community as containing four components: social interaction, a shared purpose, a common set of expected behaviours and some form of computer system which both mediates and facilitates communication. Ignoring the computer-mediation requirement, the notable difference between this and the, previously mentioned, Whittaker et al. [32] definition is that the latter does not use the term "social", instead focusing on active participation leading to shared activities or emotional bonds. This is perhaps expected, given the less inclusive nature of the Preece definition but it is interesting to note the stress on the social component of online communities which goes right back to some of the early proponents such as Howard Rheingold who defined online communities as "social aggregations that emerge from the Net when enough people carry on those public discussions long enough, with sufficient human feeling, to form webs of personal relationships in cyberspace." [28].

The rise of the social network is often seen as a recent phenomenon with sites such as MySpace, Facebook and Orkut opening the way for new research into online social connections. Even sites such as LiveJournal in which the social network element is both secondary to, and confused by, the journalling aspect provide a fertile ground for research into the connections that exist in the virtual world. However, the focus on the many one–one relationships that exist between users within those sites intended explicitly for social networking creates a very different social structure to that seen on the fora within which the early virtual communities were recognised or even sites such as LiveJournal which actively promote community as well as individual spaces. Even when the social networking sites provide community areas such as the groups on Facebook, the individual-individual relationships are often strongly promoted over any group links, for example through the types of notifications which users receive which privilege the reporting of actions done by individuals over those which occur within the group setting.

If we compare the Preece [25] definition of an online community with a semantically based social network such as the Web Based Semantic Networks (WBSN) defined by Golbeck [12, p. 13], both have a social aspect and are computer-mediated. What is missing from the requirements for a WBSN is any requirement, explicit or implicit, for a shared set of behaviours or a shared purpose. It could be argued that wanting to be part of a WBSN is a shared purpose but that seems indefensibly vague.

If social networks exemplify the network of relationships that exist within a group but without the necessity of a shared goal, a Community of Practice (COP)

Table 12.1 Comparison of Links between communities of practice and social Networks

Community Type	Links	Focus	"Community"
Community of Practice	Inferred	Practice	Social Interaction not required
Social Network	Explicit	People	Shared purpose and behaviours not required
IBSC	Explicit and Implicit	People as community members	

gains its community application through the inferred links that develop among a group that have a common task: "What is shared by a community of practice – what makes it a community – is its practice. The concept of practice connotes doing, but not just doing in and of itself. It is doing in a historical and social context that gives structure and meaning to what we do. When I talk about practice, I am talking about social practice." [31]. More recently the definition has lost even that much social notation to become "a relatively loose, distributed group of people connected by a shared task, problem, job or practice" [23].

We can see (Table 12.1) that while a COP or a social network such as a WBSN *may* describe a community, it is not a guaranteed assumption which can be made about the system described by either type of network. For this reason we identify a third type of group, the Internet Based Semantic Community (IBSC). An IBSC might be drawn from either a COP and a social network or both, but at the same time it can be shown to fulfil the definitions for a virtual community. This is an important distinction because services can then be designed and implemented with the assumption that the network acts in ways specific to a community rather than a random gathering of users. In addition, it can be argued, by identifying those attributes and behaviours that are unique to a IBSC, we can return to the non-community based networks and consider how other observations seen in IBSCs, and regarded as beneficial can be applied.

12.3 Visualising Community

We saw above that there are distinctions that can be drawn between networks of acquaintance or co-location, communities of friends and communities based around both social interaction and shared interest. To illustrate this further, we present a visualisation of the structure of online relationships as seen within the online journalling site LiveJournal.

LiveJournal includes a network with explicitly stated links between users' journals. In this it differs from many social networking sites because the stated links represent the desire of the linking user to subscribe to the journal being linked. While this is called "friending" it does not necessarily represent a social link between the two users who may not know each other at all. However, from a modelling perspective it serves the same function and since most social networks do not differentiate between strong social links and casual acquaintances the relationship derived from the linking of the two journals can be deemed sufficient to model a valid communal interaction.

LiveJournal allows for the creation of two different types of journal - personal, or user, journals, which are owned and used by individuals, and community journals, which are a shared resource between multiple users. Other research has been carried out using LiveJournal as a base [8, 24] but this research has focused on personal journals and personal interests rather than considering the interaction between user and community journals. An important facet of the LiveJournal network is that it does not privilege the relationships between personal journals over those between personal and community journals. This presents the opportunity to study these relationships in conjunction.

The example given centres on a journal set up by the author as a means of interacting with the research case study community, among others. The community in question is that of online media fans for many of whom LiveJournal represents a means through which they can gather and exchange information, opinions and media objects they have been inspired to create. For privacy reasons all the names of the journals have been removed. Where specific nodes are referenced, they are either identified by a letter (personal journals) or two letters (community journals). This identification remains consistent throughout.

Data was gathered from the starting journal, Node "F", and then those that were directly connected to it. A routine identified nodes which were within community groups through an iterative process which calculated the number of shared neighbours for any two nodes. For ease of analysis, nodes representing generic Live-Journal related communities were removed as were nodes not connected to any of the identified network groups. In addition to gathering information about the links between the various journals, both community and individual user, information about the interests that were specified within the journal profile was also collected. This information was aggregated across nodes found to be in a group which allowed for the identification of the top fifteen interests held in common within a group.

The following colour schemes were used within the visualisation:

- Nodes representing community journals are displayed in red while those representing user, or personal, journals where shown in blue.
- Bi-directional links between nodes are shown in black, mono-directional links are shown in grey with an arrow to indicate the direction.
- Community groupings of users are shown in blue, the darker the blue the more tightly-knit the community.
- Community groupings of users and community journals are shown in green, the darker the green the more tightly-knit the community.

Six clustered groups were identified as relating to node "F". These were numbered 1 – 6 (see Fig. 12.1 for identification). Of those six groups, one contained no community journals, Group 5, two were weakly connected to community journals, Groups 3 and 5, and three showed strong links, Groups 1, 4 and 6 (see Fig. 12.1).

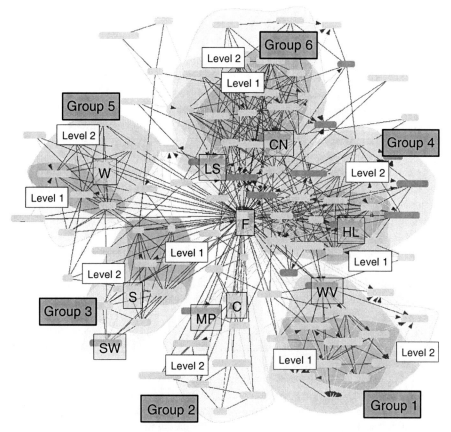

Fig. 12.1 Social Network Groups on LiveJournal with Central Node "F". Main image highlighting groupings containing community journals (*green areas*) and those the groupings not including community journals (*blue areas*). (*See* Online version for color details)

We will now consider the various facets that make up the definitions of virtual communities, COPs and WBSN and each of these groups in relation to those facets:

1. Members have some shared goal, interest, need or activity that provides the primary reason for belonging to the community:

Taking the first requirement for community proposed by Whittaker et al. [32] as covering Preece's [25] requirement for a shared purpose and being comparable with Wenger [31] for a shared practice we consider the evidence for a primary reason that any given nodes were part of identifiable groups within the visualized network structure.

One would expect that the users in those groups which contain strong links to community journals, Groups 1, 4 and 6, would share a practice or interest. Correlating the visualization with the analysis of the interests we can see that this is the case with Groups 4 and 6 but not Group 1. With Groups 4 and 6, we can see a pattern of the more closely knit area of the group (level 1) having strongly popular interests even in comparison to the more weakly connected area (level 2) and these shared interests, for the most part, relating to a theme. This contrasts with the other groups where there are either more noticeably popular interests as there are more people involved, or show no uniting trend within the shared areas of interest.

As Group 1 appears to contradict the expected results being strongly linked to a community journal but not having any discernable shared interests, we will consider it more closely. There is strong similarity in the interest trends between Groups 1 and 5. In both cases the more central nodes do not share any common interests. However investigation into the specifics of the case reveals that Group 1 represents fictional characters created for a collaborative writing project. This is interesting because it demonstrates that the social network of fictional people strongly resembles one of non-fictional users. The only difference between this network and that seen in other social networks is that one represents a deliberate creation by a community, hence the strong linking to the community journal. As a creation of the community rather than a representation of users within the community, Group 1 is more closely related to the type of social network that can be seen illustrated by Group 5. However, at the same time, the group focuses on and is controlled by the shared interest embodied by the community journal even though the interests stated, representing those of the characters rather than the players, are not explicitly shared.

Having considered the groups, which are strongly linked to community nodes, we now look at those which are weakly linked. Both Groups 2 and 3 have networks that are only partially linked to a community node. In neither case is there a strong theme within the interests that are shared between the users. If we select nodes within each of these two groups, S and C, and map the network that surrounds them (see Figs. 12.3 and 12.2) we can see even less emphasis on the community journals suggesting that they have little influence over the surrounding nodes and while those journals may represent some shared bond it is not a strong one nor does it extend with any significance into the social connections that surround it. This shows that it is not merely the presence of a community journal that signifies a difference but the way in which the personal journals around it interface with it.

Finally, we consider Group 5 which represents a network of purely personal journals. As we noted previously, the trend within the interests is similar to that in Group 1 with the most closely connected individuals having no shared interests but common ground being found when the larger group is considered. There is a general theme to the interests at the wider level which suggests that there may be some commonality beyond chance. Since the visualisation is limited in its distance from the primary node and every other group has had a community journal associated with in to a greater or lesser extent, there is the possibility that a community journal exists for this group but is hidden. As with Groups 2 and 3, we locate a central node and expand the visualisation to centre on this new journal, W (see Fig. 12.4).

As with the previous cases, the further visualisation confirms the strong social links without the presence of a central community hub. While those networks may have many social links and have some shared interests they have no demonstrably focused interest or goal that can be determined from the information available as we would expect to see this more strongly in the more tightly connected area of

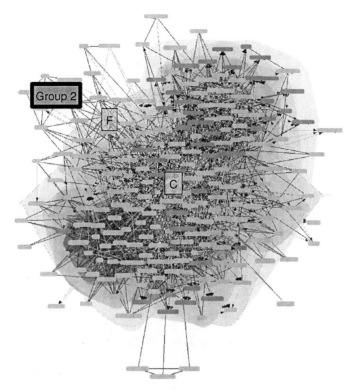

Fig. 12.2 Social Network Groups on LiveJournal with Central Node "C". Image shows all personal journals and those community journals which were identified as being within a group. Groupings containing community journals highlighted in green, groupings not including community journals highlighted in blue. Areas identified in Fig. 12.1 are labelled in purple. (*See* Online version for color details)

the network. It seems likely that Group 5, like Groups 2 and 3, represent friends or colleagues for whom the social and/or co-locational bond provides the linking factor and whom we would expect to have some interests on common but for whom those interests are not the primary reason for the connection.

2. Members engage in repeated active participation and there are often intense interactions, strong emotional ties and shared activities occurring between participants:

It can be argued that this second requirement given by Whittaker et al. [32], which corresponds to that of social interaction which was the first requirement named by Preece [25], can be seen between all the nodes that are identified as being within groups. While the emotional content of the links cannot be derived from the information available to us and, as we have previously stated we cannot assume a social bond, the links represent one user's desire to interact with another even though that interaction may be as basic as reading the other user's journal on a regular basis. Boyd [5] compares the "friend" links on LiveJournal with those of other social networks. She concludes that because there is no structural requirement for receptivity in the friend links (the mono-direction links, shown in grey in our visualisation) and the connection between friend links and privacy setting, there is

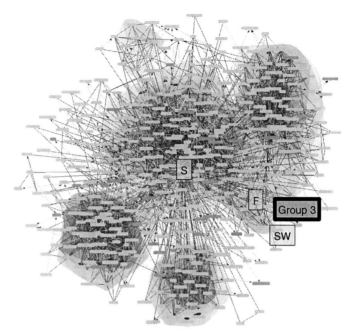

Fig. 12.3 Social Network Groups on LiveJournal with Central Node "S". Image shows nodes identified as being within groups. Groupings containing community journals highlighted in green, groupings not including community journals highlighted in blue. Groupings of personal journal nodes highlighted in blue. Areas identified in Fig. 12.1 labelled in purple. (*See* Online version for color details)

a greater social weight inherent in the bidirectional links (those shown in black on the visualisation). This supports our hypothesis that the links between the nodes, especially those identified as bidirectional, satisfy this requirement.

3. Members have access to shared resources and there are policies for determining access to those resources:

The definition by Whittaker et al. [32] is the only one to require shared resources. In the pre-social networking online landscape archives, websites and mailing lists acted as points of contact for members of an online community and places through which information, media objects and other resources can be shared as well as social norms being set, agreed on and enforced. While access was mostly controlled through obscurity, a scheme that is growing less effective due to improvements in search utilities, many of these community site required users to join or otherwise have an account to gain full access to resources. As we are working within one site this basic entry requirement can be assumed to be met, by all journals under review. For this condition to be met, the shared resources must go beyond those gained through the act of signing up to the site.

In the case of our visualisation, these shared resources are best represented by the community journals. While many have open membership the option is available for membership to be restricted and investigation of the communties reveal that

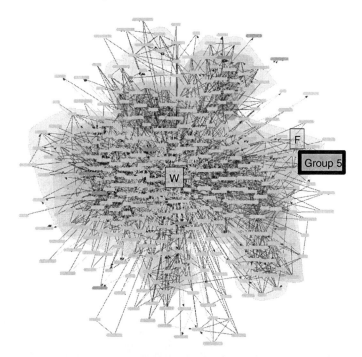

Fig. 12.4 Social Network Groups on LiveJournal with Central Node "W". Image shows nodes identified as being within groups. Groupings containing community journals highlighted in green, groupings not including community journals highlighted in blue. Areas identified in Fig. 12.1 are labelled in purple. (*See* Online version for color details)

some have additional access policies such as age restrictions or some proof of good standing. For this reason we can conclude that those groups where the community journals act as a central shared resource for the group meet this requirement, specifically Groups 1, 4 and 6.

  4. Reciprocity of information, support and services between members:

  As with the previous requirement, this aspect is exclusive to the Whittaker et al. [32] definition. It could be argued that reciprocity is seen within all the networks that exist, both between exclusively personal journals and those which include communities, as the rational behind the site is that users can post to their own journals as well as read from others'. This allows for an exchange of information and, one must assume, support and assistance when needed. However the reciprocity of posting in one's own journal is much more amorphous than to the community journals which exist as places for uses to gather, request and share information. Beyond this, the profile pages of the various community journals seen in the visualisation reveal that they act as specific places for discussion and for the exchange and review of media objects created by members of the community, again a reciprocal activity with members providing media in exchange for the provision of other media and of comments and feedback on their work.

Table 12.2 Most common shared interests of nodes within community groups with central node "F"(Fig. 12.1)

Group	Top Interests	Nodes (of total nodes in group)
1		Level 1
	5 Nodes, No Shared Interests	
		Level 2
	Magic	3/9 (33.3%)
		1 of 5 shared interests listed
		Community Level
	Magic	3/8 (37.5%)
		1 of 5 shared interests listed
		Community Nodes: WV (collaborative writing journal)
2		No Level 1
		Level 2
	Stargate	3/7 (42.9%)
		1 of 20 shared interests listed
		Community Level
	Slash[1]	3/6 (50.0%)
	Stargate	3/6 (50.0%)
	Writing	3/6 (50.0%)
		3 of 21 shared interests listed
		Community Nodes: MP (writer's support site)
3		Level 1
	Over 15 of 21 interests shared by 2/5 nodes (40.0%)	
		Level 2
	Over 15 of 34 interests shared by 2/8 nodes (25.0%)	
		Community Level
	Writing	3/5 (60.0%)
		1 of 11 shared interests listed
		Community Nodes: SW (university writing group)
4		Level 1
	Duncan/Methos	5/5 (100.0%)
	Highlander	5/5 (100.0%)
	Methos	5/5 (100.0%)
	Peter Wingfield	5/5 (100.0%)
	Slash	5/5 (100.0%)
		5 of 81 shared interests listed
		Level 2
	Highlander	10/10 (100.0%)
	Methos	10/10 (100.0%)
		2 of 121 shared interests listed
		Community Level
	Highlander	9/9 (100.0%)
	Methos	9/9 (100.0%)
		2 of 104 shared interests listed
		Community Nodes: HL (fan community journal)
5		Level 1
	3 Nodes, No Shared Interests	
		Level 2
	Anime	4/7 (57.1%)
	Babylon 5	4/7 (57.1%)
	Manga	4/7 (57.1%)
	Utena	4/7 (57.1%)
		4 of 65 shared interests listed
		No Community Level

Table 12.2 (continued)

6		Level 1	
	Reading	3/4 (75.0%)	
	Slash	3/4 (75.0%)	
	Writing	3/4 (75.0%)	
	BDSM	3/4 (75.0%)	
			4 of 13 shared interests listed
		Level 2	
	Slash	6/9 (66.7%)	
			1 of 28 shared interests listed
		Community Level	
	Slash	3/15 (86.7%)	
			1 of 70 shared interests listed
			Community Nodes: LS, CN (fan offline meetup journals)

5. A common set of expected behaviours:

The requirement given by Preece [25] for shared expectations of appropriate behaviour can be correlated with the concept proposed by Whittaker et al. [32] of a shared context within which the community exists. While maintaining a link to another journal suggests that a given user finds the behaviour of the subscribed journal acceptable, this acceptance is on an personal level. There is no control over behaviour other than unsubscribing from journals whose behaviour an individual finds offensive.

Conversely, community expectations set both the type of posts allowed to the community and the type of information and level of detail which members are expected to include with any media items they provide. A number of the community journals, as identified in the case study, explicitly described or otherwise referenced a required ettiquette in their profiles. These understood expectations went beyond those commonly found in standard netiquette [6, 10]. As these community journals act as a central hub for the nodes which link to them, it seems reasonable to argue that the standards of behaviour laid down at the community nodes are at least acknowledged by the users being represented by the connecting nodes even if the rules only apply to interaction that occurs on the community journal itself.

6. System must support the creation of the intra-community relationships/links and relationships/links between users must be directly stated, editable and browsable:

The final requirements are drawn directly from the definition proposed by Golbeck [12] for a Web Based Social Network. The majority of the requirements for the identification of a WBSN relate to the relationship links that exist between the various nodes within the network. Since the expression of these links are within the electronic space this encompasses and goes beyond the requirement given by Preece [25] for some form of computer mediation. The visualizations were created through automatic processing of the LiveJournal links proving that they were stated, visible and browsable. That this was possible at all shows that the system supports the creation of defined relationships as codified as mono- or bidirectional links.

12.4 Communities, Groups and Networks

From the above, we can see that while the network groups within the visualisation might be definable as Communities of Practice and all represent Web Based Semantic Networks, only those with both user and community nodes fulfil all the conditions laid down by the traditional definitions of community such as we discussed at the beginning of the chapter.

Group	1	2	3	4	5	6
Shared goal, interest or activity	√			√	?	√
Repeated active participation	√	√	√	√	√	√
Shared resources	√			√		√
Reciprocity of information, support, services	√	?	?	√	?	√
Shared expected behaviour	√			√		√
Stated, editable and browsable intra-community links	√	√	√	√	√	√

Groups 2, 3 and 5 represent social networks, and indeed WBSNs. In the case of Groups 3 and 5 no further inference can be drawn from them however the positioning of Group 2 between a number of strong and related communities suggests it might represent a section of inter-community space where social ties are bridging the gap between two areas of strong but not shared interests. These networks are noticeably different from those such as Groups 4 and 6 which represent communities. It is only those networks which have both social interaction and shared interests which fulfil the traditional social science definition of community. Group 1 represent special case as it models a social network which was created specifically by a community and while the fictional characters represented by the journals are part of a social network, the players behind the creations are part of the community. .

The recognition of the difference between network groups and network groupss that are also communities can inform the inferences and assumptions that we can make on a social level when analysing and processing data from them.

12.5 Community Trust

While social networks model the social bonds between people, they do not intrinsically differentiate between close friendships and casual acquaintances. This differentiation can be achieved through additional structures such as trust values or extending the link information to describe the social level of the connection. While these extensions can be used to facilitate the identification of groups to filter at an individual level, the definition of community allows us to regard the groups so identified as closely knit areas in which there are internal policies as to behaviour and thus, within the context of the communities shared values, a high-trust area.

Trust on the Internet takes many different forms. Commerce, communication, interacting with other people, all the types of actions where trust occurs without much thought in the real world, are replicated in the digital world. The majority of the research that has been done has concentrated on issues related to trust in electronic commerce, especially authentication and security. This focus is at least partly due to the corporate interests involved and the increased risk that is associated with the involvement of money. The non-commercial nature of the systems that are being considered in this chapter result in the emphasis falling first onto lower risk systems and secondly onto the other domains in which trust is a factor.

To consider these problems we have to first consider what is meant by "trust". In many respects that is a question for the philosophers. It is certainly one they have been discussing since the discipline first arose and they reluctantly started taking notes [21, pp. 30–36]. The dictionary definition is long and contains at least three totally distinct meanings depending on context. Academics who have investigated trust in social, philosophical and security contexts frequently define the term in such a way as to fit the point they are making – whether it is to do with fulfilling expectations or acting within a role [21]. The majority of these definitions are firmly based on the idea of an interaction between two individuals and, while history may be taken into account as an indicator of probable future behaviour, the greater context is not often seen as a part of that equation. Fukuyama is one of the few that is firmly placed within a larger group setting. Possibly because his interest in economics he describes social trust, that is the level of trust in a society, as "the expectations that arise within a community of regular, honest cooperative behaviour, based on commonly shared norms, on the part of the members of the community" [10]. Further he emphasises this trust as a contributing factor to economic success [10].

The small world concept, that within a social group of any size a short path of acquaintances can be found to link any two nodes, was opened up for study by Milgram [19] in the 1960s. More recent work has shown that the Internet follows similar patterns and can be considered a small world system [1, 2, 15, 30]. Barabasi [3], in their study of random networks, showed that in expanding networks popular nodes would attract more links than outliers in what they referred to as "preferential attachment". This allowed the network to grow with a power-law degree distribution. This is especially relevant to the focus on community in this chapter as it can be assumed that the "hub" nodes seen in a community network would be shared community spaces rather than those of specific individuals as these are the areas which act as general bonding areas for community members.

Trust ratings allow the build up of a trust network by modelling the trust between the individuals that make up a given system. However, if we consider Fukuyama's definition of trust in comparison to this system, then the trust is not just between two individuals but is also between each individual within that community and the combined mass of individuals that make up the community. That bond of trust is a simple one; the individual is trusted to abide by the *mores* of the community while the community is trusted to include the individual with whatever advantages that may bring. Inappropriate behaviour on the part of the individual will result in removal of trust in that individual by the community until the point is reached where the individual is no longer considered part of that community. This puts the user in a situation where they either have to regain that trust or rejoin the community with a new identity (and hope no one is able to make the link between the two). Depending on the cost of identity creation [9] and the trust given to new members, this process can be more or less prejudicial both to the individual and the community. Even in the case of the offender rejoining with a new identity the lesson can be learned and the community standards of behaviour adhered to [17] and if not the pattern repeats.[2] Conversely inappropriate behaviour by the community will result in denunciation of that community until the point is reached where the community is changed or a new community is set up either as a replacement or an alternative.

As we have already seen, according to both Whittaker et al. [32] and Preece [25], part of the definition of an online community involves a shared understanding of appropriate behaviour then it logically follows that this type of trust must be present within that type of community structure.

This would suggest that when the context of trust is related to agreed upon behaviours within the community then the level to which someone is known and trusted within that community might be used as a measure of how unlikely they are to act in a way that goes against the etiquette of the community. Conversely if a person is not known and trusted by the community then it can be seen as a sign that they either cannot be trusted to act in accordance with the community's standards or have not yet been within the community long enough that they can be trusted to know what those standards are.

Membership of a group is often seen as a clear cut division, one is either part of a given set or not. However using the logic described above, community trust can be seen as a function of membership, but as part of a fuzzy rather than an absolute set. We provide an illustration of these two different ways of modelling community membership, binary and gradual, in Fig. 12.5.

In his paper on trust strategies for the Semantic Web, O'Hara [22] suggest five scenarios that agents might follow: optimistic, pessimistic, centralised, investigation and transitivity. If we consider membership of a group as a binary state, then we can compare it to a combination of pessimistic and optimistic strategies. Prior to gaining membership trust between community members is in a pessimistic state, that is interaction is restricted until additional reasons for trust are given. However, if the two agents, or users, are both members of the same community then interaction becomes optimistic and trust is assumed as a default state (labelled as "binary" on Fig. 12.5). This system, while workable, does not take into account the idea of membership of a community as a process with community practices being learned through involvement.

Transitive trust systems [22] rely on the idea that in some systems, especially social ones, trust can be calculated through opinions gained from a network of interconnected contacts. This conceptualisation allows for both the idea of a gradual absorption of a new user into an existing network and a gradual increase in trust as the user becomes known (labelled as "gradual" on Fig. 12.5). The necessary compo-

---

[2] In most cases, until the troublemaker decides that the effort required is not worth the time taken just to cause trouble.

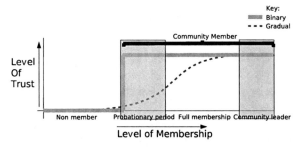

Fig. 12.5 Diagram illustrating trust as a component of community membership.

nent that O'Hara [22] identifies for this system to work is context. By working with a community network, and having the context relate to knowledge and compliance of community standards these conditions are met.

How would one measure how well someone is known and trusted within a community? The most obvious way would be to consider the number of potential paths between that community member and another. Working on the small world principle just as the previously mentioned web of trust does, it is clear that each person within the community who trusts a member of that community in a specific context represents the first link in a potential chain between that community member and another.

In many respects, if trust is seen a reduction of cognitive complexity in times of uncertainty this is a further reduction since a person is not trusting another person but is instead trusting the community to which they both belong to tell them whether or not trust can be given.

Similar structures can already be seen in use in the buyers and sellers rating schemes on sites such as eBay While "users of eBay" is a very broad and loose-knit community, decisions about whether to trust sellers are made at least partially on the relative number of positive and negative comments that have been previously made about that seller by other buyers, that is, other members of that community [4]. Considering it as a community trust system, we can see that the community standards are that the goods are as advertised and are dispatched in a timely and appropriate manner in exchange for the money that the buyer sends the seller. The buyer has more trust in the seller the more affidavits they have accumulated since these show that the seller is known to the community and vouched for. This is despite the fact that the buyer does not necessarily know any of the people who are giving these recommendations. If someone does not live up to the community expected standards, then the seller receives bad reviews, lowering their reputation and therefore, the likelihood that a buyer will choose to do business (i.e., trust) with them. In severe cases the seller's account is suspended – in effect the person is ejected from the community.

The system works on the basis of a "x number of people can't be wrong". There are two main immediate problems with this. First, history has repeatedly proved that sometimes all those people can be wrong. Due to the system by which reputation is calculated [27, 26] it is possible to build up a good reputation with small items in order to set up a scam on an expensive item. While this may result in the seller being suspended, this does not help the buyer who has been defrauded. There are also cases of faked reviews or groups getting together to bolster each other's rating in return for their own ratings being padded rather than in return for the services offered [4, 13, 20]. This effect can be seen in other reputation based systems, for example Google's page ranking system which uses the number of links to a page as a gauge for its relative importance. However, due to this use of popularity to indicate reputation, a number of websites working together (either intentionally or unintentionally) can unfairly elevate the popularity of a link in the Google page rankings [11, 14, 18, 29].

Second, as we have mentioned, there is the probationary period when a newcomer must build up initial trust to be accepted by the community. In community terms this parallels the introduction of a newcomer into a community. While this period exists to allow the two way process of evaluation, the user evaluating the community and vice versa, the trust evaluation is more biased towards the community needing to assess the potential member. A number of possible strategies have been developed for this and recommendations for which should be used depend on the risk associated with the particular activity.

Reputation can be defined as the social standing of either an individual user or a group, that is, how that party is seen by others. Reputation can be gained through actions seen as positive by the group or lost though actions which are seen as negative such as breaking the community rules. "Reputation causes people to cooperate in the present in order to avoid negative consequences in future interactions with the same people. Reputations spread information about people's behaviour, so that expectations of future interactions can influence behaviour even if the future interactions may be with different people than those in the present" 9. Reputation and trust are intricately linked, in that reputation is often used in the calculation of trust; however, the two are not interchangeable.

Now consider a tightly knit community such as a hobbyist group, as seen in our visualisation above, or a gaming clan. The community by definition has codes of acceptable behaviour and those who break these rules will be shunned with the word being spread to related groups by overlapping membership. It has been shown that when reputation is a factor within a community then it can act as part of the social control mechanism. For example "Gossip allows the dominant hierarchy to be kept under the group's control, and illegitimate or dangerous figures to be replaced. Thus, it allows social control while fostering social cohesion and promotes social order while ensuring legitimacy" [7, p. 193]. Within such a community, there is no other commodity for exchange except for reputation.

12.6 Conclusion

When the possibility of online communities was first discussed the debate was over what defined a community since there are vital difference between a community and a group or even a network of people. Now the idea that physical space defines community seems unlikely, but the necessity to discuss what is and is not a community is still important. That discussion has happened for the Internet and now it must happen for the Semantic Web and its associated group structures.

One recent trend has been the ease with which people can make connections with other people. Many of these linkages are weak, webs of acquaintances rather than webs of friendship, and it can be hard to pick out the meaningful links within the many. The debate over whether something is or is not a community is important because it not only allows us to differentiate the group from other looser structures but it also allows us to make certain assumptions which we could not make otherwise. Looking at the definitions for communities which have been used in the past, the groupings most commonly seen as communities within Semantic Web research, communities of practice and social networks, may be but are not definitively communities. The Internet Based Semantic Community represents those networks, whether social, communities of practice or something else, which do meet the commonly accepted community definitions.

Throughout this chapter we have tried to ensure that the social aspect of computing is considered an significant part of the system. The user and the social environment, in which the user is working, are components that need to be taken into account during any analysis of existing networks and in the design of future networking systems. Recently, the social aspects of computer use have been highlighted with laws and campaigns directed at the way technology can be used; however it is necessary not to fall into the fallacy of completely separating social and technical solutions. As technology opens up new possibilities, so the human element becomes increasingly important as what we can do gives way as a barrier to what we should do. Online communities represent a place where social control exists in parallel with technology, but it is a social control that has largely developed from within the community rather than one imposed by external decree. As social networks become more ubiquitous, the communities within them are going to become increasingly important as they represent organised and motivated forces. The question that faces us in the future is, having recognised that these structures exist within the semantic as well as the online world, how we use that information?

References

1. Lada A. Adamic. The Small World Web. In *Proceedings of european Conference on Digital Libraries '99*. p. 443–452, 1999.
2. Réka Albert, Hawoong Jeong, and Albert-László Barabasi. Diameter of the World-Wide Web. *Nature*, 401:130–131, September 1999.
3. Albert-Laszlo Barabasi and Raka Albert. Emergence of Scaling in Random Networks. *Science*, 286:509–512, 1999.
4. Rajat Bhattacharjee and Ashish Goel. Avoiding Ballot Stuffing in eBay-like Reputation Systems. In *Third Workshop on the Economics of Peer-to-Peer Systems*, 2005.
5. Danah Boyd. Friends, Friendsters, and Fop 8: Writing Community into Being on Social Network Sities. *First Monday*, 11(12), December 2006. http://www.firstmonday.org/issues/issue11_12/boyd/(06/02/2007).

6. Rhiannon Bury. *Cyberspaces of their Own: Female Fandoms Online*, volume 25 of *Digital Formations*. Peter Lang, 2005.

7. Rosaria Conte and Mario Paolucci. *Reputation in Artifical Societies. Social Beliefs for Social Order.* Kluwer Academic Publishers, Dordrecht, 2002.

8. Li Ding, Lina Zhou, Tim Finin, and Anupam Joshi. How the Sermantic Web is Being Used: An Analysis of FOAF. In *Proceedingd of the 38th International Conference on System Sciences*, January 2005.

9. Eric J. Friedman and Paul Resnick. The Social Cost of Cheap Pseudonyms. *Journal of Economics and Management Strategy*, 10(2):173–199, 1990.

10. Francis Fukuyama. *Trust: The Social Virtues and the Creation of Prosperity.* Penguin, 1995.

11. Mark Glaser. Companies Subvert Search Results to Squelch Criticism. *USC Annenberg Online Journalism Review*, May 2005. http://www.ojr.org/stories/050601glaser/(05/02/2007).

12. Jennifer Golbeck. *Computing and Applying Trust in Web-based Social Networks.* Thesis, University of Maryland, College Park, MD, April 2005..

13. Lee Gomes. How Sellers Trick EBay's Rating System. *The Wall Stree Journal Online*, 22 December 2006. http://startup.wsj.com/ecommerce/ecommerce/20061222-gomes.html?refresh=on(05/02/2007).

14. Google Blogoscoped Team. Googlebomb watch. Google Blogoscoped, 2004. http://blog.outer-court.com/googlebomb/(05/02/2007).

15. Elizabeth Gray, Jean-Marc Seigneur, Yong Chen, and Christian Jensen. Trust Propagation in Small Worlds. In Paddy Nixon and Sotirios Terzis, editors, *Proceedings of the First International Conference on Trust Management*, 2003.

16. Hellekson and Kristina Busse, editors. *Fan Fiction Communities in the Age of the Internet.* McFarland and Company, 2006.

17. Richard C, Mackinnon. Punishing the Persona:Correctional Strategies for the Virtual offender. In Steve Jones, editor, Virtual Culture: Identity and Communication in Cybersociety. Sage Publications Ltd., Londan, 1997.

18. Marissa Mayer. Googlebombing 'Failure'. GoogleBlog, 16 September 2005. http://googleblog.blogspot.com/2005/09/googlebombing-failure.html(05/02/2007).

19. Stanley Milgram. the Small World Problem. Psychology Today, 2:60-67, 1967.

20. Eilinor Mills. Study: eBay Sellers Gaming the Reputation System? C-Net, January 2007. http://news.com.com/2061-10803_3-6149491. html(06/02/2007).

21. Kieron O'Hara. Trust, from Socrates to Spin. Icon Books, 2004.

22. Kieron O'Hara, Harith Alani, Yannis Kalfoglou, and Nigel Shadbolt. Trust Strategies for the Semantic Web. In Proceedings of 3rd International Semantic Web Conference (ISWC), Workshop on Trust, Security, and Reputation the Semantic Web, Hiroshima, Japan, 2004.

23. Kieron O'Hara, Hairth Alani, and Nigel Shadblot. Identyfying Communities of Practice: Analysing Ontologies as Networks to Support Community Recognition. In IFIP World Computer congress. Information Systems: The E-Business Challenge, 2002,

24. John C. Paolillo, Sarah Mercure, and Elijah Wright. The Social Semantics of LiveJournal FOAF:Structure and Change from 2004 to 2005. in Proceedinds of the ISWC 2005 Workshop on Semantic Network Analysis, November 2005.

25. Jenny Preece. Online Communication- Desining Usability, Supporting Sociability. Jhon Wiley and Sons, Ltd., New york, 2000.

26. Paul Resnick and Zeckhauser.Trust Among Strangers in Intenet Transactions: Emprial Analysis of eBy's Reputation System. In Michel R. Bay, editor, The Economics of the internet and E-Commerce, Volume 11 of Advances in Applied microeconomics, Amsterdam, Elsevier Science, 2002.

27. Paul Resnick, richard Zeckhausar, Eric Friedman, and Ko Kuwabara.Reputation Systems:Facilitating Trust iin internet Interactions. in Communications of the ACM, pp.45–48. ACM, December 2000.

28. Howaed Rheingold.The Virtual Community:homesteading on the Electronic Frontier.Secker and Waeburg, 19963.

29. Clifford Tatum. Deconstructing Google bombs:A breach of symbolic power or just a goofy prank? First Monday, 10(10), October 2005.http://firstmonday.org/issue/issue10_10/tatum/index.html(05/02/2007).
30. Duncan Watts and Steven Strogatz. Collective Dynamics of 'small World' networks. Nature, 393:440–442, 1998.
31. Etienne Wenger. Communities of Practice:Learning,Meaning and Identity. Cambridge University Press Cambridge, MA, 1997.
32. Steve Whittaker, Ellen Issacs, and Vicky O'Day.Widening the Net:Workshop Report on the Theory and Practice of Physical and Network Communities.SIGCHI Bulletin, 29(3), July 1997.

Index

Printed in the United States
148731LV00001B/108/P